NEW COLLEGE
OXFORD
1379–1979

1. The Founder and distinguished alumni: the Founder at the top; on his right Chichele and Beckington; on his left Cranley and Waynflete; below, standing, from left to right Chaundler, Holes, Norton, Sugar, Say, Andrewes, and Selot.

NEW COLLEGE
OXFORD
1379–1979

Edited by
John Buxton and Penry Williams

PUBLISHED BY
THE WARDEN AND FELLOWS OF NEW COLLEGE, OXFORD
IN COMMEMORATION OF THE SIXTH CENTENARY
1979

British Library Cataloguing in Publication Data

New College, Oxford, 1379–1979.
1. New College, *Oxford* – History
I. Buxton, John   II. Williams, Penry
378.425'74   LF655

ISBN 0–9506510–0–1

Designed and produced by Oxprint Limited, Oxford

CONTENTS

Preface   viii

List of Illustrations   x

Acknowledgements   xvi

Abbreviations to End-of-Chapter References   xvii

PART ONE

The History of the College

I   The Foundation and the Medieval College, 1379–1530   3
By R. L. Storey, *Professor of English History, University of Nottingham*

II   From the Reformation to the Era of Reform, 1530–1850   44
By Penry Williams, *Fellow of New College*

III   Transformation, 1850–1914   72
By Alan Ryan, *Fellow of New College; Reader in Politics, University of Oxford*

IV   New College Between the Two World Wars

[i] INTRODUCTION   107
By Sir William Hayter, K.C.M.G., *Warden of New College, 1958–1976;
Honorary Fellow, 1976*

[ii] THE MID-TWENTIES: AN ECONOMIST'S
VIEW   112
By Lord Robbins, C.H., C.B., F.B.A., *Fellow of New College, 1927–1929;
Professor of Economics in the University of London, 1929–1961*

[iii] MEMORIES OF NEW COLLEGE, 1928–1931   120
By Goronwy Rees, *Fellow of All Souls College, 1931; Principal, University
College of Wales, Aberystwyth, 1953–1957*

v

[iv] THE WARDEN'S LODGINGS BETWEEN THE   127
WARS
By Mary Bennett, *Principal of St. Hilda's College, Oxford*

[v] A TRADE UNIONIST AT NEW COLLEGE,   132
1931–1933
By George Woodcock, P.C., C.B.E., *General Secretary of the T.U.C.,*
1947–1960; Honorary Fellow of New College, 1963

[vi] REFLECTIONS ON AN UNDERGRADUATE   138
DIARY
By John Buxton, *Fellow of New College; Reader in English Literature, University*
of Oxford

PART TWO

The Architecture of the College

V   The Building of the Medieval College
By Gervase Jackson-Stops, *Architectural Adviser to the National Trust*
1. INTRODUCTION AND NOTE ON THE   147
    SOURCES
2. WILLIAM OF WYKEHAM AND THE ARCHI-   149
    TECTURE OF NEW COLLEGE
3. THE MASONS AND CARPENTERS: WYNFORD,   156
    HERLAND, AND YEVELE
4. A TOUR OF THE FOUNDER'S BUILDINGS   164

VI   Gains and Losses: the College Buildings, 1404–1750
By Gervase Jackson-Stops
1. THE FIFTEENTH AND SIXTEENTH CEN-   193
    TURIES: CHEQUER, THE LAW LIBRARY,
    AND THE TUDOR ADDITIONS
2. THE SEVENTEENTH CENTURY: THE   202
    LAUDIAN REVIVAL AND BYRD'S GARDEN
    QUADRANGLE
3. THE EARLY EIGHTEENTH CENTURY: THE   220
    GARDEN QUADRANGLE COMPLETED

VII   Restoration and Expansion: the Buildings Since 1750
By Gervase Jackson-Stops
1. THE LATE EIGHTEENTH CENTURY: 233
    REYNOLDS AND WYATT

2. THE MID-NINETEENTH CENTURY: SCOTT'S   244
'RESTORATIONS' AND THE HOLYWELL
BUILDING

3. THE LAST HUNDRED YEARS   254

PART THREE

Traditions and Possessions

VIII Music and Musicians   267
By Paul R. Hale, *Assistant Director of Music, Tonbridge School*

IX   The College Plate   293
By Charles Oman, *Keeper of the Department of Metalwork, Victoria and
Albert Museum, 1945–1966*

X   Thoughts on the Archives   306
By Francis W. Steer, *Archivist of New College, 1965–1978*

XI   The Medieval Library   317
By R. W. Hunt, F.B.A., *Keeper of Western Manuscripts, the Bodleian Library
1945–1975*

XII   Memorials at New College   346
By Francis W. Steer

Epilogue   363

By Penry Williams

Further Reading   369

Appendix: Wardens of New College   370

Index   371

PREFACE

In 1973 the college decided to publish a book to commemorate the sixth century of its foundation, and appointed us as editors. We drew up a table of contents that would cover the history of the institution and of its buildings, together with chapters on certain aspects of the college's life and its possessions; and we invited contributions from eleven members of the college and from others with special knowledge. We did not invite anyone to write about the stained glass in chapel because Dr. Woodforde's book, *The Stained Glass of New College, Oxford*, provides a recent and comprehensive account. We are grateful to our contributors for their tolerance of editorial suggestion and interference. We owe thanks to colleagues and others who have helped to improve the book, especially to Sir Folliott Sandford, for his knowledge of illustrations of the college and of its recent history; to the Rev. Dr. G. V. Bennett, the Librarian; and to Dr. Francis Steer, until recently the Archivist, both for his catalogue *The Archives of New College, Oxford*, and for much help to us and to contributors over historical matters. We also wish to thank Miss Harding, the Assistant Librarian, Mrs. Willson-Pepper, the Assistant Archivist, and successive Assistant Librarians and Fellows' Secretaries for much practical help. Finally we are deeply indebted to Mr Eric Christiansen for compiling the Index.

The book was not intended to be a formal, learned history of the college, since the time for that to be undertaken will be when the new *History of the University* is nearer completion, but we hope that we have provided a worthy and accurate record of the first six hundred years of the college for the instruction and pleasure of its members past, present and yet to come. For the inter-war years (which many regard as the most distinguished in the college's history) we preferred to make use of personal reminiscences, since a more formal treatment of a period within living memory would have provoked dispute. 'It wasn't at all like that', is a natural response to a record of what we ourselves remember that has the effrontery to claim to be detached and judicious, whereas the idiosyncrasies of personal recollection will be accepted, even if with a shrug of the shoulders here and there. Besides, they may provide material for later historians, and prompt others to record their memories of the college. For even in the seventh century of its existence some will find their years here exhilarating and rewarding.

New College   J.B.
July 1978   P.H.W.

It is with deep regret that we have to record the death of Dr. Francis Steer in August 1978. We greatly valued the work that he had already done and much missed his advice in the later stages of preparing this volume.

LIST OF ILLUSTRATIONS

1. *Frontispiece.* N.C. MS (Bodley) 288 (The Chaundler MS.) f. 4r. *c.* 1461–5. Above in the centre is William of Wykeham seated. On his right are Henry Chichele, Archbishop of Canterbury (founder of All Souls College) and Thomas Beckington, Bishop of Wells; on his left, Thomas Cranley, Archbishop of Dublin, and William Waynflete, Bishop of Winchester (founder of Magdalen College). Below, standing, from left to right, are Thomas Chaundler, Andrew Holes, John Norton, Hugh Sugar, William Say, Richard Andrewes, John Selot.

Between pages 206 and 207

2. New College and its members, drawing on vellum in Warden Thomas Chaundler's manuscript, *c.* 1461–5 (N.C. MS. (Bodley) 288).

3. Engraving of New College, by David Loggan, *c.* 1670, published in *Oxonia Illustrata* (1675).

4. Engraving of the Great Quadrangle, by David Loggan, 1675, published in *Oxonia Illustrata* in the same year, and showing the additional storey built in 1674.

5. Aerial view of New College from the east (Aerofilms).

6. Drawing by Joseph Dixon of the Great Quadrangle, from the south-west corner, made for the 1793 Oxford Almanack (Ashmolean Museum, Oxford).

7. The Great Quadrangle from the west.

8. The Chapel and Bell Tower from the Slype.

9. The Cloisters, Bell Tower, and west end of Chapel.

10. The Ante-Chapel.

11. The Chapel, looking westwards, from a drawing by Frederick Mackenzie, engraved by J. C. Stadler, (published in R. Ackermann's *History of the University of Oxford*, 1814).

12. The east end of the Chapel, *c.* 1870 (National Monuments Record).

13. Preliminary design for the new Chapel roof by Gilbert Scott (N.C. MS. 3230).

14. The east end of the Chapel.

15–18. Medieval wood carving: four fourteenth-century misericords from the Chapel. Top to bottom: William of Wykeham welcoming scholars to Oxford; a female centaur and hedgehogs; scholars fighting with daggers; and a doctor delivering a lecture.

19–21. Medieval stone carving: (above) a Bishop and King, from the Hall; (below) a corbel in the Treasury.

22–5. Medieval glass: Judah and St. Athanasius from the Antechapel windows; and a Wise Virgin and Angel, from the upper lights of the Choir windows.

26. Detail of a window on the south side of the Choir, by William Price, 1740.

27. Detail of a window on the north side of the Choir, by William Peckitt, 1771.

28. Watercolour design by Biagio Rebecca for figures in the north windows of the Choir, *c.* 1773 (Warden's Lodgings, New College).

29.   Oil sketch by Sir Joshua Reynolds for the central Nativity in the west window of Chapel, *c.* 1778 (private collection).

30.   Oil sketch by Sir Joshua Reynolds for the figure of Charity in the west window, *c.* 1778 (Ashmolean Museum, Oxford).

31–3.   Medieval stone vaults: the Muniment Room; the staircase to Hall; the Beer Cellar.

34 & 35.   Medieval timber roofs: the Kitchen and Long Room.

36.   The Hall.

37.   Detail of the panelling in Hall, *c.* 1533–5.

38.   Detail of the carved spandrel above the buttery door.

39.   The Gatehouse and Warden's Lodgings from New College Lane.

40.   The staircase in the Warden's Lodgings.

41–3.   Jacobean carving: panelling in the Warden's Hall, and overmantels in the Warden's Study and one of the Fellows' Chambers.

44 & 45.   Preliminary design for the Garden Quadrangle by William Byrd, engraved by Michael Burghers, 1678 (N.C. MS. 1153); the elevation on a hinged flap applied to the ground plan.

46–9.   Alternative schemes for the Garden Quadrangle by William Byrd, *c.* 1678–81 (N.C. MSS. 526, 1133 and 1171).

50.   Engraving of the Garden Quadrangle, probably by George Edwards, 1682 showing Byrd's final design (N.C. MS. 951).

51.   Pen and wash drawing of the Garden Quadrangle, by

Michael Burghers, probably used as the basis for an engraving published in 1708 (Ashmolean Museum, Oxford Almanacks volume).

52.   The Garden Quadrangle from the Mount.

53.   The gatescreen, made by Thomas Robinson in 1711 photographed before its reconstruction in 1894 (Oxford City Library).

54.   The Senior Common Room.

55.   The Warden's summerhouse.

56.   The Garden, detail from a unique engraving by Michael Burghers, dated 1708 (Bodleian Library, Oxford).

57.   The Garden, from an engraving in William Williams's *Oxonia Depicta*, 1732.

58.   The Founder's Library.

59.   The Upper Library.

60.   The Holywell Buildings, from a photograph of *c.* 1880 (National Monuments Records).

61.   Staircase well in the Holywell Building.

62.   Design by Basil Champneys for the Robinson Tower and Pandy, from *The Builder*, 8 April, 1899.

63.   The Sacher Building, with sculpture by Barbara Hepworth.

64 & 65.   *The Annuciation*, two panels by Bartolommeo Montagna (*c.* 1450–1523).

66.   *St. James*, by El Greco.

67.   *Lazarus*, by Jacob Epstein.

Between pages 302 and 303

68. The Founder's Pastoral Staff.

69. The Warden's Grace Cup: silver-gilt, *c.* 1480.

70. Warden Hill's Salt: silver-gilt, *c.* 1490.

71. Coconut cup mounted in silver-gilt, *c.* 1490.

72. Coconut cup mounted in silver-gilt, *c.* 1500.

73. Archbishop Warham's Salt: silver-gilt and crystal, *c.* 1500.

74. Pax: silver, *c.* 1500.

75. The Spanish Ambassador's cup: silver-gilt, 1680.

76. College pot or tun, 1675.

77. Tankard, 1677.

78. Tankard, refashioned in 1732 from one given in 1680.

79. Tankard, refashioned in 1749, from one given in 1695.

80. Book donated by the Founder. (N.C. MS. (Bodley) 17, f. 92 r.) *Numbers*, with the *glossa ordinaria*. Mid-thirteenth-century English (?). The initial shows the Lord speaking to Moses (*Numbers* I. 1). Moses is horned and nimbed.

81. Book showing inscription of ownership of John Russell. (N.C. MS. (Bodley) 211, f. 1 v.).

82. A book from the circulating collection. (N.C. MS. 289 f. 74 v.). The inscription reads: 'Liber Novi Collegii Winton' in Oxon' deliberatus Johanni Dobbes vero et perpetuo socio eiusdem per manus Vic(ecustodis) et aliorum offic(ialium) xxix die mensis Aprilis Anno domini M¹ CCCC lxxxviii⁰, John Dobbes was admitted scholar on 9 April 1486 and became a full fellow 1488–9.

83. Memorial brass to John London, fellow 1494–1508. (This John London should not be confused with his later namesake who became warden in 1526).

84. Memorial bust of Michael Woodward, Warden 1658–75.

LINE DRAWINGS IN THE TEXT

a. Ground plan of New College (reprinted from *Victoria County History*).   150

b. Portraits in stained glass of Herland, Wynford and Membury from the east window of Winchester College Chapel.   158

c. Elevation and plans of typical Fellows' Chambers in the south range of the Great Quadrangle. Drawn by Gavin Stamp.   168

d. Stained glass roundel of a peewit in the window of the Old Bursary.   181

e. Plan of the first floor of the Warden's Lodgings (reprinted from *Country Life*).   186

f. Tudor chimneys over the kitchen, from an early nineteenth-century drawing by J. C. Buckler (British Museum, Add. MSS. 36423, fo. 32).   196

ACKNOWLEDGEMENTS

'The Mid-Twenties: An Economist's View' is reproduced from Lord Robbins' *Autobiography of an Economist* by kind permission of Lord Robbins and of Macmillan (London & Basingstoke).

The following have kindly given permission for the reproduction of illustrations: Aerofilms Ltd. for pl. 5; the Ashmolean Museum, Oxford, for the jacket illustration and pls. 6, 30, 51; the Bodleian Library, Oxford, for pl. 56; the British Library for fig. (f); Christie, Manson and Woods Ltd. for pl. 29; Country Life Ltd. for pls. 39–41 and fig. (e); Sir William Hayter and Chatto & Windus Ltd. for pls. 7, 8, 10, 31, 33–6, 58, and for fig. (b), taken from William Hayter, *William of Wykeham, Patron of the Arts*; Professor Luke Herrmann for pl. 57; Oxford City Library for pls. 53, 60; the Royal Commission on Historical Monuments (England) for pls. 4, 9, 12, 15–18, 32, 42–3, 62, and for fig. (a) (all Crown Copyright); the Victoria and Albert Museum for pls. 24, 25, 69, 70, 74.

Thomas-Photos, Oxford, took the photographs for pls. 3, 7, 8, 10, 11, 14, 29, 33–8, 52, 54, 58–9, 63–8, 71–3, 75–9, 84 and for fig. (d); the photographic department of the Bodleian Library for pls. 1, 2, 13, 44–50, 56–7, 80–2; the Ashmolean Library for the jacket illustration and pls. 6, 30, 51; Mr. A. C. Cooper for pl. 29; Mr. Sidney Pitcher for pls. 19–23, 26–7. Mr. Gavin Stamp executed the drawing for fig. (c).

ABBREVIATIONS TO END-OF-CHAPTER REFERENCES

Archives	Francis W. Steer, *The Archives of New College* (1974).
B.L.	British Library.
Colvin	H. M. Colvin, *Biographical Dictionary of English Architects, 1660–1840* (2nd edn., 1978).
D.N.B.	*Dictionary of National Biography.*
Emden, *BRUO*	A. B. Emden, *Biographical Register of the University of Oxford to A. D. 1500* (3 vols., Oxford, 1957–9), and *1501–1540* (1 vol., Oxford, 1974).
George	Hereford George, *New College, 1856–1906* (Oxford, 1906).
Harvey	John Harvey, *English Medieval Architects: a biographical dictionary to 1550* (1954).
N.C. MS.	Document in New College Archives (see under *Archives* above).
N.C. MS. (Bodley)	New College Manuscript deposited in Bodleian Library (see chapter xi, n. 4).
Rashdall and Rait	H. Rashdall and R. S. Rait, *New College* (1901).

rub.	Rubric number of Founder's Statutes (see under *Statutes* below).
Smith	A. H. Smith, *New College and its Buildings* (Oxford, 1952).
Statutes	Founder's Statutes, printed in *Statutes of the Colleges of Oxford* (1853), vol. i.
V.C.H.	A. H. M. Jones, 'New College', in *Victoria County History, Oxfordshire*, III (1954), 144–62.
Wood, *Ath. Ox.*	Antony Wood, *Athenae Oxonienses*, ed. P. Bliss (4 vols., 1813–20).
Wood, *Colleges*	Antony Wood, *History and Antiquities of the Colleges and Halls in the University of Oxford*, ed. J. Gutch (Oxford, 1786).
Wood, *History*	Antony Wood, *History and Antiquities of the University of Oxford*, ed. J. Gutch (2 vols. in 3, Oxford, 1792–6).
Wood, *Life*	A. Clark (ed.), *The Life and Times of Antony Wood* (Oxford Historical Society, 5 vols., 1891–1900).
Woodforde	C. Woodforde, *The Stained Glass of New College, Oxford* (Oxford, 1951).

Unless otherwise stated the place of publication is London and the figures in the references refer to page numbers.

PART ONE

The History of the College

I

The Foundation
and the Medieval College
1379–1530

R. L. STOREY

New College is a spectacular memorial to a spectacular career. The contrast between the humble obscurity of William of Wykeham's origins and his eventual grandeur and wealth is rarely equalled and never surpassed in the biographical records of late medieval England. Royal favour dispensed the greatest prizes, and one route to this fountainhead was by service in the administrative departments of the King's government. In Edward III's time this employment was largely the preserve of clergy whose holy orders qualified them to receive the King's ecclesiastical patronage. Wykeham's qualities as an administrator and councillor must have been outstanding, for he attained the highest office and received the greatest preferment at the King's disposal. Within twelve years of leaving Hampshire he became the dominant figure in the administration of Edward's household. In 1367 he was appointed Chancellor of England and consecrated as Bishop of Winchester. He was now the wealthiest prelate in England, with a revenue perhaps less only than that of John of Gaunt, Duke of Lancaster, and the King himself. A bishop's life-style, of course, was less costly than that of a prince. A Bishop of Winchester could amass a private fortune, subject to a vital proviso. The last and, for his colleges, not the least important of Wykeham's triumphs over contemporary records was the longevity which allowed him to enjoy his rich temporalities for thirty-seven years (1367–1404).

It was an accepted practice enjoined by the Church's teaching that the prosperous should found ecclesiastical institutions on a scale commensurate with their affluence; by providing for the celebration of divine service they would earn heavenly bliss. Wykeham could contemplate making a foundation of unusually great proportions. At first he seemingly considered founding a monastic house, but dismissed the idea on discovering that none of the orders were properly observing their pristine rules. In fact, the old religious orders had by this time ceased to attract the charity of substantial benefactors. Foundations for secular clergy were the fashionable recipients of pious charity, and several of Wykeham's clerical predecessors in royal government had promoted the advancement of learning by endowing collegiate societies at Oxford and Cambridge. His experience as a bishop helped to direct his purpose in this direction. Despite his continuing activity in government affairs, Wykeham was a conscientious diocesan: although he could have employed a suffragan, he preferred regularly to celebrate general ordination services in his diocese. He was thus able to observe the small and still dwindling numbers of ordinands, a threat to the well-being of the Church which he attributed to the heavy mortality caused by continuing outbreaks of the Black Death and also to the rival attractions of war, commerce and industry.[1] He cited these reasons for the reduced numbers of scholars at Oxford in his charter founding New College, and declared his resolve to provide a remedy. The college was founded to honour the names of the Crucified and the Virgin Mary, exalt the Christian faith, profit the Church, and increase divine services and the study of arts and liberal sciences. As his charter continues, learned men were valuable to the Church and useful and necessary to the King and kingdom.[2] Wykeham was seemingly less interested in pure scholarship than in the utility of university education as a professional training. The majority of his seventy scholars were directed to study theology and so prepare themselves for the parochial ministry. He knew well enough that there were few careers open to graduates in theology. Royal and ecclesiastical government preferred to employ graduates in laws. By restricting the number to read laws to twenty, Wykeham was obviously not designing New College as an administrative staff college. Indeed, in his mind its fundamental purpose was as a great chantry to make intercession for the repose of his soul. He provided for the service of the chapel by ten chaplains, three clerks and sixteen choristers, and he ordered that they alone were to be retained if the college's income failed (rub. 68).

As Wykeham was not himself a university graduate, the most plausible reason for his choice of Oxford was its closer proximity to Winchester. There were vacant sites available for building because the town's population was suffering at least an equal share in the national decline which began in the first half of the fourteenth century and was violently accelerated by plague from its middle years. By English standards, Oxford had been a large town long before students settled there; from the eleventh to the thirteenth centuries, it ranked approximately sixth in size and wealth, with at least 5,000 inhabitants. The rebuilding of the town walls in 1226–40 marks the end of the medieval borough's period of greatest prosperity.[3] By 1377 the urban population had fallen to 2,357 adults.[4] The student population, as Wykeham observed, had also declined, although scarcely from 60,000 to 3,000 as his contemporary John Wycliffe claimed: more realistic modern calculations provide a generous maximum of 3,000 in the thirteenth century and near confirmation of the university's own statement in 1438 that 'hardly one thousand remain'.[5] Despite the high proportion of students in Oxford's overall population, the university had made little impression on the town's topography in the first two hundred years of its life as an academic community of international repute. The dominant building was still the castle, St Frideswide's Priory the largest within the walls. The university had long enjoyed the legal status of a self-governing corporation, able to make its own regulations for the education and conduct of its members, and to judge them in its own court without oversight by any higher authority, lay or ecclesiastical; but it was not endowed with buildings or an income adequate to finance such capital developments. Most undergraduates lodged with townsmen or rented rooms from them; others resided with masters who took leases of entire town-tenements which were thereafter dignified with the name of halls; for lectures and other university business use was made of churches and other domestic tenements, thus called 'schools'; even the chancellor had to find his own accommodation.[6]

This lack of public buildings appeared likely to persist because wealthy benefactors were now preferring to establish autonomous societies. The constitution of Merton College, finally revised in 1274, became the model for subsequent foundations, but the other five colleges for secular clerks had a total membership of little more than Merton's initial provision for over thirty fellows, while its chapel and gradually forming quadrangle made it the most substantial of Oxford's academic buildings. The purpose of these foundations was to enable graduates in arts to study theology, for unless a student had sufficient private means or a church benefice he was unable to stay for the many years necessary to read for a higher degree; indeed, poverty forced many to leave without a first degree. Only Exeter College (1314) admitted undergraduates, but they had to be natives of its founder's diocese who had already spent two years at the university. At Merton and Queen's (1341) the statutes provided for boys to be taught grammar (i.e. Latin), but these schools disappeared for lack of funds. Oxford was, however, already supplied with grammar schools of considerable fame, and doubtless many of their pupils subsequently became students in the university, when knowledge of Latin was essential for the study of all disciplines. These academies were run by independent masters renting halls; since their young pupils boarded, these masters often married. In contrast, the regent masters with halls for undergraduates would generally have remained celibate because they hoped subsequently to be beneficed clergy. Their pupils would have been little older than the boys in the grammar schools, perhaps in their mid-teens, and to their charges the masters would have been tutors as well as guardians. Grammar schools and undergraduates' halls must have been small: since each generally occupied only one tenement, few can have accommodated more than twenty pupils.

The scale alone of Wykeham's foundation was without parallel in Oxford. The original quadrangle of New College was the largest building erected in Oxford since the twelfth century, and its seventy scholars nearly equalled the total of fellows in the six older colleges for secular clergy. In addition, Wykeham's final design included all stages of education, from the initial grounding in grammar to ultimate specialisation in any of the disciplines studied at the university. These plans were developed over a number of years. In 1369, two years after becoming bishop, he began to buy properties, part of the future college's site. He formed a community of scholars, under a warden, who were temporarily housed at his expense in five contiguous halls at the west end of New College Lane.[7] At the same time he initiated a similarly informal precursor of his other collegiate foundation by housing a group of poor boys at Winchester; in 1373, he engaged a master to teach them grammar.[8] Wykeham aimed to ensure that his scholars at Oxford were competent Latinists by establishing Winchester College for the purpose and ordering that only its scholars were to be admitted to New College. He thus created a double foundation, a grammar school and a university college for all his scholars, who would be maintained by his foundations from their entry to Winchester at about the age of thirteen and for as long as they remained in New College. The concept of provision for both Latin teaching and university studies, including the tuition of undergraduates, may not have been entirely novel, but Wykeham was the first to give it formal and assured continuity by the munificence of his building and by the endowment of two colleges.[9] It was also unlike previous founders for Wykeham to have specified the number of scholars to be maintained: at Merton and Queen's the numbers of fellows had been reduced for economic reasons.[10] The first clause of the statutes for New College begins with the decree that there should be a warden and seventy scholars *for ever*. (Although formally the seventy were called 'scholars', all were fellows: in practice, the description 'scholar' referred to a member of under two years' standing, who was a probationary fellow, after which he normally became a member of the governing body and thus a full 'fellow'.)

The formal establishment and building of Wykeham's colleges followed a temporary eclipse in his fortunes. The offence he gave in the Good Parliament of 1376 to John of Gaunt and the clique ruling the senile Edward's court led to his banishment from the capital, the sequestration of his revenues, and the disbandment of his Oxford scholars.[11] Rescued and restored by the accession of Richard II, Wykeham may well have been made aware that the fulfilment of his aspirations required their urgent translation into legal and architectural reality. In 1379 he obtained the Crown's licence to found and endow a college of a warden and seventy scholars in Oxford, and five months later, on 26 November, he granted his own charter, giving his community the legal symbols of a corporate body and the name of 'St. Mary's College commonly Seynte Marie College of Wynchestre'.[12] The foundation stone was laid on 5 March 1380. The society was able to leave its temporary accommodation on 14 April 1386. On that day, the Saturday before Palm Sunday, the warden and fellows walked in procession, following a cross and singing the litany, and thus entered and began residence in the completed quadrangle. The name New College was soon being used to distinguish it from the older college of St. Mary (Oriel).[13] From the following year Wykeham diverted his resources to his second college at Winchester.[14]

It was fortunate for New College that Wykeham lived so long. The original endowment consisted only of the grounds in which the college was to be built. It appears that Wykeham was not yet able to give his foundation an adequate permanent endowment, for the two earliest substantial properties he gave—the rectories of Adderbury (Oxfordshire) and Steeple Morden (Cambridgeshire)—actually belonged to his bishopric, which he undertook to compensate. By 1381 he had acquired some more lands for the college, but until 1392 it was being supported by receipts from lands legally still in his own possession, some of which he was to retain for his natural heirs. The endowment was nearly doubled between 1389 and 1394. Wykeham arranged to purchase the English estates of a hospital in Rome and four French religious houses which had been sequestrated by the Crown because of the war: his plan to buy three Wiltshire manors from Boscherville Abbey seemingly fell through, but the college was in possession of the remainder in 1392.[15] Most of this property was in Essex, whence the college's receipts in 1396–7 amounted to £185 11s. 6d. Property in London, Kenninghall (Kent) and Tingewick manor (Buckinghamshire) acquired from the same sources yielded £18 14s. 0d., and the two Wiltshire manors of Colerne and Stert which had recently reverted to the college produced £59 16s. 4d. These latest acquisitions provided a large proportion of the year's total income of £627 12s. 8¾d.[16]

Until his death in 1404, Wykeham was actively concerned with the college's well-being. He appointed a commission in 1385 to investigate reports he found hard to believe, that wild grapes were growing in his vineyard, with odious comparisons giving rise to strife and indiscipline. Next year, he ordered the warden to admonish fellows who were disobeying certain of his statutes. He gave new statutes in 1389 which probably transferred executive responsibility for the college's finances from the warden to the three bursars. A visitation by the Founder's commissioners in January 1393 was followed by a further reform of the statutes and immediately afterwards, in May, the college began to record fellows' oaths in a 'great register'.[17] Another innovation was that from 1396 the office of warden was filled by election by the fellows; the Founder had appointed the first two wardens, Nicholas Wykeham in 1379 and Thomas Cranley in 1389.[18] More amendments had been authorised by 1398 when payments were first made to fellows who had tutored scholars, at 9d. a head for a term. Wardens and fellows were frequently required to visit Wykeham at various places in his diocese. Warden Cranley was twice called to London as well in 1395, once to preach before the King on Whit Sunday.[19] Four months later Richard II granted charters of privileges to Wykeham's two colleges; this was done in recognition of the Founder's long record of service to the Crown, but the warden's sermon may have helped to win the King's favour because it was also followed by his own promotion.[20]

It was presumably at Wykeham's instance that in 1399, three years after the college gained full possession of its endowment, a calculation was made to show whether the actual receipts of this period would have been sufficient if expenditure had been at the maximum level permitted by the statutes for the whole three years, and it was possibly as a result of this exercise that he added the last clause of the statutes.[21] This justifiably states that he had given much thought to ensuring that the goods he had given to his scholars should endure to fulfil his purpose. The statutes were therefore to be immutable; Wykeham allowed only their literal interpretation, and he pronounced anathema and God's wrath on any member who might fraudulently violate them. Realistically, however, he envisaged a possibility that the value of the college estates could so far decline that their revenue became insufficient to support the full establishment, and he ordered a sequence of economies to be made as the college's impoverishment worsened, down to a reduction in the numbers of fellows and scholars; only the chaplains and clerks of the chapel were exempted from redundancy (rub. 68).

The close ties Wykeham maintained with New College in its first twenty years, in addition to the munificence of his provision for it, helped to create a tradition in which his memory was to hold a place in the minds of his scholars equivalent to that accorded by monastic communities to their patron saints. His life also was eulogised in literary form.[22] To ensure full knowledge of the statutes, he ordered their public reading in chapel three times a year, and that every member should read them in his chamber once annually, either privately or with his two or three companions (rub. 60). As a number of the rubrics gave Wykeham's reasons for making certain provisions, members would have been impressed with his deep concern for the well-being and harmony of his society, with his piety, wisdom and generosity. In a spirit of affectionate veneration, members of the college adopted the adjective 'Wykehamist'. The warden and fellows sent a plea for assistance to Archbishop Warham in 1526, 'ex collegio tuo Wychamensi', and in return they promised to celebrate his memory in chapel as they did 'pro Wycamo nostro'.[23] This sense of personal attachment is uniquely illustrated by John Russell's coat of arms. Having none of his own when he became a bishop in 1476, and in the manner of a twelfth-century knight publicising his loyalty to the lord of his fee, Russell adopted Wykeham's two chevrons between three roses.[24]

The endowments, accumulated by Wykeham's piecemeal and fortuitous purchases, consisted of estates of varying extent in nine counties. Apart from the spiritual profits of the appropriated rectories and a few tenements in Oxford, the college's revenue came from agricultural land, either as rents from the customary tenants of its manors or as farms for the leases of the larger properties, including the rectories. Like all other substantial proprietors at this time, the college did not retain any of its land to grow crops for its own consumption. It might be supposed that the farms whereby estates were leased for stipulated charges would have assured the college of certain income. As England's rural economy was generally stagnant if not declining until the close of the fifteenth century, the long terms of these farms (often for twenty years) would not have been to the college's disadvantage. In practice, however, receipts from every property varied from year to year, sometimes very considerably. Beside the vagaries of tenants with their rents, the level of receipts might be affected by an occasional bonus like the sale of timber, or adversely by a bill for repairs to buildings; allowances had to be made to farmers for expenses and losses, like those suffered by the farmer of Hornchurch from the ravages of the Duchess of Buckingham's rabbits.[25] Happily for the college, and perhaps in consequence of the wide distribution of its properties, the revenues were generally protected by a dispensation of 'swings and roundabouts' and annual accounts mostly closed with a balance in hand. This comfortable situation would have been impossible had the college not been exempted from taxation by Richard II.[26]

There was little need for the Founder's injunction that the warden and fellows should show all diligence in defending the college's property: they must have been sufficiently aware that their corporate income was only just adequate. As if the college had no credit, or feared to incur the smallest debt, revenues were received from its properties in small portions throughout the year: some were delivered by local officials, others collected by the warden during his progresses, and once or twice a year a fellow would be sent into Essex, and another to Wiltshire, 'to get money'.[27] All the fellows were required to meet in the chapel when important business had to be decided, such as resort to litigation, presentations to benefices and grants of farms, for which Wykeham prescribed the maximum terms of years; disputed issues were to be determined by the will of the majority, provided that it included ten lawyers (rub. 10, 47–8). Three fellows were to be annually appointed as bursars to receive payments from farmers and manorial officials under the oversight of the warden, subwarden, five deans and three senior fellows, while expenditure was to be authorised by a majority of fellows (rub. 49). College property was to be inspected by the warden and a fellow twice annually, after Easter and in September, and in October all the farmers and other accounting officers were to come to New College for an audit of their records by the warden (or subwarden), the deans and five other senior fellows (rub. 54). After the audit, the warden, subwarden, deans and bursars were to draw up an annual *valor* of the college's lands, and this was to be inspected by thirteen seniors (rub. 56).[28] All the fellows must thus have taken part in the college's administration, and most of the seniors were actively and regularly engaged; the Thirteen became the college's standing committee of management.

Wykeham described the college as a community of poor scholars—in the worldly sense, of course—and he intended that they should so remain. Beside forbidding that members should have private means above a very modest level, he required them to live in a restrained clerical style; it was unseemly, he wrote, that the poor living on alms should feed and possess dogs, ferrets or any birds of prey, nor should they engage in dishonourable games like chess or football (rub. 2, 25). In order to promote mutual charity, he decreed that fellows should be uniformly dressed, but he would not have them appear indigent and therefore required that a livery of cloth should be given to every fellow at

Christmas, as well as 6s. 8d. for fur; these clothes were not to be sold within five years, although they could be given to new fellows (rub. 22). The annual bills for cloth and furs show that liveries were also given to college retainers, among them some incumbents of its livings and manorial officers; they amount to about £90 in the fifteenth century, a sixth of the total at the bursars' disposal.

The largest item in a year's expenditure was the cost of commons, the allowance for food which Wykeham stipulated should normally be 12d. a week for fellows. The ten chaplains of the chapel had the same allowance, and when this was the current rate the allowance for servants was 8d. and for choirboys 4d. (rub. 15). The fellows who took it in turn to act as steward of the hall for a week thus had about £5 at their disposal. A stewards' book for the year 1508–9 shows their weekly accounts: for most days they bought salt-fish or beef and mutton, eggs, bread, butter and one pennyworth of mustard, and they made a single purchase of the week's supply of salt, logs, sometimes of candles, and beer, the last of which usually amounted to a fifth of the week's total bill. The Founder allowed an addition of 6s. 8d. for each of thirteen feast-days, when the warden would dine in hall (rub. 11). For these occasions the steward bought a greater variety, including 'currys', 'larcks', 'ploverys', 'blackebryddes', 'rabettes', pork, cheese and wine.[29]

Wykeham provided for inflation and its reverse, the *varietas temporum* which caused prices to rise and fall. The rate for commons was to be determined by the price of wheat: if this rose, the weekly allowance could be increased to between 13d. and 16d., and even to a ceiling of 18d. when the price of wheat in the Oxford district was above 2s. 0d. a bushel (about 50 lb.) for twenty days (rub. 15). In most years of the late fourteenth century, in fact, wheat usually cost less than 8d. a bushel, but it had been nearly double this price in 1390, and Wykeham no doubt recalled that in 1369 the price had approached the disastrously high figure envisaged in the final version of his statutes.[30] The college's economy would certainly have been ruined by a sustained famine con-dition of this order. The calculation of college expenditure in the three years 1396–9 shows that if the fellows' weekly allowance had been 18d. in the whole period, the total cost would have been £1,077 14s. 10d. The actual total cost in those years was £694 9s. 6½d. because the number of fellows in residence was always below seventy and the weekly rates obtaining were well below 18d.: in the year 27 September 1398 to 26

September 1399 the rate was 15d. in the first six weeks, and thereafter 14d., except for 16d. in the last two weeks of 1398; while the number of fellows in receipt of commons was over fifty in no more than fifteen weeks and averaged forty-two over the year. Other expenditure in this three-year period included £273 for cloth and furs, £124 for the expenses of the chapel including the chaplain's wages, £120 for the warden's stipend of £40 p.a., and numerous miscellaneous wages, allowances and expenses, and a bill of £91 14s. 0d. for unspecified building work (the belfry?) in 1398–9 alone, in all amounting to £1,034 13s 8¾d. At the end, the bursars could report a credit balance of £46 0s. 2¾d.: it would have been a debt of £337 5s. 0¾d. if the maximum payments for commons had been made continuously throughout the period.[31]

For the next thirty years it must have seemed that this calculation was unrealistically pessimistic. Then in 1428 and 1429 the price of wheat stood at over 1s. 0d. a bushel, nor did it soon return to its normal previous level of about 6d. The college remained solvent by not paying Warden Estcourt his stipend from 1432, and after his arrears had been paid, the credit balance in September 1435 was a mere £5. He had still not been paid in full when he resigned that year, nor could the college's bill for cloth be met. In September 1436 the debts amounted to £63, but net income rose to £650 with a payment of £80 for arrears by manorial collectors, and the year's account closed with £51 in hand. The college may have felt that the crisis had passed, but there followed the most disastrous harvest in English history since the famine years of 1315–22. In 1438 the price of wheat did reach 2s. 0d. a bushel. The next surviving bursars' account shows debts of £139 in 1440, while receipts from the estates were down to £510, doubtless as a consequence of the impoverishment of tenants, some of whom may have died from starvation.[32]

Wykeham had given the college £2,000 in cash which, he ordered, was to be kept as a secret reserve in an inner coffer in the chest for the college's most important records. This money was to be reserved for emergencies, such as lawsuits, the repair of buildings destroyed by fire, or the acquisition of property (rub. 50). Apart from a loan of £40 to the Founder's heir, Thomas Wykeham, in 1420, the college had faithfully refrained from making any use of this enormous treasure: none of the specified contingencies for its employment had arisen. Payment of debts in a period of acute financial stringency was not one of these permitted causes, but an indirect and allowed method of its employment to recover solvency was to increase the college's revenue by the purchase of more land. An opportunity to do this was now provided by the former fellow Thomas Beckington, the King's secretary, who persuaded Henry VI to grant the college the five manors and other property of the confiscated alien priory of Newton Longville, Buckinghamshire. The college paid £648 13s. 5½d. from the reserve to obtain this grant in 1441, and at least another £100 for contingent costs were paid from income in the following years; for the grant itself the cost was 500 marks (£333 6s. 8d.), but the college also had to settle with a royal creditor who had been given a charge on the property.[33] Bishop Beckington's later gift of 100 marks, some smaller bequests, and the tardy repayment of Thomas Wykeham's loan, were placed in the chest and regarded as contributions to the purchase price for Newton Longville.[34]

This estate added about £90 to the college's annual income. In 1442–3 this reached the record level of £734 and the debts were repaid. The relief was only temporary. In the following years receipts from the estates averaged about £650, the lowest point of £569 being reached in 1464–5.[35] It is possible that the breakdown of public order associated with the Wars of the Roses contributed to the uncertainty of the college's finances. Fortunately throughout the period 1440–80 the price of wheat generally remained in the range of 6d. to 8d. a bushel. There were few weeks, moreover, when the number of fellows and scholars in residence was over sixty. Consequently annual expenditure on commons stayed close to a mean of £220. In 1482, however, the price of wheat reached its highest level since 1438, and the bursars described the three years 1481–3 as a time of *caristia*; they had to spend £271 on commons in 1483–4, and £277 in the next year, when the account closed with £6 13s. 2½d. in hand.

By this time it is probable that the reserved treasure was no longer available. The last record of its existence is dated 1463. This was when Edward IV repaid most of a loan of £160 made to him on 18 October 1461. The college had never made a loan to one of the Lancastrian kings. To have done so would, of course, have broken the security about the treasure which Wykeham had ordered. That Warden Chaundler and his colleagues should have been more complaisant towards their new Yorkist king is suggestive of their sympathies—or fears. How Edward could have known of the treasure's existence is less mysterious.

Two former fellows, John Russell and William Porte, were employed in the administration of his personal finances. If either was indeed responsible for this loan being made, he may equally have ensured that it was repaid. The total in the chest was now over £1,300. There is no record of its disappearance. A plausible explanation is that it was seized by one of the political factions in the disturbances attending the Earl of Warwick's brief restoration of Henry VI in 1470–1. There is apparent confirmation of its loss from 1486 onward, because now legacies to the college, previously stored in the chest, were received by the bursars and considered as part of income, as were gifts. One of £40 came from John Russell, now Bishop of Lincoln. It is tempting to conjecture that Russell's conscience prompted him to make this gift because of his betrayal of the college's secret and its disastrous consequence; whatever his motives were, his entertainment by the warden in February 1486 doubtless helped to stimulate his generosity.[36]

After the penurious years 1481–5, the pattern of the college's finances changed. This was nationally a period of improving fortune for landed proprietors; they were able to raise rents and farms because of the increasing demand of an expanding population. Over the next sixty years the general level of college revenue, from no more lands, gradually rose by 30 per cent, but expenditure also rose, and at a greater rate.[37] The bursars rarely completed their accounts at Michaelmas with as much as £50 in hand, and after 1521 this annual surplus rapidly disappeared: there was none at all by 1525, and from 1531 to 1537 the college was in debt.

The annual bill for commons was now between £250 and £300. It rose to £309 in 1527–8, when the maximum weekly rate allowed for fellows, 18d., was being spent. It seems that at this time it was necessary for scholars and fellows to supplement their maintenance from their own resources, because between 1518 and 1522 three resigned 'through poverty'.[38] Until 1536 the price for wheat was often just over 1s. 0d. a bushel, in fact at about half Wykeham's figure for famine-level. Even so it was seemingly agreed that his regulations about commons were no longer realistic. From 1532 the accounts show weekly allowances of 12d. for every fellow, but the bursars were permitted to make additional issues beyond the statutory rates 'propter caristiam temporis'.[39] The higher cost of the fellows' diet, which was obviously less farinaceous than the Founder had contemplated, is not the only explanation for this higher expenditure on commons. The number of fellows being maintained, either in college or in its country estates, was now closer to the maximum of seventy than it had been before the sixteenth century. Their furs and livery were also more expensive, and the college was spending more on legal costs and fees. The rise in revenue had not kept pace with inflation. No doubt the college's administrators were much concerned to devise remedies for this situation. It was at this time that the college became a sheep-farmer, renting a pasture at Headington for over 100 sheep.[40] Solvency returned in 1538 and was marked by a payment of £134 for an extension to the warden's lodging in 1540–1.

Despite the occasional crises in the college's finances it never failed to maintain its full complement of members. In every summer vacation, the warden or subwarden and two fellows visited Winchester to investigate the state of the college. They also examined its senior pupils on their proficiency in Latin and their other qualities so they might determine the order in which they should come on to New College. Wykeham's statutes, if strictly observed, provided that every vacancy in New College would be filled within a fortnight: a boy was allowed only twenty-four hours' notice to set off from Winchester and he was required to arrive in Oxford within eight days (rub. 3). It would seem that the journey was not without hazard, or perhaps some chose to defect *en route*, for between 1394 and 1478 some thirty scholars failed to arrive in Oxford.[41] At their admission, the freshmen had to take an oath to defend the integrity of both Wykeham's foundations. To maintain the harmony of the community, a theme to which the statutes frequently recur, the new scholar undertook not to speak contemptuously about any of his colleagues or to make disparaging comparisons about other faculties, parental status or places of origin. He further promised to join no confederacy directed against any fellow or against the college's statutes, either in England or outside the country (rub. 5). These last words are most suggestive. Presumably Wykeham could only have had in mind the possibility that a scholar might engage agents at the Roman curia to obtain a papal dispensation allowing him not to observe certain statutes. The oaths prescribed for fellows and the warden specifically renounced the freedom to seek dispensations from oaths (rub. 7, 9). Wykeham would have been well aware of the way discipline in monastic communities was being undermined by the readiness of the papal court to grant dispensations to individual monks. As a member of the King's Council, Wykeham doubtless had some part in preparing the statutes of *Praemunire*. His injunctions, intended to exclude the permissive influence of papal authority from New College, are in keeping with the temper of anti-papal legislation by late fourteenth-century Parliaments.

The admission of a scholar was recorded in the register of protocols.[42] Against his name was given that of the fellow or scholar he was replacing and often the cause of the latter's departure. These registers indicate that New College was markedly a community of young men: with the annual total of admissions averaging ten, it is obvious that few members were over twenty-five years of age. That a society of seventy members should need so many recruits every year reveals what is, by modern standards, an appalling rate of student wastage. Of 1,382 scholars admitted between 1386 and 1540, one in ten (140) died within their first four years, by the age of twenty and before taking a degree. Another 115 fellows died in college, of whom only five were more than forty years old. The younger men were buried in the cloister, their seniors in the antechapel. This level of mortality is not remarkable in an age notorious for its violent and insanitary society, when the average expectation of adult life in the English population was about thirty-five years. Epidemic disease obviously accounts for the particularly heavy toll in some years; the worst were 1420 and 1472, each with eleven deaths, while this figure was nearly equalled in 1435, 1479 and 1508. From 1501 the bursars' accounts sometimes show pre-cautionary measures being taken. From April to October of that year, the college was evacuated but for the staff of the chapel and, at most, a dozen fellows. 'For fear of the pestilence', the statute requiring full attendance (rub. 24) was disregarded and the majority were sent into the country with their tutors; the college paid for their keep on the conditions that they behaved as honest clerks and attended lectures and disputations.[43] There were only two deaths in college that year, but the mortality-rate did not fall significantly until after 1528.[44] In the next fourteen years, rustication to the college manors in south Buckingham-shire was frequent, sometimes extending over twelve months, and the total number of deaths in those years was six.[45]

Death thus accounted for a fifth of all vacancies. Many more were caused by the constant premature exodus of scholars and young fellows. At their admission, scholars promised to remain for at least five years (rub. 5). In fact, one in seven left before completing the requisite two years to qualify for election as a fellow, and the same proportion of fellows departed in their first two years, none having a degree. The statutes allowed for early withdrawal if the reason was approved by the warden and other seniors, and the registers record certain categories of causes, as well as a very few instances of expulsion. For about half the younger members to go, however, no cause at all is registered. From 1415 the cause 'having no mind to study' first appears, but whether it indicates a voluntary withdrawal must be uncertain: when it was known that capable boys were waiting to come from Winchester, college tutors would not have been anxious to retain unpromising pupils. None of the bursars' accounts show ex-members making any refund of their costs, as the statutes required of those who left for unapproved causes. A few went to enter religious houses. William Bere's entry into a convent in 1416 may have been the result of personal distress about the fate of his companions: of the fourteen scholars who had entered, as he did, in 1414, five were already dead and three more had abandoned their studies. The casualty-rate at New College, scholastic as well as literal, would certainly be deemed intolerable in a modern university. In medieval Oxford, however, it may be supposed that the general level of undergraduate wastage was higher than in New College, because Wykeham's scholars were maintained and enjoyed better living conditions than other Oxford undergraduates, who lived in halls or town lodgings and were more exposed to plague and poverty. Members of New College were housed three or four to a room, and the Founder had provided that all should have separate beds.

As the foundation was made to support poor scholars, members who inherited property worth five marks (66s. 8d.) a year were required to resign; only two or three fell into this category, which suggests that most came from humble homes or were younger sons. The most common registered reason for resignation of a fellowship was preferment to a benefice. The statutes required resignation on obtaining a benefice with a minimum annual value of ten marks (rub. 38). In making this regulation, Wykeham was thinking of a benefice as a source of revenue. Many senior members of the university were supported by their income from offices in the Church, although obviously they were non-resident and had to employ deputies to perform their spiritual duties. In Wykeham's day, the curate who served an absentee rector received a stipend of eight marks. A benefice worth less than ten marks clearly could not both pay a curate and provide its non-resident rector with an income to keep him at university. Members of the college instituted to rectories below this value would be obliged to reside in them for otherwise they would be deprived by their bishops for failure to perform their duties; they therefore had to resign from college. Those who acquired wealthier livings, however, would have had the means to remain in Oxford.

About a quarter of fellows who resigned on being beneficed are known to have taken degrees later or otherwise to have continued in Oxford. Even a few scholars were fortunate enough to have been given benefices. John Gome, one of the first scholars, left in 1390 when he became a rector, and his bishop licensed him to remain in Oxford for two years. A century later, Henry Rawlings enjoyed the patronage of bishops who gave him cathedral prebends, so allowing him to reside in Peckwater Inn and study canon law until 1508, twenty years after he had left New College. One or two scholars, like John Trill, with parents resident in Oxford, took degrees after leaving college. An occasional fortuitous notice reveals a former scholar's continuing presence in Oxford. Obscurity covers the career of Andrew Newport between his resignation in 1398 and his imprisonment six years later because bills in his name demanding a woman's release from Oxford gaol had been attached to the castle gate and the doors of two churches; he was able to prove himself innocent of this dubious act of chivalry. Sampson Hussey left college after three years for an unknown reason. Four years later, in 1510, he was convicted of carrying arms in Peckwater Inn; inappropriately, he was studying canon law. These Wykehamists who could continue their studies with the aid of parochial or private revenues can be regarded as mitigating the high level of academic wastage in college. It is noticeable, however, that none of these men who took higher degrees in Oxford after leaving the college achieved much eminence, with the exception of John Kingscot; fellow from 1434 to 1437, he continued in Oxford to become a doctor of canon law and, through service to the House of York, briefly held the bishopric of Carlisle (1462–3). One may suspect that these retired fellows, studying at greater ease than in college, lacked the stimulus to strive for further advancement, nor did they gain the administrative experience which came to longer-resident fellows by taking their turns to manage the business of the college as bursars and subwardens.

According to the statutes, the majority of fellows were required to study theology after becoming bachelors of arts. Wykeham stipulated that there should always be twenty fellows studying law. Of the remainder, he allowed that two might read medicine if there was a regent doctor in the university, and another two could study astronomy (rub. 1, 8); this last provision was a remarkable innovation, because the university did not have a faculty of astronomy. In fact, a total of eight fellows became bachelors or doctors of medicine before 1542, but only John Walter, one of the original fellows, was an astronomer. Those reading theology were required first to proceed in arts to the degree of master. While so doing, many rented schools and thus took an active part in the teaching work of the university. A minority thereafter incepted as scholars of theology, fewer still remained to take the baccalaureate. Most left Oxford when they obtained college livings or fellowships in Winchester College. Others went to Winchester to be warden, headmaster or usher in the college.

Wykeham's double foundation was obviously admired as an educational institution. In 1441, when Henry VI was planning his own twin-foundation, he paid the first of a series of visits to Winchester College, and soon afterwards its headmaster, William Waynflete, was appointed provost of the King's newly begun college at Eton. Waynflete and the Wykehamists Thomas Beckington and Richard Andrew were actively engaged in the foundation of Eton and King's College, Cambridge, helping to prepare statutes modelled on Wykeham's for Winchester and New College. Because all four colleges had been dedicated to the Virgin Mary and had similar purposes and achievements, their heads, fellows and scholars entered into the *Amicabilis Concordia* of 1444, whereby each party undertook to provide aid and counsel when required by another, and to give support in litigation in all courts of law, lay and ecclesiastical.[46] 'Maintenance' was the contemporary description for associations of this kind, and they were very necessary when titles to property were frequently challenged by claimants able to pervert legal processes in the notoriously corrupt judicial system of mid-fifteenth-century England. After five years at

Eton, Waynflete was promoted to the bishopric of Winchester and almost immediately, from 1448, began preparations for the foundation of Magdalen College and School; he likewise turned to Wykeham's statutes when drawing up his own.

These and other schools frequently recruited their teaching staff from New College. William Westbury, B.D., was Headmaster of Eton from 1443 to 1447 and then provost until his death in 1477.[47] John Stanbridge, M.A., Headmaster of Magdalen College School from 1488 to 1494, was the foremost grammar teacher of his day and his textbooks were widely adopted by other English schools. Another writer of textbooks on classical composition left New College in the same year as Stanbridge (1486): this was William Horman, M.A., who went to be Headmaster of Eton, next of Winchester, and finally Vice-Provost of Eton. Their contemporary John Rede, B.D., was Headmaster of Winchester from 1484 to 1490, when he was engaged by Henry VII to be tutor in classics to Prince Arthur; he was later Warden of Winchester (1501–20) and New College (1520–1). Other fellows, mostly in the early sixteenth century, became masters in various grammar schools. New College, through its theologians, thus made a useful contribution to the demand for qualified schoolmasters, but it should be noticed that the former fellows concerned rarely regarded teaching as a profession for life; after a few years, they moved on to church livings.

Most of the fellows who remained in Oxford long enough to receive degrees in theology also eventually retired to single benefices for the rest of their lives. William Snareston, M.A., a fellow for thirteen years, was Rector of Upper Heyford from 1447 to 1492. The record for longevity must, however, belong to the lawyer William Packett, resident in the college from 1428 to 1450 and then Rector of Radclive until his death in 1496. The oldest fellow to die in college, William Holmegh, aged 48, was a doctor of theology. His thirty years as a fellow were exceeded only by Robert Hansford, another theologian, who retired to a rectory after thirty-two years. One theologian had this to say about his years in college: Hugh Palmer, fellow from 1526 to 1545, wrote in his will: 'I was fellow of the New College in Oxford a longe span and bare office there, executing the same sumwhat negligently, and taking largely more peradventure than with good conscience I ought to have.' After Nicholas Wykeham, B.C.L. (1379–81), all the wardens were theologians until 1526. Only Walter Hill spent his entire adult life in

New College, where he died in 1495, aged about sixty-two. The other wardens were former fellows recalled from pastoral cures or from Winchester. Thomas Chaundler was Warden of Winchester for four years before his election to New College in 1454; he resigned as warden in 1475 but remained in Oxford, being Chancellor of the University, until his final departure for the deanery of Hereford in 1482. His predecessors had likewise preferred to end their days as beneficed clergy.

Few of the college's theologians became prominent outside Oxford. The second warden, Thomas Cranley (1389–96), apparently made some mark in the King's court with his sermon in 1395 because six weeks later he was given a prebend in York Minster. In 1397 he was sent on a mission to Rome, when the Pope provided him to the archbishopric of Dublin. Next, Richard II appointed him Chancellor of Ireland, and he was retained in this office by both Henry IV and Henry V. Cranley left Dublin in 1417, died in Berkshire, and was buried in New College chapel. A century later Hugh Inge, a protégé of Cardinal Wolsey, held the same Irish office and archbishopric (1523–8). Three other doctors of theology held more appropriate appointments in the King's household. William Say was obviously no partisan of Lancaster or York for he held the office of Dean of the King's Chapel under both Henry VI and Edward IV. Geoffrey Simeon held the same position under Henry VII. Richard Mayhew, appointed President of Magdalen by its founder, served Henry VII as almoner and ambassador until his promotion to the see of Hereford in 1504. More unusual for a non-mendicant theologian of his time was the career of John Young. In 1513 he became the suffragan of the Bishop of London and was accordingly consecrated as 'Bishop of Gallipoli', a title he retained until his death as Warden of New College (1521–6).

The Founder's emphasis on theology explains why more fellows took the degree of M.A. than any other higher degree, while the hard fact that there were few professional opportunities for a theologian other than the cure of souls accounts for the small proportion of masters proceeding to more advanced degrees. In contrast, the college's lawyers did have cause for greater persistence. Although they were much fewer in number than their theologian colleagues, they attained nearly an equal total of degrees higher than B.A.[48] Wykeham's statutes tried to ensure that there would be equal numbers of fellows engaged in the two branches of law studied at the university, namely ten in civil law and ten in canon law (rub. 1). In practice, the former predominated: the baccalaureate in civil law was taken by more members than any other higher degree save M.A., while many a fellow who left without a degree was registered as a *civilista*. Those who continued after taking the B.C.L., usually in the seventh year of a fellowship, mostly chose to spend another three or four years reading for a second baccalaureate in canon law, some of whom went on to become bachelors 'in both laws'. Only a score confined themselves to canon law alone. A very small proportion continued specialising in the law, canon or civil, of their baccalaureates until they were admitted as doctors.

A graduate in law was equipped for service in both secular and ecclesiastical government. He certainly could not practise or hold office in the country's courts of common law: they did not require a training in Roman law, and their practitioners and judges could only be trained in the Inns of Court. There were, however, many other courts requiring the civilians and canonists whom only the universities produced. The heavily judicial apparatus of the church establishment consisted of a network of nearly a hundred courts, those of archdeacons and jurisdictional peculiars at the lower levels, a consistory in every diocese and the audience of its bishop, and at the summits the provincial courts of the Archbishops of Canterbury and York. These courts and litigants in them employed graduates in laws as judges, advocates and proctors. Non-resident bishops and archdeacons engaged these ecclesiastical lawyers as their vicars-general and officials, who ended their days in the affluence of pluralism. Civil lawyers were also required in certain specialised royal courts, the courts of admiralty and chivalry. Roman jurisprudence regulated mercantile and other issues to which foreign nationals were parties. Likewise the conduct of international diplomacy, the concepts and language of negotiations and treaties, demanded that the King should employ civilians as members of delegations in meetings with foreign diplomats who would also include civil lawyers. To obtain this expertise, the King usually employed doctors of laws already engaged in the church courts in London who were thus, one might say, recruited to the diplomatic service on an *ad hoc* basis. It was only at the papal curia that fifteenth-century English kings were represented by permanently resident agents; for relations with other foreign courts, embassies and less formal missions were appointed when need arose. Doctors of laws who were regularly engaged on these commissions benefited from the Crown's ecclesiastical patronage, and the more distinguished of these clerical diplomats were appointed to the King's Council, some to high offices in his administration, such as keeper of the privy seal and chancellor; by this avenue these ecclesiastical lawyers won the royal favour which eventually made them bishops and archbishops.

One of the earliest fellows of New College stood for his successors as the prototype of civilian-diplomat. Henry Chichele was one of the scholars maintained by Wykeham in Winchester and Oxford while the colleges were being built. He was admitted B.C.L. during his tenure of a fellowship (1387–92). He resigned on being beneficed, became principal of the civil law school in Oxford, and proceeded to a doctorate. Then he departed to be an advocate in the Court of Arches and was soon acting as vicar-general in the diocese of Salisbury, rapidly acquiring canonries and other benefices. From 1404 Chichele was employed by Henry IV as envoy to the court of Rome and also in negotiations with France and Burgundy. He became Bishop of St. David's in 1408 and a member of the King's Council in 1410. Four years later Henry V had him advanced to the archbishopric of Canterbury. Thus by royal service—and longevity—Chichele acquired the means to found All Souls College in 1438, five years before his death. Four other fellows of twelve years' standing or more, and doctors of laws before their resignations from college, made their way into the King's service and consequently achieved episcopal rank. Thomas Beckington, from being Dean of the Arches, became Henry VI's secretary and keeper of the privy seal, and finally Bishop of Bath and Wells (1443—65). John Russell, a canonist, left Oxford after Henry VI's deposition to hold the same offices under Edward IV, who had him appointed Bishop of Lincoln (1480–94); he served Richard III as chancellor and Henry VII as a diplomat. Thomas Jane was a councillor of Henry VII and Bishop of Norwich (1499–1500). William Warham's career closely resembled that of Henry Chichele; he also left charge of the university's civil law school for practice in the Court of Arches, and then by service to Henry VII as a diplomat became Archbishop of Canterbury (1504–32). Robert Sherborne, although a bachelor of medicine, followed a career more appropriate to a lawyer, first as secretary to Cardinal Morton, then as a Canterbury administrator, and finally as the King's secretary and councillor, ending as Bishop of Chichester (1508–36).

The promotion of ex-fellows to bishoprics was a great asset to the college. Relations with them were cherished so that, if need arose, they could be called upon for material assistance or to use their influence at the King's court on the college's behalf. Strong personal ties of loyalty and affection were formed in New College. It was perhaps natural that ordained clergy, with no children of their own, should regard the society in which they had lived for sometimes up to twenty years from boyhood as their real family. The central bond between members of the college, however, was their loyalty to the Founder himself. Episcopal Wykehamists readily patronised their former colleagues.[49] Some were given openings to distinguished careers. Chichele gave offices in the Canterbury administration to Beckington, Richard Andrew, D.C.L., the first Warden of All Souls, later secretary to Henry VI and finally Commissary-General of York, and John Norton, D.Dec., who served in the admiralty court for many years, was Chancellor of the University in 1439, and ended his career as Vicar-General of York. In his turn, Beckington made Hugh Sugar, D.C.L. his chancellor, and Robert Hurst, bachelor in both laws, his commissary-general in Bath and Wells, and he introduced William Say to royal service by taking him on an embassy to France. Other fellows, including Warden Chaundler, were given canonries of Wells and other benefices at his disposal, while half a dozen boys from his native village of Beckington possibly owed to him their nominations to Wykeham's foundations. Bishop Russell likewise gave places in his cathedral chapter to members of the college, among them Nicholas Mayhew, D.C.L., and his more eminent kinsman Richard, Geoffrey Simeon and Henry Ainsworth, D.C.L. (of Bologna?), while he may have introduced Thomas Brent, D.C.L., to royal service. Brent was the Queen's almoner in 1479, and like Ainsworth and Simeon became a councillor of Henry VII. With William Warham, Thomas Jane, Richard Mayhew and Robert Sherborne, they formed a strong Wykehamist contingent among the small company of doctors of law and theology who, in regular attendance on the King, constituted the conciliar group which was later institutionalised as the Court of Requests.

This patronage enabled a number of intellectually ambitious fellows to escape from the conservative atmosphere of the Oxford schools. Few Englishmen of the early fifteenth century showed much interest in the

Italian revival of classical studies known as humanism, but among them were two former fellows, Thomas Beckington and Andrew Holes. Both were lawyers who entered royal service as diplomats and thus encountered Italian scholars, in Beckington's case as a member of the household of Humphrey, Duke of Gloucester. Beckington was more a patron than a practitioner of humanistic letters, but it is possible that he inspired Thomas Chaundler's interest in classical studies. Chaundler entered New College in 1435, the year when Duke Humphrey began the series of gifts which gave the university the first great English collection of manuscripts, including recent translations into Latin of Greek classical authors. The establishment of Duke Humphrey's library helped to stimulate interest in humanism at Oxford, and as warden from 1454 to 1475 Chaundler took a leading role in the promotion of these studies. His own literary work, some of it dedicated to Beckington, was pretentious and devoid of elegance: he remained essentially a schoolman. One of his protégés, however, did develop a capacity to write in a humanistic style and calligraphy. This was John Farley, another theologian-fellow who was appointed scribe of the university when Chaundler was its chancellor. There is cause to believe, moreover, that Farley was the first Oxford graduate of this period to learn Greek.[50] He may even have been more like the Italian humanists in his private life and philosophy, for he is not known to have been ordained or to have held a benefice, but as he was still a fellow at his death in 1464, he may be presumed not to have taken a wife.

Shortly after Chaundler's resignation, his successor Walter Hill and the seniors found themselves in difficulty. On 5 December 1475 they spent two hours trying to elect a subwarden and discovered, to their distress, that it was impossible to do this without violating the Founder's statutes. In their perplexity they wrote to seek the guidance of four distinguished ex-fellows, one of them Chaundler himself. The actual cause of the problem is not stated in their letter, but it may well be connected with the unusually high rate of vacancies in the preceding years, including the heavy mortality in 1472. In consequence, nearly all the fellows in college in December 1475 had been admitted after 1468: at Hill's election on 5 September five of the fellows were bachelors of laws, seven were masters of arts, six more were bachelors, and the other thirty-two fellows were undergraduates.[51] This was the minimum number of lawyers for the election of a subwarden (rub. 13), and there were not enough masters to make a total of thirteen seniors.

The four ex-fellows were asked to formulate a decree appropriate to the matter which could be added to the college's statutes.

And for as moche as statutes oftyn tymys be in grete dowte in ther sense by termys of Latyn, sum tyme in equivocacion, sum tyme in adverbyall or conjunccionall determinacion, but mooste ofte of erronyus undrestondyng by selfe wyll of men, we wryte unto yow undre playne and rude forme, praying yow when hytt shall lyke yow to make us an exemplar for the decree, that hyt be wrote under such wyse that our clowdy undrestondyying blemyshe nott your clere and bryght wysdome.[52]

The use of English in this letter is most interesting. The statutes required that members should use only Latin when speaking to each other (rub. 17), yet here is an admission of inability to interpret Latin with precision. The reasons given for the unsuitability of Latin as a language for exact definition, however, indicate that there was a specialist in the study of grammar in New College. His criticism of Latin as it was commonly used in the later middle ages was presumably due to his knowledge of the then novel methods of literary analysis practised by the humanists. His appreciation of language certainly enabled him to achieve an outstanding English prose-style. It is not difficult to identify this grammarian among the college's seniors in 1475. William Grocyn had entered the college in 1465, after already winning a reputation as a Latinist at Winchester. He was one of the five seniors appointed to act as scrutators at Warden Hill's election, and he was chosen to make the record of those proceedings. It is therefore almost certain that he drafted this letter three months later. Grocyn resigned as a fellow when he was beneficed in 1481, but for a while he remained in Oxford as reader in divinity in Magdalen College. It was perhaps under his tuition that the future schoolmasters Stanbridge, Horman and Rede developed their expertise as grammarians.

The difficulty of electing a subwarden was resolved by July 1476, when William Holden, M.A., is known to have been in office. He apparently was a conventional Oxford theologian, for he was to bequeath the college a manuscript of Duns Scotus. Grocyn also was a theologian, although he is not known to have been ordained. He was instituted to the college's rectory of Newton Longville, and in 1485 Bishop Russell granted him a prebend in Lincoln Cathedral. Their revenues allowed him to travel to Italy. He was not the first ex-fellow to study there, but his precursors John Boner and Richard Coole had gone respectively to Bologna (*c.* 1425) and Padua (1450) to become doctors of laws. Grocyn spent two years in Florence perfecting the knowledge of Greek which he probably first acquired in Oxford. On his return, he gave the first public lectures on Greek in the university, probably in Exeter College, where he rented a chamber in 1491–3. He also lectured in London, applying his techniques of textual criticism to challenge accepted theological learning. It was as a teacher, for he wrote little if anything of substance, that Grocyn made his name as the first outstanding English humanist.

In his later years Grocyn enjoyed the patronage of Archbishop Warham, whose time at New College (1473–88) coincided with Grocyn's, and it was possibly because of the latter's influence that Warham became England's Maecenas for humanists. Apart from his well-known patronage of Erasmus, Grocyn and other established scholars, Warham did much to enable younger men to study in the Italian fountainheads of humanism by using the patronage of his archbishopric as a fund for travelling scholarships. Those of Warham's New College protégés who later achieved distinction, however, preferred to study for conventional degrees in Italian universities. John Young—another of that name—returned as a D.C.L. from Bologna and Ferrara, and after serving Warham as chancellor became Master of the Rolls in 1508; frequently engaged in royal diplomacy, he was on the road to a bishopric when he fell to sweating sickness in 1516. William Knight, D.C.L., had a similar career as a diplomat and secretary to Henry VIII, ending as Bishop of Bath and Wells (1541–7). Others returned from Italy to remain members of Warham's entourage, Thomas Woodington, D.C.L., as Dean of the Arches, and Thomas Wells, D.D. (Turin), as the archbishop's dispenser of funds to humanists; he declined election as Warden of New College in 1520. Two other former fellows served Warham as secretaries. The diocese of Canterbury had a fair sprinkling of Wykehamist parsons and officials in Warham's time.

Numerous grants were made to the college by former fellows who had prospered outside Oxford. The four Wiccamical prebends in Chichester Cathedral were the benefaction of Bishop Sherborne to provide further patronage to support fellows. Clement Harding, D.C.L., official of the Archdeacon of Canterbury, left the college his lands. The college treasures and library were enriched by testamentary bequests, most notably by Warham's great collection of printed books and manuscripts. Richard Lavender, D.Dec., Archdeacon of Leicester, bequeathed all those of his books which a review body headed by the warden considered 'useful and necessary'. By this time (1508), many works of this category had been received, digests and commentaries on civil and canon law, doubtless much worn as their owners had practised and held courts in many places. Medical treatises were also received; the theologian John Green, a protégé of Chichele's, provided *Rosa in Medicinis*, presumably the work by John of Gaddesden (d. 1315). Less useful and necessary, perhaps, was the gift of Albrecht von Eüb's *Margarita poetica* by Robert Mason, D.C.L., Archdeacon of Northumberland, or the allegorical and theological exposition of Ovid's *Metamorphoses* from the canonist William North. North also gave a copy of that popular choice of 'the general reader', Higden's *Polychronicon*, as did Robert Thurbarn, D.M., Warden of Winchester. Another Warden of Winchester, Michael Cliffe, D.Dec., bequeathed a standing piece of silver of which the cover had 'ly knappe blew amelyd', and in 1509 William Speckington, D.C.L., added to the college's substantial collection of plate a silver nut set with the figure of St. John the Baptist on its cover. As well as plate for hall and chapel, vestments also were received. Bishop Beckington gave the college his best cross, the second best going to Winchester. The less prosperous ex-fellows made bequests too, like the twenty shillings from a Vicar of Rye or the simple piece of silver plate from William Snareston, the long-lived Rector of Upper Heyford.

The vast majority of Wykehamists did not have careers which brought material prosperity. Perhaps as many as half of the fellows spent most of their lives as parish clergy. Some taught in the grammar schools which were increasing in number throughout the country to meet an expanding demand for literacy. This great silent revolution of fifteenth-century England itself provides one reason why so small a proportion of Wykehamists won employment in secular administration, with its opportunities for eminence and wealth so amply exemplified by the Founder himself. The day for clerical administrators like Wykeham passed within two decades of his death: by 1430 most careerists in bureaucratic service were preferring to remain laymen and were adopting the personal description of 'gentleman' instead of 'clerk'. Except for graduates in laws and a smaller number in theology, few of the Crown's ministers and officials were now ecclesiastics.[53] The clergy had lost their near-monopoly of the skills of literacy and numeracy requisite for civil administration. Because many of the laity were now better educated than their forebears, they were less inclined to tolerate inadequately trained parochial clergy. This shortcoming was a familiar one, and founders of university colleges appreciated that it was a cause of the spread of heretical opinions. New College helped to provide a remedy for this problem in the parishes where its members exercised the cure of souls.

The college held the advowsons of a score of benefices because they were appurtenances of the manors either received from Wykeham or bought in 1441, and on nearly half the occasions when the warden and fellows made presentations they nominated one of themselves to fill the vacancy. The churches attached to the Founder's endowment were modest livings, most assessed at under £10 p.a. The fellows presented were thus not being given sinecures: they would be unable to employ curates and must therefore have accepted their presentations in the knowledge that they would have to reside in their benefices and apply themselves to their pastoral responsibilities. Undoubtedly other fellows obtained benefices which could be used as means of support while they continued their studies or began careers as ecclesiastical lawyers, but most of those who obtained college livings were obliged to regard them as vocations for the remainder of their lives. As nearly all the Wykehamist clergy in this category had read theology, one may presume that by the standards of the day they were well prepared for the parochial ministry. This had been Wykeham's major objective when founding his colleges. The statutes required fellows to be ordained and provided an incentive to take orders by allocating the sum of 40 marks to be divided annually among graduate-priests up to a limit of 40s. each; they were to be given instruction so that they could celebrate mass in the college chapel (rub. 29, 30).[54] The Founder's concern was less to enable clever boys to achieve lucrative careers than to educate poor scholars for the service of the Church. Thomas Kynow was a notable example of this kind of Wykehamist: after fourteen years at Winchester and New College, he served as Rector of Alton Barnes,

Wiltshire, from 1415 until his death in 1463, with an income of £6 p.a.[55]

The proportion of members who achieved distinction undoubtedly compares unfavourably with the records of other Oxford colleges. Fellows of other colleges, however, were usually graduates at the time of their election; they had already given proof of their competence for academic study. Admission to New College was of course restricted to scholars from Winchester, and the number admitted there was designed to match the places available at Oxford. When boys were chosen for admission to Winchester, it must have been difficult to discern which would have the potential to attain baccalaureates fifteen years later. There were statutory directions that priority was to be given to the Founder's kinsmen, next to natives of the estates of the two colleges, then to candidates from the diocese of Winchester, and finally from other counties in a certain order (rub. 2). The observation of these rules made New College a restrictively regional community: overall, more than two-thirds of all known members came from the five counties of Hampshire, Wiltshire, Oxford, Somerset and Berkshire. Most of the remainder came from London and Middlesex, Bristol and Gloucestershire, Essex, Surrey, Dorset and Buckinghamshire. Founder's Kin were not numerous: six were admitted in Wykeham's lifetime, another five in the following century; of these one, Thomas Gilbert (d. 1503), proceeded to a doctorate of canon law and became a diocesan official. It seems reasonable to suppose that the uneven level of academic attainment by members of the college was to some extent a result of these constraints in recruitment. A representative sample of the range of intellectual ability among New College men is provided by the members who came from Adderbury, the college-owned village which supplied the largest total of entrants: of the fourteen, one died young, six left without degrees, three ended as bachelors and two as masters of arts, and two took higher degrees, one being Richard Andrew, D.C.L., the first Warden of All Souls.

The society of New College was also 'comprehensive' in another way. Contrary to the intention indicated by the statutes, the college was responsible for introducing a new element into the traditional society of an English medieval university. Wykeham had required that his scholars should be fit to become fully ordained clergy (rub. 2). He allowed fellows to defer taking priests' orders, theologians for three years after incepting in arts and lawyers for up to fourteen years from the start of their studies; failure to comply was to incur immediate loss of commons and expulsion after three months (rub. 29). It seems that in practice fellows chose their own time to be ordained. Some became priests in the same year in which they became bachelors of arts, but then left college soon afterwards. Higher graduates ordained priest within three years of incepting likewise departed after a short interval. Those who remained, particularly the lawyers, but sometimes a theologian like John Farley, enjoyed some dispensation. Laurence Cox, D.Dec., was a fellow from 1450 to 1471 and three times subwarden; he was holding two cathedral prebends and a parish church when he was ordained priest in 1477. William Cruston, Richard Hayward and John Lichfield were all doctors of civil law before resigning their fellowships after fourteen years or more, but none was then a deacon. The future prelates, Chichele and Beckington, postponed their assumption of priests' orders until after their departure from New College, while Warham only reached the subdiaconate five years after his resignation, when he was forty-five years of age, beneficed and already launched as a diplomat. These doctors were primarily lawyers and they did not make a final commitment to clerical status until after establishing themselves in careers which could earn high preferment in the Church.

The college's most distinguished *alumni* were thus apparently reluctant priests, without any urgent sense of vocation for holy orders. There was seemingly no pressure of opinion in college to make them fall into line. One of the earliest fellows avoided all orders while in college. Ralph Greenhurst, admitted as a scholar in 1389, resigned in 1401 and in the following year received the first clerical tonsure. He eventually became a doctor of civil law but abandoned his clerical status by taking a wife. He was employed in embassies by the King and in 1411 was appointed Protonotary of Chancery, an office which made him responsible for diplomatic correspondence. His appointment required a relaxation of Chancery's rules barring married men from its senior positions. Dr. Greenhurst is a significant figure in the history of Chancery as one of the earliest in its soon increasing number of non-ecclesiastical officers. He was joined there by a junior contemporary at New College, Richard Sturgeon, who gave up his studies as a *civilista* in 1405 and was to be clerk of the Crown in Chancery for over thirty years;

he also married, and in his will, dated 1456, is described as a 'gentleman'.[56] Other fellows resigned to enter 'secular employment': there was John Barell in 1412, for instance, and William Benbury two years later. Further details of their careers have not been traced nor whether they retained clerical status. Unless a man was appointed to high office, his record comes to an end with his departure from college. The many others who left to take an appointment, or without registered cause, may well include some who lived as laymen. William Porte escaped this blanket of darkness. He resigned his fellowship in 1423, after six years as an artist and student of theology, and next returns to view as a servant and executor of Cardinal Beaufort, Bishop of Winchester, in 1447. Then after another interval he was holding the royal offices of treasurer of the chamber and keeper of the jewels under Edward IV. He continued his association with the college, gave a score of volumes to the library and many furnishings including an organ to the chapel; with his wife, Porte was enrolled among the college's benefactors.

Because a somewhat reserved attitude to the priesthood was tolerated in New College, it seems in keeping that some of its members should become early examples of lay members of the civil service. It was for the same reason, perhaps, that the college admitted scholars who not only never became clergy but of whom it was probably known at the time that neither they nor their parents were willing that these young men should have any kind of clerical career. This was apparently the case with Thomas Wykeham, the Founder's great-nephew. He was admitted as a fellow in 1390, registered as a *civilista*, but resigned after four years. He then entered royal service and in 1404 inherited the bishop's personal estates, estimated to be worth £400 p.a. Thomas Wykeham built Broughton Castle, was knighted, and represented Oxfordshire in four Parliaments between 1402 and 1425.[57] Also admitted in the Founder's lifetime were Edward and John Brocas, neither of whom remained long enough to become a fellow. They were kinsmen of Wykeham's friend Sir Bernard Brocas and so members of one of the leading families of Hampshire and Surrey. John Brocas married; his son, a commoner at Winchester who did not go on to New College, was also a member of Parliament.[58]

A fair proportion of the boys admitted to Winchester as commoners apparently belonged to knightly families and their academic careers were often brief. After one or two years at Winchester, they were admitted as scholars there and were able to proceed to New College in due course. One of the earliest was John Lucas of Hampton-on-Thames, whose record ends in 1408, after four years in New College. When the term 'being minded to give up study' first appears in the college register in 1415, it is applied to a scholar admitted in the previous September. This was Richard Hankford, a commoner at Winchester from 1408; there he was excused payment 'in respect to William Hankford, the king's justice', who was his grandfather and had been personally acquainted with Wykeham, presumably as a legal adviser. By 1415 Sir William was Chief Justice of England and hoped to found a knightly dynasty in his native Devonshire. Richard, now his heir, was doubtless removed from New College to assume the role of a youth with his expectations, and in July 1415 this would require his enlistment in one of the companies which Henry V led to Agincourt. By 1421, Richard Hankford was sufficiently experienced a soldier to be engaged by the King with his own retinue for the French war and subsequently, at the time of the siege of Orleans, he was on the staff of the Earl of Salisbury, whose daughter he had married after the death of his first wife. Wykeham had deplored the departure of Oxford men to the French wars, but it is unlikely that Hankford was the only member of the college to answer the call to arms: why else should a Wavell have left in the year of Bosworth? One of the few treatises written by a fifteenth-century Wykehamist was *De Officio Militari* by Nicholas Upton, D.Dec.; Upton had come to Oxford the year before Hankford and he also was a member of Salisbury's entourage in 1428. Hankford was another early Wykehamist to be a member of the House of Commons, as shire-knight for Devon in 1423, and but for his early death in 1431 he would probably have been called to the Lords, for his first wife was heiress to a barony. The Hankford dynasty failed for lack of male issue, but this fleeting member of New College was a direct forebear of Queen Elizabeth I.[59] Other commoners at Winchester included John Kingscot and John Farley, whose academic careers have already been noticed. One of the last in the fifteenth century was Geoffrey Kidwelly of Odiham, a scholar of New College for fifteen months, who may have been the son of Richard III's attorney-general. New College also had commoners during Chaundler's wardenship: one who was a kinsman of Bishop Beckington was deflected from study by marriage.[60]

Contemporary with Richard Hankford was Richard Wallop. He also abandoned his studies in the autumn of 1415. A namesake left in 1442 after two years as a fellow, while a third Wallop, Robert, is only known to have been admitted to New College in 1469. None of these members of successive generations of the Wallop family is known to have been ordained as clergy, and this was certainly not the case with a fourth, Giles, who resigned his fellowship in 1512 after telling the warden that he had a wife. The Wallops doubtless returned to their native Hampshire to the life of estate-management and participation in local government which was the lot of gentry families. With the second Richard Wallop the cause of resignation was registered: he went *ad curiam*, that is to one of the Inns of Court where, as his contemporary Sir John Fortescue wrote, many young men of good birth came to acquire social accomplishments as well as a training in the common law. By no means all of these students at the inns became professional lawyers but, like their peers the Pastons, they had good cause to believe that a knowledge of common law was essential to all men with expectations of property in that corruptly litigitious and disorderly age. The Inns of Court already had the role of England's third centre of higher education although obviously, unlike Oxford and Cambridge, they were not part of the clerical establishment. Some other students at the inns in the fifteenth century are known to have previously spent a few years at Cambridge—like the Pastons—or Oxford, but it is probable that they were studying grammar with private tutors rather than following courses with junior members of the university; nor, of course, were they fellows of colleges.

The first fellow of New College whose cause of resignation was registered as *ad curiam* was Bartholomew Bolney, who went to Lincoln's Inn in 1423 and was a reader and treasurer there; presumably he built up a legal practice in Sussex, where he served on many judicial commissions and was its shire-knight in the Parliament of 1460.[61] There may well have been other members of the college whose unexplained departures marked their entries to the profession of common lawyer, the later details of their careers being obscure because they did not practise and win advancement in the courts at Westminster. One such Wykehamist is known because in middle life he reverted to the clerical estate. After three years at Oxford, Roger Housewife had turned to the common law and practised in the east midlands, becoming a J.P. in Leicestershire and a judge (perhaps recorder) in Lincoln. By his own account, he declined the serjeant's coif and instead, by papal dispensation, was ordained priest and became an itinerant preacher. In 1437, thirty years after he had left Oxford, Convocation permitted him to proceed to the degree of bachelor of theology.[62] John Brown, Thomas Heveningham and Henry More were contemporaries of Richard Wallop who went from fellowships *ad curiam*, as did Thomas Welles in 1475. At least two other fellows resigned for the same reason in the 1470s, although it is not given in the register. John Newport left for Lincoln's Inn and ended as its governor and a serjeant-at-law, and John Kingsmill, a fellow for three years until 1479, crowned his career as a justice of Common Pleas (1504–9).

Wykeham had intended New College to educate men in accordance with his diagnosis of the needs of society and government in his own day. The careers of individual members, however, show that his society of scholars, although restricted by his statutes, was not unresponsive to new requirements from its changing national environment. Some met the public demand for more teachers of grammar, a few were prompted by the challenge to traditional scholarship launched by Italian humanism. By the first decade of the sixteenth century, a considerable proportion of the Crown's servants entrusted with executive power were common lawyers, not clerks or graduates as in Wykeham's time. Against this background, John Kingsmill is as significant a figure in the college's history as William Grocyn. While Grocyn was the first outstanding example of the traditionally educated Oxford theologian to adopt humanistic techniques to dispute the accepted learning of his discipline, Kingsmill was the first Wykehamist to abandon the law schools of the university and reach the summit of the profession of common law. The departure of Kingsmill and other fellows *ad curiam* foreshadowed the triumph of common law over other branches of jurisprudence, and thus of the sovereignty of the Crown over the English Church. The Henrician Reformation was not achieved by the *diktat* of a monarch possessed of absolute power: it required the consent of a substantial proportion of a political nation jealous of its traditional liberties. That this consent was forthcoming indicates that opinion was not unprepared for the legislation of the Reformation Parliament. Part of this process of preparation was the gradual erosion of adherence to certain aspects of the ecclesiastical structure which had long prevailed in pre-Reformation society.

Increasing departure from traditional clerical *mores* can be illustrated from an examination of the crude statistics of admissions to New College before and after 1480, the mid-point between the resignations of Kingsmill and Grocyn. By taking the figures from then to 1529, the year when the Reformation Parliament met, and comparing those for the previous fifty years, it emerges that in the later period many more men were passing through college. At the same time, members were being recruited from a wider geographical area: twenty-two counties were represented in 1430–79, thirty-one in 1480-1529. This suggests that Winchester was unable to attract sufficient recruits from its customary 'catchment area' despite a slight rise in the population; it cannot be argued that standards for admission had been raised, because a higher proportion of New College men were leaving within a few years of entry. In fact, in the half-century from 1480 there were twenty or more scholars in residence in each of twenty-nine years and often more than half the total of seventy members were undergraduates.[63] This was therefore a sustained trend implying a reduced degree of motivation for the fruits of university education, but unfortunately the registers are silent about the causes of most withdrawals. A fair number of scholars and junior fellows are said to have given up their studies. From 1514, others made the same decision less courteously, being excluded after absence beyond the statutory limit of two months and two days. More were now leaving 'to study the laws of the realm'; there were four such defections to the Inns of Court in 1518 alone, including two fellows in their fourth or fifth year in college.[64] They were not the only members to prefer lay status. The first recorded instance of resignation to marry occurred in 1508: Thomas Bentley had been a fellow for twelve years and was reading medicine. Other fellows whose qualifications were more appropriate for a clerical profession also left to marry; there were, for instance, Henry Watts, M.A., in 1519, and James Edyall, B.C.L., in 1525. Another possible indication that the tide of opinion in New College was turning against the conventional standards of the medieval Church is that from 1494 onward the bursars never had to pay the graduate-priest's fee to more than twelve fellows in any one year.[65]

A further omen is the appearance from 1510 of another category of cause for resignation, 'to transfer to civil law', and a little later, perhaps meaning the same, of 'having no wish to study arts'. Robert Chalner was seemingly the first thus to revolt against the Founder's limitation of the number of fellows who might read law; Archbishop Warham came to his rescue with a benefice so that he was able to proceed to B.C.L. and take a doctorate abroad. Almost annually from 1514 there was a resignation to witness a preference of civil law to theology.[66] Then in 1526 the college for the first time elected a lawyer as warden. John London, D.C.L., has an unsavoury reputation as a prosecutor of Protestants and suppressor of monasteries. Possibly Thomas Cromwell, as Henry VIII's vicar-general, would still have employed him if he had not been warden: he had been engaged in ecclesiastical jurisdiction before his election. His electors in 1526 could not have foreseen their candidate's notoriety, yet they did choose a man suited to serve his time and so again show the college responding to the changing character of English public life. Warden London received twenty-eight of a total of fifty-one votes. The college's theologians were in complete disarray, a few supporting London, the others dividing their votes among five other candidates. Their disunity may reflect the contemporary crisis in theological studies, the division between traditionalists and humanists; some fellows may even have been influenced by Luther's recent challenge to orthodox doctrine. The heavily outnumbered civilians were obviously more united in purpose, also more distinguished in leadership: there was only one bachelor in theology but seven in laws, of whom Robert Hunt was soon to become principal of the university's civil law school. Headed by the subwarden, all seven voted for London, with the bulk of their following provided by the more junior fellows.[67]

This victory of lawyers over theologians at New College is significant in the national context. Six years later the English clergy made their submission to Henry VIII, accepting his judicial sovereignty in ecclesiastical causes. The acquiescence of bishops to the King's will, their failure to defend papal supremacy, are more readily explicable when it is considered that the majority of them were graduates in civil law and thus intellectually committed to the doctrine of the sovereign state and the overriding claims of princely authority. It was appropriate that their leader, William Warham, Primate of All England, was a member of the society founded by that great 'king's clerk', William of Wykeham.

REFERENCES
1. R. L. Storey, 'Recruitment of English Clergy in the Period of the Conciliar Movement', *Annuarium Historiae Conciliorum*, 7 (1975), 293–6.
2. *Liber Statutorum Collegii Beate Marie Wyntoniensis in Oxonia* (1797), preamble; N.C. MS. 5567. The final version of the Founder's statutes is also printed in *Statutes of the Colleges of Oxford* (London, 1853), i. Further references to them will be given by citing rubric numbers in brackets. The college's muniments [hereafter cited as N.C. MSS.] are admirably listed in Steer, *Archives*. N.C. MS. 5567, Wykeham's charter of 30 November 1379, with other foundation documents, was printed for the college to commemorate the fifth centenary.
3. H. C. Darby, *An Historical Geography of England before A.D. 1800* (Cambridge, 1948), 218, 220, 222; and *Domesday England* (Cambridge, 1977), 306; H. E. Salter, *Medieval Oxford* (Oxford Historical Society, 1936), 23, 31–2, 87–9; Royal Commission on Historical Monuments, *City of Oxford* (1939), 159.
4. I.e. men and women aged fourteen and more. E. Powell, *The Rising in East Anglia in 1381* (Cambridge, 1896), 122.
5. H. Rashdall, *The Universities of Europe in the Middle Ages*, ed. F. M. Powicke and A. B. Emden (Oxford, 1936), iii, 326–33; cf. T. H. Aston, 'Oxford's Medieval Alumni', *Past and Present* 74 (1977), 6–7.
6. Rashdall, op. cit., iii, 164–5; Salter, 90–110; W. A. Pantin, 'The Halls and Schools of Medieval Oxford', *Oxford Studies presented to Daniel Callus* (Oxford Hist. Soc., 1964), 30–8, 82–7, 98–100.
7. N.C. MS. 7711; H. E. Salter, *Survey of Oxford* (Oxford Hist. Soc., 1960, 1967), i, 147–50.
8. *V.C.H.*, 155; G. H. Moberley, *Life of William of Wykeham* (London, 1893), 121–2.
9. A. B. Cobban, *The King's Hall within the University of Cambridge* (Cambridge, 1969), argues that Wykeham's double foundation was modelled on King's Hall and the choir-school of the Chapel Royal, but does not show that boys regularly proceeded from the chapel to King's Hall (46–65).
10. Rashdall, op. cit., iii, 192–210; Salter, *Medieval Oxford*, 93–7.
11. Wykeham is said to have dismissed sixty scholars being maintained at his expense in Oxford (*Chronicon Angliae* (Rolls Series, 1874, lxxx), but N.C. MS. 7711, the earliest surviving warden's account, shows forty to sixty scholars being kept in the year from 18 September 1376 without any break in their maintenance. The financial records cited in this chapter are listed in Steer, *Archives*, 16–24. The series listed as 'Coll. Acct.' are the central annual records of receipts and expenditure; they are entitled 'Warden's Account' initially, but from 1388–9 as 'Bursars' Account'.
12. *Calendar of Patent Rolls, 1377–81* (H.M.S.O.), 379; N.C. MS. 5567.
13. *V.C.H.*, 154, 155 and *n*. 97.
14. Moberly, op. cit., 215–19.

15. *Cal. Pat. Rolls, 1337–81*, 412, 621; *1381–5*, 63, 575; *1385–8*, 211, 368–9; *1388–92*, 262, 265, 386, 390, 407, 417; *1391–6*, 51, 62; *V.C.H.*, 155; N.C. MSS. 7330–41.

16. Including nearly £60 received from the bursars for 1395–6 (N.C. MSS. 7343–5). These are receipt rolls. Each of the three bursars kept a roll and all three for 1396–7 have somewhat unusually survived. They are indentures made from a single membrane. The central roll (i.e. indented at both margins) shows least receipts, the right-hand roll is the fullest and alone gives totals of receipts from every property. Under the heading for each manor were recorded, presumably as they were delivered by officials or fellows (see below, p. 11), up to about a dozen receipts in every year, the last being the delivery at audit. (Only the totals received from each property are shown in the bursars' main accounts.)

17. N.C. MS. 7340 (not 1394, as in *V.C.H.*, 155).

18. *Wykeham's Register*, ed. T. F. Kirby (Hampshire Record Soc., 1896–9), ii, 374–6, 383–4, 414–15, 425–6, 463–5; and see *n.* 11 above. Nicholas's relation to the Founder is not known. He is described as 'Kinsman'. He was a B.C.L. by 1372 and may therefore have been born by 1345. He died two years after Wykeham but could have been his junior by twenty years.

19. N.C. MSS. 7348, 7342.

20. *Calendar of Charter Rolls* (H.M.S.O.), v, 352.

21. Below, pp. 12–13.

22. R. Lowth, *The Life of William of Wykeham* (London, 1758), xiv–xxi; Moberly, xiv–xvi; cf. R. B. Dobson, *Durham Priory 1400–1450* (Cambridge, 1973), 12.

23. N.C. MS. 9748, ff. 229–30.

24. Converting Wykeham's *sable* and *gules* on *argent* to *or* and *argent* on *azure*. This coat-of-arms, now uncoloured, decorates Russell's chantry chapel in Lincoln Cathedral.

25. E.g. N.C. MSS. 2563–70. These are the earliest surviving examples (of 1466–82) of the series described by Dr. Steer as 'bailiffs' accounts' (*Archives*, 14, 20–1). They appear to be the records made at the annual audits. As they are written on paper, there may have been no intention that they should be preserved. Similar records were doubtless made at all audits since the foundation.

26. Moberly, 215–20; *Cal. Charter Rolls*, v, 352.

27. E.g. N.C. MSS. 7371, 7375, 2094, 1994.

28. For surviving *valors* (really annual views of account), see *Archives*, 3, 73.

29. N.C. MS. 2553.

30. J.E.T. Rogers, *History of Agriculture and Prices in England* (Oxford, 1866–1902), i, 232–4.

31. N.C. MS. 7348 (bursars' account for 1398–9). The calculation for 1396–9 is on a paper roll numbered 65 (in an obsolete series) in Box 25 of the muniments.

32. Rogers, iv, 282–4; N.C. MS. 7404–6.
33. *Cal. Pat. Rolls, 1436–41*, 359, 516, 558, 571; N.C. MSS. 7407, 7409–10.
34. N.C. MS. 4961 (Steer, 5) gives the entire history of this fund.
35. Of twenty-one known totals of annual receipts in 1443–80, three were between £592 and £599 (in 1443–4, 1460–1 and 1463–4) and two exceeded £700 (£720 in 1447–8 and £734 in 1479–80). For references, see *Archives*, 19–21.
36. N.C. MS. 7445–7; the last shows 6d. for wine at Russell's visit.
37. From £654 in 1483–4 to £860 in 1539–40, accelerating to £980 in1540–1 and £992 in 1541–2 (see 'coll. accts.' and receipts listed in Steer, 21–4). Cf. *Valor Ecclesiasticus* (Record Commission, 1810–34), ii, 256–63.
38. A. B. Emden, *Biographical Register of the University of Oxford* [hereafter cited as Emden, *BRUO*], 4 vols. (1–3, to A.D. 1500, and 4, for 1501–40), (Oxford, 1957–74), iv, *snn.* Hawarden, Ric.; Legge, John; Strett, John. Unless otherwise stated, particulars of careers of members named in this chapter are taken from *BRUO*. When I have modernised the form of a surname, its form in *BRUO* is shown in the index in italics after the form used in this chapter. My statistics are also derived from these four volumes of *BRUO*.
39. In 1532–3, the total for commons (at the weekly rates of 12d. for fellows and 8d. for servants *and* choirboys) was £255 14s. 10½d., plus an 'excess' of £49 19s. 2d. Next year the total was £265 1s. 0d. and the 'excess' over the statutory allowance was £64 4s. 5¾d. (N.C. MSS. 7485, 7488; see also 7489–90, 7493, 7495–6).
40. The largest number of sheep sheared was 190 in 1536 (N.C. MSS. 7485, 7490, 7495–6, 7498, 7501).
41. E.g. Walter Cheverell, John Greene and Lambert Wyxton disappeared in 1433.
42. N.C. MSS. 9746–8 (Steer, 100).
43. N.C. MS. 7462.
44. Deaths in 1501–28 totalled seventy-six, with nine in 1508 and six in 1510, 1513 and 1518 (N.C. MSS. 9747, pp. 343–81; 9748, ff. 256–76v.). The only other notices of rustication in these years belong to 1519 (after the deaths), the autumn of 1527, and after four deaths in July 1528 (N.C. MSS. 7476, 7480).
45. N.C. MSS. 7481, 7485, 7488, 7490, 7493, 7495, 7501 (for 1541–2, 'in the time of sweating sickness').
46. Printed in M. E. C. Walcott, *William of Wykeham and his Colleges* (1852), 141–3.
47. Modern abbreviations for degrees are given when appropriate, B.D. and D.D. for theology, and B.Dec. and D.Dec. for canon law.
48. Mr. Aston (see *n.* 5) does not take account of M.A.s and so concludes that law had 'pride of place' in New College (pp. 14–15, 20); but fifty of the seventy members were always studying arts and theology, and as their

'turnover' was perhaps more rapid than that of lawyers, they amounted to at least 70 per cent of all Wykehamists.

49. G. F. Lytle, 'Patronage Patterns and Oxford Colleges *c.* 1300–*c.* 1530', *The University and Society*, ed. L. Stone (Princeton, 1974), i, 143–6.

50. R. Weiss, *Humanism in England during the Fifteenth Century* (Oxford, 1957), 66–7, 71–80, 132–7.

51. N.C. MS. 9746, pp. 312–18. Hill did not vote. Fourteen of the undergraduate fellows were *civiliste*. Scholars (seventeen then) did not take part.

52. N.C. MS. 9654, f. 158v. No registers of college correspondence survive from this time. This and a few other letters are in this manuscript (the White Book) written over erasures of formal instruments of *c.* 1425.

53. R. L. Storey, 'Gentleman-bureaucrats', *Profession, Vocation, and Culture in Medieval England*, ed. C. H. Clough (Liverpool, 1980); see also Aston, 30–2.

54. Payments to graduate priests in the fifteenth century show annual totals of between eleven and eighteen; there were less in 1402–3 and 1476–7, more in 1414–15, 1428–9 and 1449–50 (see Bursars' Accounts).

55. *Taxatio Ecclesiastica, circa 1291* (Rec. Comm., 1802), 189b; *Valor Ecclesiasticus*, ii, 133. Snareston and Packett (above, p. 21) were equally poor parsons (*Taxatio*, 32b, 41a). Cf. Lytle, 139–40, who did not investigate the values of college livings.

56. Public Record Office: Probate 11, vol. 4, fo. 65.

57. Emden, *BRUO*, ii, 2112; J. S. Roskell, *The Commons in the Parliament of 1422* (Manchester, 1954), 239–41.

58. J. C. Wedgwood, *History of Parliament 1439–1509* (1936–8), ii, 113. See also G. F. Lytle, 'The Social Origins of Oxford Students in the late Middle Ages: New College, *c.* 1380–*c.* 1510', *Les Universités à la Fin du Moyen Âge*, ed. J. Paquet and J. Ijsewijn (Louvain, 1978).

59. His daughter Anne, Countess of Ormond, was the great-grandmother of Anne Boleyn. *Complete Peerage*, ed. G.E.C. (1910–59), v, 504–6, x, 132, 133 *n.* 137–9; Emden, *BRUO*, ii, 866, iii, xxvii; *Return of the Names of Every Member* (H.M.S.O., 1879), i, 305; Public Record Office: Exchequer 101, box 71, no. 773; Moberly, 346 (bequest by Wykeham to William Hankford).

60. *Official Correspondence of Thomas Bekynton* (Rolls Series, 1872), i, 272–3.

61. Wedgwood, ii, 91.

62. *Cal. Pat. Rolls, 1422–29*, 565; *Cal. Papal Letters* (H.M.S.O.), viii, 88; *Register of Edmund Lacy* (Canterbury & York Soc., 1963–73), ii, 195.

63. Cf. nine years with twenty or more scholars (first and second years) in 1430–79. The death-rate in college was unchanged at 20 per cent of all vacancies, *viz.* 85 of 422 in 1430–79 and 104 of 517 in 1480–1529.

64. N.C. MS. 9747, pp. 343–81, 9748, ff. 256–76; Emden, *BRUO*, iv, *snn.* Bedyll, Ric.; Brown, John; Halihen, Edw.; Heritage, Ric. See also three

Halls from Aylesbury, *viz.* George (vac. 1513), Thomas (1531) and Christopher (1535).

65. The smallest total was seven in 1500–1 (N.C. MS. 7462). Cf. above, *n.* 54.

66. Emden, *BRUO*, iv, *snn.* Rawlens, Simon (vac. 1515); Sydnam, Walter (1516); Love, Edw. (1517); Rede, Giles (1519), etc.

67. All but six of the twenty-one admitted to the college after 1520 voted for London. N.C. MS. 9757 (Steer, 47), ff. 101v–104.

II

From the Reformation to the Era of Reform 1530–1850[1]

PENRY WILLIAMS

New College had effectively adapted itself to the social and intellectual changes of the fifteenth century. Several of its members—William Grocyn pre-eminent among them—had been influenced by the new learning of the Italian humanists. Archbishop Warham, fellow from 1473 to 1488, had become a generous patron of scholarship. A small but significant number of fellows, led by John Kingsmill, had deserted the university laws schools for the common law. In 1526, for the first time, a lawyer, Dr. London, had been elected as warden. Yet the college showed itself surprisingly resistant to the two great changes of the sixteenth century: the entry into the universities of large numbers of commoners and the Protestant Reformation.

For thirty years after 1550 and again for about twenty-five years after 1615 the numbers entering the university rose steeply. From an average of 220 freshmen per annum in 1520–9 for Oxford as a whole, admissions had fallen to 120 a year in 1546–52. Then they began to rise until they reached 445 per annum in the 1580s. Further expansion in the early seventeenth century raised the average to 530 in the 1630s. Many of these recruits, probably most, were young men of humble origin, but a growing number came from the ranks of the nobility and gentry. Most Oxford colleges responded to this rising demand for university education: commoners were admitted in addition to fellows and scholars; tutors were appointed to educate them; and new buildings were erected for their accommodation. Only two colleges stood aside from this tide of expansion: New College and All Souls. Admittedly some commoners were allowed into New College—notably the second

Earl of Pembroke and Sir Henry Wotton–but they were few in number and did not live within the college walls. The college remained, until the nineteenth century, a society with a warden and seventy scholars, which had been considered large in 1379, but was now relatively small.[2] In part this conservatism was probably a consequence of the traditional and genuine reverence for the Founder's statutes. In part it may have stemmed from the lack of any incentive for change. New College was wealthy; it held the right of presentation to several substantial benefices; its fellows enjoyed comfortable lives and the prospect of suitable preferment. They had no reason to burden themselves with the duties of supervising or teaching additional students.

The response of the college to the pressures and conflicts of the Reformation was more complex and, in the end, more flexible. When Henry VIII established the Crown's supremacy over the Church in the early 1530s, the college was headed by Dr. London, elected warden in 1526. London has long had an evil reputation as one of the most odious of the Visitors appointed by Henry VIII to inspect the monasteries; but perhaps his energy and his ambition have made him seem more brutal than he actually was.[3] Even so, he combined an oleaginous subservience to his political masters, especially to Thomas Cromwell, with a ruthless, and sometimes cruel, bullying of those beneath him.

His task at New College was not easy, for the fellows were divided into hostile and quarrelsome factions. The early Protestants of the college included John Quinbey, deprived of his fellowship for heresy in 1528, Dr. John Man, later Warden of Merton, Ralph Skinner, briefly Warden of New College under Edward VI, and John Philpot, martyred under Mary. The Catholics in London's time were intellectually more powerful: the two brothers, John and Nicholas Harpsfield, Thomas Harding and Thomas Martin were among their number.

London's own views, in spite of his enthusiasm for clearing relics from the monasteries, were doctrinally conservative. Before the breach with Rome he had already dealt savagely with the heretic Quinbey, imprisoning him in the bell-tower until he died 'half starved with cold and lack of food'. By 1532 London's conservatism was presenting a target for his enemies. He wrote anxiously to Cromwell protesting that any rumours of his hostility to royal policy were false: he had, he claimed, publicly consented to the divorce before the whole university.

Two years later he appealed for Cromwell's support in disciplining the fellows, who were becoming restive under his authority. London was indeed treading a rough and difficult path. He had to enforce the anti-papal policy of the Crown, but he was determined not to allow heresy and innovation. The behaviour of his nephew, Edward, caused him special embarrassment, through his adoption of reforming doctrines. In July 1536 London took his nephew for a long walk, starting at 5 a.m. According to the nephew, London warned him of the dangers of heretical opinions, complained that Bishop Gardiner would be disturbed to hear that the university is 'corrupted of one of his own (London's) college', and, resorting to a shameless piece of moral blackmail, told the young man that when his mother heard 'what an abominable heretic she hath to her son . . . she will never eat more bread that shall do her good'. London then suggested that although the King had 'conceived a little malice against the bishop of Rome . . . yet I trust the blessed King will wear harness on his own back to fight against such heretics as thou art'. He ended with a crude threat: 'If thou wilt not make revocation, thou shalt be expelled thy college and utterly undone.' Since the whole conversation was then reported by Edward to the Council, it is hardly surprising that London feared for his own safety and insisted to Cromwell that he had always been a supporter of the royal supremacy.[4]

The submission of the university to the authority of the Crown was finally achieved in 1535 by the two royal Visitors Dr. Legh and Dr. Layton, who imposed a series of changes in line with the reforming policy of the Crown. They established various lectureships, including one for Greek and another for Latin in New College, forbade the use of the traditional Duns Scotus as a text—setting 'Dunce in Bocardo [the town gaol]'—, ordered regular attendance at lectures and abolished the study of canon law. They also secured the destruction of many medieval manuscripts and rejoiced to see the sheets of Duns Scotus's works blowing round the college quadrangle, where a Mr. Greenfield from Buckinghamshire was gathering them up to make 'blawnsherres', a device for keeping deer within a wood.[5]

Under Henry VIII then, New College allowed the old learning to be thrown aside and accepted secular control over the Church. However it remained not merely hostile to Protestantism, but also the chief Oxford stronghold of the humanist exponents of the Catholic faith. John

Harpsfield, who entered New College in 1532, became Regius Professor of Greek, wrote a series of homilies and held the post of Archdeacon of London under Bishop Bonner. His younger brother, Nicholas, was of greater scholarly distinction. His *Life of Thomas More* has been described by R. W. Chambers as 'the first formal biography in the English language'. Of still greater importance for the Catholic cause was his *Historia Anglicana Ecclesiastica*, a work of major learning. Thomas Harding, Nicholas's exact contemporary, Professor of Hebrew, was to be the foremost Catholic antagonist to Bishop Jewel in the great literary debate over the Elizabethan Settlement. Nicholas Saunders, who entered New College in 1546, was regarded by Antony Wood, with good reason, as 'the most noted defender of the Roman Catholic cause in his time'. His major work, *De Visibili Monarchia Ecclesiae*, was in a sense the Catholic answer to Foxe's *Book of Martyrs*: it listed the Englishmen who had suffered for the Roman faith and justified the papal excommunication of Queen Elizabeth. Owen Lewis, during his exile after 1559, became a professor at Douai and ultimately Bishop of Cassano. Thomas Stapleton, whom Wood calls 'the most learned Roman Catholic of his time', was Professor of Divinity at Louvain and a major controversialist whose literary output was both massive and scholarly. These men were the leaders of a large and formidable band of Catholic priests and writers who were trained in New College during the mid-century turmoil, and remained its most influential members until the purges under Elizabeth.

They did not, however, oppose the destruction of papal supremacy. Nor do they seem to have actively opposed the Edwardian movement towards a Protestant Church. London's successor as warden, Henry Cole, at first conformed to the new regime. The new Books of Common Prayer, printed in 1549 and 1552, were bought for the college chapel. The royal visitation of Oxford in 1549 brought about the destruction of many manuscripts, although the fellows saved the stained glass windows in the chapel by pleading that the college was too poor to allow their replacement by plain glass. The fellows were also able to ward off another scheme of reform by which its civil lawyers would be transferred to All Souls, and the All Souls artists and theologians moved to New College.[6] During Edward's reign several fellows were admitted who later showed themselves to be strong Catholics—Owen Lewis, Thomas Stapleton, John Rastell, John Marshal among them—and the

Crown apparently made no serious attempt to restrict entry to Protestants or to deprive existing Catholic fellows. The one serious dispute involved the warden, Henry Cole, against whom the fellows lodged a complaint in 1550, demanding his removal. The charges were sufficiently serious for the Privy Council to order the royal Visitors to investigate the grievances of the fellows and, if they found them substantiated, to eject the warden from office. Evidently the case against Cole was strong, for he ceased to be warden, either through resignation or deprivation, early in 1551.[7] The grounds for the objections to Cole are unknown, but, since he revealed himself to be an ardent Catholic in the following reign, it seems likely that they stemmed from the Protestant faction within the college.

That faction was certainly successful in the election of Cole's successor, Ralph Skinner. A protégé of the Marquis of Dorset, who patronised several Protestant scholars, Skinner was elected warden in May 1551 with the approval, and possibly at the instigation, of the royal Visitors. He was the first married warden of the college, but was not to hold the post for long. In May 1553, after Stephen Gardiner had been restored as Bishop of Winchester and Visitor of New College, Skinner resigned. A year later he figured prominently in the second Marian parliament, speaking strongly and bravely against a bill declaring that the regality of a queen equalled that of a king: to endow Mary with such powers would, Skinner argued, enable her to seize the lands of her subjects.[8]

The new warden, Thomas White, was a civil lawyer who had spent the years from 1534 to 1552 as an unobtrusive and apparently conformist fellow of the college. Presented to the Buckinghamshire living of Newton Longville in 1552 he returned to New College as warden in September 1553, holding both posts in plurality. He found no difficulty in bending to the religious wind of the times. But the new ecclesiastical regime of Queen Mary was much more exacting than its predecessor. While Edward's government had allowed Catholics to remain in their fellowships, Mary's agents were not prepared to tolerate Protestants: seven fellows were deprived during the first year of her reign, and no fewer than fifteen new fellows admitted, many of them Catholics who were to leave the college after the accession of Elizabeth. The account-rolls show that chapel services were quickly restored to their old orthodox form: albs were bought; vestments, organs and windows repaired; altars set up and painted.

Elizabeth was perhaps rather more patient than her sister had been in demanding conformity, but in the end she and her bishops refused to tolerate those who dissented from the Protestant settlement. Visitors were sent down to Oxford in 1559 and within two or three years all but two heads of houses had been removed. One of the survivors was the flexible Thomas White. Yet even he was under threat, for the new Visitor, Bishop Horne of Winchester, returned from exile in Strasbourg, was evidently uneasy about leaving him in control at New College.[9] In the end, White remained as warden until 1573, when he left New College to be Chancellor of the diocese of Salisbury. Many of his colleagues were less fortunate. However, Elizabeth and her ministers did not force the issue and the purge of Catholics from New College was gradual. During the first two years of the reign four men left of their own accord and fled overseas: Nicholas Saunders, John Rastell, Thomas Stapleton and John Fowler, who became a printer in Louvain and Antwerp. These four were probably the most distinguished Catholic fellows of New College at the time, the Harpsfield brothers and Thomas Harding having already moved on to higher positions. Five other fellows were expelled during the first two years. There was then a brief lull until 1562, when eleven men were deprived of their fellowships, and nine more were removed in 1564–8. In addition, nine fellows who entered New College after the accession of Elizabeth were deprived, two of them—John Mundyn and John Body—being later executed for treason. Thirty-three fellows of the college were thus extruded during the first decade of Elizabeth's reign, evidently for Catholic beliefs, and five more were expelled after 1568. New College lost many more fellows than any other college and has therefore traditionally been regarded as having suffered more heavily than the rest. But one has to remember that it had more fellows to lose. Thirty-three fellows out of seventy is not proportionately as severe a loss as Merton's nine out of a fellowship body that seldom exceeded fourteen. The real catastrophe for New College lay in the quality rather than the number of its deprived Catholics.

The gradual but ultimately decisive movement towards Protestantism was also reflected in the chapel accounts and in the records of visitations. Sixty communion-books were bought in 1559; altars and images were destroyed in 1560. Yet the rood-loft was not taken down until 1571–2. Long before then Bishop Horne had initiated a series of visitations. He made a personal visitation of the college in September 1561 and ordered every fellow to subscribe to the Oath of Supremacy and to the Book of Common Prayer: those who refused were pronounced contumacious. In the following year Dr. George Acworth, acting as commissary to the bishop, continued the visitation, at which various fellows were reported to have neglected to take communion and to possess popish books. Four years later, in September 1566, Acworth began the most elaborate of all these enquiries. It was clear that the earlier investigations had taken little effect, for Acworth uncovered an immense heap of abuses, ranging from the trivial to the genuinely disquieting. Some of the changes had no connection with the enforcement of Protestantism: one fellow had assulted a colleague 'with a great stick'; the warden was charged with administrative negligence and moral laxity. But there was enough evidence of popery to cause anxiety to a stern Protestant like Horne. Several fellows were said to possess popish books; twenty-three refused to subscribe to the articles of religion; John Mundyn had not communicated since the accession of Elizabeth; John Fisher was said to have laughed throughout the services and to have drunk all the wine 'in mockery of the Holy Supper'. The visitation was resumed in March 1567, when most of the fellows were charged with some offence. Again, these varied from getting into college after the gates were closed or keeping birds to the denial of transubstantiation. At the close of the proceedings Horne issued a set of sixty-two injunctions. Some of them were intended to improve the administration of the college or secure the observation of the statutes: the long room, or 'bog-house', was to be cleansed; no birds or dogs were allowed in college; no water or urine was to be thrown from the upper windows; no female should be admitted to the buttery or other rooms. But many were concerned with the enforcement of the Anglican liturgy and the royal supremacy. All fellows were to attend communion at least four times a year; no one should possess the books of the English papist exiles; turning to the east during the service was forbidden; execration of the state of the realm and its religion should cease; the images in chapel were to be removed and burned; the articles of religion were not to be questioned; papistical doctrine must not be taught. The issue of such orders indicates that as late as 1566 popish practices and doctrines were still entrenched.[10]

Ten years later Horne ordered a second visitation, conducted by John Kingsmill and Thomas Bilson, Headmaster of Winchester. This time the charges brought against the fellows almost entirely concerned moral, rather than religious, offences. One man had stolen books; another was a 'frequenter of taverns'; several kept dogs; there was a general excess in dress and in the playing of games. Horne's injunctions show that there was no longer any need to strike at popery: he dwelt on the need to eliminate corruption from elections; on the length of disputations; on the enormity of bursars taking dripping from the kitchen for their own use. Seventeen years after the settlement of religion by Elizabeth, New College could be regarded as a Protestant institution, though not one ardent in its faith or spotless in its conduct.[11]

In the thirty years after the death of Henry VIII the New College community had undergone a major and convulsive transformation. The illustrious Catholic scholars who had made it a centre of humanist learning under Henry VIII had departed, many of them overseas, to continue the fight against heresy. It is difficult to explain the moral strength, numbers and quality of the New College Catholics. In a small community the accidents of personality can be all-important: the tradition, formed perhaps by the Harpsfields and Harding, probably depended very heavily upon personal teaching and example. The severance of that tradition can only have been a serious blow to the learning and devotion of the college. New College produced a few eminent Puritans, notably John Garbrand, Prebendary of Salisbury and editor of the works of Bishop Jewel. But the leadership and inspiration of Oxford religion passed away from New College during the reign of Elizabeth to Magdalen, Christ Church and Corpus Christi, the three principal centres of Puritan teaching.

The order-books of the college and admonitions of its Visitor suggest that a certain laxity and indolence prevailed at New College between the middle of Elizabeth's reign and the Civil War. The society was now firmly governed by its senior members, the Warden and Thirteen, who made almost all the important decisions. For the most part they were concerned with the management of the college estates, appointments to benefices and the granting of leave of absence to fellows. No longer was residence in college an essential duty of a fellow: he could generally obtain permission to reside elsewhere while continuing to enjoy his fellowship.[12] More serious was the growing practice of 'corrupt resignations'. Since the number of fellows was limited to seventy, new fellows could only be elected when a vacancy occurred. The posers, who chose the roll of scholars at Winchester, were in practice drawing up a waiting list, and there was no guarantee that its members might actually gain admission to New College. From this situation arose the sale of places: existing fellows waited until shortly before the posers went down to Winchester and then offered their resignation, for a consideration, to those waiting on the existing roll. In 1610 the Visitor wrote in strong terms to the warden ordering these 'scandalous corruptions' to be ended. But persisting complaints throughout the seventeenth and eighteenth centuries show that the bishop's attempts were vain.[13]

A second threat to the quality of the fellowship body emerged from the claims of Founder's Kin. Wykeham had made provision for some priority to be given to his kin, but in his own lifetime and during the next century it was not much exploited. However, the Founder had imposed no limits upon the degree of consanguinity at either of his colleges, and in consequence the number of possible claimants was very large. By Elizabeth's reign several landed families—most notably the Fiennes and the Wykehams—saw the advantage of gaining precedence on the Winchester and New College rolls. In 1586 Bishop Cooper was asked to pronounce upon the claim of the Fiennes family. He avoided this issue but ordered instead that the number of Founder's Kin admitted to either college should not exceed two in each year, and that there should never be more than ten at Winchester or eight at New College at any one time. This limitation was not effective for long, and in 1651 the quota was raised to twenty at each college. For the next two centuries the number of Founder's Kin remained high. In 1853 the warden and twenty-one of the seventy fellows claimed consanguinity with William of Wykeham.[14]

Archbishop Laud spoke harsh words about the state of New College in 1635. He said that he had often wondered why so many good scholars came from Winchester to New College, and 'yet so few of them afterwards prove eminent men'. He attributed this failing to an excessive study of Calvin's *Institutes*.[15] But it seems likely that other explanations are more plausible. Non-residence, corrupt resignations and the privileges of Founder's Kin all helped to slacken the endeavours and lower the quality of New College men.

The truth is that New College was a comfortable institution, with good rewards to offer to its members, and no great efforts were called forth for success. The income of the college rose steadily from about £900 per annum under Edward VI to an average of £1,100 per annum in the first five years of Elizabeth. It then climbed steadily to average £3,330 in the second half of the 1630s. After about 1590, the fines on entry paid by tenants were divided into five parts: one part went to the warden, two to the college, and the remaining two-fifths for allocation to the fellows. From about the same date the fellows also shared among themselves the surplus of revenue over expenditure, known as the 'increment'. Fines and increments provided a useful addition to the somewhat meagre rewards provided by the Founder.[16] This material affluence is reflected in the buildings of the college. The Warden's Lodgings were greatly extended during the sixteenth century, probably in the days of Warden London. The fellows soon followed this example. Cramped by living with their juniors in the original chambers, the senior fellows built attic rooms, known as 'cocklofts', in the roof of the southern range, where they could enjoy greater privacy.[17] Although life in the college became more comfortable, most fellows, anxious for an independent life, sought posts outside it. They were well placed to succeed, for the college had been amply endowed with the right of presentation to benefices: the Founder had bequeathed fourteen advowsons and eight more were acquired in the course of the fifteenth century. By 1642 the college held the presentation to twenty-six clerical livings, which provided desirable posts for its members.

Even so, although there was not much incentive during Elizabethan and early Stuart times for New College men to exert themselves, the college produced rather more men of eminence than Laud's characteristically acerbic comments would suggest. Warden Robert Pincke, elected at the King's insistence in 1617, was an old-fashioned scholar of some distinction, who played a major role in the government of the university. Thomas James, described by Camden as 'wholly dedicated to learning' was the first librarian of the Bodleian. Pincke and James, together with another New College man, Richard Zouche, were chosen for the committee of four which drew up the Laudian statutes for the university. A man of altogether different distinction was John White, fellow from 1595 to 1606. He left Oxford to be Rector of Dorchester, Dorset, where he was highly successful in raising money for the poor. But his main significance lay in a series of imaginative schemes which led to the foundation of the Massachusetts Bay Colony in 1630, which White described in his *Planters' Plea*. Colonies, he claimed, should not be 'emunctories or sinks of states to drain away their filth', but the resort of persons who were both godly and industrious. He proved his point by the success of the colony.

Richard Haydocke, who became a probationer fellow in 1588, won distinction in two separate fields, art and medicine. His original fame sprang from his alleged ability to preach in his sleep, a pretence that was exposed by James I. Much more interesting is Haydocke's ability as an engraver and as the translator of Lomazzo's *Trattato dell' arte de la pittura*, the earliest treatise on painting in English, which he illustrated himself. He also executed the memorial brass to Sir Thomas Hopper in New College chapel, skilfully combining allegory and emblem in the design. For most of his life he practised as a physician in Salisbury. Haydocke was a near contemporary of John Hoskyns, probationer fellow in 1586, who acted as *terrae filius* in 1592, and had then to resign his fellowship because his satirical wit had bitten too deep. His expulsion did not prevent him from achieving a successful career as lawyer, writer and politician. In his *Direccions for Speech and Style* (*c*. 1599) he says that 'I have used and outworn 6 several styles, since I was first fellow of New College and am yet able to bear the fashion of writing company'. The suggestion that the fellows of New College regarded writing as an important craft is borne out by the group of epigrammatists who collaborated in 1587 to produce a collection of elegies to Philip Sidney, entitled *Peplus Illustrisimi Viri D. Philippi Sidnaei*: Hoskyns was one of their number.[18]

It would be pleasant to claim that New College contributed something to the education of Sir Henry Wotton, one of the most versatile men of his age. Friend of John Donne, he wrote plays, investigated optics, published *The Elements of Architecture*, acted as secretary to the second Earl of Essex, and served as ambassador in Venice. But his stay at the college was brief. He matriculated in 1584 as one of the few commoners in New College, but moved after a short time to Hart Hall and then to Queen's.

The prosperous and comfortable life of the college was abruptly broken in September 1642 when parliamentary troops under Lord Saye and Sele, an old member of New College and Founder's Kin at that, entered Oxford. The vice-chancellor, Dr. Prideux, had fled and Warden Pincke was left to defend, as best he could, the interests of the university. The New College connection with the parliamentary commander did not much help him, for his study was searched for papers and, although he appealed for help to the chancellor, Lord Pembroke, he was arrested. However, following the battle of Edgehill, Oxford became the head-quarters of the royalist army for the remainder of the Civil War and Pincke returned. New College was made into the King's major arsenal: the cloisters and the bell-tower were filled with weapons and ammunition. The school was moved from its position between chapel and cloisters to a room at the east end of the hall—'a dark nasty room very unfit for such a purpose', according to Antony Wood, one of the most distinguished alumni of New College School.[19] Most of the academic life of the university was suspended for the next four years. Numbers declined, lectures fell off, the annual degree-giving Act was suspended. Worse still, rents became hard to collect. From an average of £2,970 per annum in the five years preceding the outbreak of Civil War, the revenues of New College fell to the low point of £1,059 in 1643-4.[20]

Oxford surrendered to Parliament in June 1646. Its sympathies had been overwhelmingly royalist during the war and substantially Laudian before it: the new regime was bound to institute a purge. In May 1647 Parliament issued an ordinance establishing a board of twenty-five Visitors who were to be supervised by a parliamentary committee in London. In all, three sets of Visitors were appointed: the first from September 1647 until April 1652; the second from June 1652 until January 1654; the third from January 1654 until about 1658, when their activities lapsed. Their task was to discover and expel those who opposed the new regime and to regulate the general conduct of university business.[21]

On the death of Warden Pincke in November 1647 the Visitors expressly forbade the college to elect a successor until he should be approved by themselves. The fellows disobeyed and elected Henry Stringer, Regius Professor of Greek, on 17 November. His rule was brief, for the Visitors had him removed in the following August. By then they had proceeded to their main business. In May 1648 the fellows of New College were asked whether or not they would submit to the visitation. Only one fellow, Dr. Vivian, submitted, and it is ironical that he should later have been removed from his fellowship for various misdemeanours by the second set of Visitors in 1653. The remainder all stated that the college statutes expressly forbade them to submit to any Visitor who was not a member of the university, although one or two softened their refusal by an acknowledgement of the power of Parliament and the Visitors 'over the university in general'. Two senior college servants, the head cook and the barber, submitted. Of all the Oxford colleges only All Souls equalled New College in its nearly unanimous refusal to accept the visitation.

Expulsions began in June 1648, when seventeen fellows were deprived of their positions. During the next few years further expulsions were made: at least fifty fellows, four chaplains, twelve choristers and thirteen servants were ejected from their places, while about fifty-five fellows were appointed by the Visitors to fill the vacant posts. In the university as a whole the fellows submitting exceeded in number those expelled; in New College, by contrast, four times as many fellows were expelled as submitted. In January 1649 a new warden, George Marshall, an M.A. of St. John's College, Cambridge, was imposed upon the reluctant college. This was of course quite contrary to the statutes, which insisted that only a fellow or ex-fellow of New College could be warden. Marshall had been a chaplain to the parliamentary forces during the war and this was no doubt his reward for loyal service. The purge was far more drastic than any previously experienced by this or any other college: within the space of three or four years at least two-thirds of the fellowship was removed and a new collection of men put in its place. The expulsions were accompanied by some attempt to tighten the discipline and conduct of the fellows. In May 1650 the hours during which bowling was permitted were limited to the periods from dawn to 5 a.m., from 11 a.m. to 1 p.m., and from 6 p.m. to 9 p.m. In June punctual attendance in chapel was demanded at 5.30 a.m. in term, at 7 a.m. in vacation, and at 5 p.m. throughout the year.

The Restoration of the monarchy in 1660 produced a further upheaval, when several of the 'intruded' fellows were expelled and ten of the deprived men restored. There was, however, no change in the headship of the college. Marshall had died in 1658 and the college had elected as his successor Michael Woodward, Rector of Ash in Surrey and Brightwell in Berkshire (plate 84). Woodward seems to have been a man of few scholarly attainments and fewer political or religious convictions. He was, however, a first-class administrator, determined to place the affairs of the college upon a stable footing.[22] His task was not easy. The senior fellows quarrelled among themselves and tried to get the better of their warden. Two of them, Hobbes and Pelham, disputed the office of outrider, whose duty was to accompany the warden on progress. 'By such cunning tricks as these they impose upon me', wrote Woodward, 'and as in this so in all affairs of the college.' They dined and kept fires in the Chequer; gave no lectures at all or only at times that suited them; and Hobbes refused to get out of bed in the winter.[23]

Woodward was tireless in his management of the college's estates and archives. In August and September 1660 he visited college property in Cambridgeshire, Norfolk, Essex, Middlesex, Wiltshire, Oxfordshire and Buckinghamshire. In this trip he covered most of the college's manors except for those which lay in Berkshire, Hampshire, Gloucestershire, London and Kent. His tour gives a good impression of the disposition of the college lands. The greater part of its income came from Oxfordshire, Wiltshire, Buckinghamshire and Essex, with relatively small contributions from the other counties.[24] Thus the general topography of the college properties had not greatly changed since the fifteenth century.

Woodward's interest in the estates was minute and precise. He went on his progresses armed with specific questions about leases, repairs to buildings, enclosure of commons, and the felling of timber. Permission to tenants to fell trees for specific purposes was not casually granted; and if it was given Woodward would want to know on his next visit whether the timber had been used as intended. The record of his activities shows that the warden and fellows of New College were at least as much the administrators of a great estate as they were teachers in an educational establishment: probably much more so. Woodward's efforts are reflected in the bursarial accounts of his day. Rents had recovered quickly from the disastrous years of the Civil War, and during the first half of the 1650s they reached an average of £2,680 per annum. In the first five years of Woodward's tenure they reached £3,380 per annum, before falling slightly in the mid-sixties. According to Wood, New College ranked third in the taxation lists of the university: Christ Church was assessed at £2,000, Magdalen at £1,200 and New College at £1,000; the next college, All Souls, lagged far behind at £500.[25]

The contacts of New College with the outside world were not restricted to its rural acres and tenantry. For Restoration Oxford, being nearer to London than Cambridge and possessing a quantity of habitable buildings, was often a place of resort for the royal household and its entourage when London became unhealthy. In the plague year of 1665 Parliament met in Oxford and the colleges were filled with courtiers and M.P.s. Antony Wood regarded the visit sourly: 'the greater sort of the courtiers were high, proud, insolent, and looked upon scholars as no more than pedants. . . . Rude, rough, whoremongers; vain, empty, careless'. But New College was luckier than most, since it lodged the Spanish ambassador, Count Molina, a man of learning and courtesy, who presented the warden with a cup on his departure. The cup was unluckily stolen a few years later, but replaced by a later ambassador, Ronquillo (plate 75).[26]

New College at this time was becoming more aristocratic both in its membership and in its style. The fellows demanded greater comfort for themselves and built the additional storey in the main quadrangle to provide more rooms. Celia Fiennes observed that her nephew's tutor, Mr. Gross, had 'a very pretty apartment of dining room, bed chamber, and study, and a room for a servant'—provision far more luxurious than the Founder had intended. In 1677 the college allowed the admission of sixteen noble and gentlemen commoners who would pay fees for their residence. The garden quadrangle buildings were erected to house them.[27] The scholars were generally of higher social origins than they had been in the previous century, partly because the number of Founder's Kin was increasing. The abuse of corrupt resignations— and thus in effect the sale of places—gave an advantage to the well-to-do and weighted the scales against the side of the poor: all attempts to end this practice seem to have been futile.[28]

Although New College produced a few eminent men in the Restoration period—notably Bishop Ken and Lord Chief Justice Herbert—it was for the most part easy-going and indolent. The Visitor,

Bishop Morley, attributed this to the large number of benefices in the gift of the college, which gave its members guaranteed employment without the need for exertion. Some of its critics accused the fellows of worse than indolence. Wood commented in 1682 that New College needed thorough reform, since its fellows were 'much given to drinking and gaming and vain brutish pleasure. They degenerate in learning'. The priggish Lord Ashley reported to his father in 1689 that there was only one sober fellow, Palmer, in the whole fellowship: and Palmer resigned in the following year.[29]

But Ashley admitted that in this respect New College was little different from the other foundations. Indeed in most respects the contrast between New College and the others diminished after 1660. Following the Reformation New College had been exceptional in remaining a small society of scholars, while most other colleges competed to attract commoners and grew in size. With the Restoration, the universities became less attractive to all sections of society and a long contraction of numbers began. The enrolment for freshmen into Oxford fell from 460 per annum in the 1660s to only 200 per annum in the 1750s. The university had become too expensive for the less well-to-do and trained only for one career, the Church. Most colleges shrank in size and attracted either intending clerics or aristocrats devoted to pleasure. Thus New College, by remaining an institution primarily intended to provide parochial clergy, came to resemble the other colleges much more closely than it had done in the years 1550 to 1640. Its newly aristocratic outlook and conduct were also mirrored elsewhere. A French visitor of the early eighteenth century described the colleges as 'palaces compared with the Tuileries, occupied by rich idlers who sleep and get drunk one part of the day, and the rest they spend in training, clumsily enough, a parcel of uncouth youths to be clergymen'. No doubt he was being unfair, but the attractive scent of luxury in Restoration Oxford is inescapable.[30]

That does not mean that the university was unimportant in the life of the nation. It contained many profitable and valued posts, while continuing to train the bulk of the nation's clergy. As a source of patronage and the nursery of preachers it was vitally significant to the politicians who sought to control the government and the country. From about 1690 Oxford therefore became a battleground constantly fought over by rival political interests.[31]

New College was closely contested at the beginning of the eighteenth century between the two parties, with the Tories holding a narrow lead over their opponents. The critical moment came with the election as warden of Thomas Braithwaite in 1703. Having prudently voted for himself, Braithwaite was elected by a majority of one over his rival, Charles Trimnel, who had been tutor to the powerful Earl of Sunderland. Trimnel was the candidate of the Whigs, and the Archbishop of Canterbury, Thomas Tenison, was determined to secure the wardenship for him, thus giving his party five heads of houses. The Whig minority in New College, encouraged by their political patrons, therefore absented themselves from the meeting at which the formal document of election had to be sealed. Since some of Braithwaite's party were also absent and the sealing necessitated a majority of all fellows, not merely of those present, the decision 'devolved' upon the Visitor, Peter Mews, Bishop of Winchester. The Tory interest in Oxford, led by Dean Aldrich of Christ Church, mobilised support for Braithwaite and, through the agency of Francis Atterbury, a Mr. Butler was sent down to the bishop to present their case. In July both parties appeared with legal counsel before the bishop, who decided, after a long and tiring day's argument, in favour of Braithwaite. Much of the credit for this was attributed by Atterbury to the shadowy figure of Mr. Butler. Writing to Bishop Trelawney, Atterbury remarked: 'Your Lordship can hardly imagine how far this matter was driven into a party cause, and how much concerned the great men of both sides were for the event of it.' 'There was', wrote Atterbury in another letter, 'a mystery of iniquity in the management of that matter.'[32]

In spite of Braithwaite's success in 1703 and the election of another Tory, John Cobb, in 1712, there was a sizeable Whig minority in the college. One of its most colourful and tempestuous members was Dr. John Ayliffe, who attacked the privileges of the university and the House of Stuart in a pamphlet entitled *The Ancient and Present State of the University*, published in July 1714, in which he criticised New College for the 'supine negligence of a late warden [Braithwaite], and the discouragements arising from domestic quarrels'. Ayliffe was summoned before the University Court in November and prosecuted by the vice-chancellor himself, Dr. Bernard Gardiner, and by Thomas Braithwaite, now Warden of Winchester. After a confusion of writs, arrests, escapes and appeals, Ayliffe was deprived of his degrees and banished from the university. He was then summoned to appear before the warden and seniors of New College, where he still remained a fellow. Surprisingly perhaps, he was acquitted, the warden and five fellows voting for his expulsion, nine voting against. Evidently the election of a Tory warden did not guarantee the condemnation of an errant Whig: party alignments were too complicated for that. The warden then appealed to the Visitor, the Tory Bishop Trelawney, who ordered Ayliffe to recant. Ayliffe refused to do so and forestalled expulsion by resigning: according to Hearne, whose evidence is not very reliable against a Whig, he sold his fellowship. Finally, Ayliffe was rewarded by the Whig government with the office of commissioner of hawkers and pedlars.[33]

While Ayliffe was engaged in these legal embroilments, his political friends were involved in more violent activities. Early in the reign of George I some New College Whigs had founded the Constitution Club under the leadership of George Lavington, later Bishop of Exeter, and a certain Captain Thomas. The club contained at least ten members from New College. In May 1715 it met at the King's Head Tavern in the High Street to celebrate the King's birthday. A mob of Tory students and townsmen surrounded the tavern with cries of 'No George', 'James for Ever', until the Constitutioners fled in some disorder. One of them, Thomas Hamilton, sheltered in New College and fired his pistol at his pursuers. But, although the Whig press was able to make some capital out of the riots and the trial of a Constitutioner which followed, the incident suggests that the Whigs were in a minority, both in New College and in the university as a whole.[34]

The election of Henry Bigg to the wardenship of New College in 1725 might suggest that the political complexion of the college had changed, since he is described by Hearne as 'a great Whig'. But this election was unscrupulously rigged by one of Bigg's opponents, Thomas Prince, who promised to withdraw and to persuade his supporters to vote for the third candidate, Thomas Lee. In the event, Prince played a 'knavish and treacherous part', by failing to tell Lee of his withdrawal until too late. In Hearne's view, had Bigg's opponents stood together they would have carried the day, but the election was contrived by William Bradshaw, Dean of Christ Church and Bishop of Bristol, who had once been chaplain to Braithwaite's old rival, Charles Trimnel.[35]

Bigg did not in any case have much influence upon New College politics. He quickly tired of the duties of the wardenship, having a large fortune as well as a pretty and rich wife; five years after his election he was chosen Warden of Winchester.[36] For the rest of the century New College showed itself to be generally Tory and independent in its politics. The wardens of both Winchester and New College protested strongly at the issue of royal letters of *mandamus* nominating scholars and fellows to the two institutions; they alleged in 1726 that William III and Anne had both promised to abandon the practice.[37] In 1748 Warden Purnell, then vice-chancellor, refused to condemn some undergraduates accused of toasting the health of King James III. Purnell was censured by the government and the undergraduates imprisoned in London. But Purnell's tolerance of drunken young Jacobites had serious consequences for New College. Since the time of Warden Nicholas (1675–9) it had been the constant practice of the fellows of New College to elect their own warden as Warden of Winchester. Originally, the Winchester post had been inferior, but by the middle of the seventeenth century it was worth some £300 per annum more than the wardenship of New College. In 1757, when Dr. Coxed died, Purnell was elected Warden of Winchester in his place, as the previous six New College wardens had been. He had, however, reckoned without the Visitor, the notorious Whig, Bishop Hoadley, now at Winchester, who was determined to secure a reliable warden at the school and perhaps to punish Purnell for his conduct in 1748. Hoadley refused to accept Purnell and installed Dr. Christopher Golding in his place. Since then the wardenships of the two colleges have been severed and wardens of New College have had to look elsewhere for promotion.[38]

In the second half of the eighteenth century New College continued to be Tory and independent in its politics. In the election of a chancellor in 1762 a majority of the fellows supported the unsuccessful Tory candidate, Lord Foley. Ten years later New College was the principal hope of the equally unsuccessful Tory, Lord Radnor, who withdrew before the all-powerful Lord North, elected chancellor without opposition. In parliamentary elections the college usually backed the undistinguished but frequently successful Tory, Francis Page, an old member of the college. When a proposal was mooted in 1772 that lay undergraduates no longer be required to subscribe to the Thirty-Nine Articles, the Warden of New College was one of six heads of houses firmly opposed to change.[39]

A detailed impression of life in eighteenth-century New College can be gained from the informative but colourless diary of James Woodforde, who matriculated from Oriel in 1758, transferred to New College in 1759, and finally resigned his fellowship in 1776 after securing the coveted living of Weston Longville. In his day there were three categories of fellow at New College: scholars or probationary fellows, who remained in this status for two years after matriculating; junior fellows, who had passed their probation and were either under-graduates or B.A.s; and senior fellows, who were M.A.s. Each of these groups had its own common room: the J.C.R., founded in about 1680, for the probationers; the B.C.R. for the juniors; and the M.C.R.—masters' common room—for the seniors. Woodforde's diary shows that as an undergraduate he received the normal kind of tuition necessary for the B.A. But once he had acquired that degree he seems neither to have received nor to have given any academic instruction, beyond delivering a few formal lectures, although he remained a fellow of the college for another thirteen years. Indeed academic matters receive little attention in the diary and general intellectual concerns still less. Cricket, bowls and billiards were Woodforde's principal recreations; much of his time and most of his money were spent on food and wine, whose consumption he chronicles with zest: 'I carried off my drinking exceedingly well indeed', he remarks in July 1774. He was, however, genuinely devoted to music and enjoyed playing on the harpsichord and attending concerts.[40]

Life proceeded at much the same ambling pace throughout term and vacation. Indeed, except during the year when Woodforde was pro-proctor, 1774–5, there was no apparent distinction between them. Even when Woodforde joined the executive body of the college, the Warden and Thirteen, in 1773, he incurred very occasional extra duties, for the committee met only about once a month. As pro-proctor he had more to do, quelling undergraduate riots, attending Encaenia, and going to a meeting of the delegates of the Clarendon Press; but this was an exceptional year. For ten out of the fifteen years during which Woodforde was a full fellow of New College he spent almost the whole of his time away from Oxford. In 1763, having taken his B.A., Woodforde accepted the curacy of Thurloxton, near Taunton. For the next decade he lived mainly as a Somerset curate, visiting Oxford about once a year to vote in elections or to go through the formal exercises required for his M.A., which he took in 1767. He records in 1771 that his fellowship brought in £58 15s. 6d. of which £31 6s. 6d. was left after he had paid his debts.

Then, in 1773, he came back to New College in the hope of being elected Headmaster of Bedford School, the 'third best thing in the gift of New College'. He lost the appointment, but decided that if he were to secure a permanent living he must stay in Oxford. In the following year the benefice of Weston Longville, in Norfolk, fell vacant and Woodforde began to canvass for it on hearing that the most senior fellow did not want it. His chief rival was John Hooke, who had beaten him in the contest over Bedford School. This time the result was reversed and Woodforde was elected to the living by 21 votes to 15, after 'many learned and warm arguments started and disputed'.

The life revealed by Woodforde's diary was probably fairly typical of a New College fellow at that time. In his early years he received some tuition for the B.A., though from outside tutors, not from fellows of his own college. Once he became a B.A., Woodforde was required to give certain formal lectures but he had no responsibility whatsoever for teaching New College men, though he might provide some general supervision of their lives as a 'moral tutor'. Essentially an eighteenth-century fellow used the college as a base, from which he could hold curacies, and as a source of patronage, which would ultimately supply him with a permanent living. Life was a matter largely of filling in the time and deciding by vote upon the disposal of offices in the gift of the college.

It is not surprising, in these circumstances, that New College produced few men of distinction in the eighteenth century. Joseph Spence, fellow in 1722, became Professor of Poetry and of Modern History. Friend of Pope, author of *Polymetis* (a treatise on classical mythology) and of a valuable collection of literary 'Anecdotes', Spence spent little time in Oxford, preferring his living at Birchanger in Essex, travel in Europe, residence in the canonry at Durham and at his house in Byfleet, Surrey. Robert Lowth, who also became Professor of Poetry, wrote a scholarly life of the Founder, became Bishop of London, and made himself into an expert Hebraist, apparently because he believed that Hebrew was the language spoken in Paradise. Finally, one might mention William Howley, fellow from 1783–94, who ultimately became Archbishop of Canterbury, though Greville considered him 'a very ordinary man'.

More New College men went into the Church than followed any other career: probably this was by then usual in most colleges. Between 1701 and 1725, 134 fellows were elected, an average of just over five per annum, of whom sixty-six went on to hold parochial livings. They were not for the most part distinguished men, but they were following the intentions of the Founder. The lack of distinction at New College may partly be attributed to difficulties at Winchester, where the fellows, who had no duties, consumed most of the income, leaving the masters few and underpaid. The hold of Founder's Kin over both Wykeham's foundations probably excluded men of ability: Joseph Warton and William Collins, both scholars of Winchester, were excluded from New College and had to go elsewhere.

Early in the nineteenth century changes were beginning to come over Oxford. The number of freshmen entering the university rose from 230 per annum in the years 1805–9 to 410 per annum in 1820–4. In 1801 a group of reforming dons instituted a new examination statute setting up a competitive test for an honours degree. The demand for higher standards posed fresh problems, since the existing system of teaching— if it can even be called that—was wholly inadequate for honours work. There thus began a warm debate, which lasted for about three-quarters of a century, over the best means of transforming the university and its colleges into institutions of teaching and scholarship.[41]

For fifty years New College took little part in these developments. Its numbers remained fixed at the maximum of seventy fellows. Its members mostly held aloof from the debates over the functions of fellows, methods of teaching and establishment of chairs. They were much more concerned about the college's finances, which were running into deficit after about 1810. The increments paid to fellows were increased in that year from £2,711 to £4,797 in spite of gloomy, and probably sensible, warnings from Warden Gauntlett that the revenue could not stand it. After 1830 the increments began to fall steadily, to £4,060 in 1832, £3,456 in 1838, down to £1,440 in 1849.[42]

However, some proposals for change and even some actual reforms were made in New College during the first half of the century. Augustus Hare, later to become a man of some literary distinction, having entered the college as an undergraduate in 1810, published a short pamphlet in 1814 urging that New College surrender its privilege of sending men up for degrees without their having first taken university examinations or supplicated for graces to Congregation. This privilege rested upon rubric XXVI of the original statutes, in which Wykeham forbade any of his scholars to plead for graces in order to obtain exemption from the conditions laid down for degrees. What had been intended to ensure the strict performance of academic duties later became a means of escape from them. The right was attacked by members of other colleges in 1608, but upheld on appeal by the chancellor. It had come under fire intermittently in the next two centuries. Hare's criticism was the first to come from within the college. He argued that public university examinations promoted literature and encouraged distinction; New College's isolation from such a stimulus deprived its members of a valuable opportunity. His appeal was in vain.[43]

In 1822 the reforming minority within the college was strengthened by the election of Warden Shuttleworth, a strong Whig who had been tutor to the son of Lord Holland. Samuel Parr greeted his election as 'a triumph of learning over pedantry and of constitutional principles over sacerdotal intolerance'.[44] Shuttleworth was a man of wit and distinction: as a boy at Winchester he had written a prize poem on 'The Progress of Learning' which concluded with the couplet

> 'Oh! make me, sphere-descended Queen
> A Bishop, or at least a Dean'.

By the time he became warden he knew all the intellectual lions of his day: none of them visited Oxford without dining at New College.[45]

Although Shuttleworth was a man of much greater distinction than any of his predecessors for at least 150 years, he found it an arduous business to reform his own college. A proposal put forward by Augustus Hare in 1829, probably with Shuttleworth's support, for reducing the privileges of Founder's Kin was defeated.[46] In the following year Shuttleworth tried to persuade the fellows to raise his income: he claimed that the warden's annual revenue amounted only to £860, whereas the President of Jesus received £1650 and the Provost of Oriel £2,500. The fellows offered an increase, but Shuttleworth was dissatisfied and appealed, at considerable length, to the Visitor. The outcome of his efforts was an agreed increase, made up partly in cash and partly in kind. In 1832 he stirred up ferocious opposition among his seniors when he expelled a junior fellow, George Heathcote, who belonged to an influential Hampshire family. Heathcote had failed college collections twice, had been absent for part of the summer term of 1831, and seldom attended chapel. After a year's rustication he continued to be idle and disobedient and the warden finally resorted to expulsion. The young man's family appealed to the Visitor, asserting that their kinsman had been extremely nervous about his examinations and had eventually been driven to a state of distraction. The senior fellows insisted that they should have been consulted. The issue, Shuttleworth claimed, lay not merely between the authority of the warden and the seniors, important though that might be. It was 'between the total absence of any machinery of education which existed at the time of my assuming my present office and the improved habits which I trust I have been instrumental in introducing'. After years of perseverance Shuttleworth had introduced three tutors into New College. But, he commented sadly, 'the leaven of former times is not yet extinct. . .', for many still cherish the 'uninspiring indolence of their earlier life'. The standards of the college could be ruined if a lazy and disobedient undergraduate could successfully defy the warden; their improvement hung upon a thread. Shuttleworth's reply evidently convinced the Visitor and Heathcote's expulsion was confirmed.[47]

This fracas may have marked a turning-point in the progress of reform. In 1834, the college, frightened perhaps by the newly-acquired reforming zeal of the chancellor, the great Duke of Wellington, surrendered its right of separate examinations and agreed to enter men for the university's examinations. The decision was carried by twenty-five votes to fifteen.[48] In 1838 Shuttleworth persuaded the Visitor that probationers must have their warden's permission before they were raised to the status of full fellows. After Shuttleworth had departed for the see of Chichester in 1840, cautious progress towards an improvement of academic standards continued. Money was granted for tuition in mathematics and there was even talk of appointing a tutor in the subject. In 1842 prizes were founded to reward men who did well in the university examinations: £30 for a double first; £25 for a first and second; £10 for a second. Some of these prizes were actually awarded.[49]

By 1850, when the first Parliamentary Commission was appointed, New College was still isolated from the main stream of university development. It was a small, static community within a changing and expanding institution. But it had relinquished some of its privileges and there was evidently a group of fellows anxious to see further changes. The next decades were to see rapid and radical alteration under the pressure of government enquiry.

REFERENCES

1. Acknowledgements. I am much indebted to Dr. G. V. Bennett for advice and information on the whole chapter, especially on sources for the period after 1660, and to Dr. Francis Steer and my wife for reading it in draft and making many helpful suggestions. In this chapter I have not attempted to cover all the available material for the history of New College over three centuries: I have tried instead to trace the broad lines of the college's development and to illustrate this by some of the more colourful incidents and personalities of the time. There is a great deal of information, not duplicated here, in Rashdall and Rait, *New College*.
2. L. Stone (ed.), *The University in Society* (Princeton, 1975), I, chs. i and iii.
3. See D. Knowles, *The Religious Orders in England* III (Cambridge, 1959), 354–7. In the biographical material of London and other fellows I have relied substantially upon the MS. Register of Warden Sewell in New College library, the *D.N.B.* and Antony Wood, *Athenae Oxonienses*, ed. P. Bliss (London, 1813, 3 vols.).
4. Quoted in G. R. Elton, *Policy and Police* (Cambridge, 1972), 352–3. Cf. *Letters and Papers of Henry VIII*, vol. V, nos. 289, 506, 583, 1632; VI, no. 739; VII, nos. 146, 1299, 1394; XI, nos. 96, 118; XII, ii, no. 429; Add. I, no. 1085.
5. T. Wright, *Letters relating to the Suppression of Monasteries* (Camden Soc., 1843), 70–2. Below, ch. XI, pp. 335–6.
6. Wood, *History*, II, 104, 107.
7. *Acts of the Privy Council*, ed. J. R. Dasent, III, 139, 204. H.M.C., *Salisbury MSS.*, I, 81.
8. Jennifer Loach, 'Opposition to the Crown in Parliament, 1553–1558' (Oxford D.Phil. thesis, 1974), 299–300.
9. State Papers Domestic, Elizabeth, vol. 19, nos. 55, 56.
10. Bursarial Rolls (N.C. MSS.) nos. 7532–48. State Papers Domestic, Elizabeth, vol. 19, nos. 55, 56. A full transcript of the visitations is in Bodley MS. Top. Oxon. C. 354: I am grateful to Dr. Jane Roscoe for

making an abstract of part of this for me. Other visitation documents are in N.C. MSS. 3093, 3688. The visitations are very fully described in Rashdell and Rait, 115–33, and I have not therefore given a detailed treatment of them here.

11. N.C. MSS. 3093, 3688. Rashdall and Rait, 133–9. Bodley MS. Top. Oxon C. 354.

12. N.C. MS. 957: order-book for 1611–36.

13. Ibid., p. 13 from end.

14. G. D. Squibb, *Founder's Kin* (Oxford, 1972), ch. ii. Joseph Phillimore, *A Report of an Appeal to the Lord Bishop of Winchester* (1839). State Papers Domestic, Elizabeth, vol. 90, nos. 5, 6. *Calendar of State Papers Additional, 1580–1625*, p. 1. Below, pp. 77–82.

15. Quoted in Rashdall and Rait, 148–9.

16. Figures for college income are taken from the account-rolls, nos. 7512–667; order-book no. 957, p. 16 from end. I am grateful to the late John Cooper for helping me to elucidate some of the problems of college finance.

17. See below, ch. VI, pp. 199–201.

18. David Ogg, *New England and New College, Oxford* (Oxford, 1937), for White. K. J. Höltgen, 'Richard Haydocke, translator, engraver, physician', *The Library*, XXXII (1978). John Hoskyns, *Direccions for Speech and Style* printed in *The Life, Letters, and Writings of John Hoskyns* (ed. Louise Brown Osborn, New Haven, 1937), 152–3: I am grateful to Mrs. Anne Barton for this reference.

19. Andrew Clark (ed.), *The Life and Times of Antony Wood* (Oxford Hist. Soc., 1891), I, 69.

20. N.C. MSS., Bursars' Rolls, nos. 7657–669.

21. For the action of the Visitors and their dealings with New College see Montagu Burrows (ed.), *The Register of the Visitors of the University of Oxford* (Camden Soc., 1881), *passim*; N.C. MSS. 9655 (The Great Register) and 988 (order-book for 1650–5). The succeeding two paragraphs are based upon these sources.

22. For Woodward, see R. L. Rickard (ed.), *Progress Notes of Warden Woodward for the Wiltshire Estates of New College, Oxford, 1659–1675* (Wiltshire Record Society, vol. XIII, 1957), intro. Mr. Rickard has also edited Woodward's *Progress Notes* for Oxfordshire (Oxfordshire Record Society, vol. XXVII, 1945) and Norfolk (Norfolk Record Society, vol. XXII, 1951). Transcripts of Woodward's papers by David Ogg are kept in the New College library and throw some light on Woodward himself, more still on the history of the college.

23. Rickard, *Progress Notes . . . for the Wiltshire Estates*, xviii.

24. Ibid., p. xix. Bursars' Rolls, *passim*.

25. Mr. Rickard's three volumes (cit. *n.* 20) illustrate this point fully. Bursarial Accounts, 7673–686. Wood, *Life*, II, 565.

26. Wood, *Life*, II, 67. Woodward Transcripts, 45ff. Below, ch. IX, p. 301.
27. See below, ch. VI, pp. 212–17, 220–4. *The Journeys of Celia Fiennes*, ed. Christopher Morris (1947), 37.
28. Transcripts of Woodward Papers, 28, 74, 77. N.C. MS. 993: Warden Beeston's declaration of 1686; no. 1087: Morley's visitation.
29. Woodward Transcripts, 28. Wood, *Life*, III, 3. Rashdall and Rait, 189–90.
30. L. Stone, *The University in Society*, 37–59, esp. 45.
31. For Oxford politics in the eighteenth century see W. R. Ward, *Georgian Oxford* (Oxford, 1958), *passim*.
32. J. Nichols, *Epistolary Correspondence . . . of . . . Francis Atterbury* (1st edn. of 1784), III, 107; (2nd edn. of 1799), I, 222–36. I am grateful to Dr. G. V. Bennett for this reference. N.C. MSS. 5063, 5079. Some accounts give Braithwaite's majority as two, but it seems clear from subsequent events that it must have been only one. On Atterbury and the general background to clerical politics see G. V. Bennett, *The Tory Crisis in Church and State, 1688–1730* (Oxford, 1975), esp. chs. iii and iv. I have been unable to identify 'Mr. Butler'.
33. Rashdall and Rait, 198–204. Ward, *Georgian Oxford*, 110–12. C. E. Doble (ed.), *Remarks and Collections of Thomas Hearne* (Oxford Hist. Soc., V, 100). Anon., *The Case of Dr. Ayliffe* (1716). John Ayliffe, *The Ancient and Present State of the University of Oxford* (1714, 2 vols.), 323.
34. Ward, op. cit., 55, 71–2, 88, 111, 280 *n*. B.
35. *Remarks and Collections of Hearne*, VIII, 314–16.
36. Ibid., IX, 67.
37. British Library, *Additional MSS.*, no. 36,136, ff. 65–109.
38. Ward, *Georgian Oxford*, 170, 185 and *n*. 38. There is a large number of tracts on the wardenship issue. The most informative are Dr. Brindle, *A Letter to the Reverend Dr. Lowth* (1759) and Anon., *An Impartial Bystander's Review of the Controversy concerning the Wardenship of Winchester College* (1759).
39. Ward, op. cit., 222–3, 228–35, 258–9, 264, 285 *n*. Bb. On Foley see G.E.C., *The Complete Peerage*, V. 535.
40. Edited by W. N. Hargreaves-Maudsley as *Woodforde at Oxford, 1759–1776* (Oxford Hist. Soc., n.s. XXI, 1969). This and the following paragraphs are based largely on this diary.
41. See the chapters by L. Stone, S. Rothblatt and A. Engel in Stone (ed.), *The University in Society*, vol. I, and also W. R. Ward, *Victorian Oxford* (1965), for the general background.
42. N.C. MS. 51: Account-book for 1800–55. New College finances in the late eighteenth and early nineteenth centuries present something of a puzzle. In the five years 1775/6 to 1779/80 revenue averaged £4,420 p.a. and expenditure £4,450. In the first five years of the nineteenth century average revenue had increased to £7,175 and expenditure to £6,315. The corresponding figures for the quinquennium 1810–14 were £11,750 and £12,506. The reason for the increases and for the deterioration in the

balance after 1810 are not yet clear. Proposals for retrenchment were still being made in the 1830s and 1840s (N.C. MS. 9637, order-book for 1815–50).

43. Augustus Hare, *A Letter to George Martin Esq.* (1814). N.C. MSS. 1023; 11,765.
44. Quoted in Ward, *Victorian Oxford*, 338, *n.* 151.
45. *Gentleman's Magazine*, 1861, ii, 245–8. Nesta Webster, *Spacious Days: an autobiography* (1950), 22.
46. Joseph Phillimore, *A Report of an Appeal to the Lord Bishop of Winchester* (1839). N.C. MS. 1086. Squibb, *Founder's Kin*, 69, 120.
47. Winchester Diocesan Records (Hampshire Record Office) E/8/A–1, 2. I am grateful to Dr. Ronald Pugh of King Alfred's College, Winchester, for telling me of these documents and for showing me the draft of his article on 'Post-Restoration Bishops of Winchester as Visitors of Oxford Colleges', to appear in *Oxoniensa* for 1978. That article adds considerable detail to what I have written above.
48. Ward, *Victorian Oxford*, 95. N.C. MS. 3504.
49. N.C. MSS. 1086, 9637.

III

Transformation, 1850–1914

ALAN RYAN

The years from the appointment of the first University Commission to the outbreak of the First World War are among the most interesting in the whole history of the college. They were years in which New College experienced what was to all intents a second foundation; and if there was no one person in New College who played the role of second Founder in quite the way Dr. Ridding played it at Winchester, the transformation was every bit as dramatic. New College in 1850 was a closed society, in H. A. L. Fisher's memorable phrase, a society 'at once contracted, indolent, orthodox and obscure'.[1] The melancholy evidence of the college's losses in the First World War, which exceeded those of every other Oxford college, suggests the extent of its expansion in numbers. The eminence of the fellows of 1914, and the varied ways in which they and recent undergraduates served their country in the conflict, remind us that the growth in distinction had been as remarkable as the growth in numbers. In 1850, New College was a sort of fossil; before 1900, it was universally agreed that the pre-eminent colleges of the University of Oxford were Balliol, Christ Church, Magdalen and New College.[2]

Some years ago, an anonymous graffitist scrawled on a wall of the new buildings, 'New College is a little bit like Balliol'. The theme of what follows is that it is a mistake to think that only similar institutions can put up similar buildings, and that far from being a little bit like Balliol, New College was very unlike almost every other college. Anyone writing the history of Balliol from 1850, and anyone writing the history of New College from 1885, would find himself writing the history of what we now recognise as an Oxford college. But when our period opens, New College was an entirely different creature from what it became by the 1880s. A little guidebook put out in 1906 was not exaggerating when it claimed that a New College undergraduate of the time would have found the college of 1856 much stranger than its Founder would have done, while the position in 1880 would have been the reverse.[3]

It is, of course, true that the slabs of undistinguished Gilbert Scott which make up the older portion of the new buildings look very like Balliol's undistinguished Waterhouse. And the fact that both colleges undertook new building at the same date does attest to the great growth in the numbers of undergraduates which took place in the 1870s and 1880s. But in the early 1870s, when the new buildings were under construction, the process of expansion had only just begun in New College, while it was well under way at Balliol; New College had seventy-five undergraduates only, Balliol 145. Before the First World War, both had round about 300. Conversely, New College, with its greater endowments, had thirty-nine fellows to Balliol's eleven; but, of those thirty-nine only four were college lecturers, while six of Balliol's eleven held that position.[4] As we shall see, this difference in numbers reflected in addition the peculiarity of New College's statutes before the reforms of the 1850s, and the different conception of what a fellowship was which had prevailed in those unreformed days.

By the early 1870s, the isolation of New College had been much reduced; and it was to New College that Balliol had turned in 1868 in order to establish a system of shared lectures—a system from which all subsequent intercollegiate lecturing has developed. None the less, when the lectures were begun, the Balliol undergraduates hired bath chairs and attendants for their journey to the remote and inaccessible foundation to which they had been sent.[5] Although it is a surprising and not easily explicable fact that New College changed its statutes, style, standards and ambitions with a rush, once change had been forced upon it, it was still a very distinctive institution ten years after the first great change.

In trying to discern the frame of mind in which the college faced the demands for change which the 1850s brought, the twentieth-century reader is handicapped by some of the nineteenth century's habits. Where primary sources are concerned, the most baffling of these habits is an unwillingness to give more than the conclusions of a debate, and then often in terms which are inscrutable in the absence of the agenda; the minutes of the nineteenth-century governing body are full of references to such events as: 'Mr Adams's motion was negatived'—and barren of any statement of what the motion was, let alone why it was defeated. One supposes that passionate arguments must have taken place about changes as momentous as those which the college underwent in the 1850s and 1860s; but, what they were, and who was on what side, are not at all easy to discover.

Matters are made both easier and more awkward by the excellence of the one secondary account we possess. Hereford George's little book on *New College 1856–1906* was written for members of the college, and the *Record* of the day carries warm recommendations of its virtues from Warden Spooner. But it induces ambivalent feelings in a later writer. It is, except in very small points, entirely accurate; it gives an entirely lucid and rational account of how the college set about modernising its teaching, its buildings, its methods of choosing both undergraduates and fellows, its machinery of administration, and its finances. What it does not do is tell us *who* suggested changes, and who opposed them, although it speaks of some violent conflicts of opinion. Only three names cross the threshold of anonymity, and George apologises for mentioning even those three. They are the names of E. C. Wickham, Alfred Robinson and Warden Sewell—and none of them is referred to by name after the first few pages.[6]

Even if it is mostly the debasement of taste in the intervening seventy years which makes this impersonality so frustrating—and what follows is itself essentially 'Institutional' history—there are two things to be said against it. It suggests, what evidently was not true, namely, that the college progressed steadily under the guidance of some sort of 'invisible hand'; for it is clear that some individuals made a great deal of difference, on George's own account, and it would have been a help to know which made what difference on what issues. The second complaint is that George seriously misleads the reader by underestimating his own role in the story. Hereford George was both an exemplary and an influential figure, and one of the most important of the benign forces for change. He was one of the first of the new breed of college tutors, a man who saw teaching and research as the career of a lifetime, rather than something to be undertaken while waiting for a parish. Men like him needed different rules to live under; they had to have the freedom to marry—and George was the first married fellow in Oxford; they needed somewhere other than college rooms to live in; and they needed something like the twentieth-century ladder of promotion and change of job to keep them alert. George's evidence to the Universities Commission of 1877 contains a wholly twentieth-century plea from the working college teacher; at a time when the professors were in a sulky state, and were complaining that tutors kept their pupils away from professorial lectures, George suggested that what were needed were research seminars in which those heavily engaged in teaching could take part, to have the benefit of what the professoriate was working at.[7] He was a more than competent military historian, and a *Kriegspiel* enthusiast; he was also a classical mountaineer, and the sort of tutor whose stocky figure and square auburn beard were remembered with affection for half a century. He was elected a fellow under the old statutes in 1856, and apart from a brief career at the Bar, he devoted the rest of his life to New College. He was responsible for the success of the new Honours School of Law and Modern History, and then of the separated School of Modern History. To leave himself out of his history of the changes he had done so much to help was a sin against both himself and his readers.

The proper starting point for the story of these changes is not easy to settle. The Reform Act of 1832 had served notice of a wholesale inspection and renovation of Church and State, and perhaps the surprising fact is not that university and college reform came about in the 1850s, but that it came so long after 1832. For, after 1832 there had been a flurry of attacks on endowed institutions; radicals like John Stuart Mill could claim the support of conservative thinkers like Coleridge for the demands they made—did endowed institutions fulfil the terms of the bequests of their pious benefactors; if not, by what right did they enjoy the revenues of those ancient trusts? Readers of Trollope know the story as intimately as readers of Mill. Charities, old schools, the finances of the Established Church, were all in the reformers' minds; the colleges of Oxford and Cambridge could hardly expect to escape scrutiny.[8]

In the eyes of liberals, the state of the university at large was peculiarly odious. To them it seemed that the role of the University of Oxford was simply to repress liberalism, Romanism and serious intellectual activity among the Anglican clergymen who were its senior members, and to keep up pressure on the Tories whom the university sent to Parliament to avert all external inspection and control. Of course this was exaggeration, and in any event, heretics, reformers and liberals sprang up as fast as they were cut down. But, a realistic appraisal of the balance of forces in the university would have suggested to any reformer that reform would have to be imposed from without, by a liberal government.[9]

The colleges were implicated in the more obnoxious features of the Anglican monopoly of positions in Oxford. They chose their fellows from quaintly restricted sources; they imposed on them no obligations to teach or study; they generally imposed few restrictions on where they might reside. Even if they were to improve in these respects, the restriction of fellowships to celibate clergymen of the Established Church would make the improvement minimal. In any case, most reformers had little time for the tutorial system, on which even improved college teaching would be based. Scottish critics were apt to be particularly damning; they pointed to the flourishing state of Scottish universities under a system of professorial instruction, and contrasted this with the state of things under the 'regenting' system— that is to say, the system in which a student was handed over to a regent or tutor for the duration of his university course.[10] Others pointed to the superiority of the German universities, although polemically this was ill-advised. The German universities were known to be infected by the new biblical criticism of Strauss. Feuerbach and the Bauers, and opponents of reform were always ready to make the point.[11]

New College was not by local standards a scandalous institution. Its fellows did not misappropriate funds for private purposes; they did not take part in reactionary political adventures; they were not in the forefront of those baying for heretical blood. They were, at worst, obscure and unenergetic. None the less, New College was, by the standards of a later age, a strange place. It was a very small, closed foundation. Under the Founder's statutes, membership of New College was confined to seventy fellows, whose devotions were assisted by the services of ten singing chaplains. In 1854, there were on the books of the college, two noblemen and five gentlemen commoners in addition. Of these, not more than one or two can have been in residence, since almost all of them already possessed the B.A. Unlike most other colleges, New

College had never admitted commoners—other than a handful of gentlemen commoners, for whose benefit the garden quad had been erected; perhaps the college had always been wealthy enough to dispense with the income, perhaps fellows had always thought, as some still did, that the Founder's prohibition on strangers pernoctating within the walls ruled out the admission of commoners on any scale. Of the seventy fellows, some twenty were undergraduates—the number fluctuated between a dozen and a little over twenty. They were the majority of those in residence; in consequence a good deal of the college was unlived in. Surprisingly, there are no complaints of the bleak scenes this must have implied for life in hall and chapel, and one imagines that the chapel at least must have attracted a good many visitors and townspeople.

The intellectual life of the college was at a low ebb. Until the 1850s the level of undergraduate attainment was unimpressive. The reasons for this generally low level are simply stated. New College could by its statutes elect its fellows from only one source, the college at Winchester. That is, the choice of candidates for fellowships was not merely confined to the boys of one school, but to a small group within that school. Only the scholars of Winchester were eligible for the fellowships of New College. To obtain a scholarship to Winchester, moreover, was not a matter of intellectual achievement, but a question of patronage. Scholars had to pass a qualifying test of an elementary kind, but the decisive point was to secure the nomination of the warden and fellows of Winchester. If the boys who entered Winchester were not picked for intellectual merit, they were not given the sort of teaching which would create it, either. Nor was the examination which selected the boys who would become fellows of New College competitive; there was some alteration in the order in which boys would become eligible to fill any vacancy at New College during their years at school, but not much. In general, a boy of thirteen or fourteen would have a fair idea of his chances of a New College fellowship four or five years later. It hardly encouraged strenuous intellectual activity.[12] A final item in this gloomy catalogue of disincentives was the existence of Founder's Kin. The supposed descendants of the Founder had succeeded in quartering themselves on the two St. Mary colleges some three hundred years before; after disputes between the colleges and the interested families, an agreement had been reached that no more than eighteen Founder's

Kin should be taken on by the two colleges. In 1852, when Bishop Sumner made his last visitation under the Founder's statutes, the number had risen to thirty-one. Some indication of the intellectual abilities which were traditionally ascribed to Founder's Kin can be gleaned from the story of how Founder's Kin were selected, which is still told to visitors to Winchester. A boy claiming Founder's Kin was struck a sharp blow on the head with the flat of a stout wooden trencher; if it broke, he was Founder's Kin.

The process of reform was slow. In 1850 the first University Commisson was appointed, with power only to enquire and recommend; its recommendations were published as a Blue Book in 1852. Only in 1854 was a commission with executive powers appointed; its task was to give the university and the colleges appropriate new statutes, either by agreement or as a last resort by *fiat*. Between the publication of the 1852 Blue Book and the appointment of the executive commissioners in 1854, New College sought the advice of its Visitor about what useful changes could be made within the bounds of the old statutes. The fact that the college took such advice in 1852–3 suggests that there was no diehard resistance to change; the fact that the question put to the Visitor was what changes he thought should be made within the constraints of the old statutes suggests as strongly that there was no enthusiasm for change, either.[13]

New College refused to co-operate with the commissioners of 1850; the college would not divulge its statutes, and threw itself on the discretion of the Visitor. He did nothing, but the commissioners secured a copy of the statutes from the British Museum. After the commissioners issued their report, New College was not notably loud in protest, even though the report recommended a great loosening of the ties with Winchester, the admission of commoners, the creation of open scholarships and more besides.[14] Although Warden Williams went off to London with the Hebdomadal Council to protest about the changes proposed for the university at large, no New College men were prominent in the agitation of the next two years.

The most important agitation was that of the Tutors' Association.[15] This body defended what eventually turned out to be the twentieth-century compromise which gives Oxford its distinctive character, as a university in which tutorial instruction rests with the colleges, and lectures, examinations and the general superintendence of syllabuses and the like with the university. The Tutors' Association owed its success to its gaining the ear of a newly reform-minded Gladstone, but also to the obvious sense of its views. As against the anti-collegiate reformers with their urge to establish a professorial dictatorship and the diehards who wanted no change whatever, the compromise the association defended was an attractive one. Oxford could become a place of teaching and research if college fellows could make a career of these activities; equally, there was need for more organised instruction provided by the university, and for such a purpose there should be more professors, and they should have proper salaries rather than ludicrous sums such as forty or fifty pounds a year which served to advertise the chairs to which they were attached as the mere sinecures they had in fact become. But there was no need to turn the college tutors into mere assistant lecturers. There is no evidence of the three New College tutors playing any active part in the association's existence. Since there had been a strike by the New College undergraduates only a year or two before, in protest against the incompetence of their tutors, this is hardly surprising.

It is important to remember what the aspirations of the fellows of New College in the early 1850s actually were, and what a fellowship meant to somebody in that period. Perhaps the most important thing to clear out of one's mind is any lingering thought that fellows would naturally have wanted to become university teachers or to engage in research. A fellowship provided a young man with a modest income on which he could rely until he was able to make his way in the world, and indeed one on which he could rely for the rest of his life if he did not choose to marry, did not choose to earn a substantial income and did not have the luck to inherit one. The great majority of the fellows of New College went on to become country clergymen; so close was this tie, both at New College and elsewhere, that much of the most sincere hostility to reform came from those who thought that college fellowships and college revenues were morally if not in law the property of the Established Church. In the case of New College, particularly, the boys who went to Winchester as scholars and thus as potential fellows, were very frequently from clerical families. They were not strikingly upper class; and they would probably have found a New College fellowship with the prospect of a comfortable parish to follow a very satisfactory insurance policy. The stipends of the fellows were not large. The

Founder's statutes required the college to maintain seventy fellows, and there was no way to suppress fellowships in order to increase the individual fellow's dividend. Alhough there was a small additional payment to the older fellows, none received much more than a hundred and fifty pounds a year. Some of the fellows of Magdalen and All Souls got four times as much—at a time when agricultural labourers earned thirty pounds a year in regular employment and perhaps as much again from odds and ends, and the Northcote-Trevelyan enquiry into the civil service was told that a 'gentleman' could manage very well on four hundred. So, a New College fellowship was not a very glittering prize, even if we take into account, as we certainly should, the fact that it was the income of a single man who got most of his living expenses in kind. Hereford George reminds us, too, that apart from Founder's Kin, the fellows were on probation for the first couple of years, and got a great deal less then; indeed, he writes of them as years of some hardship for the young men and their families.[16]

The fellows, then, were neither well off by the standards of the day, nor were they the *pauperes* spoken of in the Founder's statutes. But, in any case, the college's revenues were not intended to provide for nothing more than their stipends. As a corporate landowner, and as the owner of numerous benefices, the college had obligations to the holders of its benefices and to their parishes, which diminished its available income. Where the college's income came in the form of tithe rent-charges, as it did in parts of Essex, it came encumbered by charges for the salaries of several incumbents in the parishes of the area. And the maintenance of the choir consumed as much as a dozen fellows would have done. These obligations were felt every bit as acutely as were the obligations to educate undergraduates and keep up intellectual standards among them and their seniors. All in all, it is less helpful to see New College in 1850 as a nascent institution of higher education than to see it as a corporate landowner whose revenues were by statute and tradition devoted to training and paying for the personnel of the Established Church. It was such an institution that its members wished to see preserved, and it is in such a light that their attitude to the college's educational tasks must be understood.

The effect of the report of the commissioners, when it appeared in 1852, was to stimulate the college into taking the advice of the Visitor on the changes that could be made within the old statutes. The position of the college was somewhat delicate. It was generally felt that the existing fellows of colleges were morally bound by the oaths they took on election to their fellowships to observe the statutes under which they had been elected. They had no power to alter those statutes, and there is no reason to suppose that their professions of doubt about the lawfulness of trying to do so were anything but sincere. But it was quite out of the question to try to give literal obedience to them and the 1852 Blue Book is almost amusing on the extent of the impossibility. The Founder had required five fellows to proceed to the higher degrees in canon law, but canon law had not been taught for three hundred years, and even the D.C.L. was a higher degree in name alone. The more malicious reformers sometimes suggested that it would indeed be a good idea to enforce the letter of the old rules—since even with allowances for inflation those would allow the fellows of most colleges an income of about forty pounds a year, and would thus leave a surplus which the reformers might expropriate. It was a difficult task to say just how much allowance could properly be made for the changed circumstances in which the Founder's statutes were being followed without admitting the principle of wholesale reinterpretation.

The Visitor made his last visitation under the old statutes in December 1852, and he and the college corresponded about the changes to be made. It is not easy to discover from their correspondence quite what the college wished to hear, but the impression that it leaves is that the bishop was more decidedly for change than were the warden and fellows of New College, while the real laggards were the warden and fellows of Winchester. The reason for this is simple enough. The bishop took the view that the way to improve standards at New College was to improve them at Winchester; what were probationary fellowships under the old statute should become scholarships, and should be open to all the boys at Winchester, not just the scholars. Moreover, the scholarships to Winchester should from now on be awarded by merit, assessed by competitive examination. The bishop professed himself uncertain whether the Founder had intended scholars and fellows to be selected simply from those who were *qualified* as *ydonei et habiles* or from those who were *best* qualified; but he came down on the side of competition in the present. To strengthen further the forces of competition, New College should establish open scholarships; and commoners should certainly be admitted.[17] The warden and fellows of

Winchester resisted the abandonment of their patronage, but they were overridden, and from December 1854, scholarships to Winchester were awarded by competitive examination. It remains unclear whether Sumner actually possessed the legal authority to impose his wishes on Winchester in this way; but, with the Clarendon Commission on the public schools still a long way in the future, he made a considerable difference to Winchester by doing so.[18] Paradoxically, at New College, where his authority was incontestable, his proposals were almost immediately overtaken by those which the University Commission of 1854 put forward; to take one instance only, where Sumner had suggested that the number of Founder's Kin at the two St. Mary colleges should not exceed the eighteen laid down by Bishop Cooper, the new ordinances abolished Founder's Kin outright.[19]

The Commission of 1854 was appointed with power to give colleges new statutes. Most importantly, perhaps, those new statutes gave colleges the power to revise their statutes subject to approval by the Privy Council. From the implementation of the new statutes colleges would be able to modify piecemeal the rules under which they operated whenever they perceived the need; convulsive change was no longer the only alternative to absolute stagnation. There is an odd paucity of evidence how New College set about negotiating with the commissioners for the new ordinances and statutes. The results, however, were very much in line with the proposals of 1852, and thus not very different from what Bishop Sumner had advised. In future, only graduates were to be fellows; undergraduate fellows would be replaced by scholars; the original foundation of seventy fellows would become one of forty fellows and thirty scholars. Half the fellows were to be elected from those who had studied either at Winchester or New College; the other half were to be elected by open competition. In either case, fellowships were to be awarded on examination. The ten singing chaplains were reduced to three; Founder's Kin had no privileges at all. Three things are worth noticing besides. Open scholarships were not created at once; as George points out, there was no way of paying for them other than by diminishing the stipends of the fellows. Once the new statutes had given the college the power to suppress fellowships in order to pay for them, the college did move to create open scholarships, and almost the first major change in the statutes was the reduction in the number of fellowships from forty to thirty to provide the funds. In the second place, clerical restrictions vanished instantly.[20] There must, one imagines, have been some argument about that, but there is no trace of it; instead, New College just did away with the requirement that fellows should proceed to holy orders. Lastly, the college's relationship with the university altered; it was agreed that the Savilian Professorships of Astronomy and Geometry should be a charge on New College revenues.[21]

To the twentieth-century reader, the reduction in the number of fellows from seventy to forty and then thirty conjures up visions of the summary sacking of dozens of men in mid-career. But, of course, it was not like that. In the first place, the reduction was to be achieved only gradually. In the second place, fellowships, even when awarded to graduates only, had no necessary connection with a tutorial career. In any case, a college with twenty undergraduates required no more than three or four tutors, and therefore had no particular reason to regard its fellowships as primarily intended to attract teachers for its undergraduates. Only later did it seem necessary to take powers to elect to fellowships men whose services were wanted for teaching;[22] in 1857 when the new ordinances were agreed, fellowships still seemed appropriate prizes for promising young men. Moreover, there were far fewer promising young men than there were fellowships—one estimate is that throughout the university as a whole, there were twice as many fellowships falling vacant each year as there were first classes in the schools.[23] Fewer fellowships, open to a wider competition, would have seemed an entirely proper means of improving the standard of prize-winners.

Finally, we must recall that it does not necessarily make a very great and immediate difference if thirty fellows who have not yet obtained their M.A. are replaced by thirty scholars. In the end, of course, it did, for the scholars had only a five-year tenure at best, not an expectation for life; and they did not have a share in the government of the college. Although the Warden and Thirteen had been the *de facto* governing body, and although there had been senior, middle and junior common rooms, so that it would be misleading to think of the fellows as an undifferentiated body, it is still true that they had been equal members of one corporate body in a way they were not thereafter.

But if the immediate changes were not quite so violent as one might at first glance think they must have been, it is still striking how rapid and far-reaching the changes were over the next twenty years. By 1866 open scholarships had been created; this was both for the sake of keeping the Wykehamists up to scratch, and in order to induce non-Wykehamists to come to New College as commoners.[24] Initial attempts to bring in more commoners had been frustrated by the candidates' fears that the college would be divided into a Wykehamist aristocracy of intellect and a non-Wykehamist *lumpenproletariat*. A year later the age of the married don opened; the college took powers to re-elect to his fellowship anyone whose services the college wished to keep as senior bursar, tutor or lecturer, and who would otherwise have vacated his fellowship by marrying. This was one of the contentious issues which have left their mark in the minutes of the governing body—votes are recorded over a period of two years, and the names of those on the side of change or the *status quo* listed. The intellectual standards of the college rose to such an extent that it was able to refuse to accept anyone who was not committed to reading for an honours degree. An energetic rebuilding programme was started; the hall was reroofed in 1863 with timbers from the college's own estates at Whaddon in Buckinghamshire; and land was purchased from Merton so that new buildings could be put up in Holywell. The college estates were put into order by successive bursars. And although the choir surfaces in the records as the source of anxieties about unpaid fees, unsuitable accommodation, incompetent choristers and from time to time drunken lay clerks, even, it was increasingly well-housed, well-trained and properly supervised.

The question this raises is, who brought it about, and why did nobody try to stop it? St. John's, after all, dug in for a long fight and rejected every draft of new statutes put forward by the commissioners until the Privy Council put a stop to obstruction in 1861, and imposed even less attractive statutes. Two things seem to explain why New College changed so quickly and painlessly. The first was an improvement in the standard of teaching at Winchester; it is difficult to find any hard evidence of change, but the results obtained in final honour schools suddenly improve quite strikingly in the late 1840s and early 1850s. The other was a sudden jump in resignations of incumbent fellows at the same time. The average during the first half of the century is about four resignations a year; but in 1850 and 1851 there were twenty-two resignations.[25] Only detailed biographical investigation could test the guess that those most hostile to change would have been most likely to take their chance of a country living and leave, but it is a plausible guess that they would be the most fearful of what might emerge from the commission of 1850. Sir Charles Oman's *Memoirs of Victorian Oxford* suggests that the speed with which New College adapted to the changes introduced by the ordinances of 1857 owed much to the rapid turnover of fellows, which removed the obstructive and irreconcilable. This appears to overestimate the rate at which the governing body *did* change after 1857 and to underestimate the importance of the flurry of changes around 1850.

Still, the mere absence of decided opposition to change is hardly enough to explain why change occurred. One thing that is plain is that the process did not involve pressure from above; Warden Williams, who had succeeded Shuttleworth in 1840, died in 1860; he had certainly had no appetite for change, having reposed in the belief that the Founder's statutes had served the college perfectly well for almost five hundred years and that they were therefore in no great need of improvement. He was succeeded by J. E. Sewell, a man of fifty at the time of his election, who was to go on in the office until 1903 when he died at the age of ninety-two. He was known to irreverent junior members as 'the Shirt'; his chief occupation was small-scale antiquarian research, and he sat in the lodgings, carefully annotating the statutes laid down by the Founder, while his colleagues got on with running the college under the statutes which had replaced them. As R. S. Rait mildly remarks in the *D.N.B.*: 'The chief share in the growth of New College during his long wardenship is to be attributed to his colleagues, but Sewell loyally accepted changes which did not commend themselves to his own judgment.' His great virtue was that he served as a symbol of continuity with the old order, and softened the pangs of transition. He was, however, quite formidable when members of the college visited the college estates. Fisher tells a nice story of Sewell's confrontation with a lady who thought that the insanitary state of her cottage entitled her to a reduction in its rent, and was startled that the benign old gentleman to whom she addressed the demand thought, in contrast, that she owed the college money by way of compensating it for her having let its property get into such a state.[26] Still, in college affairs, what Sewell supplied was evidently ballast—indispensable to safe sailing, but not a propulsive force.

The two dominant figures, as George's account suggests, were evidently E. C. Wickham and Alfred Robinson. Robinson was one of the first thorough outsiders to join the college. W. A. Spooner had been the first non-Wykehamist to become a scholar, when one of the Winchester scholarships was thrown open to general competition in 1861, but Robinson had been a schoolboy at Marlborough, and was a scholar of University College when he became a fellow of New College in 1864. Robinson's period of thoroughgoing ascendancy over the affairs of the college dates from his appointment as senior bursar in 1875, but he was evidently a figure to be reckoned with from the first, as the fact that he was twice President of the Union might suggest. Before Robinson became senior bursar, even, the first steps in reorganising the college's finances had already been taken, under the bursarial control of the Reverend Lancelot J. Lee; he was a rather unbursarial figure, with a passion for hunting and for driving a four-in-hand, but the policy of concentrating the college's estates within a manageable distance of Oxford began with him, as did the policy of changing from beneficial tenancies to conventional rack-renting. He was a man of some spirit, as his quarrelsome replies to the Cleveland Commission of 1873 will reveal, but he is quite properly overshadowed in recollection by his successor as senior bursar.

Quite what gave Robinson his extraordinary power is hard to tell. Spooner writes of him as someone who possessed an unusual moral authority and who seemed to his listeners to be their own consciences in another flesh. But it seems equally plausible that it was the clarity and energy of his mind that made him so formidable. He had, as his evidence to successive commissions reveals, an unusually clear idea of what the University of Oxford and its constituent colleges should be doing, and an unusual confidence that with the aid of rational policies they could do it without difficulty. Indeed, he brought all sorts of anxieties upon the college by his insistence that with rational management the college income could provide for new buildings, more undergraduates and a surplus to be devoted to university purposes. He held solid liberal convictions—Sir Charles Oman's recollection of him wavers between suggesting that this was the most abominable fault in his character and that his being a non-Wykehamist was even worse— and could evidently carry the college with him by the strength of those convictions. He would certainly have become warden if Sewell had not lived to such an unusual age, and if he himself had not died, in 1895, while still a comparatively young man.[27]

From the later 1860s onwards, Spooner, who did become warden on Sewell's death, plainly deserves a good deal of the credit for the smoothness and painlessness of the process of growth. His appearance and his own recollections of his career make it hard to treat him with the seriousness he deserves. He looked like an ineffectual sheep—Sir Charles Oman, again, thought that this was a bar to his being elected warden, on the not entirely impressive principle that heads of houses ought to look like heads of houses. He was short-sighted, very pink-faced, and with the white hair of albinism. He recalled in later life a certain embarrassment during his undergraduate career, when a visiting preacher had given a sermon on the text 'Ye who have grown grey in sin' and nobody could think of anyone but Spooner as a possible target for his address. He was known affectionately as 'the Child'—with the inevitable result that when he took for himself a much more imposing wife, the lady was known as 'the Madonna'. He summed up his career as merely that of a *moderately useful man*, and his memoirs do not give one very much evidence on which to dispute this. However, his memoirs are misleading in a crucial respect; they concentrate almost exclusively on events in the university at large, where, indeed, Spooner did not wield much influence. They contain almost nothing about his labours in New College, where it is evident that he worked incessantly as tutor, lecturer, dean, examiner. A moderately useful sheep would not have been elected warden by the distinguished body that the fellows of New College had become by 1903.[28]

We have already mentioned the part played by Hereford George from the middle of the 1860s onward. But the initial impetus for change seems to have been supplied above all by E. C. Wickham. Gladstone, whose son-in-law Wickham later became, acquired a reputation for being an 'old man in a hurry'. Wickham had the more usual reputation—that of being a young man in a hurry, filled with what Hereford George says his elders regarded as 'a spirit of abominable restlessness'. He had an equal mixture of the engineer and the pedagogue about him—he was an excellent tutor, and his attitude to all institutions was to ask what task they were supposed to perform, and then to see how they might be made to perform it better. It was no doubt proper that he went off to become Headmaster of Wellington in 1874; but before he went, he had been the driving force behind the creation of inter-collegiate lectures in 1868, and he was one of the first New College tutors whose intellectual abilities gave him any claims on the attention of pupils from other colleges.[29]

In retrospect, it seems difficult to believe that so many changes could have been set in train by a handful of tutors. But, as we have seen already, the majority of fellows would have had interests outside the college, and so long as they did not obstruct change, it could be pushed along by a very few active fellows. Until a good deal later, colleges could manage their teaching with very few tutors and lecturers; college lectures really were lectures even if they were given to no more than half a dozen pupils; and the style of teaching was reminiscent of school, with classes construing set-books or working through mathematical examples. In these conditions—as we have already seen, even in 1873 New College had only four college tutors—two or three people could make a great deal of difference.

One feature of these years which it is difficult to recapture is the place of religion in the life of the college. It is a familiar story that university reform was intimately bound up with the fate of the Anglican establishment; the one great battle which was not decided by the reforms of the 1854 commissioners was the place of religious tests. There must have been religious tensions, if nothing worse, in New College as elsewhere; there certainly were incessant arguments about the degree of elaboration proper in the college's chapel services. And, throughout the 1860s, there was a rather plaintive attempt by one—but one only—of the fellows to have the chapel roof painted in its medieval colours. But there seems to have been no greater rift on theological issues among the fellows of the college. It was, however, a fellow of New College who became the first Roman Catholic to hold a fellowship in Oxford since the Reformation. Croke Robinson joined the Catholic Church in 1872, almost immediately after the repeal of the religious tests; he eventually became a monsignor and domestic prelate to the Pope. But there is no evidence that his secession to Rome caused his colleagues much anxiety.

From the acceptance of the new ordinances and statutes in 1857, then, the college grew in numbers and changed in character. In this, it was to a large extent sharing in the experience of other colleges and of the university as a whole. In 1873, the government of the day decided to investigate—what, oddly, nobody had tried to uncover in the 1850s—the financial resources of the colleges and universities of Oxford and

Cambridge. This enquiry was carried out by the Cleveland Commission. It was a purely investigative commission, though it paved the way for the Royal Commission of 1877, which was both investigative and executive, and which was given powers for five years to revise the statutes of colleges and university alike, and in particular to make arrangements for the financing of university purposes from the surplus revenues of the colleges. Thus, since the Royal Commission relied heavily on what the Cleveland Commission discovered—or believed that it had discovered—the Cleveland Commission's results were of great importance. They are also of great interest still, because they supply the only readily accessible comparative statistics about such things as the number of undergraduates in each college, the number of benefices owned by each college, the size of their estates, the size of their tithe income and so on. That the commission did its work in 1873 turned out to be something of a disaster, for its figures all related to the years immediately before the agricultural depression of the last quarter of the century, and thus encouraged the Royal Commission of four years later to propose all sorts of expenditures which became impossible in the colder financial climate. It also did its work with a surprising degree of inefficiency; its figures for the external income of the colleges seem to be reliable—that is, its figures for rents from estates above all. But it obtained much less reliable figures for 'internal' income and expenditure—that is, income from the rent of college rooms to undergraduates, income from the charges made to them for their meals and for service. It was not just that some colleges entered gross figures and some only net figures: because there was no uniform system of accounting, there is no ready way of knowing what figures are net and what gross within a given college's accounts. The result was that the report was greeted with a fair measure of cynicism and even outrage. None the less, it paved the way for the system of college contributions to a common university fund, from which professors and university lecturers were until the 1960s supposed to receive their salaries.

New College's dealings with the Cleveland Commission present a splendidly confused picture. 1873 was a year of some activity in New College; the college joined with Balliol in agreeing to give £300 a year apiece to the infant University College at Bristol, on condition among other things that the college admitted women as freely as men, a condition that neither Balliol nor New College managed to meet for another 106 years.[30] But, the college quarrelled with the commissioners in the most embarrassing fashion. The final report singled out New College and Lincoln as the only two colleges which would not present their accounts in the form the commissioners had requested. Lincoln was in worse straits than New College—its accounts were kept in bad Latin as well as in archaic forms, and when the new system of uniform accounting procedures was introduced in 1883, it took Lincoln a year longer than any other college to fall into line. Still, Lincoln's attitude was tolerably apologetic; the Reverend Lancelot J. Lee was simply rude. He was undeniably under some provocation, for the commissioners insisted on knowing about the sources and destinations of very minor sums of money for no very obviously good reasons. Lee offered to send the commissioners every scrap of paper the bursary possessed; he would not, however, himself transcribe the college accounts into the form required by the commissioners, and when they had transcribed them, he would not agree that their transcription was correct, since he had not actually made the transcription himself. Eventually, an enquiry from the commisioners into the purpose of a fund for augmenting benefices provoked the irritated reply that he supposed the point of augmenting benefices was to make them more valuable. The commissioners thereupon declined to deal further with Lee, and insisted on dealing with the warden directly.[31] It seems possible that Lee was not in the best of health at the time, for he resigned to take up a south Oxfordshire parish a year later and died not long afterwards.

But if the combativeness of the Reverend Lancelot Lee expressed the college's anxieties about outside scrutiny—and there seems to have been a particular fear, then and later, that the choir would come under attack as an unnecessary extravagance—the college's action in laying before the commissioners the draft of the statutes they wished to live under reflects a willingness to discuss with any interested body the way the college did its work.

The draft statutes of 1873 became in essentials the actual statutes which the college received in 1882, after the Royal Commission of 1877 had done its work. They reflect what one might call the second stage of modernisation. The ordinances of 1857 are recognisably the statutes of an institution not wholly unlike the twentieth-century college; but the twentieth-century fellow of New College would find them oddly barren of references to tutors and lecturers, professorial fellows and research fellows; and he would find the emphasis on examination curious in any college other than All Souls, where prize fellows make up a substantial part of the whole body. The draft of 1873 looks like the statutes of a twentieth-century college. There was to be a maximum of thirty-six fellows, of whom five were to be professorial fellows (only two chairs were as yet attached to the college), a maximum of ten were to be tutorial fellows, who could be elected by the college without examination, and four at most could be elected for their distinction in learning as what would now be called senior research fellows; the remainder would hold ordinary fellowships, tenable for seven years and non-renewable, offered alternately for Wykehamists and for the world at large to compete for, and awarded on examination. There were no celibacy requirements, and they could be held without obligation to reside for more than one probationary year. The poverty of the twentieth century, as well as the great concentration of effort on teaching, has to all intents and purposes abolished the ordinary fellowships, although they have to an extent been replaced by research fellowships of one kind and another. Otherwise, the college which the draft of 1873 envisaged is the college which was in full existence ten years later, and has remained so since. The creation of a class of tutorial fellowships perhaps reflects two things. The first is the way in which competitive examination had ceased to be thought the only way to secure good candidates for fellowships; 1854 was something like the high tide of an enthusiasm for examination, and by 1873, it had ebbed somewhat. The other, of course, is the college's realisation that, with the new buildings coming to completion, there would be an enormous increase in the number of undergraduates needing instruction—the number of commoners in residence is hard to work out either from the *University Calendar* or from the college's own register, but it must have gone up from something in the order of sixty-five in 1873 to 180 in 1883; and it is quite clear that the college was in a condition where it could fill any accommodation it had with further commoners, especially as the effect of opening the college to non-Wykehamists was by this time the establishment of new ties with schools like Eton and Harrow, and, more surprisingly, Manchester Grammar School. Obviously, the college needed to take steps to have them taught; it seemed equally obvious that there might be no connection between the cleverness a young man needed to get a fellowship and the skills needed in a successful teacher. In fact, such fears turned out to be groundless and many of the college's most devoted tutors began as prize fellows and unofficial tutors—Spooner, Courtney, Robinson and Fisher were only a few of them.[32]

The administration of the college necessarily altered to meet the demands of the new order; under the Founder's statutes, the seventy fellows were a self-governing community, even though most matters were managed by the warden and thirteen senior fellows. Under the new regime, with the abolition of undergraduate fellows, the governing body was simply the fellows under the new statutes. But most of the day-to-day business could be managed by a small committee of the warden and college officers, while the internal affairs were left in the hands of the warden and residents. After 1870, however, things changed again, when the two main concerns of the college were entrusted to committees empowered to look after them on a day-to-day basis, and to bring proposals for change before the whole governing body. The Tuition Comittee was established once it became clear that increased numbers demanded some sort of continuous appraisal of the college's teaching needs, and some continuous control over the work of the undergraduates as well as over the arrangements made with other colleges for shared lecturing and the like. The Estates Committee was set up to provide continuous supervision of the college's property, a task which was made necessary by the changes in the legal and financial status of college property which will be discussed below. Of course, then as now, committees were set up *ad hoc*, to consider changes in the order of service, or to formulate a policy about college aid to parish schools, as well as for the usual purposes of examining candidates for scholarships and fellowships. But the establishment of these two major committees 'in 1870 and 1871 marked the college's recognition that teaching was its main task, and financing its own expansion as an institution of learning its main problem.

The way in which the college dealt with its finances has an interest of its own, which may be felt by more people than legal antiquarians on the one hand and those who send their bank statements as Christmas cards to entertain their friends on the other. The two heroes of the story are C. W. Lawrence in the 1850s and Alfred Robinson in the 1880s. The former was a sometime fellow of New College and for some years the Steward of Christ Church and New College; it was he who steered through Parliament the crucial piece of legislation—the College Estates Act, 1858—which allowed the colleges of Oxford and Cambridge a degree of freedom in managing and improving their property which was essential to expansion. The conditions under which colleges owned and leased out their property were already so quaint in 1873 that the Cleveland commissioners thought it necessary to have a barrister append a couple of pages in explanation when they presented their report. Colleges let their property on two sorts of lease; the more important was the so-called 'beneficial lease', which was for a period of twenty years, renewable at six yearly intervals—forty years and fourteen years in the case of building leases. Where a college was the lord of the manor, small pieces of property were let out as copyholds, usually held for the lives of three named persons. The money rent taken on a beneficial lease was absurdly low, although the lease afforded a rent in kind as well: this was imposed by a statute of Elizabeth I, and was intended to secure that pious donors' wishes about providing food and drink for their foundations were not frustrated.[33] But the most important element in the income it provided was the 'fine' which the college took on renewal of the lease. In principle, this was a premium paid to the owner by the lessee for the privilege of continuing to enjoy the lease. In practice, the fine provided so large a part of the income derived from such leases that it amounted to a rent in a series of lump sums. Although it was an advance payment, it was always treated by colleges as current income. The beneficial lease had various disadvantages; for one thing, it kept the land out of the colleges' hands for excessively long periods. For another, it provided neither an incentive for improvement to the property, nor—because the fine was treated as current income—did it allow the colleges to build up the capital they would have needed to become improving landlords. The forty-year building lease, in contrast, was too short to allow colleges to reap the development gains they could otherwise have taken on occasions when a demand for building land would have made ninety-nine year leases very profitable.

Now, the remedy for all this was simple enough. To get its land back into its own hands, all a college had to do was to refuse to renew a lease, forgo the fine and resume possession. Copyholds took longer to run out, but by refusing to put in new lives a college would get possession when the last existing life was over, and even if the process took fifty years, the sooner it was started the better. But no college could contemplate the sacrifice of anything like as large a proportion of its income as the absence of fines would have entailed. The solution to this was obvious also; colleges needed to be able to borrow whatever sums were necessary to buy out existing leases, to contract what were later known as 'fine loans'. Since the land in question would let at twice and perhaps three times its existing rental, once improvements had been made—these were, it should be remembered, estimates made during the agricultural prosperity of the three decades between the abolition of the Corn Laws and the depression of the last quarter of the century—the mortgages raised to meet the missing fines could be paid off soon enough, and the colleges then allowed to expand their activities without financial embarrassment. The difficulty, until 1858, was that colleges were legally debarred from doing anything of the sort; they held their land in mortmain, and were tightly restricted in what they could do with it. Until the 1820s, they were unable even to sell property for anything other than building within their own walls, and for some highway purposes—the latter giving rise to a splendid but insecure form of conveyance, whereby the seller would recite the provisions of the appropriate statute, and transfer the property in question, without the least attempt to show that the transfer was *required* for roadmaking. The College Estates Act of 1858 gave colleges power to mortgage their property for the purpose of forgoing fines, and for building for college purposes. It also allowed colleges to buy and sell land, not at will, since they had to get the approval of the Copyhold Commissioners (later and until after the Second World War, the Board of Agriculture); and money got from selling land had to be held by the commissioners until it was reinvested in land—though in the middle of the nineteenth century it was no hardship to have money in 3 per cent government stocks, unless it happened to be at a time when the college was borrowing elsewhere at 4 per cent and was left to cast longing eyes at its own capital in the commissioners' purdah.[34]

New College took full advantage of this freedom from the beginning. In the 1870s, the college's borrowings amounted to £30,000 in fine loans and £25,000 in loans for buildings, rather more than twice its gross annual income, and demanding at its height, something like £3,000 a year in repayments. Even when rental income had increased a good deal, these repayments were still a substantial charge upon it, but the fine loans at least were repaid by the time the First World War brought spectacular financial trouble upon the whole university, as inflation, the absence of undergraduates and the stickiness of rents compared to prices all made things difficult.

The college's income placed it among the richest colleges in Oxford, far outstripped by Christ Church and Magdalen, but well up in the second rank. But to a twentieth-century eye, it is the peculiar composition of that income which is interesting—and some peculiar charges on it too. For one thing, a high proportion of the gross income came from tithe rentcharges, a form of income which tended to be paid late, paid grudgingly and paid with a good many deductions. These tithes were the legacy of the expropriation of alien priories during the Hundred Years War—they had gone first to the Crown, thence by purchase to William of Wykeham and by gift to New College. The Act of 1836 which had transformed tithes into tithe rentcharges had done a little to reduce the unpopularity of tithes—and a lot to reduce personal hostility between farmers and clergymen—but tithes were usually loaded with a high proportion of the parish rate; the situation of New College was different in only one respect, but that an important one. The college was bound to appoint and pay the salaries of the incumbents at Romford, Hornchurch and Writtle, where the incumbents were notionally chaplains and employees of the college rather than rectors in the usual way. Even in the twentieth century, there have been arguments about the proper role of the college in these odd parishes, and occasional battles between the college and the Bishops of London and Chelmsford over their respective rights there.

More contentious was the expenditure on the choir. Attention was evidently drawn to this in reforming quarters; the cost seems to have been exaggerated on such occasions, for P. E. Matheson's *Life of Hastings Rashdall* talks of Rashdall's undergraduate generation fearing that the 'three thousand' a year spent on the choir might be drastically reduced when the commission of 1877 brought in its recomendations.[35] In fact the figure hovered around two thousand pounds a year, and it seems that this figure covered the whole cost of running the chapel, educating the choirboys, paying lay clerks and so on. Still, it was four-fifths of the figure said by Christ Church to cover the same costs there—and that was a college with twice the income, maintaining a cathedral rather than a college chapel.

The disparity in stipend between the warden and his fellows is another feature of the expenditure which would catch a twentieth-century eye; his salary was under the old statutes made up of all sorts of odds and ends, including the sinecure rectorship of Colerne and the rents of four houses in Gerrard Street, London, where Edmund Burke used to live and where the Post Office now rubs shoulders with a Chinese restaurant and an Indian clothes shop. This was about to be compounded for a stipend of two thousand pounds a year. This was, of course, small beer compared with the Dean of Christ Church's five thousand, but then he was a dignitary of the Established Church; it was almost three times the stipend of the Master of Balliol, and about a third larger than the stipends of most heads.

The difference in the scale of endowments between one college and another was quite dramatic. Balliol reported an income from endowments of not much more than five thousand pounds a year, even though it had twice as many undergraduates as New College—which explains why there were only eleven fellows of Balliol at that time. Balliol had, however, borrowed forty thousand pounds for new building, and had been greatly helped by a gift of nine thousand pounds from Miss Brackenbury; New College could still support its old ecclesiastical role from its endowments, and could expand without hoping for benefactions. (This is not to say that they were not very welcome when they came; the college owed its sports field by the river to the generosity of a friend of Alfred Robinson, a fact which must still gladden all those who are happy not to play games in Mansfield Road and not to see houses all along the Cherwell).[36] In the 1870s a college could survive without an endowment, if it confined itself to teaching and accommodating students; just as people opened schools for profit, it was possible to run a college with enough in hand to pay one's debts. But the history of Keble shows that it was not entirely comfortable, and, of course, it meant a very different kind of existence from that of New College.

The general level of income and expenditure depicted in 1873·was pretty much what was maintained until the war. The history of university finance from 1875 to 1914 is complex; but the salient feature of it is that the hoped for increase in agricultural rents never materialised. In the long run overall income and expenditure did rise; this was partly due to the simple increase in size of the colleges—an obvious factor in New College—so that the 'internal' income steadily rose. Endowment income did not: it fell very sharply between 1885–95, before recovering strongly up to 1914. The causes of this disappointing state of affairs are numerous. First, and most important, was the great depression in agriculture which persisted, with a short interruption during and after the First World War, until the 1940s. In 1877, Robinson was still cheerful; he told the Royal Commission that there was no reason to suppose that the fall in rents was more than a pause in the upward trend. In the event, of course, it was next best thing to permanent. The college suffered a fall in the gross rental from land right up to 1914. The net effect was nothing like as grim as this might lead one to expect. Other forms of income, particularly from building leases, more than made up for the shortfall. The colleges of both universities seem to have been unusually lucky among English landowners in owning much of their land in places where there was a demand for building.[37] New College did not do unusually well in this respect, but there was enough well-placed land to allow the college to preserve its gross income from rents intact; and as the burden of loan repayment eased towards the later 1900s, net income rose appreciably. A second problem of some importance was the condition of the college estates generally. The most optimistic assumptions about the change to rack-renting took it for granted that the estates would be in good order when they were expected to command high rents. But it took a good deal of money to bring them up to scratch, and most colleges were alarmed by the bills they faced when they got their estates in hand. To this was added the embarrassing factor of the cottages in which farm labourers were accustomed to live. It is doubtful whether colleges were generally worse landlords in this respect than their non-corporate contemporaries. They did, however, present easier and more easily embarrassed targets for criticism. Improvements and new cottages were thus a constant drain on the new rents; we may look nostalgically at cottages costing a couple of hundred pounds—but half a dozen of those a year swallowed the stipends of four or five fellows. It was factors like these which induced Robinson to press for two further Estates Acts, which allowed loans to be spread over longer periods than the Act of 1858 had permitted, and, at the same time allowed colleges to borrow the money held for them by the Copyhold Commissioners, a freedom which saved anything up to 1½ per cent in interest rates.

But some of the impression of declining income which was certainly felt by Hereford George, and was attested by the setting up of college comittees to think of ways of increasing income and cutting expenses, represents a growth in ambitions rather than a decline in resources. The college's income did not shrink, at any rate in the longer term, but it became inadequate to the demands upon it. In domestic matters, the college was undoubtedly helped by the fall in prices and wages of the times. But a major change for the worse was the urgency of the needs of the university. Alfred Robinson had assured successive commissions that all the university's needs could be taken care of from the revenues of the colleges. So far as New College went, the revenues did not rise rapidly, but the university's demands rose from a couple of hundred pounds a year in 1871 to £5,000 in 1913. This change swamped all the small gains from falling prices, and it occurred in a period when the expense of education was starting its familiar climb. The education of a man reading Greats cannot cost very much more than the salaries of his tutors and the wear and tear on books and furniture; the arrival of the natural sciences changed all that for ever. New College shared laboratory facilities with other colleges, and spared itself the worst expense, but still found itself in a new and altogether more costly age. So it was with some anxiety that the college arrived in the twentieth century, not an anxiety so urgent that anything very dramatic was done or should have been done before 1914, but nevertheless one which made the pre-war years something less than the calm and sunlit years of folklore.

The college's entire life, of course, changed in ways which reflected not only the outside world's changing fashions and tastes, but its own new openness to that world. One way of visualising this is to remember that in 1854 the centenarian President of Magdalen, Dr. Routh, was still telling undergraduates his favourite tale of going to see two undergraduates hanged for highway robbery on the 'Gownsmen's Gallows' in Holywell. In 1854 he was already a relic of barbarous antiquity; in 1884 he was almost unimaginable. New College joined in the life of the new world in every way. We have seen Sir Charles Oman complaining that Alfred Robinson filled the college with Etonians; in rowing at least, the impact was extraordinary. From 1885 to 1906, New College was never out of the first three places in Eights. As if to prove that brains and brawn could coexist in one frame, the college could boast of G. C. Bourne, who rowed in winning Oxford VIIIs in 1881 and 1882 and got a first in 1885; he became fellow and tutor in Physiology before becoming the Linacre Professor of Physiology and an F.R.S., and applied his scientific talents to his sporting enthusiasms with such effect that his design for a college boat enabled two fairly poor crews to row Head of the River. His son had the extraordinary distinction of stroking four successive winning Boat Race crews. Winchester had always produced a fair crop of cricketers, and many of these found their way into university teams: a New College man, Hine-Haycock, played in the only Oxford team ever to defeat a touring Australian side. For their benefit, new playing-fields were created—it was also felt that the young men's morals would be improved if they played closer to home, since the expedition to Cowley Marsh where they had previously played gave them too good an opportunity to drive coaches to the peril of the citizenry and to over-indulge in supper parties after their matches. New College never turned into an athlete's paradise, however; Hastings Rashdall was an avid mountain walker, but he waged something of a holy war against the cult of sport in English public schools, and his reaction seems to have been common among his colleagues.

There were, however, occasional outbreaks of rowdiness. Minutes of college meetings make fairly frequent reference to young men who denied doing mischief they had done or who failed to deny doing mischief they hadn't. Members of other colleges are from time to time barred from the premises, or a father summoned to remove a son who had thrown bottles out of the new buildings into windows across the street. But only for a couple of years around 1909–11 does the college seem to have been much affected by the upper-class loutishness which characterised the 'rags' of the day. Naturally, different tutors took it all differently; Warden Spooner, himself, seems to have behaved with an admirable mixture of calmness and determination. All this, oddly enough, appears to have gone along with a much stricter division between undergraduates and their elders than had existed in the days before the first reforms. Hereford George reminds us that when he was a new fellow in 1856 he was almost at once a member of the governing body of the college, entitled to decide its fate in the company of his seniors. It would have been quite out of place for him to call them 'Sir' as if he had been a schoolboy and they schoolmasters. There could be no question of taking off one's cap to salute graduate fellows, and a gown would have been required only for a formal lecture, never for everyday dealings with his tutor.[38] The change from the easy-going manners of the 1850s has many causes no doubt, but it almost seems that by 1910 there had come a recognition that 'boys will be boys' and a corresponding insistence that boys should never be confused with their seniors. But it is wise to be cautious about guessing what the social atmosphere of the college must have been; the degree of intimacy prevalent obviously depends a great deal on the relative ages of everyone involved. The elderly George may well have felt fairly remote from the young men of 1906; but the young men of the years immediately before the war may well have felt absolutely at ease with the youngest of the fellows, such as Heath and Cheesman.

Still, the greatest change that took place was the change in the intellectual standing of the college, if we can properly enlarge the term to embrace the expression of practical intelligence in law, government and industry. The college nurtured philosophers of some distinction, whether they were undergraduates who went on to other places, or outsiders who were brought into the college. Of these last, W. L. Courtney is one of the most attractive; *everyone* recalls him as a man with the dash and swagger of the cavalry officer rather than the 'remote and ineffectual don' he should have become. He was evidently a rather more worldly figure than some of his Wykehamist colleagues liked, and perhaps had been marked out as literary editor of the *Daily Telegraph* and eventually as editor of the *Fortnightly Review* from the very beginning. In Oxford, he was a great figure in theatrical activities and was the founder of the city's theatre; he also blotted his copy-book by bringing the novelist Rhoda Broughton down from London, for she promptly introduced Mr. and Mrs. Mark Pattison into her next novel. None the less, he was an excellent philosopher who held the unfashionable view that it was possible to defend Hegel in decent, clear English and demolish J. S. Mill in terms which any second-class man could understand. It was by no means a foregone conclusion that Cook Wilson should have defeated him in the contest for the newly established Wykeham Professorship of Logic. A. E. Taylor and H. A. Prichard were gifted undergraduates whose careers took them elsewhere. Hastings Rashdall was a less strikingly talented undergraduate, but his work on moral philosophy is still worth reading, and he was obviously a benign as well as an effective tutor. H. W. B. Joseph was not exactly a benign figure; he was evidently too tough and too fierce to be invariably successful with his pupils, but those who could stand the force of his inquisition obviously profited from it. There was a rash of ancient historians and archaeologists; nobody knows quite what made Spooner suggest to the young Leonard Woolley that he might take up archaeology, but it was evidently some sort of divine inspiration. J. L. Myres was a fellow and later Wykeham Professor of Ancient History; Alfred Zimmern taught the same subject, although he eventually became Professor of International Relations. Gilbert Murray was briefly a fellow in the 1880s, and less briefly twenty years later. In Modern History, H. A. L. Fisher and David Ogg became very distinguished tutors and authors, while Charles Oman spent much of a very long life resenting what he believed to have been the college's deliberate erection of obstacles in the way of his becoming a fellow. Out of the undergraduate 'mainstream' subjects, figures like D. S. Margoliouth come down with an awe-inspiring reputation for linguistic facility. In the natural sciences the Haldanes, father and son, appeared on the scene to considerable effect—by the outbreak of the war, J.S. was a research fellow and Reader in Physiology, while J.B.S. was still only a scholar, but had given an indication of the other side of his career by helping to organise a strike of tram drivers and conductors.

Some of the young men made a name in the great world; Lord Milner had been a dazzling undergraduate at Balliol, but transferred his loyalties when he became a fellow of New College in 1876, and came back to his new home to recruit for his 'kindergarten' in South Africa. Lionel Curtis, Philip Kerr and W. L. Hichens all made their careers with him at this time. Milner had worked briefly as a journalist while a young fellow, but the college's major contribution to that field was E. T. Cook, whose reputation as an editor was second only to that of the legendary W. T. Stead—with whom indeed he began his career.

This chapter has been in essentials an account of the changes which an *institution* underwent during a period of some sixty years. It would be agreeable, though it is unfortunately beyond the competence of the present author to provide it, to supplement this with a biographical account of the careers of large numbers of the college's members during that period. Perhaps, therefore, we may conclude with only one observation to suggest how the success of the institution is reflected in the biographies of its members. The *Twentieth Century Supplement to the Dictionary of National Biography* has only three entries under 'Z'—two of them are for Zimmern (scholar 1898, fellow 1904) and de Zulueta (scholar 1897, fellow 1907).

REFERENCES

1. H. A. L. Fisher, *An Unfinished Autobiography* (Oxford, 1940), 43.
2. Mallet, III, 469–70, 485; see also note on numbers below.
3. A. O. Prickard, *New College* (1906), 86.
4. Universities Commission, 1873, *Report*, 55, 76, 219, 380–2.
5. L. Ragg, *Memoir of E. C. Wickham* (1911), 59–60.
6. George, 6–8.
7. Ibid., 76–80.
8. J. S. Mill, 'Corporation and Church Property', *Collected Works*, IV (1967), 202, 214.
9. W. R. Ward, *Victorian Oxford* (1965), chs. I–VI, VII, 152–5.
10. J. Veitch, *Sir William Hamilton, the Man and his Philosophy* (Edinburgh, 1883), 10–11.
11. H. L. Mansel, ' "Phrontisterion" or Oxford in the Nineteenth Century', *Letters, Lectures and Reviews* (1873), 392ff.
12. George, 16.
13. Sumner Correspondence, N.C. MS. 3043.
14. Oxford University Commission, *Report* (1852), 210–11.
15. Arthur Engel, 'The Emerging Concept of the Academic Profession', L. Stone (ed.), *The University in Society* (Princeton, 1972), II, 335ff.
16. George, 16.
17. Sumner Correspondence, ibid.
18. A. K. Cook, *About Winchester College* (1924), 398.
19. *Statutes and Ordinances*, 1857, *4.
20. Mallet, III, 328–9.
21. *Statutes and Ordinances*, 1857, 21–2.
22. George, 31–2.
23. V. H. H. Green, *A History of Oxford University* (1974), 145.
24. George, 21–2.
25. Warden Sewell's Register, 294–6.
26. Fisher, op. cit., 44.
27. C.W.C. Oman, *Memoirs of Victorian Oxford* (1942), 91.
28. W. G. Hayter, *W. A. Spooner* (1976), 135.
29. George, 71; Ragg, op. cit., 71.
30. Mallet, III, 333ff.
31. Universities Commission, 1873, *Report*, 441.
32. Ibid., xiii; George, 33–4, 46–7.
33. Universities Commission, 1873, *Report*, xvii.
34. C. L. Shadwell, *The Universities and Colleges Estates Acts* (Oxford, 1898).

35. P. E. Matheson, *Hastings Rashdall* (1928), 32.
36. George, 101.
37. John Dunbabin, 'Oxford and Cambridge College Finances, 1871–1913', *Econ. Hist. Rev.*, 1975, vol. 28, 637–9.
38. George, 99.

A note on undergraduate numbers

The *Calendar* lists undergraduate numbers only from 1873. A good many of them would have been on the books but not in residence. Christ Church was, and remained, the largest college, but it was run increasingly close by New College and Balliol.

1873: New College, 95; Balliol, 174; Christ Church, 244
1884: New College, 225; Balliol, 240; Christ Church, 246
1894: New College, 253; Balliol, 236; Christ Church, 295
1913: New College, 301; Balliol, 262; Christ Church, 322

New College numbers grew fairly steadily between 1873 and 1884, but the figures indicate the way in which the college in effect stabilised after 1884.

APPENDIX

The College Finances

(i)

The commissioners' summary produces the following figures for 1871:

Income from land	£15,003 17s. 11d.
House property	£502 4s. 3d.
Tithe rentcharges	£8,322 3s. 4d.
Other rentcharges	£93 4s. 11d.
Stocks, etc	£1,530 12s. 5d.
Others and sundries	£730 13s. 0d.
	£26,182 15s. 10d.
Loans in lieu of fines	£2,369 0s. 0d.
Warden's additional income	£512 0s. 0d.
	£29,063 15s. 10d.

To this the commissioners added an 'Internal Income' which must surely have been an internal balance of £1,378 1s. 7d. £2,220 5s. 0d. went into the Tuition Account: about £1,500 from undergraduates and the rest as a charge on the college. So the college had about £32,000 to meet all its current expenses, including stipends, scholarships, payments to vicars, the choir and the maintenance and improvement of its property. The commissioners' balance sheet is lengthy, but the major items on it were the following:

Warden	£2,112 0s. 0d.
Fellows (39)	£9,382 4s. 4d.
Scholars (30)	£3,000 0s. 0d.
University/Professors	£295 0s. 0d.
Chapel and chapel service	£2,004 12s. 6d.
Vicars/Augmentation	£3,115 12s. 6d.
Interest on loans	£1,730 10s. 2d.
Management of estates	£1,048 6s. 0d.
Improvements	£1,625 5s. 4d.

The bursar's notes on the accounts pointed out that in the ten years past the college had spent £19,980 2s. 6d. on improvements to its rackrent property, which was about 20 per cent of the gross income received from it; twenty-one new cottages had been built at an average of £300 per pair. He estimated that the cost would certainly not be less in the future, and that the burden of repayment of loans, as well as the rehabilitation of copyhold property as it fell in would be very heavy. None the less, all these charges were being met out of current income.

(ii)

College property in 1871 (taken from the Cleveland Commission's figures for 1/1/1872): Total acreage, 17,057. The major holdings clustered round Buckingham and in north Oxfordshire, with others in Essex and Wiltshire. At Radclive the college owned some 675 acres (230 on copyhold tenures); at Hardwicke some 900, including 500 on beneficial leases; at Tingewick some 500, and smaller parcels at Great Horwood and Newton Longville. In north Oxfordshire, the college had between 300 and 600 acres at Adderbury, Heyford, Milcomb, Shipton, Stanton St. John, Swalcliffe and Woodperry. The Essex holdings included 800 acres at Takeley, and a good deal of Romford and Hornchurch. In Wiltshire, the main estates were at Alton Barnes and Stert. When the commission compiled its figures 7,287 acres were let at rackrent, 6,182 were let on beneficial leases, and 2,657 were out on copyhold tenures.

College benefices in 1871 were worth something over £20,330 annually to their incumbents; the college had the advowsons of forty-one benefices, of which the most valuable were Worthen in Shropshire, Donhead in Wiltshire and Saham Tony in Norfolk, all of which were worth over £1,000 per annum. The majority were worth a little less than half that figure, and the rear was brought up by the warden's rectorship of Colerne, valued at £73 19s. 5d.

(iii)

A typical entry for a beneficial lease looks like the following: Hardwicke, Bucks; 219 acres 37 poles, manor farm and buildings; lessee Baron L. de

Rothschild; last valuation 1868, annual value £550 gross; let on a twenty-year lease from 1854, rent £33 14s. 7½d.; wheat 166 gals 4 pts, malt 180 gals; fine on last renewal £1,111 0s. 0d. estimated value at rackrent £530 0s. 0d.

Tithe rentcharges came for the most part from two areas in Essex: in 1870, Writtle and Roxwell was supposed to yield £3,401, which, after property tax, poor rates, stipends of vicars and expenses of collection came down to £1,800 for the college's own use; Hornchurch and Romford yielded £4,441 gross, which, after the same deductions came to £2,493 for the college's own use. The gross figure for tithe rentcharges was among the highest for the Oxford colleges, but was dwarfed by Christ Church's £37,000 gross.

A typical copyhold entry looks like the following: Oxford, Stanton St. John, Manor of Stanton St. John; copyholders Martha Butler and Amy Butler; acreage of copyhold 51 acres 1 rod 8 poles; names and ages of lives in the copyhold M. Butler 71, A. Butler 65, H. Broughton 25.

The following rather fragmentary extracts from the published accounts of the colleges and university after 1883 may give some insight into the way sources of income and directions of expenditure changed. New College, uniquely, published a figure for 'net endowment income'. This varied as follows: 1884: £21,773; 1895: £16,431; 1905: £19,298; 1914: £22,261. Rackrent income in the same years went from £20,147 gross in 1884, to £16,431 in 1895, £16,206 in 1905 and £17,630 in 1914, while income from long building-leases rose from £664 in 1884 to £2,599 in 1895, £4,745 in 1905 and £4,845 in 1914. The total 'turnover' as nearly as one can judge, remained just about constant as between 1884 and 1913, gross income and expenditure recovered after 1895 from £41,00 to something over £45,000 per annum. This masked a quite impressive shift between income from external sources and income from internal sources: in 1884 the gross external income amounted to £33,450, and the internal income (from tutorial charges, board and lodging and so on) to £9,821; by 1905 this had moved to a gross external figure of £29,547 and an internal figure of £12,968. But, of course, this remained quite unlike Balliol's income, where internal income was twice as great as external income; and in 1905, Hertford still had no income from endowments at all, and an entirely internally-generated income of only £8,313. The pattern of expenditure matched the pattern of income. In 1884, the stipends of fellows cost New College £5,762, and Balliol only £2,520; but the costs of tutors were £4,342 in New College and £4,865 in Balliol. As noted in the text, the demands of the university grew during these years; in 1895 the figure had already grown to £1,724 per annum—including £1,200 for professorial stipends and £224 to the C.U.F. In 1905, this was £2,405, but by 1914 it had more than doubled again to £5,195. The contentious expenditure on the choir varied around £2,100 per annum throughout the period; but, and oddly enough, the total cost of the head of the college dropped by a third during the thirty years, in spite of the fact that the bachelor Sewell had been replaced by the family man Spooner. The general picture is not unexpected; tuition costs and tuition fees get bigger as the college gets bigger; agricultural rents remain level or drop somewhat, and are compensated for by building-leases; fine loans gradually vanish from the accounts, while loans for improvements and new buildings stay in. A glimpse of approaching trouble is afforded by the accounts for 1914, where the internal income drops to a misleadingly low figure—the accounts were drawn for the calendar year to 31 December, and by then many of the young men who would otherwise have been in residence were already dead.

IV

New College between
the two World Wars

[i]
Introduction

SIR WILLIAM HAYTER

William Hayter was a Winchester scholar of New College from 1925 to 1929. After twenty-eight years in the diplomatic service he returned to New College as warden in 1958, and was elected to an honorary fellowship on his retirement as warden in 1976.

When the First World War ended, New College resumed its life, under its by then venerable warden, almost as if nothing had happened, and entered what was perhaps its most distinguished period since its foundation. The two wardens of the period were the two most famous, perhaps the only famous, heads of the college. Spooner had since the turn of the century been one of the best known and best loved of Oxford figures. Fisher, who succeeded him in 1925, was a man of immense distinction, appearing among other heads of houses, as Lionel Robbins says, like a Triton among minnows, still the only ex-cabinet minister to have become head of an Oxford college. Whether because of the attraction of these great men or for some other reason, the undergraduates of the period were also a remarkable lot; my own contemporaries, for instance, included six future cabinet ministers. The Schools results were impressive, the choir was the best in Oxford, the first VIII was never lower than fourth on the river, and most university sports at one time or another had a New College captain: there was no doubt at all that we were a leading college.

There was indeed a tendency to arrogance among the undergraduates at that time, and this perhaps led them to wonder if the fellows of the college were quite worthy of them. True, when the First

World War ended two fellows of the college, Milner and Fisher, were members of the Cabinet. True, there was one undoubted genius, G. H. Hardy, among the fellows, and there were other eminent fellows, such as J. S. Haldane, D. S. Margoliouth and Hugh Allen. But these great men had nothing to do with teaching the undergraduates of the college, and we sometimes wondered whether our teachers, of whom we saw very little outside the tutorial relationship, were quite as distinguished as we thought we deserved. We knew that four of the best younger fellows had been killed in the war, and many of the survivors tended to strike us as rather tired old men. There were exceptions, of course. Joseph was still in destructive vigour. Alic Smith was clearly a remarkable man (though not perhaps a remarkable tutor). Two eminent scientists, appointed as the war ended, Julian Huxley and J. B. S. Haldane, left us early for other universities, as did Lionel Robbins. But in Fisher's time distinguished appointments to fellowships came to be made. Christopher Cox, Dick Crossman, Isaiah Berlin and David Cecil would have been adornments to any common room, and all were outstanding teachers, though as might have been expected none of them made a life-long career in college tutoring. One fellow, appointed in Fisher's time, who did was Eric Yorke, who became one of Oxford's most successful tutors in Classics. This subject was still a leading one, in numbers as well as in prestige. Of those taking Schools in 1924, thirteen were in Literae Humaniores. There were also six in Chemistry, one in Mathematics, five in Animal Physiology (i.e. Medicine), one in Engineering Science, fifteen in Law, fourteen in Modern History, two in English, two in Modern Languages (French) and three in P.P.E. Clearly there were a few new subjects growing up, but they did not look as if they were going to need fellowship appointments; help from part-time lecturers would do. Chemistry and Biology had had fellows since before the war, but when the first fellow in Physics was appointed in 1925 the *New College Record* noted that this was 'primarily to help the University'. The School of Philosophy, Politics and Economics, then known as 'Modern Greats', was clearly going to grow, and a fellow in Economics was appointed in 1922; Politics was not thought to require a fellowship appointment, but the Philosophy side was thought to need strengthening to cope with the demands of the new School. No fellow in English was appointed till 1939, and none in Modern Languages until after the Second World War.

The atmosphere in the college after the end of the First World War is admirably described in Maurice Bowra's memoirs. Undergraduates then, he writes, 'managed to combine seriousness with frivolity' (but when have they ever not done this?). 'We allowed our thoughts to be swayed more by hopes than by realities.' Warden Spooner 'seemed to possess the gift of eternal youth'. It seemed a kind of paradise to the returning warriors. In the Michaelmas Term 1918 there had been thirty undergraduates in residence. By the same time next year there were 257, and 299 in 1920; numbers eventually settled down to around 250; a project for reducing the numbers still further was mooted but never realised.

It has often been observed that of the two inter-war decades the twenties were a period when a forlorn attempt was made to revert to a pre-1914 life-style, while the thirties looked forward apprehensively to 1939. Oxford in the twenties was apolitical, the time of the Oxford aesthetes. Oxford in the thirties was nervously political. In 1926, when the General Strike took place, a kind of herd instinct took practically every New College undergraduate off on one kind of strike-breaking or another. But this was not a political gesture, more a kind of lark, and Hugh Gaitskell's activities on the other side were regarded as a minority eccentricity and not at all resented. If this had happened in the thirties he would probably have found himself in the majority, and there would have been resentment on both sides. In neither decade did New College fall into any of the fashionable extremes. None of the leading Oxford aesthetes of the twenties was at New College, nor were any of the political agitators or poets of the thirties. The typical New College product of the period went into public or academic life in a steady responsible kind of a way. The results began to show, of course, after the Second World War. I have already mentioned the six future cabinet ministers of the twenties (Gaitskell, Eccles, Crossman, Longford, Molson, Jay). Kenneth Younger might have joined them, but he left politics to become Head of Chatham House. By the 1950s five New College men of this or a slightly earlier period had become Law Lords (Lords Simonds, Cohen, Oaksey, Tucker and Radcliffe) and there was another, Richard Wilberforce, soon after. The first Ombudsman, Edmund Compton, was a New College man. David Harlech was Ambassador in Washington, and Patrick Reilly in Paris. Derick Hoyer-Millar was Permanent Under-Secretary at the Foreign Office. Shan

Hackett was Commander-in-Chief of the British Army of the Rhine. George Godber brought the Health Service to birth. George Woodcock became Secretary-General of the T.U.C., Gerald Ellison became Bishop of London, and Cuthbert Bardsley of Coventry. Max Mallowan, following the example of another New College man, Leonard Woolley, became the leading archaeologist of his day. Nowell Myres became Bodley's librarian, and numerous professorial chairs were occupied by New College academics. Six former New College undergraduates of the period became heads of Oxford colleges, one of them becoming vice-chancellor. Distinguished Americans, too, now began to appear among the college's old members. Jock Whitney was to return many years later as U.S. Ambassador to the Court of St. James, and F.O. Matthiessen became a leading American intellectual.

In addition to these products of the inter-war years who achieved distinction later, there were of course many New College men of an earlier intake who held eminent positions between the wars. There were, for instance, two Lord Chancellors (Jowitt and Simonds), and cabinet ministers like Samuel Hoare, Duff Cooper and Ormsby-Gore. The peak of Galsworthy's reputation was reached in this period. H. A. L. Fisher's great *History of Europe* was written while he was warden. Perhaps Angus Wilson was thinking of this phase in the college's history when he makes one of his characters in *The Old Men at the Zoo* say 'Winchester, New College and the Treasury are the three places where they know everything'.

The college's physical appearance did not alter much between the wars. When the tents that had sheltered a hospital in the garden from 1914–18 had been cleared away, the college reverted to its pre-war shape. The only substantial additions to its buildings were the construction of undergraduate accommodation attached to Savile House, and the new library, built as a memorial to New College men killed in the First World War and completed just as the Second World War was breaking out and the cellars were being made safe as an air-raid precaution. The conversion of a room in the muniment tower to house the college's treasure was finished in 1931.

An innovation of the inter-war years was the foundation of the New College Society, which held its first dinner in 1933. The members who attended must have felt, even in that unhappy period, that they had something to celebrate, and a college to be proud of: looked at from our own perspective it seems something of a golden age. The following five contributions describe the impression made on five very different writers by this prosperous college between the wars.

[ii]

The Mid-Twenties:
An Economist's View

LORD ROBBINS

Lionel Charles Robbins, now Lord Robbins of Clare Market, was a lecturer at New College in 1924 when the first fellow in Economics, Harold Keith Salvesen, was absent at Harvard, and was himself fellow in Economics from 1927 to 1929, when a chair in economics at the L.S.E. fell vacant unexpectedly. In his Autobiography of an Economist, *Lord Robbins devotes some nine pages to his time at Oxford and the following extract is reproduced with the kind permission of the author and his publishers, Macmillan & Co.*

My years at New College stand out in memory as among the halcyon periods of my life. The college was at the height of one of those phases in the life of academic institutions when everything seems right. It had a warden of eminence in H. A. L. Fisher. The list of its fellows included such famous names as Hugh Allen the musician, J. S. Haldane the physicist, G. H. Hardy the mathematician, Julian Huxley the biologist, H. W. B. Joseph the philosopher, R. H. Lightfoot the theologian, J. L. Myres the ancient historian and David Ogg the historian; and the quality of those who were not so well known was correspondingly high. Under Fisher and the highly efficient bursar, G. R. Y. Radcliffe—the only Oxford bursar whom Keynes was willing to praise—the administration was unobtrusive and effective; and the college meetings knew no more disharmony than that which was aroused by the presence of a stunted tree in the garden which some of us wished to remove as an eyesore and others wished to keep as reminiscent of Warden Spooner who had planted it. As for the less formal side of college life, I can hardly conceive any society less pretentious and more intellectually stimulating than that which would assemble on working—as distinct from ceremonial—nights, after hall in the senior common room. This was civilisation at its most lively and agreeable. I have known similar atmospheres at L.S.E. from time to time and in some private circles, but never anything superior or so continuous. We were not self-consciously on the crest of a wave. But unconsciously we knew it and this gave to much that we said and did that kind of exhilaration.

Of this friendly and distinguished community, certain figures are outstanding in recollection.

First, although not so intimately known as the others, comes the warden. Fisher was a truly distinguished man, both as a scholar and as an administrator. Among the heads of houses in the Oxford of that day he was a Triton among minnows; the present generation of very distinguished heads had no counterpart in those days. Beyond his academic experience, he had had a tour of duty, not without leaving some marks on history, as Minister of Education in the war-time coalition; and he brought to university politics, therefore, something of the spaciousness of a larger world. It must be confessed, however, that this was not without some corresponding disadvantages. A man of the utmost purity of motive himself, he had fallen under the spell of Lloyd George for whom he had conceived an entirely unsophisticated admiration. 'When I hear Fisher on George's administration', said the cynical Walter Roche, one of A.G.G.'s cronies, 'I think of a good man who has inadvertently found himself in a brothel—*and rather enjoyed it!*' In the senior common room we used to be at some pains to head him off reminiscences of this period of his life. His true excellence lay elsewhere. Although it would have been easy to have discharged them less thoroughly, he took his duties as warden most conscientiously. He and his talented wife were not wealthy, nor were his emoluments as warden on the lavish scale, yet in the course of every academic year he would entertain every member of the college, fellows and students alike, at parties at which, if recollections of Lloyd George did not obtrude, a mellow and far-ranging culture sensitively deployed made the occasion memorable. 'How well educated our dear warden is', remarked the fastidious young Hugh Gaitskell as we walked away together from one of these gatherings. But beyond all this, and even more impressive as an example, he maintained his status and his studies as a scholar. It was during this period of his wardenship that he wrote the work which brought him the widest fame. Among my most vivid recollections of New College is the spectacle, visible most evenings on leaving the senior common room, of Fisher's profile silhouetted against the window of his study in the warden's lodgings, absorbed in the creation of his classic *History of Europe*.

Next in importance to Fisher in the general councils of the college was H. W. B. Joseph, senior tutor and philosopher. In Sir Roy Harrod's book on Lord Cherwell and in reminiscences which I have heard recounted by others, Joseph appears as a formidable and even somewhat distasteful figure. Such is not my recollection. Formidable he certainly was: however wrong-headed his ratiocination, you had to argue with his intense sincerity and intellectual force with, as the Germans say, the hat in the hand. But distasteful surely not. Short but massive, almost square in build, with immensely muscular hands and penetrating glance, to me at least he embodied many of the virtues of the dedicated teacher and scholar. It is true that he was vigorous and uncompromising in debate and probably unaware of the devastating impact of his condemnation of what he thought to be muddled or slovenly. But *au fond* he was essentially humble: if he condemned, it was not from any assumption of personal superiority but rather in the interests of what he conceived to be truth. It is true too that he was exacting in his demands both of students and of colleagues. But he was even more exacting of himself. When the college at last imposed an upper limit of eighteen hours on tutorial obligation, he habitually exceeded it; and his teaching quarters were of quite monkish austerity, self-inflicted in the interests of the college finances. His published work, moreover, was by no means to be despised. His *Introduction to Logic*, although, like most of the Oxford philosophy of his time, out of touch with the path-breaking developments which were taking place elsewhere, was an elegant work, obviously the production of a powerful mind: it has been said to be one of the best statements of the Aristotelian tradition in this respect. Admittedly there was something slightly preposterous about some of his preoccupations. Without any special mathematical competence, he spent months picking over Hardy's *Pure Mathematics* with a view to discovering conceptual flaws and eventually discovered an unimportant blemish which it gave Hardy infinite pleasure to acknowledge in the next edition, with a fake quotation from the Latin paying tribute to him who ends by beautifying that which he sought to destroy. And his critique, *The Labour Theory of Value in Karl Marx*, in itself something of an intellectual *tour de force* for a non-economist, was written, as with characteristic candour he confesses in his preface, in complete ignorance of Böhm-Bawerk's famous polemic, whose arguments it substantially duplicates. Nevertheless, to know Joseph was to respect him, both for intellect and for character, and to know him at all well was to become aware of a sensitive, kindly spirit concealed behind the somewhat severe exterior.

Among the central body of tutors, A. H. Smith, also a philosopher, was outstanding. I would not say he was outstanding as a philosopher. Indeed I suspect that in that capacity he was not very distinguished. He certainly never gave me the impression that philosophical speculation was his intellectual centre of gravity. It is true that he wrote a book on Kant for the completion of which he forced himself to take sabbatical leave with residence at some exile at Stow-on-the-Wold. But it was virtually unreadable: no work in human history, said Hardy, had made so little appeal to the art of the harlot. He was outstanding, however, as a practical idealist, decisive, open-minded, forward-looking, and immensely influential in the councils of the college. Unlike most of his contemporaries, he had not become a teacher immediately after graduation. He had first served for a period as a civil servant in the Scottish Office and had only come back to academic life at the end of the war when the college decided that it needed someone of his personal authority to cope with the generation of ex-army undergraduates. Thus, with Fisher, he brought with him a breath of the outside world; and although in so many ways their temperaments were very dissimilar, it was the presence of their ampler backgrounds which was largely responsible for the difference of administrative atmosphere at that time between New College and other colleges. He was a force in university affairs, although decidedly in the minority. Together with E. L. Woodward (later Sir Llewellyn) he spent himself in the service of sanity and proper provision for the future in the great Bodleian controversy— alas in vain—and much of the little that was progressive and sensible in university policy of the inter-wars years owed something to his efforts. This was the period of his greatest influence. In later years his sense of duty as a son, which led him to take up residence until their death with his aged parents at Headington, brought it about that he was less inti- mate with the junior fellows; and although he ultimately became warden, it cannot be said that his period of office was a period of har- mony. But in my day, if anything had happened to Fisher, Smith would have had the unanimous support of all fellows under the age of fifty.

It would be wrong, however, to conceive of Smith's qualities as only those of an administrator; he was more many-sided than that. Although he may not have excelled as a pure academic, his was a sensitive and subtle intelligence. He had a strong feeling for personalities; and his long Henry Jamesian sentences, however deficient as a medium of abstract argument, were extraordinarily effective in the analysis of character and situations, all the more so when his sense of the absurd lent a flavour of burlesque to the exposition. To settle down in his austere but exquisitely furnished rooms for leisurely survey of the complications of the latest crusade in which he had become involved was a special delectation for his intimates, something unique but without the least suspicion of the precious. He was devoted to the visual arts, and his knowledge of, and feeling for, the history and structure of the college buildings had something of the passion which most men reserve for human relationships. Above all, he was a large-hearted, warm human being, combining strong masculine sympathy with an almost feminine quickness of intuition of moods and attitudes. Never shall I forget being met by Smith on my first arrival at Oxford as a temporary lecturer. It was a damp, windy autumn evening, the quad was gloomy and empty and my spirits were at their most diffident and apprehensive. But in a dozen paces, as he gripped my bag and welcomed me, he made me feel a full member of the college. A fine man, of a stature perhaps disproportionate to the *milieu* in which he moved, giving life and vividness to all he touched.

And then there was G. H. Hardy. Of Hardy as a mathematician, one of the most eminent of the first half of this century, it were otiose to write; in his *Mathematician's Apology*, a notable addition to the short list of classic autobiographies in the language, he has given his own account of the nature of the emotions with which he pursued his supreme aim. But there remains something to say of Hardy as a colleague and as an influence. He was a professorial fellow, so that his participation in the daily business of college teaching was negligible. But this could not be said of his presence as a member of our community. Whether caught up in the trances of mathematical contemplation, oblivious of everything save the distant peaks of abstract relationships, or the leader of talk in the senior common room, arranging with mock seriousness complicated games and intelligence tests, his personality gave a quality to the atmosphere quite unlike anything else in my experience. In appearance

Hardy was striking. He was slight of build and the ease of his move-
ments, born of long devotion to games demanding swift response,
served only to enhance the concentration of interest in the intellectual
beauty of the face, with its deep brow, its ascetic nostrils and lips and the
extraordinary quality of the rather broad-set eyes. No depiction known
to me of a saint receiving the stigmata shows greater intensity than did
Hardy's features when plunged in meditation. Nor is it easy to conceive
a more vivid exhibition of the meaning of the word 'illumination' than
was afforded by the same features lit up by the play of wit or intent on
kindly badinage. And nothing in the man belied the appearance. I
suspect that, fundamentally, when not elated by achievement either in
speculation or in games, Hardy found many forms of contact with life
very painful and that, from a very early stage, he had taken extensive
measures to guard himself against them. Certainly in his friendliest
moments—and he could be very friendly indeed—one was conscious of
immense reserves. The elaborate apparatus of serio-comic technicality
which on occasion lent such piquancy to his talk, was probably, at least
in part, another such manifestation. Nevertheless his influence was very
positive. I have never known anyone in whom there was so little of the
commonplace and so much of the genuinely individual in everything he
did and said. His sense of excellence was absolute: anything less was not
worth while. What Dr. Johnson said of Burke applied exactly to Hardy:
his presence called forth all one's powers. Hence any talk or action in
which he participated had a tone and flavour all its own. If, as I think,
the New College of those days had a very special distinction among
institutions I have known, I have little doubt that much of this special
quality was evoked by Hardy's catalytic presence.

My own relations with this remarkable man could hardly have been
more fortunate or more decisive in the establishment of criteria of
certain kinds of intellectual performance. Needless to say, I had nothing
to give him in the sphere of his own special competence. But we both
came from other universities and therefore shared some capacity to see
the peculiarities of Oxford and Oxford habits, good and bad, from the
outside. What was probably much more important from his point of
view was that, in those days, I shared some of his absorbed interest in
cricket, the second great passion of his life, for which, although myself a
very indifferent performer, ever since, as a very little boy, I used to play
in the back garden at Sipson Farm with my father, I too had had a quite

special feeling. On top of this I felt much as he did about the pretensions of organised religion and the absurd insincerity of much public life. Thus on the secondary plane of everyday existence, we had a good deal in common. Moreover, economics happened to figure in Hardy's list of comparatively 'good' subjects, as having—in contrast, e.g. to the chemistry of those days which he disliked—something of a rational basis. He did not think much of the contemporary mathematical economics: I remember that when I showed him Bowley's *Groundwork*, he was distinctly uncomplimentary, holding the exposition to be deficient in elegance and the results lacking in depth—a quality to which he attached great significance. But he thought well of the possibilities of the subject and took pains to procure me some instruction in the calculus which, although it has never led to positive contributions on my part in that section of the field, at least gave me enough understanding of the language not to feel utterly lost amid this sort of construction. He confirmed me, too, in my belief in the importance of theory as the basis of all fruitful science, however dependent on eventual empirical testing. He never ceased to urge the importance of following one's thought wherever the logic leads one, no matter how initially absurd may seem to be the consequences. Above all there was such unflinching candour and integrity in his approach to the life of the mind as to leave a quite indelible impression on all who had contact with him. If ever I were tempted consciously to use weak arguments or to conceal intellectual difficulties, I should only have to think of Hardy and the impulse would wither away.

In this agreeable and distinguished society, I spent three of the happiest years of my life—one in 1924–5 and two in 1927–8 and 1928–9. I had lively and talented pupils whom it was a stimulus to teach—I have only to mention David Eccles, Robin Hankey, Hugh Gaitskell in the first period, Reg Bassett, Evan Durbin, Gilbert Walker and John Witt in the second, to give some idea of the quality—and I ran a discussion society, the Adam Smith Society, inaugurated by my predecessor, of which other leading lights of P.P.E. were members: I remember in particular Henry Phelps Brown, then at Wadham, who eventually succeeded me at New College and later became an ornament of the professoriate at L.S.E., and Colin Clark, then a chemistry scholar at Brasenose, somewhat disillusioned with his subject, who would appear with large sheaves of statistical matter, worked up in his spare time, to illuminate and bring down to earth the theoretical discussions of his fellow members. My own work, though because of heavy teaching duties done perforce at weekends and in vacations, went well: in my second period I was beginning to publish successfully in the professional journals. So what with all this and the magic of the college garden enclosed in the ancient city walls, the bookshops, the walks in the town and the country outside, and Bach and Palestrina in the chapel after hall on Sunday evenings, I lived almost as in an earthly paradise and took comparatively little thought for the morrow.

[iii]

Memories of New College, 1928–1931

GORONWY REES

Goronwy Rees was educated in Aberystwyth and in Cardiff, and was a scholar of New College from 1928 to 1931, when he was elected to a fellowship at All Souls.

Oxford has become a very different place from what it was when I went up to New College in 1928; whether for better or worse I would not profess to say, but in either case so changed as to be almost unrecognisable. Only its memorials of the past remain much as they were; yet in a setting so transformed that the city can never again have the beauty it once had.

The stones of Oxford were very important to me when I first went up, because I was then a passionate medievalist; it would be true to say that I was in love with the Middle Ages, and the thought of living in daily and intimate contact with buildings that were the work of medieval hands was one of the reasons why I had chosen to sit for a scholarship at New College. The other was that my mother had once spent a long golden summer's afternoon sitting with my father in its gardens and had then and there decided that New College was the right place for me. These may seem rather curious reasons for a decision which was, after all, of some importance to my future, but I have never had any cause to regret it.

Not that my years at New College were a period of unalloyed happiness. Youth and adolescence, in which one is half a boy and half a man are notoriously a difficult and turbulent age; one of my reasons for gratitude to the college is that it provided a kind of haven, almost a convalescent home, in which to get over the green sickness of youth without doing more than unavoidable harm either to others or to myself. There was always a part of me that longed to be somewhere else, and felt that the college, and Oxford, actually made it harder to grow up, that elsewhere there was a world of harsh realities from which their enfolding arms shielded me too protectively. Yet in such moods the college always seemed to murmur, with a seductiveness that was hard to resist: 'Stay with me for a while. There will be plenty of time for all that later on.'

In my own case, I suppose, there were particular reasons why I should have thought of such an appeal as a seduction, indeed, because of the beauty of the college, as an almost physical one; and though I yielded it was not without a sense of guilt. For at that time the college, even more than the university as a whole, was the almost exclusive preserve of the English ruling class, a kind of pheasantry in which the products of the English public schools were reared like game birds. This gave it a social cohesiveness and solidarity which to an interloper like myself seemed to be alarming and, on first acquaintance, even repellent. This was particularly true of New College because of the very large proportion of Wykehamists among its undergraduate members, for whom the college represented, what Mark Pattison feared a century ago that Oxford would become, an extension and continuation of their schooldays, the completion of an intensive course designed, as the Founder himself would have wished, to enlist able and gifted recruits in the service of Church and State, of politics, the law, the civil service; of what today would be called the Establishment.

Wykehamists, because there were so many of them, gave New College a certain prim, slightly self-satisfied, almost ecclesiastical air, though even then modulated to meet the demands of a secular society; to an outsider there was something inexpressibly English and middle class about it all. I do not use these words in any pejorative sense; but to a Welsh grammar-school boy like myself, who had rarely crossed the border into England before, and had never met a public-school boy, the college seemed to present an almost impenetrably solid and alien front. Perhaps this was because in 1928 the English middle class was enjoying for the last time, as in some golden afterglow of an autumn sunset, that sense of confidence which came from having created a great empire. But even in the three years I spent at New College this was to change.

It should not be supposed, however, that it was wealth that distinguishd New College's little nest of gentlefolk, however privileged by their upbringing and education. There were indeed a few *richissimi* young men, but on the whole they were more often to be seen on the hunting or the polo field, and rarely graced the college with their presence. But there were many more whose education had cost their parents considerable financial sacrifices, and in later life I was surprised to learn that several had rather less money than myself, who received a perfectly adequate income from scholarships, from the college, from the state and from the city of Cardiff, where I was educated. A modest, if sufficient, competence was what most people enjoyed; few indulged in the more extravagant forms of conspicuous waste which flourished in some other colleges. Moderation in all things was the aim of the college and we were notably lacking in the eccentrics, aesthetes, poets, whose sometimes flamboyant behaviour was an amiable feature of Oxford life at the time.

Their absence tended to make life rather dull. But on the whole they were a dying generation, the last lingering ghosts of the twenties. After 1929, the Great Depression set in, and inaugurated a sterner and more serious era, in which the pressure of outside events began to make themselves felt even in Oxford. Pleasure had been the ruling principle of the twenties; in the thirties politics took their place, and young men who would once have dedicated themselves to cultivating their sensibilites now fancied themselves Marxists and revolutionaries. Even in this, however, New College clung to the principle of moderation: where other colleges produced communists, New College remained true to its own peculiarly Wykehamist brand of socialism, in the tradition which had been established in the college by Hugh Gaitskell and Evan Durbin. It might be considered the most important contribution made by the college to the government, or misgovernment, of Britain.

Its most notable exponents in my day were Richard Crossman and Douglas Jay, both older than me, both Wykehamists, both already dedicated socialists with political ambitions, both imbued with the spirit of 'doing something for the poor'. Crossman would certainly have been voted almost unanimously the man in the college most likely to succeed and perhaps it was because he was so efficiently organised for success that we found each other unsympathetic. Many years later, when editor of the *New Statesman*, Crossman reviewing a book of mine said that at New College he had thought me a young man on the make and I had thought him dull. It would have been truer to say, I think, that I was on a different kind of make from his, and he had thought me frivolous. Besides, I sometimes used to play rugby football for the college with him and he used to exasperate me by his assumption that rugby was a matter of brute force rather than intelligence, which offended all my instincts as a Welshman. Jay on the other hand, became a close friend, perhaps because he combined with his socialism and great lucidity of mind a wild streak of personal eccentricity.

It was through playing football also, though this time a different code, that I first met John Sparrow. In everything the antithesis of Crossman, what he valued on the football field, as in life, was elegance and style. He disapproved of my rather bustling methods as a centre-forward and would shake his head sadly if I scored a goal which did not come up to his exacting standards. But this did not prevent us from becoming life-long friends.

It will be seen, perhaps, that as time went by I began to lose the sense of loneliness and alienation I had felt on first arriving at the college. When the shock of confrontation with the English middle-class, public-school complex (a useful acronym would be E.M.P. on the model of W.A.S.P. in America) was over, I began to realise that its apparently rigid front was less impenetrable, certainly less hostile, than I had supposed. Indeed I discovered, to my surprise, that if only one were oneself willing, E.M.P.s positively welcomed one, with a kindness and tolerance which I have ever since regarded as essential characteristics of the English, and certainly something quite unlike the kind of response the alien and the stranger is apt to provoke in my own country.

Perhaps indeed the very difference between us added an extra dimension to the pleasure of making friends, as if we could both learn from each other things we should otherwise never have known. Certainly after the nostalgic unhappiness of my first term I gradually, and to my own surprise, began to feel at home in the college; indeed, I began to feel that I now had two homes instead of one, and each the better because they were so different from each other. The regular alternation between vacation and term was like shuttling between a wife and a mistress. It was all the easier to feel at home because, in those days, the college was still small enough for us to live in a peculiarly close and intimate domesticity, as in some extended family in which it was really very difficult not to get to know one another, unless one was stubbornly determined not to. It was more like living in some large and pleasant country house than attending an educational institution.

It was a further consequence that, in such a society, its older and more senior members were as approachable as one's immediate contemporaries; this is something which, I think, has largely disappeared from the Oxford of today. It was, for instance, very hard, if presumptuous, not to behave towards an infinitely accessible don like Christopher Cox as if one were not somehow his equal. But not all such relationships were quite as easy; my philosophy tutor, for instance, H. W. B. Joseph, was a constant source of worry and anxiety to me during my last two years in the college. It was not that I disliked Joseph; on the contrary, I was very fond of him. How could one have disliked anybody who was so interested in one's moral and intellectual welfare? But the burden of his concern sometimes weighed heavily on one who, like myself, was addicted to pleasure. Sometimes when I was enjoying myself most the thought would, absurdly, cross my mind: *What would Joseph think?*.

The trouble was that it was difficult to take him frivolously. He had an acute and powerful mind, and formidable dialectical gifts, which he did not hesitate to deploy against even the most diffident pupil; for he was so convinced that the true and the good are identical that for him error was also a sin, to be ruthlessly eradicated for the good of one's soul. And if one were equally convinced, by instinct rather than reason, that there was something wrong in all this, but could not meet him in argument, one inevitably felt oneself in a false position, like some sinner who professes virtue in public but goes away to sin happily again in secret.

In my first year in college Joseph's rooms, where I went apprehensively to my tutorials, were on the ground floor of my staircase in the new buildings. On the next staircase lived a very different kind of person, the one man of indubitable genius in the college at that time, the great mathematician, G. H. Hardy. Perhaps it was mere proximity that made us acquainted, or perhaps it was, once again, a liking for games, which in Hardy was more like a passion, so that playing tennis or bowls with him may have made up for all the disparities in age and intellect.

Hardy was certainly one of the most remarkable men I have ever met; he was what Henry James would have called The Real Right Thing, and to have known him at all would alone have made it worth while going to New College. He was both shy and deeply emotional; his mind had an elegance which made Joseph's look like a good kitchen implement, and he had the gift, which some great men have, of talking to one as if one were exactly the same as himself. Years later, during the war, I met him again by accident on the towpath in Cambridge, where he had returned to Trinity and I was a soldier posted there to instruct on an intelligence course. He greeted me like an old friend, and immediately invited me to dinner at Trinity, as if New College were a quite sufficient and permanent recommendation to his affection.

And among my seniors and elders I must not omit Warden Fisher himself, austere but benevolent, wistful and self-indulgent in recalling the days when he was a member of the Cabinet, presiding over the college in the same liberal and humane spirit that had inspired his Education Act, and somehow finding the time and the interest to invite one to come for a walk once a term, when he would discuss affairs of state, or Renan and Taine, and gravely listen to anything one had to say oneself as if one really had something of value to contribute to the conversation. And equally I cannot forget Mrs. Fisher and her invitations to Sunday lunch, which it was possible to accept only if one could decode, like some Dead Sea scroll, her totally illegible handwriting, which so far as time and date were concerned might just as well have been written in invisible ink; or their daughter Mary at whom, yellow-haired like a Lorelei, I used to gaze on Sunday evenings in the chapel, bringing the spirit of *das ewig Weibliche* into our monastic and celibate existence. The Fishers completed, as it were, that system of domestic relationships which for me constituted the college's particular charm.

And oddly enough, my final memory of the college is of the warden. I had celebrated the end of my schools by getting drunk at lunch and had celebrated again in the evening at the George, and in ebullient mood had returned in time to enter the college before the gates closed. The Fishers then had living with them in the lodgings a beautiful Home Student, with whom I was rather in love. In the front quad I saw that on the ground floor the lights were still on, and feeling that I had nothing to lose I opened the front door and, as I hoped, found the beautiful Home Student still awake. We greeted each other appropriately. She told me the Fishers had gone to bed, and we were deep in whispered conversation on a sofa when I suddenly became aware of a shadow on the stairs and looking up saw the warden, silver-haired and, by some trick of the lighting, mysteriously elongated, like some Shakespearean ghost, by the folds of his flannel nightdress. Silently, imperiously, he pointed to the door. Abashed, ashamed, I slunk away. I am glad to say that, magnanimously, the warden seemed to understand it all and never held my behaviour against me.

Of course, New College was not the whole of my life at Oxford, just as Oxford itself was only a part of my life elsewhere. Outside the college walls there were other friends, other distractions, other interests, which, as the years went by, increasingly preoccupied me. But the college performed the essential function of providing a safe and secure base for forays into a wider world, and in this sense it was genuinely my home. Returning to college as the gates closed, I used to be comforted by thinking that, however foolishly I might have spent the evening, in the morning Allnutt, who was my friend as well as my scout, would draw the curtains and light the fire and bring me tea, and I would awake to hear the children singing in the chapel, and another day would begin in which I might either work or play. In those days I was never quite sure which was which.

There is a very beautiful passage in Newman's *Apologia Pro Vita Sua* in which he describes how, after looking for the last time at the snapdragons outside his window in Trinity, he prepared to leave Oxford for his retirement to Littlemore; with sadness because, as he says, 'Trinity was always kind to me'. I might have said very much the same, when, with not much idea of what was going to come next, I finally went down. To me, certainly, New College was always kind.

[iv]

The Warden's Lodgings between the Wars

MARY BENNETT

Mary Bennett was the daughter of Warden Fisher. She was educated at the Oxford High School and at Somerville, where she read Mods and Greats. During the war she worked in the B.B.C.; afterwards for ten years in the Colonial Office. She was married to John Sloman Bennett in 1955 and returned to Oxford as Principal of St. Hilda's in 1965.

I was twelve when my father became warden and twenty-seven when he died, so that my memories of New College are those of my own growing up. At first undergraduates were remote Olympian beings, one or two of whom might unbend to the extent of helping with my weekend home-work (for my parents were no good at sums); they became equals and contemporaries; they diminished into youths to be entertained at freshers' tea parties. At all stages they flowed ceaselessly through and round the house, standing in the tower room in their gowns or thunder-ing up the stairs on the way to the warden's study, putting their heads round the green baize curtain that then divided the entrance lobby from our large downstairs hall, running along New College Lane at the turn of midnight to get in before the gate closed, or to pound on it if they were the wrong side of the hour, shouting to each other across the quad, occasionally (though seldom after Christopher Cox became dean) breaking out into nocturnal bonfires and hunting-horns. 'Graduates' had not been invented, and girls were not yet considered a useful adjunct to college life. There was no doubt about who, and what, the college was for.

While undergraduates ebbed and flowed, growing younger as I grew older, the rhythm of life in the Lodgings remained constant. It was an enchanting but singularly inconvenient house, icy cold in winter and so designed that every piece of crockery or drop of water travelled as far as

127

possible before use. No one thought of reconstructing it, and if they had they would have come up against the Gladstonian principles of Bursar Radcliffe, from whom my mother (a determined woman) proved unable to extract any amenity beyond two additional bathrooms. Colleges now provide their heads with a good deal in the way of service, heating and indeed furnishing: then nothing was provided beyond a set of pewter plates and a man to stoke the boiler when the house was thawed out at weekends. My mother ran it with six maids, of whom Rose, the parlour-maid, was as much a key figure in the lodgings as the steward, Wheeler, was in college. She was always at the pitch of achievement (sometimes at the cost of frayed domestic nerves), remembering every one and everything: it was she who welcomed new arrivals and recognised them when they returned, made sure that my father wore a gown or a surplice in chapel as the day required, suggested names for dinner parties if someone dropped out at the last moment, and produced the claret when Mr. Belloc came to tea. 'If Rose went, you'd have to retire from New College', I once said to my father. 'If Rose went, I should have to retire from life', he replied. In fact she stayed on to look after Warden Smith, retiring only when she suddenly married and went happily away.

My father seldom spoke of college business. He was a discreet man, and college politics amused him less than they were to amuse me. He prided himself on getting through meetings fast (easier, one would suppose, when they were held regularly before breakfast) but took no great pains to dispose of the problem raised by the flower beds under the chapel—did they or did they not distract the eye from the architecture?—since he found it convenient to have an issue on which fellows could be given their heads. To the undergraduates he was prepared to give apparently endless time. In earlier years, at least, he used to summon selected scholars to read their latest essays to him (did their tutors welcome this practice?) and my impression is that he kept a firm, if light, hand on the scholarship examination. One of the few indiscretions that I recall was the ejaculation 'Boys' minds rotted with piety!' when he came discontentedly down to dinner after reading a particular Winchester scholarship entry.

Our family life was based in my mother's sunny sitting room over the bridge and in the big downstairs hall, now reabsorbed into the college but then reached immediately from the quad door. In the hall we ate all meals, except at weekends when the size of the party meant moving to the upstairs dining room. As we sat at table we could see Mr. Joseph trotting or Mr. Henderson striding across the corner of the quad, while my mother at her writing table in the window was equally visible to those whom her stream of all-but-illegible notes would summon to lunch or tea. To tea undergraduates came almost daily (their appetites blunted in Hilary Term by the enormous cake, with rock-hard icing, presented every Christmas by the bursar) but weekday lunch and dinner were rapid domestic affairs, after which we vanished to our respective pursuits. As often as not someone dropped in to lunch to talk to my father about the Oxford Preservation Trust, or Rhodes House, or the New Bodleian, or to accompany him on his daily constitutional round the Parks, but there was no sitting over meals. My parents both worked extremely hard, and when I was at home I worked fairly steadily too.

In 1931 I went to Somerville (where I worked much less) and for three years was replaced as daughter of the house by Maire Lynd, 'B.J.', then a Home Student. Beautiful and intensely romantic, hoping to find a hero or a genius in each young man that crossed her path, B.J. brought a waft of poetry into our serious academic household, with new friends for me and much enjoyment for my parents who were both devoted to her. She once shocked my father profoundly by coming down in her dressing gown to receive a pair of after-dinner callers, and in the mornings and evenings we were both encouraged to use the Queen's Lane door, then opening from the ground floor of the lodgings, rather than the quad ('Girls in the quad' was an alarm cry to bring the porter from his lodge and the warden from his study with equal celerity); but I think that with her friends and mine constantly in and out of the house the lodgings must have become a gayer place for everyone. It certainly seemed lively enough to her and to me when we were young.

During vacations, spent away from Oxford in our Surrey home, where my father could get on with writing and my mother with her garden and hens—not that she failed to keep hens in New College also—weekend parties for the next term were worked out. There were spare rooms for three couples and they were normally filled. Guests arrived on Saturdays in time to dress (white ties) for a grown-up dinner party of eighteen: in early years I used to watch them process into the dining room from between the top floor banisters. Sunday lunch was also for eighteen but this time undergraduates. My father had a penchant for political ladies—Mrs. Dugdale, Lady Milner—and much thought went towards selecting young men articulate and amusing enough to put next to them at table. More undergraduates to tea: then chapel, after which the gentlemen of the party, who had at some point scrambled into dinner jackets, went off to dine in hall while the ladies supped domestically at home. My mother's elderly cousin, Margaret L. Woods ('Cousin Daisy'), widow of a President of Trinity, and herself a poet, novelist and hostess of the Rhoda Broughton period, usually came to chapel and supper: with her white curls and violet eyes she remained a great charmer, and was the only person to whom Rose allowed a second cup of after-dinner coffee. On Monday morning the visitors departed, the central heating faded away, and the working week resumed.

In retrospect I think that these weekend parties helped to keep my father going, first when he was writing the *History of Europe* against the clock and later as the European scene steadily darkened beyond us. As Rebecca West was to write of him years afterwards he was 'very amusing when he was amused'; but he relapsed easily into boredom and gloom and needed distraction. Friends from various different worlds, young married nephews and nieces, acquaintances made on Hellenic cruises, old New College men with sons and daughters up, all were scooped in by my mother who believed, optimistically but in general correctly, that a heterogeneous party would entertain each other as well as my father. I think that it worked, and that the visitors also liked meeting the undergraduates and the undergraduates the visitors. It was hard work for all of us, but fun.

Of all the arts conversation is the most fugitive. What did we talk about? I remember the baffled look on the face of a weekend guest who asked the room at large what was the use of philosophy and was answered gaily by Isaiah Berlin 'None whatever' (but my father quickly led up Dick Crossman, who enumerated several), the marvellous appearance of Virginia Woolf, smoking a cheroot in the corner of the drawing room, Elie Halévy's sharp barking laugh at the contrast between B.J.'s exquisite appearance, in satin and roses, and her communist loyalties, and the universal embarrassment of a lunch party when H. G. Wells said something to offend one of Lady Mary Murray's numerous principles and she refused to speak to him, or indeed to anyone else. But what they said has vanished.

Life in a spacious, well-ordered house before the war was in a sense an unsuitable preparation for life in Oxford today. The sound of a guest doing a little weekend cooking would not have been heard in my mother's household. But there are constants. Undergraduates remain excitable and dons quarrelsome. Things always get better in the summer term. There is a special Oxford rating of people and things, unfamiliar to newcomers and often undetected, for which it is sometimes useful to have a trained nose. But mainly, of course, those fifteen years stimulated and stretched. At every stage of life I have been grateful to have them banked up behind me.

[v]

A Trade Unionist at Oxford 1931–1933

GEORGE WOODCOCK

The Right Hon. George Woodcock, C.B.E., as he now is, came up to New College in 1931 from Ruskin College at the age of twenty-six. He obtained First Class Honours in P.P.E. in 1933. From 1960 until 1969 he was General Secretary of the T.U.C. He was elected to an honorary fellowship at New College in 1963.

I reached New College at a comparatively late age and by an unusual route. I had left elementary school half-time at thirteen and I had worked for twelve years as a weaver in a Lancashire cotton mill. I was then a student at Ruskin College, Oxford, for two years, at the end of which I was awarded a scholarship by the Oxford University Delegacy for Extra-Mural Studies. Alic Smith, who later became the warden of the college, was one of the extra-mural delegates in that year. He persuaded New College to accept me to read for the Honour School of Philosophy, Politics and Economics. When I entered the college as an undergraduate in October 1931 I was just a fortnight short of my twenty-seventh birthday.

Even at that age, I was not the oldest of the newcomers to the college in that year. R. C. Sherriff, already famous as the author of the play 'Journey's End', was admitted at the same time at the age of thirty-seven. We both had senior status, allowed by the university authorities for our past accomplishments rather than because of our mature ages. This meant that we were excused from Responsions and from the First Public Examination—fortunately for me, for I could not have satisfied the examiners in either.

Sherriff, I think, did not read for a degree, never lived in and was not often seen about the college. I met him only once, in our first term, and that meeting was arranged for us by Mrs. Fisher, the wife of the warden. My only remaining recollection of Sherriff at New College is of his surprise and alarm when I suggested that he was likely to be pursued in Oxford as a literary 'lion'.

With me it seemed more likely that my greater age and different background would tend towards setting me apart from the rest of the undergraduates, most of whom were still in their 'teens' and had come straight to New College from school. At Ruskin College, where we lived close together, taking all meals in common and all following the same course of studies, it had been impossible not to get to know each of the other thirty-six students fairly intimately—and important, therefore, at least to try to get on reasonably well with all of them. In contrast, conditions in New College allowed for widely differing degrees of association or separation among its members. In New College there were seven or eight times the number of students that there were in Ruskin, reading in a variety of schools. Undergraduates in their third year usually lived out in lodgings and might come in to the college only for tutorials. The only common meal was dinner in hall and it was possible to sign off from that on three of the seven nights in the week. In New College, even the most popular and gregarious of the undergraduates could hardly expect (or wish) to come closer than a nodding acquaintance with more than a selection of his contemporaries. I doubt if more than a few of the undergraduates knew or cared anything at all about my background. On the other hand, that was, probably, a reason for the interest taken in me by some of the dons, in particular by Henry Phelps Brown who taught me in my main subjects, by Alic Smith who was my moral tutor, and by the warden, who often nabbed me as we were both leaving college after lunch and took me with him on his afternoon walk when my intention had been to sneak off to the cinema.

I, naturally, found most of my closest friends and regular associates among the undergraduates nearest to my own age. The college had, in fact, a fair sprinkling of undergraduates three or four years above the average in age for an undergraduate—mainly graduates staying up to take one of the higher degrees and Rhodes Scholars. There were about sixteen Rhodes Scholars in residence during my time, coming from every one of the countries of the 'old' Commonwealth plus Rhodesia and the United States of America. A fair number of them came from South Africa and Rhodesia, forming a coherent but not an exclusive group. I became specially well-acquainted with the members of this group through being paired with one of them, Hugh Ashton, for regular tutorials. Bram Fischer was a member of this group. At New College he was a pleasant youth, more serious than most, reading jurisprudence and with no special interest in politics. His name became known all over the world when (in the sixties) he was imprisoned in his native South Africa for his active opposition to his government's policy of apartheid and his membership of the Communist Party.

The warden of the college, H. A. L. Fisher, looked the part—tall, spare, dignified and laconic. I remember nothing of a talk he gave to the freshmen gathered together in hall on the first day of our first term except his warning that 'Oxford is not good for everyone'. By that he meant that undergraduates in Oxford were subject to only a few specific constraints on their social lives and to little supervision in the way they set about their studies. If an undergraduate found that the combination of considerable personal freedom and plenty of opportunities for distraction was rather too much for him, it would be in the under-graduate's own interest to leave Oxford.

One of the few specific rules about our conduct was that residents should be inside (and non-residents outside) the college by midnight. One night, I had kicked on the main gate but I was still on the wrong side waiting to be admitted when Great Tom finished striking twelve. As Allsop, the head porter, opened the small door I was joined in a rush by an undergraduate in a dinner jacket who had leaped out of a taxi driven at speed down New College Lane. Allsop, usually friendly, gave us a cool 'good night' and as we walked together into the quad the undergraduate assured me that I had saved him from expulsion. The college authorities, he said, were waiting for an excuse to send him down 'just when I have got this beautiful room in the garden quad where I can entertain all my friends'. Evidently the college did not necessarily leave it to the student himself to decide that he was not suited for the liberties of New College.

There must have been available to us some written instructions and advice about the rules and customs of the college and of the university. As I recall, I learned of most of them only casually—about the wearing of gowns, drinking in pubs, permission to go outside a three-mile radius of Carfax and so on. Until this incident at the gate I had not known that it was possible for a mere undergraduate to order a special meal to be served in his own room and I was in my last term when I discovered that we had the privilege of buying two bottles of vintage port each term from the well-stocked cellars of the college at much below their price in the open market!

For a dinner to be prepared in the college kitchens and served in his own room, an undergraduate needed the dean's permission and the co-operation of the college chef. Also, he needed the money. I had £250 a year from the Extra Mural Delegacy. There were not many New College undergraduates in those days who had as much as that to cover three university terms. My scholarship, however, was intended to provide for me during vacations as well as terms. My midnight accomplice at the gate must have had richer and more indulgent parents than most of us, who were content to don black ties just two or three times a term for a dinner of one of the college clubs.

There must have been at least a dozen different clubs and societies in New College in my time, ranging from the serious to the frivolous and from the orthodox to the eccentric. Some came into being and lapsed during the course of a single term. I became a member of two of the more solidly established—the XX Club and the Essay Society. Meetings of the XX Club were occasions for speeches meant to be witty and almost invariably delivered in an attempted imitation of the style of some famous past or present parliamentary or after-dinner speaker. A treasured possession of the XX Club was the book containing the minutes written by A. P. Herbert when he was its secretary. The Essay Society was for undergraduates with other pretensions. Its purpose was to discuss learned papers prepared and read by its members. Membership was by invitation and was reckoned (at least by its members) as something of a distinction. The president of the Essay Society was Tony Andrewes, from 1953 until 1977 Wykeham Professor of Ancient History.

One of the distinctive characters of New College in the inter-war years was H. W. B. Joseph. Joseph taught philosophy to students of Greats. In addition, he was ready to argue with anyone about practically anything. During my time he was engaged in a row with Sir James Jeans through the correspondence columns of *The Times* about some of Sir James's scientific theories. Joseph had one of the Rhodes Scholars, an American, and myself to lunch at his home in north Oxford. The scholar, simply to make a contribution to the table-talk on what he took to be a social occasion, said that he would have liked to have seen more students from North America about the college than there were. Joseph immediately invited him to say how many he thought there ought to be and was disappointed when the scholar, taken aback, lifted his shoulders to signify that he would rather let the matter drop.

Joseph was more successful in prodding me into an attempt to explain some economic theories of which he was as sceptical as he was of the scientific theories of the day. I had reason to mention a footnote (relating to the use of graphs by economists) in Alfred Marshall's *Principles of Economics*. Joseph promptly produced his copy of Marshall and asked to be shown the exact reference. Like the scholar, I was flustered and I could not find it there and then. I found it when I got back to my rooms and dropped a note to Joseph who responded with a two-page letter of crisp, critical comments on the economist's conception of utility as something that can be measured as potatoes can be weighed. Obviously, Joseph was willing to continue our discussion by correspondence and I really ought not to have let go this chance of acquiring a collection of Joseph's views written in his own lucid and provocative style.

We were, as the warden had said that we would be, under little supervision and hardly any direction. In P.P.E. at any rate, it was for the most part left to each undergraduate to decide for himself not only how to set about his studies but also for what principal purpose—more or less to satisfy his own curiosity or simply to be able, when the time came, to satisfy the university examiners. Taking the three main sources of learning—private study, university lectures, and regular sessions with tutors—the first two were entirely at the discretion of the student. In my case, my method of producing an essay did not allow for extensive reading. I would read a bit, sit a bit, write a bit, sit a bit, cross out most of what I had already written, and repeat the process until the time ran out.

Since we did not need anyone's permission to attend or to avoid university lectures, it was of my own choice that I went to very few. In six terms I went regularly only to the lectures given by D. H. McGregor, the Professor of Political Economy. Otherwise, I went to a series given over one term by H. A. Prichard, the Professor of Moral Philosophy. I was attracted to McGregor equally by the style and by the subjects of his lectures. The attraction of Prichard was almost exclusively in his style.

A lecture by McGregor was usually complete in itself. He would set out to examine a question somewhat off the beaten track—e.g. 'Is the Co-op dividend on purchases a distribution of trading profits which ought to be taxed, or a rebate of price which could get the Co-ops in trouble with manufacturers who fix and maintain the retail selling price of their products?' Prichard's lectures were given really for Greats students and for a student of P.P.E. were distinctly a luxury. The series that I attended was given under the general title 'Duty and ignorance of fact' and the particular one that I most clearly remember could have been sub-titled 'Reflections on the kind of moral dilemmas that could face a man in the course of a bicycle ride'. McGregor would glance occasionally at a single sheet of paper about the size of an ordinary post-card. Prichard, so far as I could see, used no notes at all. The style of both men was the same—painfully scrupulous and tortuous. Each was, in effect, engaged in an argument with himself. I only occasionally took a note of something said. Generally, it was enough for me to sit and to observe how their minds worked.

If I were to try to describe in detail the effect on me of Oxford and New College, the result would sound pompous or merely obsequious. In brief, I revelled in the freedom to go my own way, promised by the warden on my first day. For two years my full-time occupation was to nag away happily at my own uncertainties and to argue eagerly about my own conclusions.

Coming up to New College for my last term I was in a panic at the thought of how little I had learned in the two years and of the opportunites I had wasted through my own laziness and conceit. It was then too late to make good my deficiencies so I settled down to occupy myself in the six weeks before the final examinations by alternately sitting and playing patience.

[vi]

Reflections on an Undergraduate Diary

JOHN BUXTON

John Buxton came up to New College from Malvern in 1931 as a Commoner, and read Mods and Greats. He returned in 1946 as a lecturer in English Literature and was elected to a fellowship in 1949. In 1972 he was appointed to a readership in English Literature.

The diaries which I kept as an undergraduate in the 1930s have both helped and hindered this attempt at reminiscence. I have not much taste now for the adolescent naivety which they insist on disclosing, yet they do record the conversations and concerns of a group of young men in New College at the time when Hitler came to power; and they contain impressions of Warden Fisher, of tutors and lecturers and of a society which was very conscious of its own distinctive quality—a society of which it was then exciting to be a member. Not that my own circle of friends was confined to New College, and indeed one of the surprises in reading these diaries again has been to discover how often I dined in other colleges. I had a cousin of my year at Merton, and other members of my family at Balliol, Exeter, Queen's; I had friends from home at Magdalen, Wadham, Trinity and at L.M.H. and Somerville. I was not exceptional (as I should be now) in having a social life based at home more than in Oxford: some of us even had sisters, whom we would invite down with their friends for Eights week or to Commem. balls, to make up parties with our newly acquired Oxford friends. We enjoyed each other's company and did not clamour for the attention of our elders. No doubt the segregated masculinity of New College deprived us of some essential element in the process of maturing, but since we were unaware of this, it didn't seem to matter. The friendships then made, apart from the breakages of 1939–45, remain—the most valued of all the acquisitions of those years.

No doubt, like every other generation of undergraduates, we educated each other; but I should not wish to underrate what we learnt from Eric Yorke, Christopher Cox and Dick Crossman, the three tutors whose names most often recur in my diaries. They had little enough in common apart from the one thing that mattered above all others, that they treated their pupils as if they were intelligent beings whose tastes and preferences deserved consideration even if they also deserved modification. They made us think that we were concerned, with them, in the discovery of the literature, the history and the thought of the civilisations of the ancient world. Nothing could have been more rewarding. We were not instructed by men who knew all the answers; we were partners in a quest, and were being educated. Perhaps the favourable impression which New College made upon me immediately on my arrival (in addition to the beauty of the buildings and the garden) owed something to the fact that the first person I met, apart from my own contemporaries, was Christopher Cox, who introduced himself as my moral tutor. A day or two later Warden Fisher sent for me: he seemed to have an unjustifiably sanguine view of my abilities, but if I provided the scepticism he provided the encouragement. And he advised me to explore Oxford as thoroughly and attentively as I would explore Florence.

In our first term we joined numerous clubs and societies, persuaded by their sophistical secretaries; as we got to know ourselves better we gradually resigned from them. I joined only one political society, the Friends of the Soviet Union. This was because Eisenstein's film, 'Battleship Potemkin', was being shown to them at Ruskin College: the audience consisted for the most part of plain and earnest young women wearing red scarves, and the subscription was sixpence. I was a member of O.U.D.S. when Christopher Hassall and Peggy Ashcroft played in John Gielgud's memorable production of 'Romeo and Juliet', but I never aspired to act. There were college societies also, such as the 1854 Club (a less austere affair than the Essay Society) which had been founded originally for non-Wykehamists, but in my time had been infiltrated even by Founder's Kin: the members discussed papers on such topics as the New Deal, Kipling, Laughter, the Unintelligible Element in Poetry. Eric Yorke ran a Greek play-reading society, and on one occasion H. W. B. Joseph read the part of Socrates and H. L. Henderson that of Strepsiades in Aristophanes' *The Clouds*. In Trinity

Term the New College Nomads played cricket in neighbouring villages—Drayton St. Leonard had a one-legged bowler who, with no run, hurled the ball at one with terrifying force (he was the blacksmith). After Commem. we went on tour to Devon and Cornwall. At least one American indulged in this very un-American activity, but he came to no harm, and is now an honorary fellow.

There were other long vac. pleasures: going to North America (where lumbering seemed to be the principal recreation) which I did not try, or to the Continent, which I did. One summer I went to Greece with a friend, who later became a professor at Oxford. In Athens we stayed at the British School, of which Humfry Payne was Director. He suggested a visit to the Benaki Museum, which gave me a new, but lifelong, interest in Greek island embroideries, and I bought my first pieces. (They are now in the Ashmolean.) On Crete we stayed in Sir Arthur Evan's Villa Ariadne at Cnossos. The Wade-Gerys were there too, and we met John Pendlebury, with his rangy, vigorous frame and daunting glass eye. We walked over Taygetos from Sparta to Kalamata, and went on up to Pylos and Sphacteria, and so to Olympia and across to Delphi.

The presence among us of a future Director of the British School at Rome led to participation in a series of digs at Butley Priory, Bredon Hill, Colchester and Witham—the last of prime importance for the dating of Saxon pottery. Butley Priory, with its beautiful encaustic tiles and silted-up dock, from which they had been exported, was the home of Monty Rendall, the retired Headmaster of Winchester. Parties of half a dozen or so would wield pick and shovel, or probe with trowel and knife, and so learn about the techniques of archaeology under the guidance of Christopher Hawkes, Nowell Myres and Mortimer Wheeler. One year I dug in Ireland with Tom Kendrick, later Director of the British Museum, but this unluckily prevented me from accepting Christopher Cox's invitation to join a reading party at the châlet. I did what I could to make up for that twenty years later.

My diaries record frequent visits to concerts—at one recital in the town hall by Jelly d'Aranyi, Great Tom began his damnable iteration of nine o'clock. She was not disconcerted. 'I see if I can beat him!' she said, and went on playing. In college Norman Tucker, later Director of Sadler's Wells, would play his piano in his rooms for his friends; when he was at the R.C.M. we went up to hear him perform Brahms B♭ piano concerto with Beecham conducting. There were many visits to the

Ashmolean, not only to learn about Greek pots from that master of precise and elegant appreciation, J. D. Beazley, but to look at drawings and water-colours and paintings. Among the lectures I attended I seem to have been quite discriminating for, apart from Beazley's, I especially admired those of Cyril Bailey, Roger Mynors, Gilbert Murray and Johnny Myres. The last, with black hair and grey beard, with eyes flashing from behind gold-rimmed spectacles, looked, and was, legendary. He would preface his first lecture with 'I hope none of you are going to waste your time taking notes!'; and so we sat back and listened—the eight or ten of us who had the good sense to attend lectures so little directed towards Schools—and would be astonished at the overflowing of a mind of such exceptional range and curiosity. On one of my visits to him in his last years I asked if he had seen Epstein's *Lazarus*, recently placed in ante-chapel. 'I never thought it would be so uncomfortable in Abraham's bosom', he said, and chuckled. Then there was 'Tom Brown' Stevens who, soon after I became a fellow, came up to me in S.C.R. one evening and said, 'I know you. The first lectures I gave, you were in the audience; after about four weeks, you *were* the audience'. (He had then taken me back to his rooms and given me a glass of whisky.) But probably I owe the greatest debt of all to Gilbert Murray, whose fine literary sense, polished phrasing and courteous manner are unforgettable. I was fortunate to know him well also in later years, even to play tennis with him when he was over eighty. One could not have been guided to a delight in Greek poetry with more perspicacity, or with more consideration. This too remains.

For philosophy I had a succession of tutors. H. W. B. Joseph retired after my first term in Greats and beginners were not deemed suitable material for his intellectual demolition. A. H. Smith was absent for a year on sabbatical leave, and W. G. de Burgh, R. H. S. Crossman and, for one rather bewildering term, Isaiah Berlin, were privileged to listen to my tenuous essays. Isaiah was at All Souls, and on entering his rooms I was confronted by the gaping horn of an E.M.G. gramophone: I felt as if I was about to be swallowed whole, like Jonah, and Isaiah, kind and patient though he was, seemed too exotic of speech and manner and appearance to be wholly reassuring. There was always the possibility of a sudden swirl in the surrounding element, a gulp, and. . . . I owed far the most, among philosophers, to Dick Crossman, whose clarity of exposition—it may have been superficial, but that brought speculation within my compass—led me to exclaim, in the privacy of my diary, that he managed to make the subject interesting. I was, as he observed, 'a literary gent.', but he knew what books might appeal to such a creature, and he responded with irony to a temperament very different from his own. 'Don't come in here looking like moral man in immoral society', he said one day when I went to a tutorial in the Barn. (Niebuhr was then prescribed reading.) And the last time I saw him, at a party in the cloisters, he recalled those days. 'I didn't have any influence on you, did I?', he said. 'No, thank God', I replied promptly, but unjustly.

From that first encounter I saw more of Christopher Cox than of any other fellow, since he was both moral tutor and, later, ancient history tutor. He was humane and vivacious, knew how to combine candour with encouragement, and possessed a sense of humour from which he himself was never excluded. He would relate scandalous rumours about himself, and ask us to deny them—perhaps a device to gain wider currency for his own inventions? He would apologise for bouts of winter indigestion with 'Excuse my hay-fever'. When he cut a tutorial he sent an apologetic note offering to pay me 2s. 6d. if it happened again, provided that I would pay him 2s. 6d. every time I asked for a post-ponement. He invited us to sherry or to lunch, and we asked him to our own parties: he was welcome everywhere and, in more senses than one, bulked large in the life of the junior members. And when, just before Schools, he noticed that I was looking rather wan, he took me off in his car, saying 'When we get out of Oxford we will take the first left and the first right and see where we end up'. (We ended up in a field near Witney.) He got the best out of us by cajolery or provocation—'truculent' was an epithet he administered to me; and one could talk to him, or rather, listen to him, about anything. It became a habit to seek his advice, which was always based on seeing many more sides of the question than one had thought of oneself (as with weekly essays), so that one had the means to form a decision that would not be regretted. Later, when there was a chance of my being elected to a fellowship, I discussed this too with him. 'Well', he said, 'remember that it is a very good thing *to have been*'. That was decisive.

Presiding over this varied and self-confident community was Warden Fisher. His pleasure in recalling his service in Lloyd George's cabinet was less irritating to undergraduates, who might see themselves as future members of a cabinet, than to middle-aged dons, who could not.

In my first term he told me that he thought politics, if you could afford it, was the finest career of all, but I knew already that I was too private a person to venture that way. The warden was visible at his desk in his study, day after day, writing his *History of Europe* with a concentrated devotion to a scholarly task which was not lost on us. Yet persons from the great world which awaited us outside the walls of the college might be met in the lodgings—a High Court Judge, a newly appointed Foreign Secretary, one of Milner's Young Men, a European statesman: to such we were introduced quite naturally, with never a hint that we should withdraw to our insignificant affairs. Or we would be invited to accompany him on his afternoon walk, to the Parks, or to Magdalen Grove, when talk might range (as on one January day in 1935) from the Passchendaele controversy, to the new Gospel fragments in the British Museum, to Cecil Rhodes, to the next government, to Archbishop Temple, who was to preach in St. Mary's a few days later. The warden was never patronising, never impatient, and I found him less intimidating than some, perhaps because his daughter Mary was my exact contemporary and we were both reading Greats. After I had gone down I was invited to dinner in the lodgings one evening, and the warden said to us, 'I suppose you would like to see this television set which I have been given?'. 'Yes', we said, and he led us up to his study where he turned the thing on. There was some highly unsuitable cabaret show, apparently accompanied by a talk on gardening, and after about a minute he said, 'Five minutes of this thing is about as much as I can stand', and switched it off. That was my first introduction to TV.

In April 1940, a few days after the warden's death, I went into chapel with my wife; Mrs. Fisher and Mary were there, and several of my own contemporaries, and Christopher Cox. He knew that I was on embarkation leave and, for once, found it difficult to speak. I went overseas a few days later. During the five years that followed, my thoughts often returned to New College, a reassuring symbol of the endurance of civilised values. When I came home again I visited the college, to see some of my old tutors, including A. H. Smith, by then warden. He asked me what I was going to do when I came out of the army: would I like to come back to New College 'to help David Cecil with the English teaching'? Nothing could have been more unexpected, for I had never thought of myself in an academic post (and only New College could have tempted me to it), but nothing could have seemed more attractive. So here I have been for the past thirty-three years.

PART TWO

The Architecture of the College

V

The Building of
the Medieval College

GERVASE JACKSON-STOPS

1. INTRODUCTION AND NOTE ON THE SOURCES

It is part of the fascination of most large-scale buildings in England that
they are an amalgam of so many different styles, dates and materials.
The empirical approach, and distrust of the *Grande Idée*, which is at the
heart of the English character, is a theme as strong in our architectural
as it is in our political history. Despite the occasional outbursts of a
Butterfield or a Stirling, English architects have by consequence
generally been masters of the happy juxtaposition and the ingenious
adaptation, rather than thoroughgoing idealists or great originators. If
the empirical approach is true of the country house in England, how
much more true is it of the older Oxford and Cambridge colleges! Their
architectural history is governed not only by what succeeding generations considered fashionable, but as much by constantly changing
social conditions within the universities, and by the sheer chance of
what funds were then available, of what odd-shaped plot of land had to
be used, or of what buildings already existing had to be matched or
balanced.

But whereas the development of a country house has generally to be
traced from a few fragments only of documentary material—a couple of
architect's designs, the owner's bank books—forming, nearly always, a
jigsaw puzzle incomplete without analogy and conjecture, the history of
a college is quite as difficult for entirely different reasons. With the
wealth of material, from the circumstantial detail of bursars' books to
the endless college meetings (making resolutions one week to be broken
the next), and the constant small changes made yearly to the buildings

and gardens, a general survey of the buildings and the major periods of activity is hard to assimilate, or to present in any logical order.

New College is no exception to this rule. Its collections of manuscripts, covering the six hundred years of its existence, are still kept in the Founder's muniment tower, but they have long since overflowed the great oak chests intended for them and, contrary to his statutes, caused the gold and silver, the chapel vestments and ornaments to be moved elsewhere. This *embarras de richesses* is, however, mitigated by the existence of three published works of primary importance for the architectural history of the college: Hastings Rashdall and R. S. Rait's *New College* in the 'College Histories' series, published in 1901, A. H. Smith's *New College and its Buildings*, 1952, and Professor A. H. M. Jones's account in the *Victoria County History of Oxfordshire*, vol. III, 1954. So comprehensively do these authors cover the subject, that there might at first seem little to add to their findings. But it would be strange if twenty-five years were to have passed without either new sources coming to light, or attitudes to different styles of architecture changing.

If an excuse for attempting a fresh account were needed, the publication in 1974 of Mr. Francis Steer's *The Archives of New College* would alone provide an excellent reason, revealing as it does so many documents that have escaped the notice of previous writers. But in addition it is perhaps easier now than it was a generation ago to see the architectural development of the college as a whole, if not more objectively, then in a more distant perspective. Rashdall and Rait, Smith, and to a lesser extent Jones, display a natural bias in favour of the Founder's buildings, and regard later additions and alterations largely as unnecessary incursions. The first of these, a pioneering study which contains some omissions and inaccuracies, was written before the revival of interest in Georgian architecture; but the last, whose approach is factual rather than narrative, is also, in the archaeological tradition of the *Victoria County Histories*, noticeably fuller on the earlier than the later buildings. Warden Smith's delightful book, in many ways a model of its kind, is again so imbued with infectious enthusiasm for the Gothic that it pays scant attention to eighteenth-, let alone nineteenth-century work.

On the other hand, the debt of this new account of the college buildings to its immediate predecessors will be obvious—particularly in the sections dealing with the medieval college, where the researches of

Mr. John Harvey and Mr. E. A. Gee have also been freely used. The passages on the stained glass are based even more closely on Dr. Christopher Woodforde's study, *The Stained Glass of New College, Oxford*, published in 1951.

A chronological has been preferred to a topographical survey partly because it sustains the narrative better and avoids the necessity for much repetition, partly because it helps to express the outward expansion of the college in geographical terms. The only exception to this rule is the final section of Chapter V which, after the bald chronology of William of Wykeham's building activities, and an account of the masons and sculptors employed, is in the form of a tour of the college as he must have left it on his death in 1404.

2. WILLIAM OF WYKEHAM AND THE ARCHITECTURE OF NEW COLLEGE

Throughout its long history the Office of the King's Works has held a central place in the development of English architecture—and perhaps nowhere is the strength of its influence clearer than at New College. Just as Byrd's garden quad of the 1680s was closely based on Wren's never-completed Winchester Palace, and Scott's Holywell building derived in many respects from his rejected Foreign Office designs of 1858, so with the very beginnings of the college, not only its planning and its style of architecture, but even the training and organisation of the craftsmen engaged on it, can be traced directly back to the mid-fourteenth-century building activities of Edward III.

Despite the series of devastating plagues in 1348, 1361 and 1369 which reduced the population of this country by between a third and a half, and which resulted in a serious shortage of manpower, Edward III had embarked on a building programme unequalled in scale since the days of his grandfather and the castles of the Welsh and Scottish marches. No less than four new hunting lodges were built for the King in the New Forest, and it was perhaps at one of these that the young William of Wykeham (while in the employment of Nicholas Uvedale, the Constable of Winchester Castle) first came across the team of royal masons and carpenters who were to play so important a part in his future career, and in the three great monuments he left to posterity. How Wykeham first entered the King's service is unclear, though it was

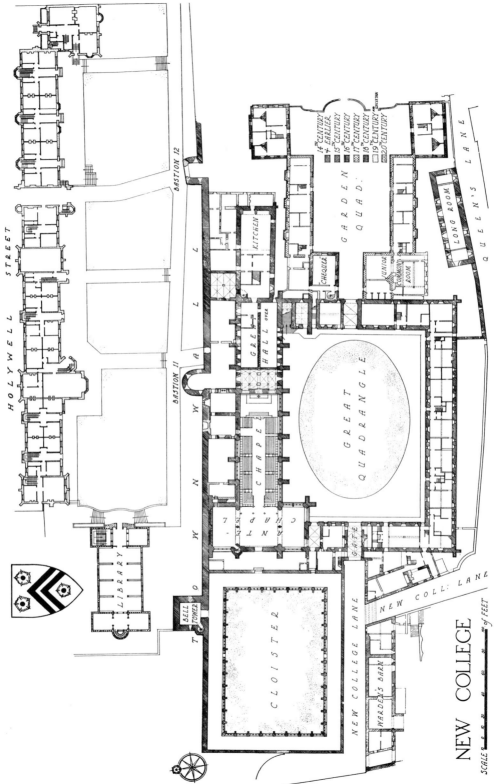

probably at the recommendation of Edington, the then Bishop of Winchester. It was at any rate in May 1356 that he received his first known appointment, as clerk at Henley-on-Heath and Easthampstead. In October of the same year he was made surveyor of the castle and park at Windsor, and by 1359 he was in charge of nearly all Edward III's major building works, in itself a far-reaching innovation, foreshadowing the regular appointment of a clerk of the King's Works after 1378.[1]

Between 1356 and 1361 over £9,000 of the King's money passed through Wykeham's hands solely for building purposes—the great majority of it spent on the new royal lodgings in the upper ward of Windsor Castle. The importance of this building for the future of William of Wykeham's two foundations can hardly be overestimated, for it was here that his first association with the master-mason William Wynford occurred, and it was here also, in the arrangement of a hall and chapel placed end to end so as to form a single unit (later combined to form the present St. George's Hall), that the key to the planning of both New College and Winchester College may be found. More than this, his practical experience as supervisor of the work at Windsor enabled William of Wykeham to form his own team of builders and craftsmen, under the leadership of Wynford, which he kept in more or less constant employment for the rest of his life, and which consisted largely of skilled men trained in the King's service. Whether or not the celebrated inscription 'Hoc Fecit Wykeham' (variously interpreted by his supporters and critics) was ever carved on the walls of the castle, Windsor certainly provided the impetus for all the bishop's later building schemes.

Although the documentation is slight, the activity of Wykeham's own team of builders probably began in 1363 (immediately after he resigned the surveyorship at Windsor) with the south-west tower of Wells Cathedral. Wynford's hand has been seen in this, and it is more than likely that he owed the commission to Wykeham who was made Provost of Wells in that year. In 1367, immediately after his elevation to the see of Winchester, he began a series of visitations in the diocese, concerned especially with the dilapidated fabric of churches and monasteries, his purchase of a number of stone quarries in the Isle of Wight showing the extent of the work planned.[2] Then, after his brief disgrace during the ascendancy of John of Gaunt in the mid-1370s, began the major enterprises of his latter years: the main quadrangle of New College from 1379 to 1386, Winchester College from 1387 to 1394, the nave of Winchester Cathedral and his own house at Highclere from 1394, and the completion of New College (including the bell-tower and cloisters) from 1396 to 1403.

The fact that the dates of these operations so neatly dovetail is itself an argument for seeing more or less the same team of craftsmen at work on all of them, quite apart from the obvious stylistic similarities between the buildings. This is also confirmed by the surviving documents, where the same names often recur: not just those of the master-craftsmen such as Wynford and Herland, but lesser masons at New College like John Wylot and John Martyn, both of whom had worked at Windsor in the 1360s, Thomas Maidstone, who was summoned back to Oxford from Wells early in 1389, and who had probably worked earlier there with Wynford, or carpenters like William Ickenham, father and son, and William Wyse, who were also employed at Winchester.[3] All this implies that William of Wykeham had, since 1363 at least, steadily built up a smaller, private version of the King's Works, far more organised and geographically wider-ranging than previous medieval bishops' establishments, and fully prepared, by 1379, to embark on the most ambitious building enterprise yet attempted in either university.

Wykeham appears to have conceived the idea of a foundation at Oxford at least ten years before the first stone was actually laid. His first purchases of land in the city occur in 1369, barely two years after his consecration as Bishop of Winchester, and by the end of 1370 he had already acquired a quarter of the site on which the college now stands. The earliest record of scholars collected under his protection at Oxford does not, however, occur until 1373, at the same time as the establishment of the first small school at Winchester; from the beginning both were to be part of the same foundation, uniform in their government as in their architecture. By 1376 there were six small hostels at Oxford, whose inmates 'went away weeping' after the death of the Black Prince and Wykeham's disgrace in that year, but who returned in 1377 with the succession of Richard II and the restoration of the bishop's temporalities.[4] Although one or two plots seem to have been bought in these intervening years it was not until 1379 that Wykeham purchased the major part of the site, evidently determined to lose no more time and to start the building work.

The complexity of the medieval city's small holdings is evident from the list of the different plots acquired: eight each from Osney Abbey, St. John's Hospital and the town, six each from St. Frideswide's and Queen's Hall, one from Godstow Nunnery and twelve from different private owners.[5] The area thus amassed formed roughly a square in the north-east corner of the city walls, its south and west boundaries formed by roads: respectively the present Queen's Lane, extended to the city wall on the east (through what is now part of New College garden), and the section of New College Lane between the warden's lodgings and warden's garden extended to the city wall on the north.

The comparative ease with which William of Wykeham was able to acquire this site within the city walls, where Balliol before this time, and Magdalen soon afterwards, had to be built outside them, was at least in part a result of the Black Death. The plague had reached its worst proportions in Oxford ten years earlier, and had reduced this quarter of the city to what the jury, appointed to examine the royal writ in 1379, described as 'full of filth, dirt, and stinking carcases . . . [with] concourse of malefactors, murderers, whores and thieves . . . a place as 'twere desolate and not included or by any occupied'.[6] It was obviously in the town's interests that this area should be rebuilt, the more so because property immediately adjoining the walls carried with it the obligation of maintenance: a royal writ described the walls of Oxford as in a state of advanced decay, and a succession of supervisors had encountered great difficulty in forcing the many smallholders along the Holywell and Longwall stretches to make their contribution. Yet despite these obvious advantages, the town still put difficulties in Wykeham's way—perhaps simply as a manifestation of that age-old hostility between town and gown which has lasted into our own times. Long after the Royal Charter of 1 August 1379, which stipulated that the college should rebuild its 'parcel of wall, towers and turrets' wherever necessary, and that it should provide two postern gates for the mayor's triennial inspection of the walls, the burgesses were still objecting to granting the necessary release. 'We are greatly surprised', writes the bishop on 28 December, 'since you well know we ask nothing else . . . [but] the said Covenants in the manner that they were agreed upon between us and you in the presence of so many good people, and as good faith and reason demand . . . in your default we shall seek remedy elsewhere against you for this cause'.[7] With the power of both Church and State behind him, this was no idle threat, and it is true to say that without the abundant help of both New College would never have been built.

Help from Richard II came not only in the form of letters patent of July 1379 granting the city a licence to sell lands for the founding of the college, and of the charter of 1 August, but also of the King's later declaration (in April 1383) that all persons and goods connected with the building of the college were under his protection and thus exempt from tolls and customs.[8] Later still, in 1397, a number of masons and carpenters employed at New College were excused the general impressment of craftsmen to work on Westminster Hall, by payment of a certain sum to John Bernard, Master of the King's Works there.[9] The fact that the tower and cloister accounts of 1396–1403 record large quantities of timber being brought from the forest of Windsor, suggests that both Richard II and Henry IV may also have given Wykeham more practical assistance in the building of his college.

Help from the Church came, as might perhaps be expected, in even stronger measure. New College was the first foundation in either university to enjoy extra-parochial rights, granted by direct papal authority. In the private chapels of the old halls and hostels mass could be celebrated only on weekdays, and there was no exemption from heavy tithes, fees for burials, marriage licences and so on. The papal bull of 1389, without actually granting William of Wykeham's college parochial status, secured for it the right to build its own cloister, adjoining the chapel, where its members could be buried, to erect its own bell-tower and to celebrate high mass in the chapel on Sundays— that is to say complete independence from the parish, setting a pattern for practically all the subsequent major foundations at Oxford and Cambridge. The bull also gave practical help to the building work by promising indulgences to those who contributed to the fabric of the chapel.[10]

This last clause is also important in establishing the early chronology of Wykeham's building. The foundation stone of the college had been laid on 5 March 1380, and the warden and his scholars took formal possession of the buildings in the early morning of 14 April 1386. It can be presumed that their living quarters were complete by this date, but there is evidence that work on the chapel continued for many years afterwards, and despite the usual dating of the whole quadrangle to before 1386 it is possible that the northern range—containing chapel, hall and muniment tower—was not finished until long afterwards. Some of the glass in the chapel windows is now thought to date from between 1399 and 1404, while the copy of the Founder's statutes made in 1405 makes it clear that many of the niches in the reredos had not yet been filled with statues. The marble floor of the chapel was not laid until 1411–12, and work on the pinnacles recorded in 1412–13 may well refer (at such an early date) to their carving, rather than to their restoration.[11]

The detailed bills which survive for the building of the cloisters, bell-tower and warden's barn between 1395 and 1403 are some compensation for the lack of specific building accounts in the 1380s. These not only reveal the names of many craftsmen (who must also have been involved in the earlier building phase), but also the sources of the materials used—lead from Winchester, timber from Windsor, lime from Witney, rough stone from Headington and freestone (or 'talstons') from Taynton in the Cotswolds. They even include one of the first documented references to a crane in the history of English building: payment to one William Willebury of 17s. 4d. for 'repairing a great wheel . . . and a large cable to run over a wheel for elevating stone and timber' during the construction of the bell-tower.[12]

The building of these extra appendages to the original quadrangle was made possible by further important acquisitions of land by the Founder in 1388–9. These consisted of the sites of Great and Little Hammer Hall, Sheld, Maiden and Temple Halls all on the other side of the road which had formerly marked the western boundary of the college. It should be remembered that at this time New College Lane was a straight road running from Queen's Lane on the south to the city wall on the north, separating the bishop's newly purchased land from his original college buildings. This did not matter as far as the southern half was concerned, for the warden's stables and paddock were best situated outside the confines of the college; on the northern half, however, it was intended to build the cloisters and bell-tower which, for obvious reasons, could not be separated from the chapel by a public highway. The answer to this problem was to divert New College Lane to its present course, turning westwards when it reached the main gate of the college, and then, after a right-angled turn at the west end of the cloisters, proceeding northwards once more. Complicated negotiations with the town had to be made once again for the diversion of the road, the replacement of one of the bastions in the city wall by the bell-tower and the closing of various small posterns in the wall itself.

The cloisters, begun about 1390, were not completed until 1400, when the petition for their consecration (by the Bishop of Dunkeld) refers for the first time to 'New College', the name by which Wykeham's 'College of St. Mary of Winchester' has been known ever since. The bell-tower was likewise long in the building, begun in about 1396 but finished only in 1403, while the warden's barn was built in 1402— sixteen years after the first warden, Nicholas of Wykeham, had taken up residence in the lodgings. By the time of the Founder's death in 1404 the college as he had planned it was practically complete; it was to be nearly fifty years before an addition of any importance was made to this original structure.

3. THE MASONS AND CARPENTERS: WYNFORD, HERLAND AND YEVELE

Warden Woodward, the methodical administrator and antiquarian responsible for putting the college on its feet again at the Restoration, first found and transcribed, in his crabbed but precise hand, the detailed accounts for the cloisters and bell-tower, together with the few fragmentary bills and records relating to the earlier main quad-rangle.[13] 'But', he concluded, 'who was ye contriver, overseer, chiefe carpenter or masons in Building ye Colledge I have not found. It may be that our Founder would have that concealed.'

In the absence of direct evidence it was held in the eighteenth and nineteenth centuries that the Founder himself must have designed both Winchester College and New College, and Wykeham thus earned a reputation as one the fathers of English architecture. This view did not, however, take into account the increasing specialisation of those involved in large-scale building work in the fourteenth century, and in particular the decisive split between the administrator or clerk responsible for paying the workmen, transporting materials and generally directing operations, and the master-craftsmen (whether masons like Wynford and Yevele or carpenters like Herland) who were without doubt responsible for drawing up plans and making models.[14] It was craftsmen such as these, directing the workmen on the site, and probably only rarely involved in manual labour themselves, who were the ancestors of the modern architect—not the clerk of the works, usually a man of higher social standing whose purely administrative role they later combined with their own.

Another equally important reason for doubting that the Founder designed his own buildings is that, surprising as it may seem, no evidence exists of his ever actually visiting New College. The hall books of the college survive more or less complete from its dedication in 1386, and are indeed a primary source for the names of craftsmen involved in its building, but neither these nor Wykeham's detailed registers as Bishop of Winchester, record a visit to Oxford between 1379 and his death in 1404.

This is not of course to deny that the bishop had any influence, even from a distance, over the architecture of his buildings. The statutes for New College with their minute descriptions of how each part of the college is to be used—from the detailed inventory of what was to be kept in the four different rooms of the muniment tower, to the injunction against ball-games in hall out of reverence for the chapel reredos immediately next to it—show that the Founder had a very precise idea of how the college looked, and how it should work. There is evidence that he was in constant touch with the master-craftsmen employed on his buildings: Wynford for instance dined at his table at Winchester no less than thirteen times during a period of only six weeks in 1393, and John Hulyn, the clerk of the works for the bell-tower at New College, travelled to London for two days early in 1397 specially to consult the bishop at his palace at Southwark.[15]

William of Wykeham's particular devotion to the Blessed Virgin Mary, based apparently on the statue in Winchester Cathedral to which he was drawn as a young boy, also found direct expression in the decoration of New College. Apart from the three groups of sculpture representing himself as a witness to the Annunciation (one either side of the main gate, the other above the entrance to hall) which are the principal decorative features of the exterior, there is the statue of the Madonna and Child within the great pinnacle surmounting the western gable of the chapel, the Coronation of the Virgin in the upper lights of the south-east antechapel windows, and the Wise Virgins (Plate 24) grouped in the north-east choir window nearest to the high altar, as well as the five scenes in the Life of the Virgin Mary placed immediately over the altar itself and the prominent position reserved for her statue in the reredos above—once again specifically mentioned in the statutes.[16] It is perhaps not too fanciful to see also in the provisions for the warden's barn, with its extensive stabling and guest quarters, a reflection of that special solicitude for travellers to which Wykeham's earliest biographers testify, and which caused him to endow hostels and wayside chapels far beyond the bounds of his own diocese.

If the Founder's role was limited to that of a knowledgeable and demanding patron, the question remains: who was responsible for the purely architectural innovations at New College, which were to be so important as a catalyst in the future development of both universities? Though long before the days of signed architects' drawings, there are fortunately a number of clues which put the answer beyond reasonable doubt. Foremost among them is a small section of stained glass in the east window of the chapel at Winchester College, showing a group of three diminutive kneeling figures: the one in the centre, with a beard, labelled 'ma[gister Guliel]m[v]s Wynfor lathomus' (William Wynford), flanked on the left by a more heavily bearded figure labelled simply 'carpentarius' (Hugh Herland), and on the right by a clean-shaven 'D[omi]n[u]s Simon Membury', the clerk of the works (Fig. b). The Winchester window, which also contains a self-portrait of its

Fig. b Portraits of Herland, Wynford and Membury in Winchester College Chapel.

glazier, Thomas of Oxford, was tragically 'restored' in 1822–8 by Sir John Betton and David Evans of Shrewsbury, who simply replaced the original glass with a careful copy. But while the colouring of the window cannot now be trusted, there is no reason to doubt the veracity of their figures.[17]

The extraordinarily close stylistic similarities between New College and Winchester alone suggest that the triumvirate here portrayed shared the responsibility for both buildings. This is also confirmed by the appearance of all three men in the books kept from 1388 onwards at New College (the so-called *Libri Senescalli*) recording the names of those dining in hall.[18] Simon of Membury, as clerk of the works, must have fulfilled the same, purely administrative, role that Wykeham himself had played during the building of Windsor—and may be discounted as an influence on the architecture of either college. The key figures were undoubtedly William Wynford and Hugh Herland, who both dined with the fellows in hall on 15 August 1388, 25 March 1389 and 16 February 1391. Wynford also paid another visit in September 1391 with a burgess from Southampton, who had probably travelled with him from Winchester, and Herland again in 1397, only a year before his death. The first of these occasions, held respectively on the Feast of the Assumption and on Easter Eve, are the most interesting, for they were almost certainly Gaudes to which many of the principal craftsmen were invited to celebrate the completion of the main buildings. At these two Gaudes, Wynford and Herland are distinguished from the other craftsmen not only because their names head the guest-list, but because their personal servants dined with the college servants on the lower table. However, they were accompanied on both evenings by a third figure of equal stature, who also brought a personal servant: the King's mason, Henry Yevele, perhaps the most celebrated of all medieval mason-architects.

Yevele's part in the evolution of the design of New College is less definite than either Wynford's or Herland's, though it deserves serious consideration. Slightly older than the other two, Yevele was trained as a mason in the City, earning his freedom as early as 1353. He became the King's mason at Westminster and the Tower in 1360, and London remained his base for the rest of his career, with commissions radiating out from there: most notable among them his work at St. Albans and Canterbury. Yevele's first known encounter with William of Wykeham occurred in 1381, when he and Wynford were both witnesses to an act of homage made before the bishop at Farnham. Their presence there could well have been to discuss Wykeham's Oxford college, then at a crucial planning stage. In 1385–6 Yevele was also responsible for rebuilding the chancel at the College of St. Martin-le-Grand, at Wykeham's expense. Later, in 1390, Wynford, Herland and Yevele were all appointed by the King for a seven-year period to direct the rebuilding of Winchester Castle: their co-operation (what the constable's accounts call 'ordinance and counsel') was not unlike that of Wren, Hawksmoor and Talman in the same Office of Works three hundred years later.[19]

Yevele's influence on the design of New College can be seen both in the overall plan of the buildings, and in at least one stylistic detail. The quadrangle plan, perhaps its most important single innovation, was, as has been seen, derived in part from Wynford's state apartments of Windsor, but it probably owed as much to Yevele's small quadrangular colleges at Cobham in Kent (begun for John, Lord Cobham in 1370) and at Arundel in Sussex (of ten years later). The formula is also found in his contemporary work on the London Charterhouse, and may indeed have been inspired by earlier Carthusian buildings. A few details of the design of New College also recall Yevele: in particular the hall windows, whose tracery and proportions are almost identical to those on the west gate at Canterbury built by him in 1378.

Despite Yevele's undoubted influence and advice, the onus of the design and building of New College fell on the mason William Wynford and the carpenter Hugh Herland; both had sons who were amongst the earliest scholars at New College, and this in itself may have been part of their reward. While there can be no doubt on purely stylistic grounds that these two were the chief 'contrivers' of the design, an entry in the Bursars' Account Roll of 1388–9—'. . . in rewardis Datis Dispensatori pro diversis victualibus per ipsum emptis custode Magistro Nicolao Wykeham Magistro Hugoni Herlond et Willelmo Wynford diversis temporibus ad Collegium venientibus iiij s.'—suggests that they were also responsible for the regular supervision of the work.[20] Between 1400 and 1402 Wynford supplied quantities of stone for Queen's Hall, though he appears to have had nothing to do with its design or building. Medieval master-masons were frequently responsible not only for feeding and housing their workmen but also for supplying materials out of their own pocket, and if the stone sold by Wynford was (as seems likely) surplus after the completion of New College, this transaction too would imply that he had directed the execution of the work, as well as giving the design.

Like his predecessor at Windsor, John Sponle, who was born at Winchcombe in Gloucestershire, William Wynford was a West Country man, presumably from the village of Winford, six miles south of Bristol. It is more than a coincidence that Richard Chevington and William Orchard, the masons responsible for New College's immediate successors, All Souls and Magdalen, were from the same part of the world.[21] Rich in stone quarries, this and the Cotswolds were also areas rich in craftsmen able to use it; and just as Oxford's supplies of stone in the fourteenth and fifteenth centuries came from the West Country, so to a great extent did its master-masons, and its architectural fashions. Wynford appears first at Windsor between 1360 and 1366, working on the great gate and the royal lodgings in the upper ward, which were to have so marked an influence on the planning of both William of Wykeham's later foundations. But his subsequent commissions were based on Winchester and the south-west, and it is interesting that he is associated with no buildings in London, which remained Yevele's main sphere of action.[22]

There is a stylistic unity about Wynford's work which leaves no doubt that he was the designer of New College, despite the dearth of documentation on the earliest period of the building work there. A piece of circumstantial evidence, the fact that his personal servant, Thomas Selby, was recorded as living in the north-eastern ward of the city in 1380, supports the view that he was directing operations from the beginning.[23] But far more conclusive are the later recurrence at Winchester College of nearly identical traceried windows, gatehouses adorned with statuary, a battlemented tower and cloister, and a chapel and hall placed back to back, this time known to have been built to his design. One decorative motif in particular, a row of narrow vertical niches with cusped heads, sometimes pierced as in the triforium of Winchester Cathedral or the parapets of the west towers at Wells, sometimes in the form of a blank arcade as in the walls of the chantry surrounding Wykeham's own tomb at Winchester, has been seen as one of Wynford's trademarks. It occurs (in abbreviated form) decorating the pinnacled buttresses which are so important a feature of the exterior of New College chapel—and which are once again nearly identical with those of the nave at Winchester Cathedral. Wynford's association with William of Wykeham after the beginning of New College included secular work such as the remodelling of the bishop's manor at Highclere in 1394. Nor did it end with Wykeham's death in 1404, for provision was made in his will that Wynford should continue the new work on Winchester Cathedral, which he did until his own death three years later.

Hugh Herland, the master-carpenter, was, like Yevele, based more in London, working at Westminster from 1360 and, after 1375 when he succeeded his father as King's carpenter, at Rochester, Queenborough and Leeds castles in Kent. It may have been at Queenborough that he first encountered William of Wykeham, and thereafter he collaborated with Wynford on all the bishop's major enterprises: at New College, Highclere and Winchester. The processes of design and construction were of course more closely linked at this date than they became later: the different trades or 'misteries' were kept entirely separate and the master glazier, smith, carpenter or mason would each have designed as well as executed his own part of the work without submitting to the dictates of an architect. The quite separate responsibility of Wynford for the masonry and Herland for the carpentry of New College is not therefore surprising. Unfortunately Herland's work, being in the more perishable material, has lasted less well: the present roofs of both chapel and hall at New College are nineteenth-century, and no accurate record remains of their original appearance.[24] One can now judge the quality of his work only by the beautiful, but simple, tied beams of the kitchen and Long Room and by the remarkable roof of the cloisters: Herland visited New College in 1397 while these were being built, but he died the following year, and the cloisters were not dedicated until 1400.

Besides Wynford, Herland and Yevele, the names of a number of other masons and carpenters engaged on the building of the college emerge from the early bursars' rolls and the *Libri Senescalli*, or hall books. Chief amongst these was the mason William Brown, who may, like Wynford, have previously been in the royal service. Brown was probably working on New College as early as 1380, when the Poll Tax returns record him living in the north-east ward. He was present at the two great Gaudes of 1389 and 1390, and also dined in hall with Wynford on two occasions in 1391; from then on he appears regularly in the hall books until 1406. In 1396–7 he took active charge of the building of the bell-tower as Wynford's warden or under-master, and he also undertook a number of other buildings in Oxford on his own account, including Canterbury College (1384–96) and Oriel chapel and gatehouse (1409–12).[25] After the completion of New College he was (until 1415) the first of a long series of master-masons responsible for routine maintenance and repair work in return for livery.

Another mason, Richard Norton, is generally associated with William Brown in the New College documents until 1397 and the two may have been in partnership. Both were fined for exceeding the normal mason's rate laid down by the Statute of Labourers, which implies that they were skilled craftsmen. Fining must by this time have been considered a matter of course for many masons and carpenters: Norton paid in 1391, 1392 and 1394, and in the first of these years was also the constable responsible for collecting the fines in the north-east ward. Simon Cerle and William Offorde are two others who are listed dining in hall with Brown and Norton, and working on many of the same projects.[26]

Set against this group of masons who, if not all natives of Oxford, were based in the city and spent the rest of their working lives there, is a number of itinerants more closely attached to Wynford and Herland, who seem to have been brought to New College for specific purposes, but who later moved on with them to other commissions. Thomas Maidstone must have been one of these—and was perhaps the father or brother of the John Maidstone responsible for hanging the bells, in the tower accounts of 1404.[27] Another, John Sampson, is of particular importance, despite what seem to be only spasmodic visits to New College between 1388 and 1396. When summoned before the Oxford justices on 15 March 1391, for receiving wages above the rates fixed by the Statute of Labourers, he was not fined like Norton and the others, because he was reported to be 'a master mason in freestone and capable and skilled in that art and in carving, and because on account of the high discretion and knowledge of that art, the wages of such a mason cannot be assessed in the same way as the wages of masons of another grade and status'.[28] This unusual justification of Sampson's claim (and the description of him as a carver) implies that he may have been responsible for at least some of the sculptural decoration of the college— including the three Annunciation groups of the main gatehouse and muniment tower, and (much better preserved) the magnificent series of corbels supporting the timbers of the hall and chapel roof (Plates 19–21).

Like Wynford's team of masons, Herland's carpenters at New College worked for him on other commissions, and do not seem to have been based solely at Oxford. The presence of 'duo carpentarii de Estamstede' dining in hall with Wynford, Herland and others on Lady Day, 1388, indeed suggests a connection with the earliest of all Wykeham's posts in the royal service, as clerk of the works at Easthampstead.[29] These two un-named craftsmen may have been William Ickenham, father and son, who were amongst the most important figures in the early part of the building of New College and who probably, as their name implies, came from Middlesex.

William Wys, who was the chief contractor for the woodwork of the bell-tower and cloisters in 1397–1400 was, according to Warden Woodward, sent from Winchester by the Founder, and this may well be so, since he was paid by Winchester College for the roofs of Heston and Isleworth churches in 1398. Another carpenter, known simply as Adam the Joiner, deserves mention since he was based in London, acting as the rent-collector for the college's estates there. From the bursars' roll for 1398–9 he is known to have ridden down to Oxford to measure work already done on the vestry and the tower, and also to have made cupboards and an altar for the chapel. Between 1400 and 1406 he was concerned with (and probably made) the canopy over the high altar.[30]

A number of other craftsmen are listed as dining in hall frequently between 1388 and about 1402, but their exact roles are nowhere specified and unless great advances are made in the study of masons' and carpenters' marks there is little hope of being able to identify their individual contributions to the remaining fourteenth-century college buildings.

4. A TOUR OF THE FOUNDER'S BUILDINGS

After six hundred years of existence, 'New' might seem an ill-chosen nickname for William of Wykeham's college. Yet from a historical and architectural point of view, it is as accurate and apt as when it was first coined. Novelty was the keynote of the buildings designed for Wykeham by Wynford, Herland and Yevele, and the formidable list of 'firsts' which they achieved here, together with the slavish imitation of so many later college builders, proves that New College was indeed a point of new departure for both universities. Here was conceived the first fully developed quadrangle plan, the first hall and chapel to be placed back to back in one range, the first T-shaped chapel, the first cloister and bell-tower, the first gate-tower with the first warden's lodgings to be placed over it, the first typical arrangement of mixed senior and junior fellows' rooms—and, as if this were not enough, the earliest surviving Perpendicular architecture in Oxford, and the first substantial building in the city to be faced entirely with dressed stone.

Before starting on a tour of the individual buildings, to see how these ideas were conceived, it is worth considering the plan as a whole, with the aid of two bird's-eye views, which help to establish the exact form of the fourteenth-century college: that in Warden Thomas Chaundler's manuscript drawn between 1461 and 1465, the earliest known representation of the college (Plate 2), and that engraved by David Loggan in 1675, just before the major seventeenth-century alterations to the buildings were begun (Plate 3).[31]

Perhaps the most important of all Wykeham's innovations is now taken so much for granted, that it has become a cliché of college architecture—the idea of a quadrangle including all the essential buildings for the life of the foundation: the chapel, hall, library and fellows' quarters catering for the daily needs of all its members, and the muniment tower, bursary and warden's lodgings for their governance. It is true that this idea had already been suggested by the gradual, and somewhat haphazard, growth of the buildings at Merton, and by the much smaller quadrangle already built at Corpus Christi, Cambridge. But the sheer scale of the New College quadrangle, housing seventy fellows as opposed to Merton's twenty-five (at that time more than all the rest of the Oxford colleges and halls put together), proclaimed an architectural venture of an altogether different scope.[32]

The buildings of New College, again like those of many of the larger early medieval monasteries, display a remarkable balance between functional and purely visual requirements. Practically no one exterior feature of the Founder's work is symmetrical: the gatehouse is for instance not in the centre of the west range, nor quite opposite the archway to the garden, while its otherwise regular elevations are off-balanced by the prominent stair-turret to the roof, placed to one side; no attempt was made to disguise the difference in size between the windows of chapel and hall, or even to build the garden archway immediately below the central window of the library in the east range. None of this, however, would have seemed in the least strange to contemporaries. Symmetry was never one of the principal aims of builders in an age when the greatest projects were often embarked upon without any thought as to how they would be finished.

Instead of following without deviation a master-plan agreed on at the outset, Wynford and Herland were probably influenced first of all by the shape of the site, then by the purely practical dictates of the Founder, and only finally by visual and aesthetic considerations. Their starting point (as with monastic buildings) would have been the east–west axis necessary for the building of the chapel. By placing the combined chapel and hall range with its precious stained-glass windows just inside the city wall, and parallel with it, they gave it the strongest position from the point of view of defence, while at the same time giving the quadrangle on the south protection from the weather. At Winchester, where the limitations of the site were not so strict (and where the lessons of New College had perhaps been learned), the entrance gatehouse was placed in the south range of the quadrangle, opposite the hall and chapel, and with an outer courtyard beyond it. The Founder's decision at New College not to have a long street elevation on the south, with a central gatehouse, like the slightly later façades of All Souls and Lincoln, may have been partly due to the narrowness of Queen's Lane, preventing anything but a sharply angled view, and making the entrance tower less imposing than it now is. It may partly also have been for reasons of defence: the city wall was still of course maintained in earnest, and provided protection on the north and east, while the high stone wall along Queen's Lane (prominent in the foreground of Chaundler's drawing), and the blank south and west walls of the cloisters, presented an almost equally stern visage towards the city itself. At all events the approach to the gatehouse down the narrow canyon of New College Lane, between great cliffs of masonry (Plate 39), still causes surprise, and was one of the few features of Wykeham's foundation not to be followed by later Oxford colleges.

The question remains—how far was the design of the college based on purely utilitarian principles, and how far thought out in visual or aesthetic terms? Inside the quadrangle itself the function of each part of the building is made more or less apparent by its fenestration. There is for instance no attempt (as there would have been in the seventeenth or eighteenth centuries) to give the chapel and hall similar windows, thus disguising the difference in both their floor levels and lighting requirements. Similarly the muniment tower, where all the college's valuables were stored, is distinguished by its arrow-slits, and the library by its row of four-light traceried windows, taller and more closely spaced than those of the fellows' rooms. Many features of the internal construction too, like the solid stone wall built at the southern end of the library, to prevent fire spreading from the neighbouring fellows' quarters (and the fact that the conduit chamber immediately below the library was one of the only chambers not provided with a fireplace) show the masons' attention to practical detail at every stage.

But although functional needs determined the planning and many of the details of the buildings, Wynford's masons cannot be accused of abandoning merely visual considerations. On the contrary they calculated extremely subtle effects within the limits imposed by the site and by the Founder's requirements. What might for instance have been a serious imbalance between the crushing weight of the hall and chapel on the north and the low two-storey chambers in the other ranges was to a great extent overcome by placing the even taller muniment tower at the angle between them, with the lesser entrance tower performing much the same role on the other side. Nor was the fenestration itself in any way haphazard: the four-light traceried windows of the library were exactly answered by those of the warden's hall in the opposite range, while the unity of the quadrangle as a whole was advanced still further by the windows of the fellows' chambers and studies. In their original form these set up a subtle rhythm of concentric arches, though strictly related to the different disposition of the ground and first-floor plans (Fig. c). A happier combination of form and function could hardly be found.

One final innovation of a general nature should be mentioned here, since it stemmed from aesthetic at least as much as practical considerations. Previous Oxford buildings had generally been executed in coral rag, the exceptionally weather-resistant rough stone found locally and so called because it consisted of the fossilised remains of coral reefs. The thirteenth-century city wall had been built of this rubble stone, and the sections that remain, bordering the college

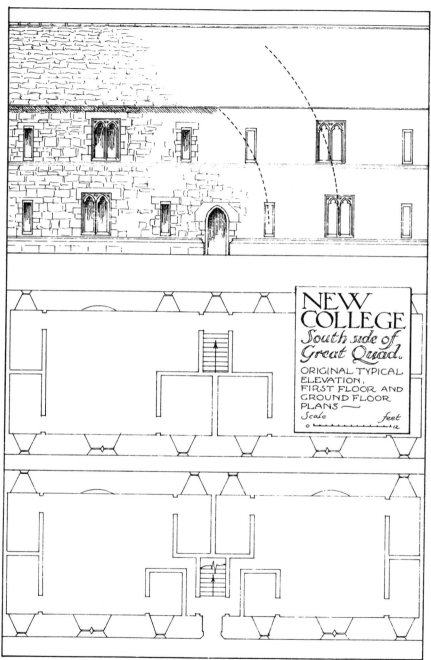

Within the figure:

NEW
COLLEGE
South side of
Great Quad.

ORIGINAL TYPICAL
ELEVATION,
FIRST FLOOR AND
GROUND FLOOR
PLANS —
Scale   feet
0 _____ 12

Fig. c Plan and elevation of fellows' chambers.

garden, still very rarely need attention. Freestone, used for window and door surrounds and for any carved detail, came from further afield, mostly from near Chipping Norton.[33] The accounts for the bell-tower and cloisters at New College record the earliest known use in Oxford of Headington hardstone for walling—a stone capable of being squared and coursed, unlike coral rag, and presenting a far neater appearance, as well as being easily obtained locally. Headington stone used in this way was admirably tough, and indeed the mason's toolmarks can still be clearly seen on the outside walls of the cloisters after almost six hundred years. However, the Founder also used rubble walling where it would not normally be seen: for instance on the north side of the chapel next to the city wall, and on the back of the south quadrangle range facing Queen's Lane. He also wisely continued to obtain freestone from the Cotswolds for carved detail, particularly from the quarries at Taynton, Burford and Barrington: he perhaps had first-hand knowledge of the former through Richard of Taynton, his assistant clerk of works at Windsor in the 1360s. Later, in the seventeenth and eighteenth centuries, freestone from Headington was used throughout the Oxford colleges in preference to Taynton, with disastrous long-term results, but the use of dressed Headington hardstone as the main building material of New College established an important precedent for the later triumphs of the Perpendicular at Oxford.

The Chapel

A tour of the Founder's college ought to begin with the chapel, not only because it is the largest, but because Wykeham himself would have considered it the most important, single building, dominating and to a large extent dictating the form of all the rest. The chapel also has the distinction of being the most revolutionary of the college buildings in its planning, and the one that has therefore excited the most controversy. The main problem concerns the antechapel, in the form of a truncated nave, one bay wider than the choir each side, but only two bays in length (Plate 10). No precedents or analogies for this form can be found: college chapels before this date had consisted solely of rectangular choirs, and while it is true that Merton was planned from the beginning to have a nave and transepts, this was because Walter de Merton specifically intended it to combine the functions of a parish church with those of a college chapel. The nave was of course never built, but even in its half-completed form Merton cannot have influenced the antechapel of New College, since its transepts were not built until 1424, over thirty years too late. Nor can the side aisles of the antechapel at New College be described in any sense as 'transepts'—they are only half as wide as the choir, and their roofs run east to west (parallel with the main roof) rather than north to south. It is also significant that the Founder's statutes refer to the antechapel consistently as the 'nave'.

A case has been put forward for thinking that the Founder first intended a much longer (perhaps seven-bay) nave, but that he was unable at first to acquire the extra land necessary on the west.[34] The most convincing evidence in support of this theory is that the masonry of the west wall of the antechapel is not bonded in with the north and south walls (in contrast with the north-east and south-east corners), implying that work came to a temporary halt here at some stage, and that the west wall was built at a slightly later date. In the absence of detailed building accounts for the chapel and hall the exact course of events will probably never be known, but it seems likely that with only two bays of the nave completed it was very soon obvious (perhaps even by 1386 when the warden and scholars first entered the college) that this was an ideal arrangement: the main part of the chapel with the high altar used by the whole college and choristers for corporate worship, the antechapel used not only for private masses at the smaller nave altars which it contained, but also for the disputations of civil and canon jurists and theologians, the meetings of the fellows, and (as is still the custom) for the election of the warden. The planning of the chapel, reflecting these various uses, was one of the most influential of all New College's architectural innovations.

New College chapel was almost as much ahead of its time in style as in planning. Perpendicular tracery seems first to have appeared at Oxford in the Canterbury College buildings of 1364 (no longer in existence), but the Decorated style was still very much alive at the time New College was begun.[35] Queen's College chapel, built between 1377 and 1379, still for instance displayed typically flowing Decorated tracery. Wynford's gigantic chapel windows introduced the 'gridiron' pattern on a large scale for the first time; the tracery is still reticulated but it has been stiffened out and made rectilinear instead of curvilinear. No doubt this was partly to give the glazier a freer hand in his designs, but the tracery is still an all-important element of the exterior architecture unlike the more advanced 'gridiron' windows (of All Souls for instance) where the mason's tracery is reduced almost to a series of bars. Wynford's stepped buttresses crowned by tall crocketed pinnacles, and his string course above the windows punctuated by carved corbels, are the only decorative features of the exterior apart from the windows, but they nevertheless produce a feeling of richness, and look forward to the more ornate Perpendicular style of Richard Wynchcombe's Divinity School.

So much of the interior of the chapel has been altered since William of Wykeham's time that a great deal of imagination is needed to form a picture of its original appearance. The original shape of Hugh Herland's timber roof is hardest of all to determine, but it can safely be said that it was nothing like either Scott's present hammer-beam roof, which is too tall for the proportions of the chapel and which necessitated the raising in pitch of the whole roof, or his predecessor, Wyatt's, shallow plaster vault (Plates 12 and 14). Evidently Herland's roof was low-pitched and may have been exactly the same as the adjoining hall roof (though the original appearance of that too is unknown): Plot, writing in 1677, drew attention to 'several other *Roofs* in this *University* also well worth the noting, whereof some are *flat* or *under-pitched*, as the . . . *Roofs* of the *Chappels* and *Halls* at *Magdalen College* and *New College*', while Thomas Warton, writing about 1760, called 'the present rafterwork . . . by no means equal to the magnificence of the rest'.[36] If this 'rafterwork' was the original medieval structure (and no evidence of an earlier alteration has yet been found) then Herland's chapel roof was probably a tie-beam and not a wooden vault like that at Winchester, slightly lower-pitched than the hammer-beam at All Souls, and probably not dissimilar to Gilbert Scott's present hall roof.

The rest of the original woodwork by Herland's team of carvers has fared almost equally badly. Of the medieval rood screen only the arched central doors with much-restored open tracery survive, and of the stalls only the sixty-two misericords, and some of the elbow-rests. The misericords are, however, amongst the college's most important treasures (Plates 15–18). Some of them provide vivid illustrations of medieval life, like that which shows a doctor delivering a lecture, with a servant carrying his books, or another which shows scholars dressed in fashionable hose with daggers at the ready. Others are drawn from the widest range of historical legend, mythology and allegory: there are scenes from the life of St. Yvain (paralleled by misericords as far away as Lincoln and Chester), a lively rendering of Jack and the Beanstalk, peacocks representing immortality (and ultimately derived from Roman mythology), harpies, female centaurs and hedgehogs with apples impaled upon their spines (referring, most graphically, to the deceits of the devil). Yet others rely on purely decorative invention, with many varieties of roses (alluding to the Founder's arms) and some fascinating architectural details, including oriels, latticed windows and towers with portcullises. One of the most charming was evidently intended as an allegory of New College itself: a bishop, presumably Wykeham, welcoming four scholars at the entrance to a walled town filled with sumptuous Gothic buildings, whence they emerge on the other side dressed respectively as a cardinal, an archbishop, a monk and a doctor.[37]

The sixty-two misericords probably represent all the stalls originally provided, despite the fact that there were to be seventy scholars. From the statutes it is clear that on feastdays, when the whole society attended, junior and probationary scholars were to stand in front of the stalls. The lay-clerks, singing priests and choristers also stood in a group below the screen and there were therefore no stalls facing eastwards as there are now—the warden and subwarden occupied those nearest the altar on the south and north sides respectively.

Just as the rood screen with its tiers of carved wooden figures must have been an obvious target for the sixteenth-century iconoclasts, so the stone statues of the medieval reredos were systematically destroyed, and the empty niches plastered over to prevent any easy return to idolatry. Wyatt's eighteenth-century plaster niches, converted into stone during the following century, were modelled on what was found behind this plaster wall, and there is no reason to doubt the general accuracy of the scheme—apart from the topmost section, included only by virtue of Scott's higher-pitched roof. Interestingly Wyatt recorded finding 'deep ultramarine blue' paint on the backs of the niches, with the carved work (the crocketed canopies and pedestals) 'richly gilt'.[38] Garish as it might seem to modern taste the woodwork, including the roof, would no doubt also have been painted in striking colours.

The only surviving medieval sculpture from the reredos is a series of five scenes from the life of the Virgin, originally placed directly above the high altar and now (in a badly mutilated state) on one wall of the song room, north of the chapel. Despite the smashed hands of the figures, and other damage incurred when they were plastered over in the sixteenth century, something of the power and directness of the medieval sculptor's art is still discernible. The magnificent carved stone corbels which support the roof timbers (here and in hall) were the only medieval sculptures inside the chapel to escape the iconoclasts, partly because they were too high to be reached easily, partly because, like the misericords, they were considered more or less secular in subject. As at Winchester they represent a series of alternating kings and bishops, a scheme later copied in the north transept at Merton, the chapel at All Souls and the hall at Magdalen. The New College corbels are of exceptional quality, however, with portrait-heads characterised perhaps to a greater extent than in any other contemporary English series (Plates 19–21). Mystery still surrounds both the carver, and the identity of most of the twelve kings and sixteen bishops represented. The two bishops flanking the west window are almost certainly William of Wykeham and Archbishop Courtenay of Canterbury, and Henry II and III, Edward III and Richard II have also been fairly convincingly identified—but these are the exceptions.[39]

The iconography and authorship of the medieval stained glass is much easier to establish, despite the fact that less than half of it survives intact. Much has already been written on the subject and here it is only necessary to summarise the main conclusions.[40] The great west window was (like the east window at Winchester) devoted to a Tree of Jesse, with a 'Doom' shown in the tracery lights above; the two flanking windows and those on the side walls of the antechapel (north and south) thence provided two different approaches to Christ—in the lower lights twenty Old Testament figures, from Adam and Eve to Moses; and in the upper lights, twenty prophets, from Jeremiah to Habbakuk, holding scrolls and messianic texts. After the Old Dispensation, the twelve Apostles representing the New Dispensation appeared in the upper lights of the two east windows of the antechapel. It is important to remember that altars stood under each of these windows: hence their lower lights contained four crucifixes, each flanked by the Blessed Virgin and St. John. The eighty main lights of the choir (or body of the chapel) were filled with single figures of saints and martyrs beneath canopies. The tracery lights of all the windows represented the nine orders of angels—seraphim, cherubim, powers, thrones and so on—

except for the great west window, with its 'Doom', the north-east window of the choir with a group of the Wise Virgins, and the two east windows of the antechapel, showing respectively the Coronation of the Blessed Virgin (south-east), and William of Wykeham kneeling before the Trinity (north-east).

Only the crucifixes appear to have been smashed as a result of the sixteenth-century visitations, and the loss of so much of the remaining glass is made the more tragic by the fact that it occurred in the eighteenth century, not long before its preservation would have been assured. In the choir none of the main lights has survived intact, though a few fragments of old glass were re-used in the windows on the south side 'restored' by William Price between 1735 and 1740. Otherwise only the tracery lights are original. Reynolds's west window is of course wholly eighteenth-century, though some parts of the original (removed by William Peckitt in 1765) survive in one of the choir aisles of York Minster. The other antechapel windows are still filled with fourteenth-century glass, although even here there has been some rearrangement, several missing patriarchs and prophets in the south and south-west windows having been replaced by saints and bishops from the choir, and missing parts of the crucifixes made up with other miscellaneous fragments. The tracery lights here again remain intact.

Despite this the stained glass in the antechapel remains one of the college's greatest possessions, hardly equalled at this date both in its design and in its technical accomplishment (Plates 22–5). The statuesque style of the main canopied figures is ideally suited to the form of Wynford's early 'gridiron' Perpendicular tracery, and in many respects more satisfying than the later, scenic style of the glass at All Souls, where the wider-spaced mullions allowed the glazier greater freedom.

It has been suggested that the scheme chosen for the glass was based on a later adaptation of the early eleventh-century *Liber Vitae* of New Minster, Winchester (otherwise known as Hyde Abbey), or some similar text emanating from the Founder's diocese.[41] Many of the more obscure saints represented—Abundius, Anastasia, Columbanus or the martyrs John and Paul—seem for instance to have appeared only because their relics were preserved at Winchester. But if this is so, the text would also have drawn on far older sources such as the 'Golden Legend'—the Greek treatise of the fifth or sixth century A.D., which first put forward the theory of the nine orders of angels.

There is no doubt at all as to the author of the New College glass. Thomas Glazier of Oxford, who made the east window of Winchester College chapel, including his own diminutive self-portrait as a kneeling figure, appears constantly in the New College hall books from 1386 until his death in 1427. His first appearance was at one of the two great Gaudes, which Wynford, Herland and Yevele attended; thereafter he dined five times in 1387–8, six times in 1388–9, approximately four times every year from 1390 to 1398, and once or twice a year after that—providing a valuable record of his progress on this important and time-consuming commission. Thomas's true identity and his origins are, however, more difficult to establish. A possibility is that he was the 'Thomas Francleyn, glazier' who, in the company of one John Tame of Henley, dined at New College with the fellows in 1401. After his death in 1427, Thomas was succeeded in the college accounts by John Glazier, who could in turn well be the 'John Frankelen, *als* Glasier, of Oxford', recorded in connection with New College in a case tried by the Chancellor's Court in 1449.[42]

Even if more was discovered about Thomas Glazier, it is unlikely that his exact role in the creation of the windows would be made much clearer. He undoubtedly carried out the major part of the work, presumably employing one Simon Glazier and 'Hykenham glazier' (perhaps a relation of the family of carpenters), who are the only others to appear in the New College accounts—in 1387 and shortly afterwards. But the design may on the other hand have been made by the mysterious Herebright of Cologne, who worked for William of Wykeham at Farnham Castle and Esher Place in 1393, and who is thought to have designed the Winchester College glass in the same year.[43] Continental influences are certainly apparent in the New College windows, as in the portrait heads of the carved stone corbels— and it would be fitting if these rare examples of the International Gothic style in England were due to Wykeham's employment of skilled foreign designer-craftsmen.

The Cloisters

It has already been seen that the bell-tower and cloisters (Plate 9) were built as an afterthought, at least a decade after the completion of the main college buildings surrounding the quadrangle—giving expression to the new extra-parochial status Wykeham had obtained for his college. Like many other features of his foundation, they obviously followed monastic precedent: the cloisters intended for processions on feastdays, and for a burial ground. This change of plan accounts for the rather awkward narrow passageway between the chapel and cloisters, for it would not have been possible to build the cloisters directly against the west wall of the chapel without the steeply pitched roof blocking the lower lights of the chapel windows. A more serious anomaly in the design of the cloisters themselves was the even number of bays provided on each side, so that the openings onto the lawn could not be central. Nor was any attempt made to conceal this, for the tracery of the open arches is of a quite different (more elaborate) pattern from the others. The diagonal buttresses in the four corners of the cloisters are also squashed awkwardly between the flanking arches, which could well have been spaced further apart. These irregularities, attributed by Warden Smith simply to 'medieval haphazardness',[44] may also be explained by the fact that Wynford is nowhere mentioned in the bell-tower and cloisters accounts and that the master-mason apparently in sole charge was his subordinate in the earlier building operations, William Brown. Wynford may well have furnished the original design for the construction and for the tracery of the arches, whose mouldings are characteristic of his work elsewhere,[45] but have left the execution (and the final details) to Brown.

The carpentry similarly seems to have been entrusted to William Wys, although Hugh Herland visited the college in 1399 and must almost certainly have given the initial design for the superb roof of the cloisters. The slender arched joists, simple, yet extraordinarily effective both visually and structurally, make the destruction of his hall and chapel roofs the more regrettable. The original stone tiles of the roof came from Stonesfield in the Cotswolds, though they have been often renewed since, and the present tiles, dating from about 1945, are from Hunters Quarry near Naunton, not far away.

The bell-tower, not finished until 1405, is functional and well-proportioned rather than an ambitious showpiece like William Orchard's later tower at Magdalen. There are at the same time strangely few close stylistic precedents for it. Yevele's tower at Westminster (of 1365) and his clock tower at St. Albans are of the same basic form, but the square-headed windows to the belfry are closer to the domestic than to the ecclesiastical architecture of the day. None of the original five bells survives, though some of the present ten, dating from the late seventeenth and early eighteenth centuries, may be recastings of the originals.

The Hall

If the cloisters were very obviously based on monastic precedent, the hall was built on strictly secular lines—indeed the Founder's statutes describe it as being 'raised above ground like a solar'. The consequent difference in height between it and the chapel allowed room for chambers below the hall (originally choristers' and lay clerks' rooms, with a fellows' set at the western end) and also brought the windows down to a much lower level on the inside. These tall two-light windows are close in style to Yevele's work, and comparable in particular with the lower windows of the tower of Southwark Cathedral (which was then a priory, under the jurisdiction of William of Wykeham's diocese); they were evidently filled with glass, for in 1402–3 Thomas Glazier was paid for three new panes, and for repairing three others.[46] The lower lights would probably have contained simple patterned quarries and the upper ones heraldic glass, of which a few fragments survive—moved in 1865 to the windows above the staircase to hall, in the west wall of the muniment tower. These consist of Wykeham's own shield, with those of St. George and St. Patrick, and the quartered arms of England and France.

The interior of hall today (Plate 36) is further from its original appearance than one might suspect: the screen and panelling are Tudor, the paved floor eighteenth century, the stained glass and the roof mid-Victorian. Hugh Herland's original roof was a low-pitched tie-beam construction, probably very similar to (if not the same as) his chapel roof, with the exception of an open louvre in the centre to take the smoke from the central hearth. This roof appears to have been ceiled in 1533–5, when the linenfold panelling was introduced. But worse was to befall, for in 1786 an entirely new one was constructed under James Wyatt's direction, with a flat plaster ceiling below it. The present timber roof was designed by Gilbert Scott in 1865 and, although the remaining evidence was too slight to reconstruct the original, is by far the most successful of Scott's attempts to 'restore' the fabric of the college. Probably only in one respect does it differ substantially from

Herland's intentions: Chalmers, writing in 1810,[47] gave the original height of the hall roof as forty feet, ten less than Scott's, and if this is so the main timbers must have sprung almost from the level of the ten finely carved medieval corbels. The corbels themselves, representing four kings and six bishops, continue the theme of those in the chapel, and are another argument for supposing that the same type of roof was intended for the hall as for the chapel.

The statutes make it clear that there was originally a much smaller · high table than is now usual in college halls, seating only the eight senior fellows. The others sat at two long tables down each side, with the stone seats in the window embrasures used by readers. The juniors sat at a separate table in the centre, probably in the upper part of the hall, and the higher college servants at another on the other side of the central hearth; the lower servants and choristers were responsible for serving at these tables. The hall was used for dinner, the main meal of the day, at 11 a.m., supper at 5 p.m., and for 'potations' after curfew on feastdays, when the statutes allowed the seniors to entertain their younger brethren with 'poems, chronicles of kingdoms and the wonders of this world'—a marvellously Chaucerian sidelight on the life of Wykeham's college in its early days.[48]

The hall may originally have been decorated with frescoes, but in 1452–3 painted hangings were brought from London and set up on rails around the walls, perhaps at the instigation of Warden Chaundler, who succeeded in the latter year. Fragments of these hangings may possibly have survived the later installation of the panelling, for Antony Wood records 'pictures of many candles or flambois in the windows, and "fiat lux" written under . . . set up by . . . Dr. Chaundler as a rebus of his own name', adding that when the French Ambassador visited New College in 1593 and was told of their history he replied that there 'might rather have been written *Fiant tenebrae*, because the painting darkened the Hall'.[49]

The Kitchen, Buttery and Pantry

The raising of the hall above a lower storey of chambers meant that it was separated from the kitchen on the east by a long and steep flight of stairs—probably only felt to be a disadvantage in modern times, when the warmth of the food and the comfort of those who served it became for the first time important considerations. The kitchen as a separate block outside the main quadrangle spared the rest of the college a great deal of noise and smell and a potential fire risk. Moreover there was plenty of space immediately to the south (where the garden quad now is) for the untidy outhouses, woodsheds and larders necessary, a direct approach to these through the 'Non-licet' gate from Queen's Lane (instead of using the main gate of the college), and easy access to the garden, which until the sixteenth century was entirely devoted to growing produce for the kitchen. Here also stood the main well, still clearly shown in Loggan's view of 1675, which served the kitchen and the garden, leaving the conduit in the arch below the library for the use of the rest of the college.

The immensely thick outside walls of the kitchen and some of its windows are original, almost certainly dating from before 1386. But the great timber wagon roof is undoubtedly the finest original feature, with its double row of arched braces to the rafters made up of vast blackened beams (Plate 34). Hugh Herland must have been responsible for the design, and while it is quite different in form from his original chapel and hall roofs, its beauty makes one regret their loss the more keenly. There was a circular open louvre in the centre of the roof (as opposed to the rectangular one in the hall), which survived well into the eighteenth century. But a document of 1402 makes it clear that as well as a central hearth there was a bread-oven in the north-east corner and two pots each fixed on the north and south walls, with smoke apparently escaping from the windows high above.[50] There were also windows on the east wall, but these were blocked up in the early sixteenth century when two large fireplaces and a chimney with a double flue were added here to replace the open central hearth. Parts of their arched frames can still be seen in the exterior masonry of the east wall.

Either side of the central stair between hall and kitchen lay two small rooms one above the other: respectively the butteries on the north, and pantries on the south, connected by a spiral staircase in the north-west corner. No original features of these rooms survive but the staircase also gives access to the beer cellar, built between the low buttery and the city wall and this is still intact, now appropriately used as a bar. The cellar is an impressive vaulted chamber with a central octagonal pillar, from which spring deeply moulded ribs, forming a star pattern at the four corners (Plate 33). Not as lofty, or as ornately decorated, as its equivalent at Winchester, which is part of the main hall range, it is nevertheless admirably placed for security, for ease of communication from hall, and for that constant low temperature necessary for the storage of alcohol.

The Muniment Tower and Bursary

The monumentality of the great tower at the north-east angle of the main quad comes as a surprise to visitors who imagine it was used simply for storing the college's documents. In reality this building, placed at the very centre of New College, also played a central part, practically as well as symbolically, in the life of the community. The tower, perhaps the least changed of all the Founder's buildings in the last six hundred years, contains four rooms, the two upper chambers occupying the whole space, save for a spiral staircase in one corner, the two lower rooms half this size to allow for the staircase to hall on the north. According to the very detailed description of the muniment tower given in Wykeham's 50th statute,[51] the rooms were used, in ascending order, as follows: the ground floor (secured by two locks) for the brass, pewter, and less valuable plate regularly used in hall; the second (with three locks) for the chests containing the college's title deeds and leases, and for the college seal; the third (with four locks) for the gold and silver used only on feastdays in hall, for the Founder's statutes themselves, and for the college's fund moneys; the highest room (with yet two more locks) for the vestments, relics, ornaments and plate used in the chapel. Today the two upper rooms are still used to house the college archives, while the ground-floor room has been adapted as a museum to display some of the gold and silver plate, relics of the Founder and the great seal itself: so that the tower still to a large extent fulfils its original function.

Enormously elaborate precautions were taken with the keys to the rooms in the muniment tower, essential in the days before banking or paper money lessened the dangers of malpractice. No less than six people were needed to take the great seal of the college out of custody: the three bursars to open the door of the room, and the warden, subwarden and dean to open the three locks of the small chest in which it was kept. Some of the medieval oak chests still remain in the two upper rooms, where the original encaustic tiles are also largely intact. The vaulted ceilings here give a suitable feeling of strength, with plain but deeply chamfered ribs providing sharp contrasts of light and shade (Plate 31).

The same is true of the more elaborate lierne vault above the stairway to hall (built into the lower half of the tower) where the ribs are moulded and meet at the centre of the arches in a distinctive pattern of four diamonds (Plate 32). This opening and closing of the liernes 'scissor-wise' has been described as a relic of the Decorated style, but it should perhaps rather be seen as an early precursor of the fan-vault, with the emphasis on the seven ribs springing from each corbel and the shallower, almost independent, ornament at the centre.[52]

The administration of the muniment tower and its contents was undertaken by the bursar, whose office immediately adjoined it on the ground floor, under the north end of the library and to the left of the conduit arch. Here from the main quadrangle tenants came to pay their rents and fellows to collect their pittances and their allowances of cloth, while from the kitchen and its outbuildings on the east those servants and tradesmen using the 'Non-licet' gate could also come to settle their accounts and claim their livery. Nothing of the original interior survives apart from a cavity in the immensely thick walls, used as a safe.[53] But the late fifteenth-century roundel in one of the windows, showing a peewit holding a string of beads and the motto 'redde quod debes' (Fig. d), is a poignant reminder of some of the financial transactions made here during the early life of the college.

Fig. d Peewit in window of Old Bursary.

The Library

On the first floor, above the bursary, the conduit arch and the first of the fellows' chambers (to the right of the arch), lay the library, originally lit by eighteen large traceried windows (Plate 58). Built initially to contain the 260 volumes given by the Founder—a substantial collection for this date—it was the first library in either university to be fully incorporated into a college plan. Bishop Reade's slightly earlier library at Merton was for instance a separate L-shaped building outside the main quadrangle, and it was not until Peterhouse at Cambridge followed New College's example in 1431 that the idea became commonplace.[54]

The library was originally approached by only one door, placed next to the south-west buttress of the muniment tower and leading up a steep flight of stairs to the northern end of the room. The books, the college's most valuable possession after its gold and silver plate and vestments, were also guarded by a series of three locks to the quadrangle door, carefully specified in the statutes: one key was to be held by the dean, and one by the bursar, while the third lock—known delightfully as the 'cliket'—could be opened by any of the fellows.

The original form of the library windows (replaced by sashes in the eighteenth century) can be judged by Loggan's engravings (Plates 3 and 4) and by the far left-hand window seen from the quadrangle, whose stone tracery was replaced about 1950 at the instigation of Warden Smith—an experiment not finally adopted for the other windows of the room. The glazier's account of 1402 reveals that the upper parts of these windows had fixed glass panes, while below the transoms the glass was set into removable iron frames, with wooden shutters. Thus when the shutters were in use, against the cold, there would still be enough light to read by from the upper halves. Each of the deep canted window recesses, whose original form was again uncovered in 1949 by the removal of the eighteenth-century plasterwork, contained a broad window seat (probably the only form of seating in the room), and between the windows were lectern-shaped desks, 5 feet 6 inches high, placed endways against the walls and projecting out into the room. The books were kept on shelves below each desk, secured by chains with links and swivels comparable with those found at Hereford Cathedral.[55]

Some of the medieval oak boards at either end of the library were also found under the eighteenth-century floor during the restoration of 1949–50, but the area in the centre, over the conduit arch, appears always to have been tiled. Warden Smith explained this as an example of medieval building practice, where boards were always laid on timber joists and tiles onto stone.[56] But this odd feature is more probably explained by a change of function, the lectern desks standing only on the timber parts of the floor, leaving the central tiled area completely free. The beams of the steeply-pitched roof were originally open to the room, probably giving much the same effect as the roof of the cloisters today, and a ceiling was not inserted here until the mid-fifteenth century.

The Fellows' Chambers and the Long Room

At King's Hall, Cambridge, most of the junior members are recorded as being housed in the main college rather than in separate hostels as early as 1370,[57] so William of Wykeham cannot, for once, be regarded as a complete innovator in this respect, even though he seems to have introduced the system to Oxford. What was entirely new, however, was the rule laid down in his statutes that seniors and juniors, who both shared the status of 'socii', or fellows, should also share rooms. The idea behind this was that the masters would have close control and exert a stronger influence on their youngers, all too easily led astray by the corrupt owners of the crowded and insanitary hostels which filled the medieval town. The more or less identical plan to which all the lodgings conformed, and their subtly related elevations looking over the quadrangle has already been discussed; in the reconstructed ground and first-floor plans, illustrated on p. 168, the large central rooms lit by the bigger windows were the 'common chambers' in which the occupants of the sets would have slept, each also having a small study to himself, partitioned off on one wall. The ground-floor rooms were designed for four fellows, but those on the first floor for only three: the upper part of the staircase taking up too much room to allow for a fourth study. Once again, this arrangement was to prove so successful that it was slavishly copied by later colleges, at Oxford and at Cambridge.[58]

As at Magdalen later in the fifteenth century, the beds were probably of two sizes, the smaller pushed under the larger when not in use, and kept in the centre of the room. The windows almost certainly did not contain glass originally, but solid wooden shutters held in position by bars would have afforded some protection from cold. Although no bills for decorative painting have survived it is likely that many of the rooms were frescoed, and that this was the origin of their curious names, which survived until at least the eighteenth century. Beginning at what is now staircase 1, in the south-west corner, and progressing eastwards these were: the Baptist's Head and the Crane's Dart; the Christopher and the Serpent's Head; the Rose and the Vine; the Green Post and the Vale; the Chamber of Three and the Conduit Chambers; and finally the Cock, placed under the west end of the hall, quite separate from the others.[59] The names of the three chambers occupying the eastern range were geographically descriptive. The Vale was probably a reference to the narrow passage adjoining it which gave access to the Long Room (containing the lavatories) in a separate building on Queen's Lane; the Chamber of Three with its staircase pushed further south than it should have been by the library, was the sole ground-floor set to have only three occupants; while the Conduit Chamber (actually under the southern end of the library) was called after the pump under the adjoining archway to the garden. The total complement of eleven ground-floor, and nine first-floor, rooms exactly accounted for the seventy fellows stipulated in the Founder's statutes.

The Long Room should itself be mentioned here. Completely detached from the quadrangle buildings, for reasons of hygiene, it lay alongside Queen's Lane, the only one of the college's buildings, apart from the warden's kitchen, not to be built either parallel or at right angles to the city wall. An L-shaped covered corridor by which it was approached is shown in Loggan (Plate 3), but this may have been a late fifteenth- or early sixteenth-century addition. The large first-floor room with an impressive tie-beam roof (Plate 35) contained the latrines, while the whole of the ground floor was occupied by an enormous cesspit. Plot, writing in 1677,[60] hoped it 'not improper . . . to mention a *structure*, commonly called the *Long-house*, I could not but note it as a Stupendious Piece of *Building*, it being so large and deep, that it has never been emptied since the Foundation of the College, which was above 300 years since, nor is it ever like to want it'. Sad to relate, this plausible story is not borne out by the fifteenth-century 'Computus' Rolls which do record the occasional cleaning out of the Long Room, for instance in 1485:[61] the proximity of the vegetable garden was perhaps not entirely fortuitous—yet another example of the rigorous logic which underlay the planning of the whole college. Earth closets were introduced on the ground floor in 1830, and bathrooms above in 1903, but by 1974-5, when the upper part was converted into a room for exhibitions and receptions, the Long Room must have had claims to be the oldest lavatory in the country still in use.

The Warden's Lodgings

This tour of the college ends where it began, at the main west gate of the college, over which lie the warden's lodgings, the earliest residence of a head of college still inhabited as such in either university. Once again the Founder's statutes established a wholly new principle; in earlier foundations such as Peterhouse, Cambridge, the master was at liberty to choose his own room from among the fellows' lodgings, and (as at Merton) dined in hall. Instead Wykeham decreed that 'the Warden . . . shall dwell apart and separate within the precincts of our College in a residence of his own, which we have provided for him and his household over the west gate . . . in order that the Fellows and Scholars may not be disturbed and annoyed in their own pursuits by those varied occupations which the Warden . . . will undertake in transacting the business of the College'.[62] Like the abbot of a large monastery, the warden was seen as the college's one contact with the outside world, and his duties included lodging and entertaining a constant stream of visitors, and travelling the country to inspect the college's different properties. For this he needed his own dining hall and kitchen, guest rooms, stables and paddock.

The warden's kitchen (again a potential fire risk) was a detached building of irregular shape fitted in at the north-west corner of the small triangular plot just outside the main gate—formed by the truncated section of the original New College Lane. It was evidently built before 1395, when detailed building records for the college first became available, but it is frustrating that its exact date is unknown. The little triangular courtyard between the kitchen and the rest of the warden's lodgings still exists (now covered with a skylight), though the heightening and subsequent alteration of all the buildings round it makes it impossible to tell what was the original means of communication between hall and kitchen. Traces of the great hearth at the southern end of the kitchen are still clearly visible, and the warden's buttery may have been partitioned off at the other end. Originally the porter's lodge lay on the south side of the main gate, with a small staircase leading up to the warden's lodgings beyond it.

The position of the warden's hall immediately over the main gate of the college was another immensely influential feature of Wykeham's building—copied at Lincoln (*c.* 1430), Exeter (1432), Magdalen (1475), and many others right up to Wadham in 1610, though curiously never imitated at Cambridge. The advantages of the arrangement were obvious: from here the warden could keep strict surveillance over both

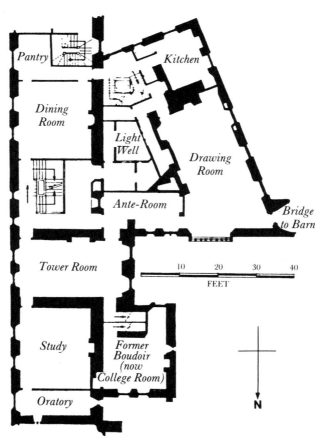

Fig. e Plan of Warden's Lodgings: first floor

the approach to the college and the quadrangle which was the hub of its life, just as from his oratory at the northern end of the lodgings he could look down into the antechapel and make sure that the masses or disputations being held there were conducted in a seemly manner. Originally the hall gave even more of an 'all-round' view than it does now—for two more windows, later blocked in by additional building, faced north and south at either end of the dais (the west end of the room), one surveying the passage between the cloisters and the west front of the chapel, the other overlooking the little triangular courtyard of the lodgings and the comings and goings of his own household and servants. Perhaps not until early nineteenth-century prison-planning and the so-called 'Panoptikon' was any building devised to give such comprehensive powers of surveillance.

The four main rooms of the original warden's lodgings still survive, though practically nothing of their medieval decoration remains. In the hall (Plate 41) only part of the base of the chimneypiece is fourteenth-century. The ceiling would almost certainly have had open beams and the walls frescoes or painted cloth hangings. The warden and his entire household took their meals here: his stewards, clerks and guests at a high table across the west end, the servants probably seated at two long refectory tables placed length-wise across the room—a miniature version of the main college hall. On certain feast days the warden was required to dine in hall itself, and when he did so was to notify the college cook in advance, requesting at the same time that better food (*epuli lautiores*) might be prepared, an indication of the elevated status Wykeham had in mind for the heads of his college. The custom was apparently maintained until Warden Spooner's retirement in 1925, A. H. Smith commenting ruefully that 'the difficulties of a later age have since led to [its] disuse'.[63]

Immediately above the warden's hall is his chamber, approached by a spiral staircase. Only the upper half of this staircase now survives, giving access to the roof of the tower, with a small door emerging under the squat pinnacle at its north-eastern corner. The warden's chamber itself was divided so as to provide a passage when extra rooms were built on either side of the tower in the fifteenth and sixteenth centuries. Originally it would have had four outside walls, and early wardens must have been thankful in winter that at least its chimneypiece shared the same flue as the fire in the hall, immediately below.

To the north of the warden's hall lay what is still his study, then lit by a tall oriel window, again shown prominently in Chaundler's drawing (Plate 2) just to the right of the gatehouse. This rested on a large carved boss, in the shape of an angel with outstretched wings bearing a shield, later moved to the adjoining south wall of the antechapel.[64] This sculptural decoration, combined with the two Annunciation groups on the walls of his chamber, differentiated the warden's from the fellows' lodgings, but a still more telling difference was the glazing of the windows—not only of the study oriel, but of the hall and oratory each side, and the ground-floor room to the north of the entrance archway (now the porter's lodge) which then also formed part of his apartments.

The oratory itself was a narrow room with a three-light tracery window almost its entire width at the east end, above the arch leading to the chapel and the cloisters. The reason for the size of this window was that an altar stood below it, and the window itself probably contained stained glass made by Thomas Glazier; open slits in the adjoining north wall gave a view down into the body of the antechapel. The partition wall between the study and oratory was removed by Warden Sewell in 1876, but later re-erected by Warden Smith in 1945.

For his frequent journeys to Winchester and the college's estates elsewhere, the statutes provided the warden with six horses and their upkeep at the college's expense. Probably by a stroke of luck rather than judgement, the southern half of the land which Wykeham had acquired in 1388–9 on the far side of the lane (primarily to build his cloisters and bell-tower) was just large enough to provide a paddock and sufficient stabling in the so-called warden's barn. The name is slightly misleading, for it fulfilled (as it does still) many different functions. The western half, approached through an arch at the north-west corner big enough to accommodate the largest haywain, contained the stables with a hayloft above; the splayed walls either side of the doors to the loft allowed them to swing right open, so that the hay and straw could be forked in without difficulty. The high gable at the west end served as a pigeon-house, another luxury to put the warden on the same social footing as an abbot, or lord of the manor. The eastern half of the barn, with a lower gate at the north-east corner, provided quarters for the groom and warden's servants on the ground floor, and guest rooms for strangers above—with their own latrine installed later in the fifteenth century behind a small blocked window still visible from the lane.

The Influence of Wykeham's Buildings

Given the scale of the Founder's building schemes, and the employment of large numbers of native Oxford masons and carpenters, it is scarcely surprising that New College was to have an overwhelming effect on later Oxford buildings of the fifteenth century. Apart from small colleges like Queen's Hall, built by William Brown, the master-mason for the bell-tower, the most obvious successors were All Souls and Magdalen, built by two archbishops, Chichele and Waynflete, who had both been at New College and who consequently took it as their model. There were of course differences in plan: in the smaller quadrangle at All Souls the hall was placed at right angles to the chapel, while the entrance tower was used to store the muniments; at Magdalen the cloisters were adapted to form the main quadrangle. But these were no more than conscious variations on the same plan, of which the essential features—in particular the T-shaped chapel—remained constant. The only major difference they, and all later Oxford colleges, displayed was the addition of a street front, even when (as at Lincoln) this was still unornamented and defensive in character, and faced onto a narrow lane.

The early Perpendicular style of the New College buildings, with its sparing use of ornament, was also to dominate Oxford architecture during the next century. In the reaction against Richard Winchcombe's north side of the Divinity School, in 1439 the new master-mason, Thomas Elwyn, was warned to avoid 'images, casements and fillets, and other idle quaintnesses' (*supervaeva curiositas*),[65] and the later austerity of Lincoln, Queen's Hall and others, can be seen as a return to Wykeham's principles. When elaborate ornament began to return at the end of the century, it was usually concentrated on one spot, such as the gatehouse of the early Tudor façade of Balliol, again on the same principle established by the Annunciation groups at New College.

Wykeham's influence was by no means confined to Oxford; his closest follower and most unquestioning admirer in the fifteenth century was Henry VI, whose twin colleges at Eton and King's, Cambridge, were directly inspired by Winchester and New College. This is clear not only in the King's frequent visits to both earlier foundations, and the increases he granted towards New College's endowment, but in his detailed instructions for his own buildings. In his so-called 'will' of 1448, the provision that King's should have a detached cloister to the west of the chapel, with a bell-tower to one side of it, was obviously derived from New College, while in the same year his second scheme for Eton stipulated a choir of 103 feet by 32 feet, exactly one foot longer and one foot narrower than New College chapel.[66] References to Wykeham's buildings and their measurements either to be followed or exceeded, abound in the surviving documents of the King's Works for these years, and it is significant that materials for the foundations of Eton, cloth for the scholars' gowns, and even its first headmaster, were all brought by Henry VI from Winchester.

Even allowing for the differences in style achieved in the intervening fifty years, and for the sophistication of Henry VI's Perpendicular, one can perhaps also sense a debt to Wykeham's own avoidance of 'idle ornament' in the King's instructions to Master Roger Keys, the mason at Eton in 1448 (and previously builder of the chapel at All Souls). Keys was to see that the chapel was 'replenysshed with goodely wyndowes and vautes leying aparte superfluite to grete curiouze werkes of entaille and besy moldyng'—in just the same spirit as Winchcombe had been rebuked for his Oxford Divinity School in the previous decade. One can safely say that, had it not been for Wykeham's example, the labour of the 'royal saint' might have been, if not in vain, then at least of quite a different order.

REFERENCES

1. R. A. Brown and H. M. Colvin, *History of the King's Works* (1963), vol. I, 162–5.
2. Smith, 5.
3. Harvey, 145, 180, 290, 311; E. A. Gee, 'Oxford Masons 1370–1530', *Archaeological Journal* (1952), vol. cix, 115.
4. *V.C.H.*, 155.
5. H. E. Salter, *Map of Medieval Oxford* (1934), map 3.
6. Wood, *Colleges*, 179.
7. Oxford City Library H5/2–3 (and a translation in N.C. MS. 14087); for disputes over the city walls see H. E. Bell, 'Longwall Papers', typescript in N.C. MSS. 10, 268, and *V.C.H.*, 144.
8. Oxford City Library H5/1.
9. E. A. Gee, op. cit., 60.
10. R. Willis and J. W. Clark, *Architectural History of the University of Cambridge* (1886), vol. III, 509; Rashdall and Rait, 31.

11. For the dating of the chapel glass, see John Harvey, 'The Wilton Diptych—a Re-examination', *Archaeologia* (1961), vol. xcviii, 21–8, reaching a rather different conclusion from Woodforde, 1–5; for the reredos, see Rashdall and Rait, 31; for the floor, *V.C.H.*, 145; and for the pinnacles, E. A. Gee, op. cit., 57.

12. N.C. MS. 9128; published in J. E. T. Rodgers (ed.), *Oxford City Documents* (Oxford Hist. Soc., 1891), 306–14.

13. N.C. MS. 2799 (Woodward's notebook entitled *Observata quaedam . . .*).

14. Brown and Colvin, op. cit., 162; influential early works assuming Wykeham acted as his own architect include C. R. Cockerell, 'The Architectural Works of William of Wykeham', *Proceedings of the . . . Archaelogical Institute* (1845–6) and Mackenzie Walcott, *William of Wykeham and his Colleges* (1852).

15. Harvey, 309; E. A. Gee, op. cit., 54.

16. For an early account of Wykeham's devotion to the Virgin, see Robert Lowth, *Life of William of Wykeham* (1758), 284–5; Statutes, rub. 63.

17. R. H. C. Davis, 'The Chronology of Perpendicular Architecture in Oxford', *Oxoniensia*, vols. xi/xii (1946–7), 80.

18. N.C. MS. 5527 (volume covering the years 1397 to 1418); the seneschal of hall was chosen from amongst the fellows, in rotation.

19. Harvey, 310; see also by John Harvey, *Henry Yevele* (2nd edn.) 1947, and 'Some Details and Mouldings used by Yevele', *Journal of the Society of Antiquaries*, vol. xxvii, 1947.

20. N.C. MS. 7333.

21. E. A. Gee, op cit., 65.

22. Harvey, 309.

23. Ibid., 301.

24. See p. 177 below.

25. Harvey, 44.

26. E. A. Gee, op. cit., 69, 115.

27. J. E. T. Rodgers (ed.), *Oxford City Documents* (Oxford Hist. Soc., 1891), 306 et seq.

28. Harvey, 239.

29. N.C. MS. 5527.

30. Harvey, 113.

31. Ed. M. R. James, *The Chaundler Manuscript*, Roxburghe Club (1906); David Loggan, *Oxonia Illustrata* (1675).

32. Rashdall and Rait, 86.

33. W. J. Arkell, *Oxford Stone* (1947), 38–9, 46–7.

34. E. A. Gee, op cit., 66–8.

35. R. H. C. Davis, op. cit., 78.

36. Robert Plot, *Natural History of Oxfordshire* (1677), 274; Anon (Thomas Warton), *Description of the City, College and Cathedral of Winchester* (*c*.1760), 25.

37. Francis W. Steer, *Misericords at New College, Oxford* (1973); see also G. L. Remnant, *A Catalogue of Misericords in Great Britain* (1969).

38. A. Chalmers, *A History of the Colleges . . . of Oxford* (1810), vol. i, 135.
39. Selby Whittingham, *Medieval Portrait Busts at New College, Oxford* (1973).
40. See Woodforde, 1–11, 67–93.
41. Ibid., 69.
42. Ibid., 7–9.
43. Herebright also painted an altarpiece for Old St. Paul's in 1398; R. H. C. Davis, op. cit., 80.
44. Smith, 58–60.
45. E.g. the gatehouse at Broughton Castle, near Banbury, built by the Founder's nephew, Sir Thomas Wykeham, about 1404.
46. N.C. MS. 7357 (from the *Computus Bursariorum*).
47. Chalmers, op. cit., i, 130.
48. Statutes, rub. 18.
49. N.C. MS. 7412; Wood, *History*, vol. ii, 256.
50. *V.C.H.*, 148, *n.* 95.
51. Quoted in full in Willis and Clark, op. cit., vol. iii, 476.
52. Jennifer Sherwood and Nikolaus Pevsner, *Oxfordshire* (Buildings of England series, 1974), 169; cf. R. H. C. Davis, op. cit. 85.
53. The ceiling must be Tudor, by comparison with that formerly in the warden's gallery, decorated with tin rosettes (pace *V.C.H.*, 148).
54. Willis and Clark, op. cit., vol. iii, 407–8. Below, ch. XI, p. 317.
55. Ibid., 422, where the Hereford chains are illustrated; two were found at New College.
56. Smith, 55.
57. A. B. Cobban, *The King's Hall, Cambridge* (1969).
58. E.g. the Old Court at Christ's College, Cambridge, as late as 1505–18; Willis and Clark, op. cit., vol. iii, 311–12.
59. Smith (pp. 50–1) puts the Vale incorrectly between the Serpent's Head and the Rose.
60. Plot, op. cit., 269
61. N.C. MS. 7399.
62. Willis and Clark, op. cit., vol. iii, 330; Statutes, rub. 11.
63. Smith, 42.
64. The present angel is a copy of the much-decayed original now at New College, Toronto; Sherwood and Pevsner, op. cit., 169.
65. R. H. C. Davis, op. cit., 78.
66. Brown and Colvin, op. cit., 271.

VI

Gains and Losses: the College Buildings, 1404–1750

GERVASE JACKSON-STOPS

1. THE FIFTEENTH AND SIXTEENTH CENTURIES: CHEQUER, THE LAW LIBRARY AND THE TUDOR ADDITIONS

With Wykeham's death in 1404, the buildings of New College were complete, a remarkable achievement compared with so many other half-finished foundations in both universities, and few major additions to this structure were found necessary during the next 250 years. Naturally, finishing touches still remained to be done, especially to the chapel, where a Purbeck marble floor was laid in 1411–12, and the altar steps were completed in 1418. The niches in the reredos were only gradually filled with sculpture, and further ornamentation was carried out in the second half of the century: more side altars were consecrated in the antechapel in 1461 (in addition to the six already mentioned there in 1455), and in 1470 the rood-beam was gilded.[1]

The sole addition to Wykeham's original buildings in the fifteenth century was the room known as Chequer, immediately behind the bursary, with the law library later built above it—now both part of the senior common room. Modest as this extension was, it was to have important consequences, both for the future development of the garden quad, and for the gradual segregation between seniors and juniors which the Founder had taken pains to avoid. While all the other main college buildings had been exactly suited to their purpose, it must soon have become clear (especially as further endowments and gifts of land came to the college) that the volume of business transacted by the bursary had been underestimated. One can well imagine that the keeping of accounts, the administration of the contents of the muniment tower, the collection of tenants' rents, and the doling out of the fellows' cloth and 'pittances', must have led to overcrowding and confusion in the small square room originally allotted to the bursary, under the library, and just to the north of the garden archway. In 1449, a larger rectangular room called the Exchequer (later shortened to 'Chequer') was therefore added to the east, outside the main quadrangle, and set back slightly to the north so as to obscure only one of the bursary's two east-facing windows.

As its name implies, the Chequer was chiefly used for outgoing payments and gifts made by the bursary, but because of its proximity to the kitchen the rather curious practice arose in the following century for the senior fellows to have their meals here together, rather than with the rest of the college in hall. Although expressly forbidden several times, for instance in Bishop Horne's visitation of 1576, this custom of foregathering in the Chequer continued, and led eventually to the formation of the senior common room itself—probably the earliest at Oxford. Nothing of the original interior of Chequer now survives, apart from the two window-frames in the south wall with two-light tracery, showing that its builder still rigorously adhered to the style of the Founder's work. The door to the left of them was intended to lead straight into the room, and the present passage and spiral staircase were partitioned off only during the nineteenth century.

The fifteenth century also saw important additions to the collection of books originally left to the college by the Founder. A ceiling was put into the library in 1445–6,[2] probably to give extra storage space under the rafters of the steeply-pitched roof, but later benefactions made an extension of the reading space itself necessary. The two principal donors were Thomas Beckington, Bishop of Bath and Wells from 1443 to 1465, and Hugh Sugar, a fellow of the college in 1435 and canon and treasurer of Wells from 1460 to 1489: both specifically gave law books, and it was Sugar who paid for these to be housed in a separate law library built above Chequer in 1480–1. Stained-glass panels with the arms of the two benefactors (unfortunately no longer in existence) were set into the east window of the new library, and that representing Sugar included in its inscription '. . . extruxit Bibliothecam librorum Judicorum' [sic].[3]

The building of the law library interfered with the existing structure to a greater extent than the addition of Chequer. Three east-facing windows at the north end of the Founder's library were rendered useless by it; the northernmost was converted into a door, but the tracery above it was retained, as were the complete frames of the other windows—the openings merely filled in with stone. Much later, in the seventeenth century, when bookcases were placed against this wall, these frames (and the doorway) were plastered over, and it was only during restoration in 1951 that they were again revealed (Plate 58). The new law library itself had no less than ten windows—five on the south (some of whose cinquefoil tracery and shutters still survive behind the present late seventeenth-century panelling), four on the north (the space for the fifth being blocked by one of the corner buttresses of the muniment tower), and one large window at the east end. No doubt it would have been arranged like a miniature version of the main library with lectern desks projecting at right angles between the windows. Two small cupboards for books survive on the east wall, but otherwise the only remaining medieval feature of the room is its shallow-pitched open timber ceiling, exposed earlier in this century, but rightly thought to be too high and too different in character for the later panelling, and now once again concealed behind a plaster ceiling.

No other important alterations were made to the fabric of the college in the fifteenth century, but two minor practical changes in the opening years of the sixteenth indicate a changing way of life, which was soon to have wider effects on the appearance of its buildings. Both the hall and the kitchen were originally provided with open central hearths, and louvres high above in the roof. By the early Tudor period, this arrangement would have been thought primitive, and accordingly, in 1500–1, a chimney was built against the north wall of hall, and another two at the east end of the kitchen. A wonderfully fanciful pair of Tudor chimney-pots, in the shape of octagonal castellated lanterns with ogee caps, pinnacles and trefoil 'windows' (for the smoke to escape) surmounted the twin kitchen flues until at least the early nineteenth century, when they were drawn by J. C. Buckler (Fig. f).[4] But whether they dated from 1501 or from later in the 1530s, when large-scale alterations to the college were in progress, is hard to determine.

The activity of the 1530s again centred on the hall, bringing it up to date by the new standards of Henry VIII's Renaissance palaces. It is probable that the medieval hall, like most monastic refectories, dispensed with the secular practice of having a screen; but between

Fig. f Tudor chimneys over the kitchen.

1533 and 1535 the present linenfold panelling of the walls, the screen, and screens-passage was installed, almost certainly at the expense of William Warham, then Archbishop of Canterbury, who died in 1532.[5] Warham earlier gave the college not only valuable books and plate, but also three large estates, of which Kingsclere in Hampshire was the most important. His arms, together with those of the Founder, were installed in stained glass in the hall windows in 1527,[6] and also appeared prominently carved in the panelling above the dais at the west end, dating from six or seven years later—along with those of Longland and Sherborne (Bishops of Lincoln and Chichester), the Tudor royal arms and those of Wykeham. In the central panel, between them, were carved the emblems of the Passion (Plates 36 and 37).

While the surrounding linenfold can be seen as a development of medieval forms, the carving of these armorial panels and of the frieze above the screen clearly shows the early influence of Renaissance ornament, with its use of paired grotesque animals and figures, and curling acanthus foliage. Even livelier are the carvings in the spandrels of the three doors leading from the screens-passage to the buttery, kitchen and pantry. The first, on the north, appropriately has figures of choristers running with bread and blackjacks of beer (Plate 38), while the larger central archway to the kitchen has elaborate Tudor roses set amongst delicate tendrils. It is interesting that in the accounts the panelling appears to have been sent from London, payment being made to one John Redyng, as well as to a Master Darnall.[7] In style and quality, it is certainly up to the standards of the best London craftsmen of the day, influenced more by contemporary Flemish than by Italian ornament. The two carpenters responsible for installing it also put up a new ceiling. After the later re-roofing by Wyatt and Scott it is difficult to know what form this took, but it probably came at the height of the medieval corbels, preserving the original medieval tie-beam roof above it.[8] All that now remains are the oak bosses, carved with grotesque masks and foliage, which were re-used by Scott in 1865 in the centre of his roof, two of them bearing the monogram of John London, warden from 1526 to 1542. The panelling, however, remains largely untouched, apart from the addition of the painted shields of later benefactors on the wall behind the dais, and Scott's removal of those sections immediately below the windows which concealed the medieval stone window seats— implying that by the early sixteenth century the medieval custom of bible-reading at each table during meals had lapsed.[9]

The increasing signs of secularisation represented by the new screen and panelling in hall—with the small panel symbolising the Passion quite outweighed by coats-of-arms and Tudor roses—were continued by the additions to the warden's lodgings, the only other large-scale structural change made to the college in the early sixteenth century. It was now becoming apparent that the welfare (and wealth) of the college depended largely on the patronage of the great men of the day, and that their entertainment by the warden must be one of his main functions. The Elizabethan portraits in the warden's lodgings—including the Earls of Dorset, Essex and Leicester, Sir Robert Sidney, Sir William Petre and Bishop Jewell—were probably gifts made to commemorate the hospitality given them by Warden Culpepper, the particular confidant of Leicester during his time as Chancellor of the University.[10] The warden also played an important part in state visits, like James I's in 1605. Obviously it was in the college's interests that he should live in some style, and that he should be able to house at least part of the retinue which accompanied such important visitors. Another reason for the expansion of the warden's lodgings came, after the Reformation, through a loophole in the Founder's statutes: since the warden was required to be in priest's orders Wykeham had not considered it necessary to stipulate (as with the fellows) that he must also be celibate. The first married warden, Ralph Skinner, was elected in 1551 and, though forced to resign two years later, set a precedent which was to be followed after 1558, necessitating extra quarters for the warden's family, as well as his servants. By the time of the college's visitation in 1566, the latter had become so numerous and uncontrollable that they were singled out for criticism as a band of 'Rybaldes and Roysters'.[11]

The exact date of the additions to the lodgings is, however, more problematical than the clearly documented changes to the hall, since a large part of the cost would have been undertaken by the warden himself and would not therefore appear in the college accounts. The 'Computus Roll' for 1540–1 lists the relatively large sum of £134 spent on the lodgings,[12] but this is unlikely to have covered more than a part of the total sum expended. On balance much the likeliest warden to have carried out the main work (despite his celibacy) was the notorious Dr. John London, a zealous persecutor of heretics and enemy of Cranmer, who finally met his deserts—dying in the Fleet prison in 1543. As a Visitor of Monasteries at the time of the Dissolution, and later Prebendary of Windsor, London would certainly have had greater means than his successor, Henry Cole. It has been seen that London's monogram appeared on the bosses of the new ceiling in hall installed in

1533–4, and it is quite possible that the enlargement of the warden's lodgings was undertaken by him in the same decade.

Despite the cramped site, which forbade any lateral extensions, new rooms were created by adding an extra storey to two existing parts of the lodgings: above the warden's study and oratory (between the gatehouse and antechapel), and above the kitchen and pantry on the west side of the small triangular service courtyard. The first of these was achieved by carrying the medieval oriel lighting the warden's study up through the second storey, as seen in Loggan's second engraving (Plate 4), and crowning this whole addition with battlements. These are just visible to the left of the gatehouse pinnacle in Loggan's earlier print (Plate 3), proving that they pre-date (and may therefore have inspired) the castellation of the rest of the main quadrangle in 1675. Magdalen, the first college at Oxford to be castellated, from 1474 onwards, was said in the sixteenth century 'to be crowned with battlements entire, in the manner worthy of gentlemen', and this wish to emulate secular building of the time evidently led to the castellation of All Souls in 1510, and to the original battlements of Wolsey's Christ Church.[13] The two extra rooms above the warden's study and oratory, still with their Tudor beamed ceilings, were approached by a door in the north wall of the warden's own tower chamber. In addition to these new guest rooms, more chambers were provided immediately behind them, one with a castellated oriel window, affording a magnificent view over the cloisters.

The other main addition to the warden's lodgings at this period was the building of a gallery over the medieval kitchen, with a bedroom at the southern end over the pantry. It is likely that these two rooms would have formed the principal guest apartment, on the model of great houses like Knole, where Archbishop Bourchier's late fifteenth-century building had a series of galleries, each leading to a bedchamber and dressing room. The shape of the warden's Tudor gallery was roughly that of the present drawing room created in recent years by Claud Phillimore, but it was probably lit only by the three west-facing windows with hood-moulds shown in Loggan's 1675 engraving and one other facing the courtyard on the east, the oriel window at the north end being a later addition. On the north side of the kitchen courtyard (where there had previously been only a wall) a connecting corridor was made between the warden's hall and this new gallery, with two very low-ceilinged storeys of servants' rooms fitted in below.[14] The windows at the north and south ends of the warden's dais now became internal doorways. The external effect of these modifications was of course considerable: the gatehouse, which would originally have given the impression of a free-standing tower, projecting outwards from the main walls of the college, assumed its present appearance of deep recession, hemmed in by masonry on either side.

Nothing of the original decoration of the warden's Tudor gallery survives apart from a section of the ceiling which was discovered above later plasterwork by W. D. Caroë during his work on the lodgings in 1903. This consisted of carved oak ribs in a geometrical pattern, with small roses carved at each intersection, backed by leaves formed of moulded tin—a rare and interesting feature. Some traces of the original red and green painted decoration could also be discerned. Caroë used this section as the basis for the ceiling of his new gallery, running east–west as opposed to north–south, and it still survives in the truncated version of this gallery which Claud Phillimore converted into an anteroom to his new drawing room in 1958–60. The similar ribbed ceilings in the warden's hall and in the old bursary were almost certainly installed at the same period, and it is interesting that the latter has alternate bosses of carved wooden Tudor roses and lion's masks, made once more of moulded tin.

While all these additions and alterations were gained largely through the increasing secularisation of the college, the losses to the chapel brought about by the Reformation showed a different side of the coin. New College was included in general visitations of the university in 1549, 1556 and 1559, and was subjected to its own special visitations in 1566 and 1576. It is heartbreaking to read in the account books what resulted: in 1547 'the servants of Master Plummer' were paid 10s. 8d., 'for work in taking down and breaking images in the high altar and remaining parts of the church';[15] in 1554, with the next swing of the pendulum, the college was forced to pay £500 to an astute Prebendary of Christ Church, to recover the vestments, altar cloths and hangings which he had bought at a cut rate in the previous reign; then, in 1559, these were again sold, and we read of two labourers working for four days destroying altars, pictures and images. The glass seems to have escaped until 1564, when an ominous entry 'pro novo vitro' probably refers to the replacement of the four crucifixes immediately above the altars on the east wall of the antechapel.[16] Two years later, the hangings were removed from the east end of the chapel, the empty niches of the reredos plastered over so as to prevent a further return to idolatry, and the wall, having been whitewashed, was painted with edifying texts.

But material rather than spiritual needs were now the order of the day. Perhaps wishing to emulate the new luxury of the warden's lodgings the fellows had begun to demand improvements in their accommodation—particularly as the seniors were, in defiance of the Founder's statutes, managing to secure chambers of their own, apart from the juniors. A start was made in 1536 when the original earth floors of the lower chambers round the quadrangle were replaced by timber. Probably some redecoration was also made about this time, though little trace of it now survives: during the restoration of the library in 1950, Tudor designs painted on thick paper were found pasted to the medieval beams of the ceiling in the Conduit Chamber.[17] Then, in Dr. Culpepper's time (1573–99), the upper chambers having already been ceiled, attic rooms called 'cocklofts' began to be constructed above in the steep-pitched medieval roofs. According to Anthony Wood these were lit by gable windows 'looking without the college' so as not to alter the appearance of the quadrangle itself, but 'no ample or uniform windows [were] made to them . . . till the beginning of [the reign of] Charles I'.[18] The cocklofts, built piecemeal in different years and to different specifications, were probably paid for (or given in lieu of their college pittances) by individual fellows. The initial idea may again have derived from the warden's lodgings, for gabled rooms are shown in the roof just to the south of the gatehouse in Loggan's first engraving, and it is possible that these dated from as early as Warden London's alterations. At any rate the principle had been extended to the library by about 1585: the roof space here had already been ceiled off in the mid-fifteenth century, and perhaps used for storage, but now gables were added looking eastwards, and reading desks presumably installed, since an account exists 'for lxij chaynes for the upper librarie'.[19]

Apart from the building of the choir school, first mentioned in 1587, in the narrow dark space between the chapel and cloisters, no other changes were made to the structure of the college in the sixteenth century. If the Founder could have returned to his college two hundred years after his death he would, standing in the quadrangle, have seen no external change at all, apart from the small rooms added above the warden's study and oratory. Greater differences would have become apparent, however, had he walked either through the main gate and seen the rest of the warden's additions, or through the conduit archway opposite and seen the garden as it is today beginning to take shape.

Warden Woodward was undoubtedly right in saying that 'the garden was ancyently not for pleasure and walking but for proffit': there are records of planting vines here as early as 1390, and as late as 1576, Ralph Agas's bird's eye view of Oxford clearly shows the main part of the garden divided into strips either side of a central path, with a single tree in each rectangular plot as the only ornamental feature.[20] In 1500 the college bought from Magdalen the gardens at the east end of St. Peter's-in-the-East, but these seem to have been orchards until the early seventeenth century, when they became the fellows' bowling green. The first signs of any activity besides routine husbandry occurred in 1529–30 when four masons, one 'rough mason or dauber', and nine labourers were working on new garden walls, 500 wagon loads of rubbish were tipped into the garden, and there were other heavy bills for manure and labour.[21] While this quite probably marked the beginning of an ornamental rather than a purely kitchen garden, the rubbish was probably used simply to level the ground (which formerly sloped quite steeply to the south) and to build up the terrace walks around it, rather than as foundations for the mount.

Mounds, or mounts, seem not to have come into fashion until the middle years of Queen Elizabeth's reign, though they had become almost inevitable in large gardens by the end of the century—Sir Thomas Tresham's layout at Lyveden in the 1590s, for instance, had a mount at each of the four corners, two pyramidal, and two with spiral paths.[22] The £3 paid to the gardener at New College in 1594 'towards ye making of ye mount', is the first specific reference to what is still the dominant feature of the garden, and probably marks the beginning of its construction—not to be completed for another half-century.

2. THE SEVENTEENTH CENTURY: THE LAUDIAN REVIVAL AND BYRD'S GARDEN QUADRANGLE

The greater comfort sought by both the warden and the senior fellows in the sixteenth century, and their emulation of the new houses of the gentry, continued in the seventeenth, though it was not until the last quarter of the century that this actually resulted in additional buildings. Just as individual fellows had begun to build themselves gabled 'cocklofts' as studies in the roof space above their chambers, so, slightly later, they began to panel some of their chambers: thus a payment is recorded in 1598 'for wainscot in Mr. Hussen's chamber', and in 1629 'to Mr. Oldis ... for the wainscotting of his chamber £5.10.0'.[23] Late sixteenth- or early seventeenth-century panelling can still be found in what was the Crane and Dart, the Christopher (and the 'cockloft' above it), the Rose, the Green Post and the Chamber of Three. The Rose also has a particularly elaborate carved Jacobean chimneypiece with an arcaded overmantel (Plate 43), obviously by the same hand as three more in the anteroom, hall and study of the warden's lodgings.

The chimneypiece in the warden's study (Plate 42), originally at the southern end of the gallery (when it shared the same flue as the hearth of his kitchen below), is carved with the arms of Bishop Bilson quartered with the see of Winchester, which dates it to between 1599 and 1616. This also accords with surviving accounts for the first decade of the seventeenth century, referring to furniture made for the gallery, including walnut tables and a court cupboard, together with eighty-five yards of wainscot.[24] The warden responsible for the three chimneypieces, and the oak panelling which survives in the anteroom, hall (Plate 41) and elsewhere in the lodgings, must therefore have been George Ryves (1599–1613), a highly respected figure who was a supervisor of James I's Authorised Version of the Bible, and later vice-chancellor. That he was rich enough to afford these additions is proved by the bequests of communion flagons to the chapel, and of pictures to the lodgings, made in his will. Stylistically, all four chimneypieces are closely comparable with the pulpit and vice-chancellor's seat in the cathedral made in 1608 and 1613 respectively by William Bennett, a master-carpenter who was elected to the City Council in 1605.[25]

The idea of forming new rooms in the college's wasted medieval roof-spaces was taken to its ultimate conclusion in the early seventeenth century. In 1626–7 new attic chambers for the clerks and choristers were formed in the roof between the hall and kitchen (above the buttery, pantry and central staircase); and finally in 1631–3 the random cocklofts already built by individual fellows were replaced by a row of

twenty uniform gables at the back of the south range, with three more
each at the southern end of the south and west ranges, built at the
expense of the college.[26] These provided all the senior fellows with
separate studies for the first time, without actually altering the
appearance of the main quadrangle.

Meanwhile yet another change in the religious climate of the times
caused further alterations to the chapel, bringing it into line with
Laudian High Church precepts. The sixteenth-century visitations had
evidently done their work only too well, and in 1636 the archbishop is
found writing to the Bishop of Winchester, perhaps a shade naïvely,
that he has 'often wondered why so many good scholars came from
Winchester to New College, and yet so few of them afterwards prove
eminent men', going on to ask whether the bishop would use his
influence with Warden Pinke ('a learned and discreet man') to make
sure that probationers were not examined so thoroughly in Calvin's
Institutions.[27] This personal interest of Laud's in the college may
explain the hurried refurbishing of the chapel during the next two years.
This included the first documented restoration of the medieval stained
glass, the provision of new stalls for the choir in front of the old ones, a
new screen supporting a handsome new organ case, and the laying of a
black-and-white marble floor throughout the whole building.

The 'Dutch pencill man' who was paid 'for making newe 18 faces in
the church windowes, some of which were wanting, others broken or
defaced', was probably one of the van Linge brothers of Emden, who
had been specifically encouraged to settle in England by Laud and his
predecessor Archbishop Abbot.[28] 'Mr. van Linge', in all likelihood
Abraham, who made the beautiful Jonah window in the cathedral in
1630 and the glass in University College chapel ten years later, also
supplied '25 pieces of glasse for the librarie windowes' at New College in
1634–5. After later restorations, few signs of his work can now be
discerned in the chapel windows.

The fifty-eight new stalls and two rows of reading desks, their ends
decorated 'with pummells on ye topps of them like Globes', were
intended for the first time to seat the whole society, including the
choristers, who had formerly stood beneath the screen. They were
executed (in 'heart of Poland oake of the best') by a joiner named
William Harris, of St. Cross, who promised that they should be
executed 'in as decent or rather in a more beautifull and comely manner

than . . . is expressed in ye draughte', and who charged £170 15s. 4d.[29] Harris was probably also responsible for the 'very fine screen curiously painted and sumptuously gilt', which Anthony Wood records being erected at the same time. An otherwise unknown artist named Francis Doone was commissioned in 1636 to decorate the screen and to paint 'figures of the Apostles, Saints etc.' on the back panels of the sixty remaining medieval stalls.[30] This work has fared little better than van Linge's stained glass: the screen and organ seem to have been dismantled during the Commonwealth, and Wyatt later redesigned the stalls, keeping only fragments of Harris's work which he placed against the walls of the antechapel. Of Doone's painted stall-backs, only seven now survive, badly damaged.

The first half of the seventeenth century also saw continuing activity in the garden, particularly on the mount, begun in 1594. The gardener received £5 'for carrying Earth for ye makeing up of ye mount in ye common garden' in 1616, and further work was done in 1623.[31] Though it seems a strange time for it to have been completed, during the rapid fluctuations and uncertainties of the Civil War, Warden Woodward recorded that in 1648–9 the mount was 'perfected with stepps of stone and setts for ye Hedges about ye walke'—presumably much as it appears in Loggan's print of 1675. Two years earlier, the clerks and choristers had lit 'a Bonefier on the Mount in the College walks' to celebrate the Prince's birthday.[32] A tradition later grew up that the mount had been built as a gun emplacement during the Civil War, and it is quite possible that it was adapted to this purpose for a time.

In all it is surprising that more damage was not done to the structure of the college in the Civil War. The fellows must have heartily regretted the money they had spent on repairs to the walls between 1621 and 1625 (as part of the Founder's original bargain with the city), for both sides in turn established their main garrisons here, considering it better capable of defence than the dilapidated castle. In September, 1642, the college was occupied and searched by the Parliamentarians. Then, only two months later, the King himself 'caused his magazine to be put into New College cloister and tower etc', knocking down a section of the cloisters so as to allow direct access from the lane on the west.[33] One can only be grateful that a stray spark from an absent-minded fellow's tinder-box did not at this time reduce much of Wykeham's buildings to rubble.

Nor was the college spared in the final stages of the war; when in 1651 it was feared that Charles II might attack Oxford, the Parliamentary commander 'took in New College for his garrison, plucking down 2 or 3 houses joyning to the cloister by Hart Hall, and also built a new fort in the middle of New Coll: Lane to defend it and plucked downe Queen's Coll: wall that stood before it, and made great havock of their gardens lying close thereby'.[34] Little evidence now remains of any damage, however, and even the Laudian redecoration of the chapel seems to have survived, apart from the dismantling of the organ. Evelyn, who visited the college in 1654, found the chapel 'in its ancient garb, notwithstanding the scrupulositie of the times'. Perhaps even more surprising, four of the peal of bells in the tower (the third, fifth, eighth and tenor) bear the inscription 'Michael Barbie made me 1655', which suggests that the new warden and fellows installed by the Protector were not as radically sectarian in their sympathies as one might have expected.[35]

With the Restoration, and under one of its most able wardens, Michael Woodward, the college set out on a period of expansion, equalled in its history only by the last half of the nineteenth century. This started modestly enough with the installation of a new organ in chapel (by the well-known maker Dallam), the 'scheame or draught of the organ case and loft' being drawn up once again by the joiner William Harris. For the decoration of the new case Woodward recorded that 'Mr. Dalham . . . named unto us one Taylor liveing by Hart Hall whom hee knew . . . [had] abilitie to do it. Hawkins he said could lay gold, but draw noe pictures, whereof hee said, there must be about eight'.[36] Taylor is an otherwise unknown decorative painter (like Francis Doone), but the gilder Richard Hawkins referred to here was a well-known Oxford craftsman, who executed the graining and gilding of the interior of the Sheldonian in 1669 and who became mayor twenty years later. Both were paid £100 for their work in the chapel in 1662, Taylor's including extra paintings on, and under, the organ loft. Two years later, in 1664, again according to Woodward, William Harris was called back to the college to restore the panelling in haĺl, which 'ye Painters', probably Hawkins's team once more, 'colord & varnished', gilding the panel above the dais carved with the symbols of the Passion and also 'ye letters or writeing about ye Hall'.

Some kind of a reredos must have been reintroduced into the chapel

2. New College in the fifteenth century, from Warden Chaundler's manuscript, *c.* 1461–65.

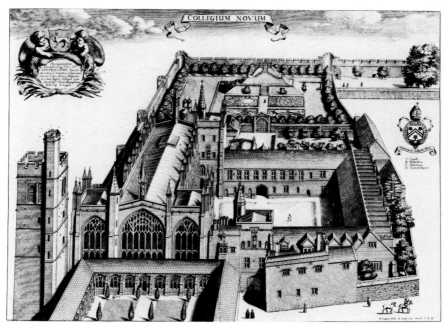

3. Engraving of New College, by David Loggan, *c.* 1670.

4. Loggan's engraving of the Great Quadrangle in 1675, after the addition of the second storey.

5. Aerial view of New College from the east, showing Longwall and the Sacher Building in the foreground, and Holywell on the right.

6. The Great Quadrangle, by Joseph Dixon: a drawing made for the 1793 Oxford Almanack (Ashmolean Museum, Oxford).

7. The Great Quadrangle, showing the Chapel, Hall and Muniment Tower on the left, the Founder's Library and Upper Library over the archway leading to the garden, and fellows' chambers on the right.

8. The Chapel and Bell Tower from the Slype, with the City Wall in the foreground, and the Library on the right.

9. The Cloisters, Bell Tower and west end of Chapel.

10. The Antechapel, with Reynolds' west window on the left.

11. The Chapel, looking westwards, from an engraving of 1814 showing Wyatt's roof, stalls and organ screen, with Reynolds' window beyond.

12. The east end of the Chapel, *c.* 1870, before Scott's restoration, showing the plaster reredos by Bernasconi.

13. Preliminary design for the new Chapel roof by Gilbert Scott, 1875.

14. The east end of the Chapel, with Scott's hammerbeam roof and stalls, and the stone reredos completed by Pearson in 1888.

15–18. Medieval wood carving: four fourteenth-century misercords from the Chapel.
15. William of Wykeham welcoming scholars to Oxford.

16. Female centaur and hedgehogs.

17. Scholars fighting with daggers.

18 Doctor delivering a lecture.

19–21. Medieval stone carving: (above) a Bishop and King, from the Hall; (below) a corbel in the Treasury.

22–25. Medieval glass: Judas and St. Athanasius, from the Antechapel windows and (right) a Wise Virgin and Angel, from the upper lights of the Choir windows.

26. Detail of a window on the south side of the Choir, by William Price, 1740.

27. Detail of a window on the north side of the Choir, by William Peckitt. 1771.

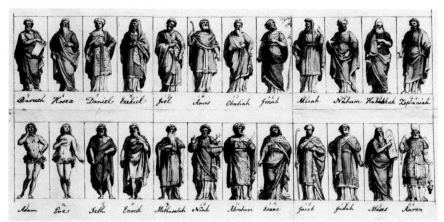

28. Design by Biagio Rebecca for figures in the north windows of the Choir, *c.* 1773.

29. Preliminary sketch by Reynolds for the Nativity in the centre of the west window, *c.* 1778.

30. Reynolds' full-size sketch for Charity in the west window, *c.* 1778 (Ashmolean Museum, Oxford).

31–33. Medieval stone vaults: (above) the Muniment Room; (below) the Beer Cellar; (opposite) the staircase to the Hall.

34 & 35. Medieval timber roofs: (above) the Kitchen; (below) the Long Room.

36. The Hall, showing the linenfold panelling of 1533–5, and Scott's roof of 1862–5.

37. Detail of the panelling above the dais in Hall, showing the Tudor royal arms in the centre, and the emblems of the Passion on the left.

38. Detail of the spandrel above the buttery door, showing a chorister running with blackjacks of beer, and a basket of bread.

39. The Gatehouse and Warden's Lodgings from New College Lane, with Byrd's bridge (of *c.* 1675–9) on the right.

40. The staircase in the Warden's Lodgings, constructed by Richard Frogley between 1675 and 1679.

41–43. Jacobean carving: (above) panelling in the Warden's Hall; (below left) overmantel in the Warden's study; (below right) overmantel in one of the Fellows' chambers.

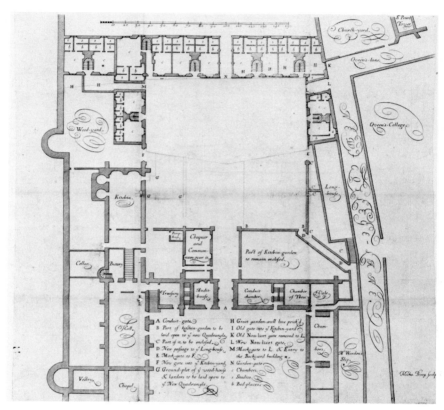

44–45. Byrd's preliminary design for the Garden Quadrangle, engraved by Burghers, 1678. The elevation (above) is printed on a hinged flap, to show its relation to the ground plan (below).

46–49. Alternative schemes for the Garden Quadrangle by William Byrd, *c.* 1678–81.

50. Byrd's final design for the Garden Quadrangle, from an engraving of 1682.

51. Drawing of the Garden Quadrangle by Michael Burghers, showing the two new wings added in 1700 and 1707 (Ashmolean Museum, Oxford).

52. The Garden Quadrangle from the Mount.

53. The gatescreen, made by Thomas Robinson in 1711, photographed before its reconstruction in 1894.

54. The Senior Common Room, panelled in 1678 by Francis Butler, with Warden Shuttleworth's 'port railway' in front of the fireplace.

55 The Warden's summerhouse, attributed to William Townesend, c.1720.

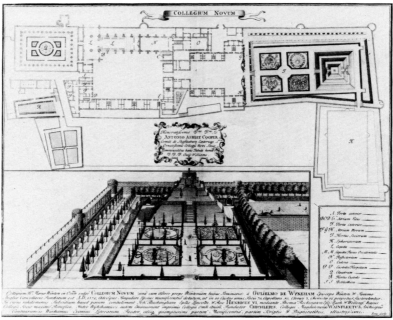

56. & 57. The Garden: (above) detail from an engraving by Michael Burghers, 1708; (below) from an engraving in William Williams' *Oxonia Depicta*, 1732.

58. The Founder's Library, now used as the S.C.R. dining room. The original gothic windows on the left were restored in 1951.

59. The Upper Library, designed by James Pears, with the advice of James Wyatt, c. 1777–80. The globes, by George Adams, were presented by Warden Oglander in 1770.

60. Scott's Holywell Building, from a photograph taken *c*. 1880, before the addition of the Robinson Tower and Pandy.

61. A staircase well in the Holywell Building.

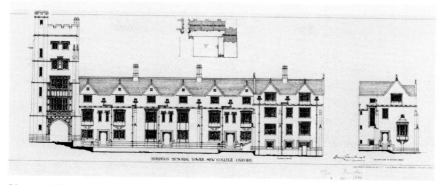

62. Basil Champneys' design for the Robinson Tower and Pandy, from *The Builder*, 1899.

63. The Sacher Building, designed by David Roberts in 1961, with sculpture by Barbara Hepworth in the foreground.

64. & 65. The Annunciation, two panels by Bartolommeo Montagna (*c.* 1450–1523).

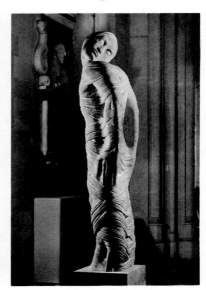

66. *St. James*, by El Greco.

67. *Lazarus*, by Jacob Epstein.

in the 1630s, though we have no record of its appearance. Like the organ, it was probably a casualty of the Civil War, for 'ye Adorneing of ye East End' was a problem which exercised the fellows continuously from at least 1664 until 1671. The saga, reported in great detail by the meticulous Woodward,[37] is worth summarising here for its curiously modern-sounding account of college meetings, and the difficulties of securing agreement on architectural or artistic matters. It began with one of the fellows, named Turner, recommending 'some rich hangings', representing 'Melchisedech his entertaining of Abraham with bread and wine', belonging to the Dean of Worcester. But whereas the tapestry was too big for the east end of Worcester Cathedral, it was slightly too small for New College, and the fellows, worried by the extra cost of 'pillars on each side . . . a crest and canopye above and some wainscott below', turned it down.

Meanwhile, 'some of ye Senior company being at London and discourseing with one Mr. Hugh May (a Courtier) . . . he told them yt beyond the seas there was an Excellent Artist who . . . would make for ye Coll: an Excellent peece . . . Theodore van Thulden at S'Hertogen-Bas'. Hugh May, Charles II's Comptroller of Works and the surveyor for his alterations to Windsor Castle, had spent the last four years of the Interregnum in the Netherlands with his close friend, the painter Lely—so that it is interesting to find both May and Lely now signing a letter to van Thulden, on behalf of the college, requesting him to send a 'modell' in oils, at an agreed price of £20, and an estimate for the completed picture. Van Thulden, born in 1606 and formerly a pupil of Rubens in Antwerp, replied that he would be happy to paint the picture, coming to Oxford only 'to see it upp . . . for I have done peeces as big as this in my owne house for the Duke of Brandenburgh and other German Princes'. His *modello*, representing the 'offering of the three Kings', was duly sent, but his estimate of £700 'was thought by some an impudent price', and this scheme in turn was swiftly abandoned, the artist himself dying shortly afterwards in 1669.[38]

Back where they started, the fellows began to wonder whether they had not turned down the Worcester hangings too hastily. Negotiations were reopened with the dean, but although the tapestry was actually hung in the chapel on Easter Day and the following Monday in 1668, it was finally rejected on three counts—that it was old and worn ('ye lustre perished'), that 'ye great man in ye Arras had noe name and they knew not who he was especially at some distance', and finally that the cost of a carved wooden surround would be £180. At this all-too-familiar point in the proceedings, there seemed no possibility of the fellows agreeing on any general course of action. A small committee was therefore elected with independent powers, and in 1670, after much further deliberation, a joiner named John Wild made a 'frame of Wainscott', which Richard Hawkins again painted and gilded, and into which was set a 'Remnant of Cloath of Gold . . . offered unto ye colledge by Dr. Yates, Principall of Brasenose'. If, after the initial involvement of such celebrities as May and Lely, this conventional reredos seems something of an anti-climax, it is only fair to say that its total cost—£75 to build, £130 to Hawkins, and just under £30 to Dr. Yates[39]— represented a mere third of van Thulden's projected painting, and that, with funds already being raised for extensive additions to the fellows' chambers, the college needed every penny it could save.

It is noteworthy that, while additions to other colleges (such as Peckwater Quad at Christ Church) were financed by single rich benefactors, money for the seventeenth- and eighteenth-century extensions to New College came through annual levies on the fellows and subscriptions by past and present members of the society. Contributions to the heightening of the main quadrangle between 1670 and 1675 ranged from £1 per annum from the impecunious philosopher Thomas Hobbes, now in his eighties, to £40 from the public-spirited Warden Woodward.[40] The need for more space, long urged by the senior fellows, was reinforced by several plague epidemics in the 1660s, with a number of deaths in the college blamed on overcrowding. If the fellows' own libraries and possessions rivalled Aubrey's, they must also have overflowed the tiny cubicle studies provided by the Founder. The problem was tackled, if not entirely overcome, by the heightening of the three quadrangle ranges in 1674–5. Because it was more economical than removing the old medieval roofs and cocklofts, and building a whole new storey, this heightening was achieved simply by extending the principle of the cockloft gables for the first time to the inward-facing roofs. The gable-ends were then concealed behind a masking wall, with a parapet which was castellated, taking its cue perhaps from the Tudor battlements above the warden's study and oratory.

To this day the roofs of the three quadrangle ranges are formed by endless rows of transverse ridges, with all the problems of internal guttering and the maintenance of extra leadwork that involves. The heightening of the quad was also to give constant trouble for another reason: the outer walls were constructed in the local Headington freestone which was to prove far less resistant than the medieval stone (probably Wheatley) of the two lower storeys. The two can never have blended well, and the upper storey finally decayed so badly that in 1906–7 it had to be entirely refaced in Box Ground stone, with Clipsham dressings. Even after cleaning in the 1960s there is still a noticeable dividing line between the fourteenth- and seventeenth-century work. The additional storey was also unfortunate architecturally, robbing the warden's gatehouse and the muniment tower of much of their dominance in Wynford's original design, and losing the warm colouring of the Cotswold tiles which remains so important a feature of the cloisters. Nevertheless the exact repetition of the medieval first-floor windows and string-course in the new storey was more tactful than might have been expected at this date—and it was only the later introduction of sashes that radically altered the proportions, and the medieval style, of the whole quadrangle.

The two engravings of New College by David Loggan, both included in his *Oxonia Illustrata*, published in 1675, are particularly useful in showing 'before-and-after' views of the quadrangle. The bird's eye view from the west (Plate 3) was probably made about 1670, before plans for the alterations had been drawn up; the second (Plate 4) shows the extra storey, and records in the inscription below that it was built in 1674. A rare early version of this second print, with an inscription in French, shows an intermediate stage, with the third storey added only to the eastern range—and this agrees with the contract of the master-mason John Dew, of Marston, who was to work from 'the east side of the Library to the west side of an upper chamber or cockloft in the warden's lodgings'.[41]

Apart from John Dew, the principal craftsmen involved were the slater and plasterer Job Dew (probably his brother or cousin), the carpenter Richard Frogley, the plumber Bernard Rawlins and the smith William Young, with the indispensable 'Mr. Hawkins ye Painter . . . making ye old and new wainscott all of one colour'.[42] A designer is nowhere mentioned but was in all likelihood William Byrd, the Oxford carver and mason who shortly afterwards built the warden's bridge across New College Lane, and who later acted as architect for the garden quad. Born in Gloucester in 1624, Byrd had moved to Oxford about 1647 and established a yard in Holywell, later playing a leading part in the building of the Sheldonian Theatre.[43] He not only made the model for Wren in 1662, but was also 'carver to the theatre', whose work almost certainly included the so-called Emperors' heads on the piers of the surrounding railings.

Byrd's employment by New College began as early as 1663–4 when he repaired the Founder's monument in Winchester Cathedral at the fellows' expense;[44] he recurs in the accounts for various small jobs in 1671, and in 1674 'for building up the chequer chymney'. This apparently minor modification in fact heralded a change of great significance. With the addition of an extra full storey above the library it became possible to move here all the law books. Thus vacated, the law library was then converted into a senior common room, Byrd opening up the flue of the chimney on the north wall to provide a hearth. At Cambridge the idea of 'combination' rooms had been adopted early on, as a natural progression from the solars, or parlours, found in domestic architecture, and usually placed therefore off the hall at the dais end.[45] Oxford common rooms were much slower to develop. Wood records that the first appeared at Merton in 1661, followed by that at Trinity in 1665—'to the end that the Fellows might meet together (chiefly in the evenings after refection) partly about business, but mostly for society's sake, which before was at each chamber by turns'. At New College, the fellows were assured of warmth and comfort not only by Byrd's chimneypiece but the installation of panelling blocking the old windows on the south side, and a new false ceiling below the fifteenth-century beamed roof. The walnut panelling, which was installed by a joiner named Francis Butler in 1678, probably to Byrd's design, makes this far the most important seventeenth-century interior to survive in the college (Plate 54). The distinctive carved drapery hanging in thick folds over each panel, is found in other senior common rooms, for instance above the overmantel at Merton, made by Arthur Frogley in 1680, and round the whole room at Wadham, previously thought to be of about 1725, but probably at least forty years earlier in date.

Richard Frogley, another of the craftsmen habitually used by Byrd, was responsible for the new staircase to the warden's lodgings in 1675. Earlier in the same year, John Nicholas had succeeded Woodward as warden, and in the brief period he held the post (before accepting in

1679 the richer wardenship of Winchester, with even greater opportunities for building),[46] he managed to leave his mark on the lodgings to a greater extent than most. The steep and narrow medieval staircase to the warden's anteroom must have seemed to him a mean approach, and one of his first acts was to annex part of the porter's lodge (then on the south side of the gate), giving back to the college in exchange the chamber in the south-western section of the lodgings. Frogley's new staircase (Plate 40) ingeniously consisted of two separate flights up to the first-floor level, one rising from near the quadrangle door, the other from the corridor to the kitchen, giving servants access to the warden's hall. From here a single wide flight led up to the second floor, allowing the medieval spiral staircase which awkwardly cut off one corner of the hall to be removed.

Warden Nicholas's other main contribution was the creation of the garden in the paddock to the south of the barn, with its own means of access from the lodgings by a bridge across New College Lane. In order to provide privacy for the garden a high wall was constructed parallel with the barn on the south, leaving a narrow yard behind, for access to the stables. On the southern side this wall was constructed with a series of shallow bays providing shelter for espaliered fruit trees, as recommended in gardening manuals of the day—an early example of the so-called 'crinkle-crankle' walls which came into fashion early in the next century. The charming little garden house at the far end of the lawn has in the past been attributed to Warden Nicholas, but, with its heavy Baroque parapet and keystones, and its sash windows (Plate 55), is far more likely to have been built early in the eighteenth century.

As with the heightening of the quadrangle, the architect of Warden Nicholas's bridge is not given in the college accounts, but fortunately William Byrd's responsibility is made clear by his testimony in a case heard before the Chancellor's Court in 1691:[47] 'since he has been a Master workman', he declared, he 'hath in diverse counties work'd at severall noble buildings too many to be here mentioned and lately in Oxford he built the Arch at New College and Edmund Hall Chappell'. The bridge presented a difficult task of construction for it had to be parallel with the Founder's new lane approaching the college gate, but also to cope with the slant of the warden's kitchen and barn bordering the remaining section of the medieval lane. It says something for Byrd's skill that his solution is satisfactory both practically and visually (Plate

39). The luxuriant Baroque scroll (similar to those he had carved ten years earlier for the Sheldonian), at the point where the bridge meets the slightly lower roof of the barn, is a particularly nice way of disguising a difficult technical problem. Byrd's skill as a stone-carver can also be seen in the auricular cartouche surrounding Warden Nicholas's arms, which is set above the arch leading into the barn on the inside. The building of the bridge necessitated some alterations to the internal planning of the lodgings. A passage was partitioned off the north end of the Tudor gallery as a means of approach—an improvement, in that it made the gallery rectangular in shape for the first time—and the guest room at the east end of the barn was converted into a lobby, from which a long flight of stone steps led straight down into the garden.

Although Warden Nicholas moved to Winchester in 1679 he may have taken part in the initial discussions for a much larger extension to the college than had hitherto been contemplated. A list of payments dated 6 March 1678, and endorsed 'Money left in ye Chest by Dr. Nicholas' includes £4 10s. 0d. paid 'to Mich. Burghers for a copper plate'. This almost certainly refers to a rare engraving, of which two copies remain in the college's possession (Plates 44 and 45), representing a preliminary design for the garden quadrangle, again by Byrd, probably ordered with a view to raising subscriptions. The engraving shows a closed quadrangle plan of a conventional pattern, but with the unique feature of three extra slips hinged (in the manner of nineteenth-century children's books) so as to show the effect of the new elevations.[48]

The need for a new quadrangle so soon after the heightening of the old one was due partly to the demands of the junior fellows and probationers, who were still squashed, four to a room, in the lower chambers, and who were envious of the seniors' spacious second-floor studies and of their common room. But it was also due to the acceptance of gentlemen commoners, as an additional source of revenue for the college. The Visitor's approval of this principle (contrary to the Founder's statutes) was gained in 1679, but may have been considered a foregone conclusion to judge from the large number of new chambers proposed in Burghers's engraving of the previous year: thirteen on the ground floor as compared with the seven finally built.

Between 1678 and 1681 several different alternatives by Byrd were considered, and a group of interesting elevations in his hand survives in the college archives.[49] The first two, showing longer ranges than the others, not entirely symmetrical, and sparsely ornamented, may have been intended either as freestanding blocks screening off the garden, or to have stood at right angles to the Founder's east range, screening the Long Room (Plate 46). The other three (Plates 47–49) are obviously alternatives for the central range as shown in the 1678 engraving—one shows a two-storey front with a hipped roof in the Dutch style; another a more up-to-date three-storey façade with the roof concealed behind a parapet; and the third (and most accomplished), alternating segmental and triangular pediments to the first-floor windows, and frames with scrolls and central masks to those on the second floor, an early use of an Italianate form associated with another provincial architect in the 1680s, Henry Bell of King's Lynn.[50]

There were, however, drawbacks to Byrd's preliminary scheme for the New College quadrangle: first there was the basic lack of symmetry on the north and south, despite the architect's ingenious provision of 'mock gates' and walls, to provide the appearance of a balanced composition; and secondly there was the sheer size of the quadrangle, substantially larger than the Founder's, and with more chambers than the college could afford either to build, or to support. A second engraving (Plate 50), almost certainly made by George Edwards in 1682 after a 'draught of ye designed buildings in pirspective' by a Mr. Crown,[51] and again published to raise subscriptions for the new building, shows the wholly different solution to the problem which Byrd eventually arrived at: an open-ended courtyard with an answering block to Chequer built on the south side of the garden archway, and two narrow flanking wings, set back so as to touch these shorter and lower blocks only at the corners. The result was a triumph of planning, for the wings screened off both the kitchen and outhouses on one side and the Long Room on the other, and provided a total of eighteen new chambers on three storeys. A new junior common room (again with claims to be the earliest in either university) was created in the western half of the two-storey block balancing Chequer, with a light-well above it (screened simply by a wall with a false mullion and transom) so as not to block the windows at this end of the library; while the eastern half was occupied by two more fellows' chambers.

How did this new, and unconventional, plan come about? In all probability the answer lies in the continuation of William Byrd's close

relations with Christopher Wren, long after the latter had left Oxford
and been appointed Surveyor of the Works by Charles II. Wren had
long advocated the abandonment of the conventional quadrangle,
writing in 1665 to Dr. Bathurst, the President of Trinity: 'I perceive the
name of Quadrangle will carrie it with those who . . . may possibly be
your Benefactors, though it be much the worse for the Chambers, and
the Beauty of the Colledge. . . .' If they insist, he continues, then 'let
them have a quadrangle, though a lame one, somewhat like a three-
legged table'.[52] By the early 1680s Wren was himself beginning to put
this idea into practice in the much larger context of a royal palace for
Charles II at Winchester. Appropriately, since this great scheme was
largely to be financed by the King's subsidies from Louis XIV, his early
plans, thought to date from about 1682,[53] were strongly influenced by
the entrance front of Versailles—a *cour d'honneur* formed by wings
stepped gradually inwards. It is significant that when work on the
palace finally began in the autumn of 1683, Byrd was summoned by the
Surveyor to Winchester to act as one of the chief contractors.

The similarity between the garden quadrangle and the general plan
of Winchester Palace was well known to contemporaries. John Ayliffe, a
fellow of the college, writing in 1714 (well within the lifetimes of most of
those concerned) describes the quadrangle as 'erected according to the
model of the Royal Palace at *Versailles*, saving that it is not built upon
pillars; or to come nearer home, 'tis of the like plan with the Queen's
House at *Winchester*, with its several projections and fallings back in a
uniform and elegant manner'.[54] What is intriguing, however, is the
slight discrepancy in the dates. Byrd's articles of agreement for the
southern half of the new quadrangle, to be built 'according to a Modell
of ye same drawne by himself, and delivered in', were made on 3
January 1682, and those for the northern half on 12 April of the
following year.[55] It was not until the autumn of 1683 that the master-
mason was summoned to Winchester, presumably leaving behind a
team of workmen at Oxford with instructions as to how to complete the
new quadrangle. One can only conjecture that Byrd had been shown
some of the preliminary designs for Winchester Palace by Wren at an
earlier date, some time in 1681. It is possible that the catalyst here was
the architecturally-minded Dr. Nicholas, who continued to employ
Byrd after he had exchanged the wardenship of New College for that of ,
Winchester, and who is also known to have sought the advice of Wren

for the new school building, erected there in 1683–7.

Despite the novelty of Byrd's overall scheme, both in style and in planning, his garden quadrangle blocks are, as one might expect, relatively old-fashioned. The windows, pedimented on the first floor (rather in the style of the Old Ashmolean), are connected in vertical strips by the projecting panels below them—an old obsession, already seen in Byrd's preliminary designs, and also found at Kill-Canon and in the long-demolished Fell's Buildings at Christ Church.[56] The string-course between the two floors of the Chequer building was continued round the new wings, and the battlements were also continued in the same form as those of the heightened main quadrangle, so as to tie the old and new buildings together visually, an example of that tactfulness already seen in Byrd's earlier work for the college. The new windows throughout had mullion-and-transom frames rather than the newly-fashionable sashes, except for the very narrow ones at the ends of the wings, which had transoms only. Plainer doorcases than those shown on Edwards' engraving were adopted, perhaps for reasons of economy.

The interior of the garden quadrangle was by no means as adventurous as the exterior. Byrd's chambers in fact differed little in plan from their medieval predecessors, consisting of a large central room with three small cubicles partitioned off at the far end, and a fourth behind the staircase. What made them infinitely more comfortable, however, was the fact that they were intended to house two rather than four fellows or commoners, each having his own study and 'bedplace'. The staircases themselves 'of Oake-timber with Railes and Ballisters thereunto, with Easy Rises' were also far lighter and more spacious than those provided by the Founder. Another refinement was that some of the uniform mullion-and-transom windows on the principal façades were ingeniously split in two, so as to light separate cubicles, belonging to rooms on different staircases. This meant that there need not be two different sizes of windows, one for chambers and one for cubicles—as there had been in the main quadrangle and in Byrd's own earlier designs.

Full details of the expense of the two blocks can be found in the college archives: the south range was described as 'almost finished' in April 1683, at a cost of nearly £1,600; the north range, completed by about September 1684, came to just over £1,300, cheaper because it necessitated only minor alterations to the existing Chequer building.

The south range itself contained nine double rooms (with two more in the junior common room block) exclusively for fellows, 'for easing ye ground chambers' in the main quadrangle. In the northern range, the ground-floor room next to Chequer was assigned to two chaplains and that above it to a senior fellow 'impowered to inform of all Misbehaviour in ye New Quadrangle', while the other seven were to be occupied by 'noblemen and fellow commoners', whose fees and rents (£6 per annum for each room) were seen as a return on the college's investment. The four staircases with their sturdy walnut balustrades still survive unaltered, though the rooms themselves were panelled in 1734–5.[57]

The finishing touches were being put to the building in December 1684, when Byrd presented a final bill for items outside the original agreement, including the eighteen small shields (representing benefactors) in the pediments over the first-floor windows, and the large coat-of-arms of George Morley, Bishop of Winchester from 1662 to 1684 above the archway to the Founder's quadrangle.[58] Bishop Morley's shield and those of two later benefactors flanking it perform an important function, distracting the eye from the asymmetrical position of the library windows. The engraved plan of Byrd's quadrangle (Plate 50) shows a screen across the eastern end of the courtyard, and it is probable that this took the form of a balustrade. The account of December 1684, already referred to, includes '24½ yards of Raile and Ballusters' and also '500 yards of pitching between the Raile and Ballusters and Garden wall'. It should be remembered that the usual means of approach for tradesmen and kitchen supplies was still (until the opening of the back gate in the city wall in 1700) through the Non-licet gate from Queen's Lane. The 'Garden wall' was probably that shown by Loggan (Plate 3), which had been retained parallel with the balustrade and beyond it, though with ironwork replacing the wooden gates shown in the central pedimented archway. Other gateways were probably made in this wall too: £63 18s. 6d. was expended on 'the Gates of Garden and two other paire of Gates Iron worke. . .', while Byrd also erected several pairs of stone piers surmounted by 'potts', 'pine-Aples' or 'Globes & Necks'.[59] Unfortunately no illustration of Byrd's completed quadrangle before the addition of the two early eighteenth-century blocks survives to show what must have been an important integral part of his scheme; but the very existence of a screen across its east end is nevertheless significant, for it establishes beyond doubt that the two later blocks were an afterthought and not (despite their enhancement of the Winchester Palace-Versailles plan) part of a long-term master scheme originally devised by Byrd.

William Byrd's last appearance in the college archives occurs in February 1687, when, after he had sent a plaintive letter to the bursar, Dr. Traffles, justifying the 'dearness of Each Chamber', and analysing the various costs of the new buildings, he was given £10 by the college 'in consideration of his Poverty and pretended losse in our Buildings', and a further £10 from Traffles himself 'to satisfy his importunity'.[60]

When the accounts for the garden quadrangle are so complete, it is disappointing that those for the garden itself are so fragmentary, and that the exact date of the parterre shown by Loggan in 1675 (Plate 3) is still something of a mystery. It has been seen that the mount was 'perfected' in 1649, and since its purpose was partly to give a view of the intricate parterre beds from above, it might be that these were already in existence. In a letter written in 1658, Wood refers to 'the garden, where Wm. of Wickham's Arms was cutt in a box platt, and not long since was seen this Motto "Manners Maketh a Man quoth Wm. of Wickham" '.[61] 'Not long since' implies that the parterre had been created before the Civil War, but that the royal arms with Charles I's monogram had led to its destruction during the Commonwealth—only to be recreated in honour of his son at the Restoration. Both the topiary sun-dial in the north-east corner, and the Founder's arms in the south-west, seem to have been even more elaborate than indicated by the engravings of Loggan, Burghers and Williams (Plates 3, 56, 57): von Uffenbach who visited the college in 1710 recorded that the former had 'a great wooden stake supplying the index finger', while 'above, as the circle is not quite filled up by the twelve hours, appear the words: *sic vita*, also cut out of box';[62] and Mrs. Lybbe Powys who, as late as 1759, still admired the garden as 'a curious specimen of the old parterre taste', noticed the same inscription as Wood in the arms of the Founder.[63] The fourth quarter was laid out as a knot garden or 'Labyrinth'.

The mount itself is described by von Uffenbach as 'a fairly steep bank called *Parnassus* covered with trimmed hedges and trees'. Probably at the same time as the sun-dial was being laid out below, it was crowned with a wind-dial, whose appearance in Loggan's engraving (Plate 3) exactly coincides with the 'ingenious contrivance' later praised in

Plot—'the *Dials* made upon a Pile of *Books* formerly on New-College Mount, with *Time* on the top, exactly pointing out from what *Quarter* the wind blows, upon the 32 points of the *Compass*, depicted on a *cylinder* of *stone*'.[64] Plot's use of the word 'formerly', and Celia Fiennes's description of a summer-house on top of the mount in 1694,[65] suggests that this charming feature, so typical of the Oxford of Wren, Boyle and Halley, was short-lived, although it seems to appear again in Williams's perhaps not altogether accurate engraving of 1732 (Plate 57).

The large walnut trees shown by Loggan in the middle of the bowling-green, to the south of the mount, were cut down in 1682, when the college earned £18 from the sale of the timber, and two years later £4 15s. 0d. were spent on 'mending ye bowling green wall and gate'.[66] It was probably about this time that Celia Fiennes's 'close shady walk . . . and cutt hedge' was planted here; half a century later Mrs. Lybbe Powys described the bowling-green as 'shady'd on one side by tall sycamores, whose branches are so enwoven from end to end as render them justly admired as a natural curiosity'. If Williams's engraving can be trusted in this respect, the pleached line of trees on the north side of the parterre just inside the city wall, cut into the shape of arches, must have been an even more remarkable sight.

Although the garden was, until the turn of the century, still sealed off from the rest of the college by a high wall, and by the right of way from the kitchen to the Non-licet gate, the austerity of the Founder's buildings was already beginning to be softened by flowers and grass. Loggan shows what appears to be a lawn in the centre of the main quadrangle in 1675, and four grass 'plotts' with trees at the corners in the cloisters. By the early eighteenth century (shown in Williams's engraving) these had been replaced by a large circular bed within a square, perhaps edged by box, which the somewhat jaundiced von Uffenbach described as 'a poor garden in the centre [of the cloisters] surrounded by a walk'. The more impressionable Celia Fiennes was, however, pleased to find the fellows taking 'much delight in greens of all sorts Myrtle Oringe and Lemons and Lorrestine growing in potts of earth, and so moved about from place to place and into the aire sometymes'. Set outside the doorways to the staircases, rather in the manner of the humbler geraniums and aspidistras still to be seen in summer on the steps of almshouses, they must have lent a festive air both to the new quadrangle and to the 'old colledg', which Byrd's men had 'washed' in 1684.[67]

Apart from some minor alterations—the refitting of the two vestries north of the chapel as a fellows' set about 1690, the building of a stable at the end of the Long Room in 1691, the erection of a large sun-dial on the south face of the muniment tower in 1696 and of a new brewhouse next to the kitchen the following year—the last decade of the seventeenth century saw a major decorative addition to the chapel.[68] After all the earlier arguments about a suitable reredos, the panel of cloth of gold put up in 1671 cannot have provided a sufficiently strong emphasis for the great blank east wall. In October 1692 the engraver Michael Burghers was paid £1 for 'sketching ye upper end of ye Chappell', and though neither the drawing nor an engraving of it appears to survive, this may have been made (like his earlier print of Byrd's quadrangle design) to raise subscriptions for a wholly new scheme of decorative painting, which the college finally commissioned from 'our ingenious countryman Mr. Henry Cook'.[69] In August 1695, Wood records that 'the plastering of the High Altar of New College was pulled down and old broken statues discovered',[70] but this was almost certainly an unintentional development during the preparation of the wall for Cooke's mural; the restoration of the medieval reredos was not seriously considered for another hundred years. The appearance of Henry Cooke's painting, which was paid for in 1696, is unfortunately known only from a description in the *Pocket Companion to Oxford*, published in 1753. But this is detailed enough to suggest that it was one of the most ambitious *trompe l'oeil* schemes, in the style of Verrio and Laguerre, ever attempted by an English painter.

The altarpiece represented

the Concave of a Semi-Rotunda in the Ionic order, with a Cupola adorned with curious Mosaic work, in which the East End of the Chapel seems to terminate. The Altar, which is partly built of wood and partly painted, intercepting in some degree the view at right Angles, greatly favours the *Deceptio*; particularly two large open Pannels in the lower part thereof, which have a wonderful Effect. In the upper part of the Altar, which is painted in such a Manner as to seem the finishing of the woodwork that supports it, between two columns of the composite order . . . is represented the salutation of the Virgin Mary; and above the Entablature hangs hovering a most beautiful cloud with great Numbers of Angels and Cherubs in various Attitudes waiting the return of the Angel Gabriel.

Very few examples of the work of Henry Cooke (?1642–1700) now survive: he completed the large painting over the dais in the hall of Chelsea Hospital, begun by Verrio, about 1690; and an oval ceiling painted for the board room of the New River Company at Islington still exists. His other known commissions have all perished, together with his easel pictures, which were equally celebrated in their day. Having spent two periods of seven years each in Italy, where he is thought to have studied under Salvator Rosa, and where he made a valuable collection of books and pictures, Cooke should be better known, and it is sad that not one engraving of New College chapel before Wyatt's alterations exists to show more clearly the form, and scale, of his masterpiece.

The same sort of mystery surrounds another gift made to the college in 1696, a lead statue of Minerva set up in the centre of the front quadrangle at the expense of Sir Henry Parker, Bart., the builder of Honington Hall in Warwickshire—perhaps an early work by Van Nost, who first popularised life-size lead statues in this country, and who probably made the Muses (to Thornhill's design) for the parapet of the Clarendon Building in 1715. The statue was seen by Mrs. Lybbe Powys in 1759 but sold about thirty years later, when the present circular grass plot was laid out, the proceeds being added to the library funds.[71] Like the near-contemporary statue of Mercury set up in Tom Quad at Christ Church, Minerva at any rate provides a suitably secular close to the seventeenth-century building history of New College. The Founder would doubtless have thought her an unsuitable rival to the Blessed Virgin over his entrance archway, but he would have been even more shocked to find commoners and noblemen living in a second quadrangle beyond his garden gate, and to know that plans for accommodating more, and in still greater comfort, were already afoot.

3. THE EARLY EIGHTEENTH CENTURY: THE GARDEN QUADRANGLE COMPLETED

The extension of the garden quad eastwards in the first decade of the eighteenth century involved a new challenge to the Founder's statutes, almost as important for the further development of the college as the acceptance of commoners had been, twenty-five years earlier. The impetus for further new building, so soon after Byrd's two ranges, came partly from the senior fellows, who wished for still more comfortable sets of single rooms than they already occupied in the upper chambers of the main quadrangle, but also from the desire to house the wealthiest and most influential noblemen and commoners, to fill the college's coffers and to gain suitable preferment for the ever more worldly fellows. The obvious way to gain this extra accommodation was to add another pair of blocks to the new quadrangle beyond Byrd's, and stepped back still further so as not to mask any of the existing windows. The main drawback to this scheme was that it would effectively seal off the medieval kitchen and its outbuildings from the Non-licet gate at the top of Queen's Lane, originally built to enable the City Council to make its annual survey of the walls, but also used by tradesmen and college servants. The solution hit upon by the fellows in April 1700, after long 'thoughts concerning the New Buildings', filled with 'pros', 'cons' and 'quaeres', was to open a new gate through the city wall at the bastion just to the north-east of the kitchen, and to make a passage from here through into Holywell, on land bought from Merton.[72]

The Visitor's leave had to be obtained, and complicated new covenants made both with Merton and with the city, the latter made more difficult because of the Founder's agreement to 'ye Annuall Entertainment of ye Corperacion wch (to th^r great dissatisfaction) is now layd aside'. But the expense of all this was more than justified: the new gate (in the fellows' own words) brought 'our wood and other things directly to kitchen, cellar, and woodhouses without disturbing ye Collidge'; it gained 'Two Roomes for ye New Buildings, otherwise . . . taken upp in 2 Arch'd Gates' (which could not necessarily be placed opposite each other); it meant the high garden wall could be removed and the parterre opened up to the college for the first time; and it finally provided room for new stables, a granary and other outbuildings on the land bought from Merton just outside the city wall, known as the Slype.

The local masons, Richard Piddington and George Smith, who had taken over Byrd's yard in Holywell in about 1692, signed the final contract for the south-east block on 2 August 1700.[73] In it they undertook to reproduce exactly all the decorative details of Byrd's new ranges 'except the Italian Mouldings about the windows which is to be done wth Ionick Architrive'. The windows themselves, apart from those at the back facing Queen's Lane ('wch shall be transtrum windows with two upright Iron Bares'), were to be 'shashes'—specified in the earlier agreement as being 'hung on box pullies with hemp line'—the first documented use of sash windows in Oxford, and an innovation which was to have important consequences for the rest of the college.

Although a ground plan for one sample staircase is attached to the contract, and mention is also made of a 'draught or modell agreed on' for the whole building, it is not clear who was actually responsible for the design. 'Mr. Martin May of Kiddlington', who was appointed 'the pson to direct and determine any differences' between the college and the contractors, and who was also to approve the size of the roof timbers, received a 'present' of £10 14s. 0d. for his trouble in May 1704[74] and later performed the same function for the second wing. On the other hand he appears neither to have been a relation of the architect, Hugh May (whose advice the college had sought thirty years earlier), nor to have designed other buildings in his own right. The two new blocks could well have been devised by as accomplished a mason and statuary as John Piddington, but are perhaps even more likely to be by William Townesend, his fellow contractor for the north block, built in 1707. Townesend built, and perhaps designed, the fellows' building at Corpus Christi in 1706–12, and was later the executant architect for both Peckwater quadrangle at Christ Church and the front quadrangle at Queen's College. His close relations with New College over a period of thirty years, and the fact that he was also employed to make alterations at Winchester in 1727–9, suggest that he acted, like Byrd in the previous generation, as the master-mason regularly consulted by the fellows over matters of design as well as construction.[75]

Although the façades of the two new blocks seem at first sight to follow Byrd's originals very faithfully, a number of subtle changes become apparent on closer inspection: the pediments over the central windows are broader and less angular; an extra string-course between the first and second floors stresses the horizontal as opposed to the strongly vertical lines of the inner ranges; while the two central doorcases, with bracketed architraves breaking out over them, are much more powerful than Byrd's. The most noticeable difference, however, is in the wider, and at the same time more widely spaced, windows. Although dictated by purely practical reasons (respectively the new sash frames, and the far larger chambers provided behind them) these give the finished garden quadrangle a distinctly Baroque air. Seen from the mound, the narrower, more crowded fenestration of Byrd's ranges gives the illusion that they are recessed far further than they actually are (Plate 52). Whether this was a matter of luck rather than judgement is hard to say, but both Burghers (Plate 51) and later Vertue were to take full advantage of the visual possibilities it presented. An illusion of a different sort, but managed with equal skill, is the apparent symmetry of the two new buildings. To make space for the south-east block the wall between the Long Room and the Non-licet gate had to be pushed out a few feet into Queen's Lane (making this, in the days before traffic restrictions, one of the most dangerous blind corners in Oxford); even then there was not quite room for the wide rectangular building, and with wonderful *insouciance* it was therefore built at a slight angle to Byrd's range, five or six feet out of true. This must have led to some head-scratching seven years later when the answering north block was begun. Had it been set exactly parallel, or at right angles to Byrd's block, it might have drawn attention to this irregularity, so a compromise was reached and it was built about three feet out of true. It says much for the eighteenth-century masons' rule of thumb that this discrepancy is almost unnoticeable, except when seen on a ground plan (Fig. a).

The long interval between the building of the two blocks is probably explained simply by shortage of money. The south block, containing six fellows' chambers, was to be financed entirely from benefactions, but the total (estimated at £600, but in the end nearer £800) was not immediately forthcoming and the difference had to be borrowed from the college treasury. It must have been with a view to whipping up further support that the engraver, Michael Burghers, was paid £15 in August 1702 'for 300 prints of the New Buildings', almost certainly based on a drawing which is now in the Ashmolean Museum (Plate 51).[76] The new gate through the city wall and the connecting passage to Holywell was constructed in the autumn of that year, but although the bill sent in by Piddington and Smith included 'bringing in of stone for the 2[d] pile of Building', five years went by before the treasury had gathered together sufficient funds to pay for the remaining block. The six chambers that it provided were reserved for noblemen and gentlemen commoners and were looked on as an investment, like the north range of Byrd's buildings, though still more lucrative. Mr. Wharton and the Marquess of Hartington, given rooms here in 1715, were for instance asked to pay £20 each as a 'benefaction' at their entrance, and a further £7 per annum as rent.[77]

The interiors of the two wings have been much less altered than those of the two earlier ranges of the garden quadrangle, perhaps because they established a standard of comfort that has never entirely been surpassed. The staircases were a great improvement on Byrd's, better lit, and easier to climb for senior fellows after those immense repasts that were now a regular feature of college life. That in the north block is still more spacious than its fellow, and has elegant twisted balusters in place of the simpler turned pattern established by Byrd. Each set of rooms contained a chamber lit by three windows, a study with two and a bedroom with one window (these having corner-chimneypieces in the fashion established by Wren and Talman, at Hampton Court and elsewhere), and finally a closet behind the stairs, saving a cold journey to the Long Room. The deeply moulded bolection panelling in the north block, which still survives in the ground- and first-floor rooms, was installed in 1710.[78]

As a final embellishment to the quadrangle, the gift of £100 in November 1710, from James Brydges (later Duke of Chandos), the builder of Canons, enabled the college to commission a magnificent wrought-iron gate screen at the entrance to the garden (Plate 53) from one of the foremost blacksmiths of the day, Thomas Robinson.[79] His agreement, dated 7 February 1711, gives a detailed description of the screen 'according to the draught here annext' (now unfortunately lost), specifying that it should be sent down from his workshop at Hyde Park Corner and set up 'before the first Sunday after Easter', a remarkably short space of time for so complicated a work. He was paid £160 (for some reason £10 less than the agreed sum) on 29 June. Robinson had, from 1697 onwards, worked with Tijou on the ironwork for St. Paul's, and his gates betray the influence of the French smith, particularly in the *repoussé* work of the overthrow—the grotesque mask above the Founder's arms and the acanthus scrolls each side—and in the finials to the gate piers with their stylised flowers. Apart from the great height of the central gate, appropriately vertical in emphasis as a counter-weight to the horizontal spreading wings, the design of the screen, 130 feet long, is also ingenious in the way it disguises the asymmetry of the quadrangle. The gate is placed neither on the axis of the archway below the Founder's library, nor exactly equidistant between the two new blocks; yet the eye is tricked into accepting the screen as perfectly balanced by the deep outward bow of the railings in the centre, and its inward-curving sides, of different lengths.

The New College screen makes it virtually certain on stylistic grounds that Robinson was the author of the splendid gates (or more properly *clairvoyée*, since they cannot be opened) at the east end of the garden at Trinity, erected in 1713. A smaller gate made by him for the entrance to the bowling-green at New College no longer exists, and it is disappointing to relate that even the screen itself is not the original, as has previously been thought. By the late nineteenth century it had evidently rusted beyond repair, and in 1894 a replica was made by an Oxford firm, William Lucy & Co., of the Eagle Iron Works. The skill with which this work was done (convincing many later experts on wrought-iron work of its authenticity) still enables it to be seen, to all intents and purposes, as an eighteenth century artefact—indeed as one of the supreme examples of the blacksmith's art in this country.[80]

The completion of the garden quadrangle, and the consequent opening of a vista from the middle gate right through to the parterre and mound, precipitated new work on the garden. A statement of expenditure from the 'Building Chest' made in 1707 included payment 'for carrying the Rubbish of the New Building into the Garden' and an obviously related payment 'for raising the walks and work done in the garden'.[81] It was probably at this time that the grass slopes shown by Loggan to the north of the parterre and behind the mound were converted into level terraces, with the avenues shown in Williams's engraving of 1732 (Plate 57).

Robinson's agreement for the gate screen in 1711 gives an interesting clue as to the identity of the college's garden designer in these years, for it stipulates that any dispute arising should be settled by 'Mr. Townsend and Mr. Bobart'.[82] While the former is undoubtedly William Townesend, the mason (and probably also architect of the two new blocks flanking the screen), the latter must be Jacob Bobart, who succeeded his father as Keeper of the Botanic Garden in 1680. The 1708 engraving of the garden quad by Michael Burghers has a fascinating vignette of the garden in one corner (Plate 56), which may represent a more radical new scheme of Bobart's, never entirely achieved. It shows a central flight of steps leading down to the parterre between two gazebos—perhaps not surprisingly Dutch in feeling, given the ancestry of both gardener and engraver.

The changes made by Bobart probably involved the planting as much as the design of the garden, though sadly few horticultural details can be gleaned from the bursars' rolls. The garden seems therefore to have remained static for well over half a century, and there is no evidence that its formality began to be eroded until the very end of the century. Poynter in 1749 described the 'lofty artificial Mount, encompassed with several Hedges of Juniper adorn'd with Trees cut into several Shapes, with Stone Steps and winding Walks up to the Top, and the Top encompass'd with Rails and Seats, and a Tree growing in the Middle'; but in the context it would be absurd to think that his 'winding Walks' signified an informal serpentine ascent, any more than Celia Fiennes's 'round of green paths' had done in 1694.[83] The eighteenth-century fellows were much too conservative to adopt new-fangled theories of the 'Picturesque'.

In another respect, by replacing the Founder's Gothic windows with sashes, the warden and fellows perhaps bowed too easily to fashion, though they were only following a general trend from which very few residential buildings at Oxford or Cambridge escaped. The original fourteenth-century windows of the fellows' lodgings were made purposely narrow, since they were not intended to be glazed. The study rooms, lit by no more than slits, were particularly dark, and probably made more so by Tudor leaded lights. There is evidence that old windows were being enlarged during the seventeenth century: £40 was for instance given by Sir Lambert Fitch in 1695 'ad amplicanda et ornanda ffenestrarii lumina collegii'.[84] What precipitated a wholesale change, however, was the adoption of sash-windows for the two east blocks of the garden quadrangle, shown opened to varying extents in Burghers's drawing of c. 1702 (Plate 51), perhaps to draw attention to their novelty. The contrast between these sashes and the stone mullion-and-transom windows of Byrd's inner ranges undoubtedly detracted from the otherwise uniform appearance of the completed quadrangle, and in 1718 Jeremiah Franklin was paid £257 'for sashing ye windows in lower Court, Comon Room, Library, Lodgings &c'. The problem was where to stop. It was obviously impossible to introduce sashes on the east side of the Founder's library (and upper library) but retain the Gothic tracery on the other side of the room, overlooking the main quadrangle; equally the medieval windows of the fellows' chambers needed enlarging for purely practical reasons. A further £267 was therefore spent in 1721 on 'sashing . . . in ye Old Court'.[85]

There is no doubt that from a purely architectural point of view the destruction of the fourteenth-century tracery and enlarging of the windows upset the balance of the original composition, already prejudiced by the addition of the second storey in 1674. The deeply chamfered reveals and sills were entirely cut away, so that the new sashes (with thicker glazing bars and more panes than the present, late eighteenth-century, ones) rested rather unsatisfactorily on the string-course below. The larger windows of the chambers were also considerably heightened, and the narrow study windows marginally widened, both being recessed in an awkward manner in the immensely thick medieval walls. Particularly sad losses were the double traceried windows of the warden's hall over the main gate and the beautiful oriel window lighting his study, extended up to the floor above in the Tudor period. The three-light window of the warden's oratory next to the antechapel, filled with stained glass, escaped for the time being (and is still shown in Williams's engraving of 1732), but it too was destroyed later in the century.

Other alterations were made to the interiors of the fellows' chambers at this time: three new staircases with twisted balusters on the model of the north-east garden quadrangle block were installed in the south range of the Founder's quadrangle (now nos. 2, 3 and 4), and around this period the gables at the back of this range overlooking Queen's Lane were replaced by a continuous wall. The Founder's library was partially refitted in 1718, and four years later the staircase at the southern end of it (between the old Conduit Chamber and Chamber of Three) was enlarged to serve as the principal entrance to both libraries, piercing the solid wall which the Founder had intended to decrease the risk of fire.[86] The new doorcase to the library on the first floor has an arched stone frame with a large carved shell in place of a keystone, almost certainly designed by William Townesend and influenced by the Baroque style of Hawksmoor and Vanbrugh, for whom he had worked at Blenheim. It is interesting that the east-facing windows on this staircase have the same small square blocks at the intersections of the sash-bars found in the summer-house at the far end of the warden's garden (Plate 55)—probably also built by Townesend in the early 1720s.

William Townesend's other main work for the college was the renewing of the hall floor in Portland stone with squares of black marble, and at the same time the remodelling of the chambers below it, in 1722.[87] Whether the medieval walls of the ground floor were insufficient for the weight of the stone floor above is not clear, but the mason's bill includes wholly new foundations, and the construction of the present pair of sturdy brick tunnel-vaults below hall running parallel from east to west. The two new rooms below hall were intended for the eight chaplains but seem not to have been a success: described by them as 'damp and unwholesome cellars', they were vacated four years later in favour of new rooms made above the kitchen stairs. Whether the chaplains felt much safer in their new eyrie is open to doubt, given Hearne's account of a great gale early in the following year, when 'the wind being extraordinarily high . . . in the Forenoon the kitchen chimney of New College fell down, and broke the Ribs of the Man that turned the spit (but 'tis hoped he may be recovered) and spoiled all the Meat at the Fire. It was a very odd, rotten, old chimney'. If this was the fanciful Tudor chimney at the east end, with its twin ogee-domed turrets, it was presumably rebuilt on exactly the same lines.[88]

It is unfortunate that none of the chapel fittings introduced in the early eighteenth century are recorded in engravings, as is Wyatt's later work. The most important of these was an elaborate wrought-iron communion rail made in 1718, probably to replace carved wooden balusters of the 1660s, which were thought too simple for the richness of Henry Cooke's painted *Deceptio* on the east wall. The railing was made by the London smith, Richard Booth, who in the following year made railings for the west end of St. Paul's, Covent Garden. Booth may have succeeded to Thomas Robinson's position in the Office of Works after the latter's death in 1715, and this would explain how he came to be employed by the college. His bill includes an undertaking 'to finish ye iron work att each end according to ye modell below'—a small sketch of value in that it shows one complete panel of the balustrade, thus enabling one to picture how the whole screen may have looked.[89] At the same time William Townesend paved the sanctuary with black and white marble, and, between 1731 and 1733, Jeremiah Franklin supplied panelling, including sixteen Doric pilasters richly gilded, for the north and south walls between the stalls and reredos. The warden, Dr. Coxed, also settled a substantial bill in 1733 for carved and gilt chandeliers and wall-sconces, ordered from the London makers, William and Charles Sparke.[90] Ablaze with candlelight, and with gilded ironwork and panelling, black and white marble, and fat crimson velvet cushions lining the stalls,[91] the chapel must have presented a colourful spectacle in Parson Woodforde's day.

REFERENCES

1. The stone for the paving, brought from London, was supplied by John Borde of Corfe, carver of the celebrated Beauchamp tomb at Warwick; see *V.C.H.*, 145; E. A. Gee, 'Oxford Masons 1370–1530', *Archaeological Journal* (1952), vol. cix, 62, 64, 67, 70.
2. N.C. MS. 7409.
3. Woodforde, 64.
4. B.L. Add. MS. 36423, fol. 32.
5. No direct evidence for this survives, but the tradition was established by the early eighteenth century; see John Ayliffe, *The Antient and Present State of the University of Oxford* (1714), vol. I, 322.
6. Woodforde, 10; six more unidentified coats-of-arms in stained glass were installed in 1534.
7. N.C. MSS. 1739, 1740.
8. A. Chalmers, *A History of the Colleges of Oxford* (1810), vol. i, 130, records that the roof was 'forty feet high before the modern ceiling was placed there'.
9. A central 'ambo' or pulpit was bought in 1540 for 'reading of the Bible' (Smith, 61–3), but the custom seems to have lapsed again after 1558.
10. Mrs. R. Lane-Poole, *Catalogue of Portraits in . . . the University . . . of Oxford* (1925), vol. II, 151 et seq.
11. See copies of Bishop Horne's injunctions in N.C. MS. 3688.
12. N.C. MS. 7500.
13. R. H. C. Davis, 'The Chronology of Perpendicular Architecture in Oxford', *Oxoniensia*, vols. xi/xii (1946/7), 81.
14. These rooms, only 5 feet 8 inches high, were still in use in the nineteenth century—one of them being lived in by Warden Sewell's housekeeper; for this, and a more detailed account of the Tudor warden's lodgings, see Smith, 69 et seq.
15. Woodforde, 11.
16. N.C. MSS. 7523, 7530, 7538.
17. N.C. MS. 7493; Smith, Appendix III, 167.
18. Wood, *Colleges and Halls*, 193.
19. N.C. MS. 7568.
20. See Woodward's *Observata quaedam. . .*, N.C. MS. 2799; Agas's map is reproduced in the Oxford Historical Society portfolio of maps, 1884.
21. N.C. MS. 7481.
22. J. M. Steane, 'The Development of Tudor and Stuart Garden Design in Northamptonshire', *Northamptonshire Past and Present* (1977), 385.
23. *V.C.H.*, 151, *n*. 51.

24. Smith, 66–7; but Smith mistakenly calls the chimneypiece in the warden's study Tudor.

25. W. G. Hiscock, *A Christ Church Miscellany* (1946), pl. 68–9.

26. *V.C.H.*, p. 151.

27. Ed. L. M. Quiller Couch, *Reminiscences of Oxford* (Oxford Hist. Soc., 1892), vol. xxii, 4–5.

28. Woodforde, 12–14.

29. N.C. MS. 1193.

30. Rashdall and Rait, 68, wrongly attribute the painting to the gilder Hawkins; a copy of Doone's estimate (made in 1747 'from a Mss Book at ye wardens of Winton') is in the archives, N.C. MS. 993.

31. N.C. MSS. 7619, 7633.

32. Woodward's *Observata quaedam. . .*, N.C. MS. 2799; Rashdall and Rait 170.

33. H. E. Bell, 'Longwall Papers', N.C. MSS. 10, 268; Wood, *Life and Times*, 64 et seq.

34. Ibid.

35. Ed. Quiller Couch, op. cit.; 'Mr. Fletcher's account of bells' (watermark 1802), N.C. MS. 2452.

36. N.C. MS. 989 (Woodward's memorandum in the back of the account book).

37. Woodward's 'Account of what was done as to ye Adorneing ye East End of ye Colledge Chapell', in N.C. MS. 989.

38. For Van Thulden, see *Connoisseur*, vol. 56 (1920), 169; U. Thieme and F. Becker, *Allgemeines Lexikon der Bildenden Künstler*, XXXIII, 1939, 110.

39. N.C. MSS. 1188, 1201.

40. N.C. MS. 1152; Hobbes died at Hardwick in 1679.

41. The contract is dated 30 May 1674 (N.C. MS. 1152); Rupert Gunnis, *Dictionary of British Sculptors 1660–1830* (1953), 126–7, refers to him as John Dener, evidently as the result of a misreading.

42. N.C. MSS. 1162, 989.

43. Mrs. J. C. Cole, 'William Byrd', in *Oxoniensia*, vol. xiv, 1949, 63.

44. N.C. MS. 7685.

45. R. Willis and J. W. Clark, *Architectural History of the University of Cambridge* (1886), vol. III., 280–1.

46. John Cornforth, 'The Buildings of Warden Nicholas', *Country Life*, 26 March 1964.

47. Mrs. J. C. Cole, op. cit.

48. N.C. MS. 1153; the engraving is reproduced in Mrs. J. C. Cole, op. cit., plate VIII, but without the flaps raised.

49. N.C. MSS. 526, 1133, 1171.

50. E.g. the Duke's Head at King's Lynn and the Sessions House at Northampton; Cottesbrooke in Northamptonshire and Kimbolton, Huntingdonshire, also have early examples of this form.

51. N.C. MS. 951.

52. Willis and Clark, op. cit., III, 274; the idea of an open quadrangle had been current at Cambridge since the time of Dr. Caius.

53. K. Downes, *English Baroque Architecture*, 1966, 33–4.

54. Ayliffe, op. cit., vol. II, 322.

55. N.C. MSS. 1153, 1168.

56. Byrd may well have designed the Old Ashmolean (1678–83), previously attributed to the master-mason, Thomas Wood, who was (or had been) one of his journeymen—and similarly Kill-Canon (*c.* 1671–4) and Fell's Buildings (1672–9) at Christ Church, where his name appears constantly in the accounts; Hiscock, op. cit., 201–2.

57. N.C. MS. 993 (order of 27 May 1684); N.C. MS. 1141.

58. N.C. MS. 951.

59. N.C. MS. 1153.

60. N.C. MSS. 1153, 951.

61. Transcript of a letter from Wood to Mr. Crew, dated 8 May 1658, in the Bodleian (Ballard MSS.) xiv, 12.

62. Ed. W. H. and W. J. C. Quarrell, *Oxford in 1710* (1928), 8–9.

63. Ed. P. Climenson, *Passages from the Diaries of Mrs. Philip Lybbe Powys 1756–1808* (1899), 39–40.

64. Robert Plot. *Natural History of Oxfordshire* 2nd ed. (1705), 274–5. The word 'formerly' does not occur in the first (1677) edition.

65. Ed. C. Morris, *The Journeys of Celia Fiennes* (1947), 37.

66. N.C. MS. 951, 30 June and 19 April respectively.

67. N.C. MS. 1153.

68. N.C. MSS. 1151, 917; *V.C.H.*, 147; the sun-dial (bearing the date in Roman numerals) can be seen in Williams's engraving of 1732.

69. N.C. MS. 951; for Cooke see E. Croft-Murray, *Decorative Painting in England 1537–1837*, vol. I (1962), 246.

70. Wood, *Life and Times*, III, 488.

71. Ibid., 194; N.C. MS. 2449; Rashdall and Rait, 85.

72. N.C. MSS. 1138, 1150.

73. N.C. MS. 1169; a preliminary contract, drawn up in March 1700 (N.C. MS. 895) named two different builders, John Saunders and William Osborne, under the direction of a 'Mr. Fitch'—possibly the same John Fitch of London who contracted to build the west front of Chatsworth in July 1700, but who died later the same year (Colvin, 206).

74. N.C. MS. 3480.

75. For Piddington, see Gunnis, op. cit., 303; for Townesend, see Colvin, 618; J. H. Harvey, *Journal of the Archaeological Association* (1965), 3rd series, xxviii, 124.

76. This drawing of the garden quadrangle, by Burghers, is reproduced in H. M. Petter, *The Oxford Almanacks* (1974), 57, where it is dated between 1707 and 1711. It seems more likely that it was made (and first engraved) in 1702 but that no impressions of the first state survive—a second impression made in 1708 would account for the unique engraving in the

Bodleian dated 1708 (G. A. Oxon. a. 56), obviously based on this drawing, and also including a vignette of the garden (see Plate 56, and page 225 below).

77. N.C. MS. 3480.

78. Ibid.

79. Ibid.; Ayliffe, op. cit., vol. i, 322 (referring to Robinson as 'that ingenious artist'); N.C. MS. 918; for further information on Robinson's career, I am indebted to Mr. Edward Saunders:

80. An advertisement of Lucy & Co. dated 1897 with a photograph of the new gates and explanatory text is in a volume in the Bodleian (G.A. Oxon. A. 56); a letter from the firm to the bursar in 1894 containing an estimate and patterns for alternative ironwork is in N.C. MS. 3125. Authorities who have accepted the gates as genuine include J. Starkie Gardner, *English Ironwork of the 17th and 18th centuries* (1911); M. Ayrton and A. Silcock, *Wrought Iron and its Decorative Use* (1929), 172.

81. N.C. MS. 3480.

82. N.C. MS. 918.

83. *Pace* Smith, 121–2; Rashdall and Rait, 88–9.

84. N.C. MS. 1200.

85. N.C. MSS. 3480, 1142.

86. N.C. MSS. 5164, 5168, 5171, 5173 (bursars' account books).

87. N.C. MSS. 1147, 1137.

88. Ed. H. E. Salter, *Hearne's Remarks and Collections* (Oxford Hist. Soc. (1914), vol. IX, 254); the chimney is shown still intact in Williams's engraving of 1732 and in Buckler's early nineteenth-century drawing (Fig. f).

89. *Survey of London* (1970), vol. xxxvi, 107; N.C. MS. 1199.

90. N.C. MSS. 3480, 1194, 1199.

91. Supplied by 'Mr. West' in 1713; N.C. MS. 3480.

VII

Restoration and Expansion: The Buildings since 1750

GERVASE JACKSON-STOPS

1. THE LATE EIGHTEENTH CENTURY: REYNOLDS AND WYATT

Against the splendour and colour of the new fittings provided for the chapel in the early eighteenth century, the decayed medieval windows must have seemed to the fellows to present a sad contrast, and even before 1750 began the long programme of 'restoration', in which nearly all the fourteenth-century glass in the main body of the chapel was destroyed. In restrospect it is easy to criticise the college for this calamity, but the eighteenth century enjoyed neither the scientific advances that made pure restoration possible, nor the knowledge of medieval art that made it desirable. What happened at New College was paralleled in countless parish churches and cathedrals during the same period, undertaken with the best motives and at great expense. The five windows on the southern side of the chapel, more exposed to heat and light over the previous 350 years than the others, were the first to be tackled. On 4 December 1736, a contract was drawn up with William Price of Kirby Street, Hatton Garden, a member of a celebrated dynasty of glass-painters, who had recently restored the rose window and the west window of Westminster Abbey.[1] His 'repairs' at New College were not as extensive as has sometimes been represented: all the main figures appear to have been renewed, their names unfortunately being omitted, but the tracery lights and most of the canopies are original (Plate 26). The work was completed by September 1740, and Price's signature appears, with the date, in the westernmost window. Horace Walpole on a visit to Oxford in 1760 commented on the 'fine painted windows; half of them recoloured by Joshua [an error

233

for William] Price', expressing tacit approval of the results.[2]

The next restoration to be attempted did not, however, meet with universal approbation even from contemporaries. With the help of a bequest from a fellow, John Eyre, who had died three years before, the college in 1765 commissioned William Peckitt of York to repair the Tree of Jesse in the great west window 'in the same manner as the New windows in the Inner Chapel'. Peckitt was on the face of it quite as well qualified as Price to undertake this work; his surviving work in a wholly eighteenth-century Gothic idiom, as at Kirkleatham Hospital, or at Strawberry Hill, where he made Walpole's armorial panels in stained glass for the staircase, shows considerable skill as well as charm. But his treatment of medieval glass was unfortunately far more cavalier than his predecessor's. Despite the initial agreement, he removed most of the glass in the main part of the west window, accepting it in part payment for the new work. Nothing if not a shrewd businessman, Peckitt later sold much of it to the Dean and Chapter of York, and fragments of the New College Tree of Jesse can still be seen in a three-light window over the entrance to the Zouche chapel in York Minster.

Peckitt's new work in the west window was far from a literal copy of the old (Plate 27). His draughtsmanship was severely criticised by the fellows, and when the time came to attempt the restoration of the three left-hand windows on the north side of the main chapel in 1771, his preliminary drawings were rejected out of hand. There followed much discussion on the possible artists whose designs Peckitt might execute; he had recently completed some windows at Audley End after water-colours by Cipriani and it was generally held that his work was perfectly acceptable when following the designs of a 'skilfull draughtsman'. The Dean of Exeter, for whom Peckitt had recently made a window based on cartoons 'by the late famous Artist Mr. Price', acted at first as the college's adviser and intermediary. In 1772 he commissioned a drawing of John the Baptist from Samuel Wale, but this was in turn rejected in favour of designs by Biagio Rebecca, perhaps recommended by James Wyatt, with whom he had recently collaborated at Heaton Hall in Lancashire. Rebecca's water-colour design for the figures in the north windows (Plate 28) still survives in the warden's lodgings, but the canopies were apparently left to Peckitt and again earned him criticism from the fellows, one of whom, J. H. Thorpe, wrote in April 1774 that he was 'sorry to remark that the shrine-work of your Niches is not of that pure gothic I would wish, bearing too much resemblance to those grotesque designs wch should never be admitted into any serious compositions'. There was a further cause for complaint in the enormous bill Peckitt presented for the three new windows, amounting to £677 10s., nearly double the amount bequeathed to the college for this purpose by three brothers, Henry, John and the Rev. Thomas Coker.[3]

The new spirit of economy that prevailed after this extravagance was short-lived, but it resulted all the same in the preservation of the precious medieval glass still to be seen in the antechapel. In 1775 the college sought the advice of a coach-painter from Marlow named Lovegrove 'who has lately been employed upon the window at All Souls', and it was evidently he who recommended that the fragments saved from the north windows should be re-set in those on the south and west of the antechapel.[4] The work was carried out by a glazier named John Taylor, who also re-leaded the other old windows here (on the north and east); if the original iconographical scheme was largely lost in the process, the survival of representative samples from almost all the chapel windows was perhaps a more important gain for later generations. There remained the problem of the only two unrestored windows in the main chapel, those in the north-east corner, whose subdued tones must have contrasted strongly with the bright colours introduced by Price and by Peckitt. Somewhat nervously the college approached a third and equally celebrated glass-painter of the day, Thomas Jervais, on the understanding that he was only to make the second window if the first was a success, and that he was (like Peckitt) to execute the work of a 'capital Artist'. Jervais's own suggestion was Benjamin West, but through the offices of the poet Thomas Warton and his brother Joseph, Headmaster of Winchester, the college secured an even bigger name, West's predecessor as President of the Royal Academy and the most respected painter of his generation, Sir Joshua Reynolds.[5]

The great man's first visit to the college was made in August 1777, on his way to Blenheim 'to Paint the whole Marlborough Family in one Picture'. Soon afterwards Reynolds made preliminary sketches for the eight figures—representing not the obscure saints of the original scheme, but female figures as allegories of religion, the three theological virtues, and the four cardinal virtues. But the odd contrast these would have made with the existing glass, particularly as they were placed against a background of sky rather than in niches, caused the fellows to change their whole course of action towards the end of the year. Peckitt's unsatisfactory west window was to be dismantled and used to fill the two north-east windows of the chapel, where it would blend in colour (and in the incompetence of its design) with its neighbours; that would also leave the whole of the great west window for Reynolds's (and Jervais's) work. The artist was delighted by this, not only because of the larger scale of the window, and the fewer stylistic restrictions imposed, but also because he saw a chance here for a dramatic central section, in an entirely painterly style, achieved by removing some of the tracery in the upper middle lights. Any architectural objections to this were swiftly set aside, Reynolds writing that 'not only Sir Willm [Chambers] but every person to whom I have shown it approve[s] of the alteration', and that it would enable him to render a 'Christ in the Manger, on the Principle that Corregio has done it in the famous Picture called the Notte [*Night*, now in the Zwinger, Dresden], making all the light proceed from Christ' (Plate 29). In the smaller spaces either side of the Nativity were to be groups of shepherds coming to worship, and in the seven lower divisions the large figures of the four cardinal virtues (already sketched for the north windows) with the addition of Faith, Hope and Charity (Plate 30).

William Mason gives a vivid picture of the artist at work on the commission.[6] Though the agreement with the college specified drawings or cartoons, he preferred oils because 'he had been so long in the use of the pallet and brushes that he found it easier'. Whilst at work on the 'Nativity' itself, Mason 'happened to call upon him, when his painting-room presented me with a very singular and pleasing prospect. Three beautiful, young, female children, with their hair dishevelled, were placed under a large mirror which hung angularly over their heads, and from the reflections in this he was painting that charming group of angels which surround the Holy Infant'. As usual with Reynolds's religious compositions, the faces were portraits from life: Mrs. Sheridan, who had earlier been the model for 'Charity' (exhibited at the Academy in 1779) also sat for the Virgin in the 'Nativity', Harriet Burrard (later Lady Rooke) posed as 'Justice', and two of Reynolds's nieces, Frances and Elizabeth Johnson, were respectively 'Temperance' and 'Fortitude'. Reynolds and Jervais themselves appear as shepherds, the former with a staff, kneeling on a rock, the latter advancing on the left with his hands uplifted.

Reynolds's decision to produce paintings rather than drawings was in fact a shrewd business move. The *modello* for the 'Nativity' was later sold by him to the Duke of Rutland for £1,200, and the seven 'Graces' were bought by the Earl of Normanton in 1821 from another of Reynolds's nieces, Lady Thomond, reputedly for 'over £5,000'. The former was unfortunately destroyed in a fire at Belvoir in 1816, but the 'Graces', which remain in the collection of the present Lord Normanton at Somerley in Hampshire, are among the artist's finest oils. In contrast to these high prices Reynolds received a total of only £231 from the college, refusing any payment at all for the 'Nativity'. This magnanimous gesture may have been made partly out of embarrassment, for Reynolds was grievously disappointed at the final result, as were Walpole and Torrington. Jervais's work, which had cost the college the monumental sum of £1,790, was in no way answerable to the subtlety of the artist's technique and colouring, but it is also fair to say that Reynolds had made none of the compromises necessary for this restrictive medium, or for the context in which it would be viewed. Horace Walpole made the point most forcibly: 'Sir Joshua's Nativity is glorious', he reported when he first saw it in London in 1783, 'the room being darkened, and the sun shining through the transparencies realizes the illumination that is supposed to be diffused from the glory, and has a magic effect'. But two years later, seen out of these artificial conditions, and with the whole window now installed in the antechapel, Walpole thought 'the old and the new are as mismanaged as an orange and a lemon, and destroy each other; nor is there room enough to retire back, and see half the new; and Sir Joshua's washy Virtues make the Nativity a dark spot . . . which happened, as I knew it would, from most of Jarvis's colours not being transparent'.[7] Torrington went further still, preferring Peckitt's work to Reynolds's 'languishing harlots', while even Dr. Warton, one of the prime movers of the scheme, wrote a long poem of somewhat ambiguous tenor, which somewhat offended the artist.[8] Now that many of Jervais's colours have faded, and others have become still more opaque, the Reynolds window is perhaps more interesting as an art historical curiosity, than as a work of art in its own right. However, its expense and the heated controversy it had aroused had one good effect: having burnt their fingers so badly, the fellows were unlikely to want to spend more on stained glass for a long time. Peckitt's glass from the west window was finally installed in the two windows at the north-east corner in 1788–9, though this was not quite enough to fill the one nearest the altar, and extra figures were added in 1821.[9] Apart from this the chapel glass remained virtually untouched until the more scientific restoration and rearrangement of the medieval fragments in this century.

The west window was, however, only the prelude to a complete re-ordering of the interior of the chapel, between 1789 and 1794, for which the catalyst may have been Reynolds himself. The exact fate of Henry Cooke's painted *Deceptio* on the east wall is not known, but its Baroque illusionism must have seemed increasingly old-fashioned, and in 1773 Lord Radnor presented a large Carracci School canvas of the Nativity (now in hall) to hang in its place over the altar. For some unknown reason two joiners were employed in 1779 'to cutting out the Panel in the wainscott in the Altarpiece and Cutting out the Stone work'—that is to say revealing the remains of the medieval reredos and its niches, as had been done in 1692. According to Daniel Prince, writing exactly ten years later, in 1789, this 'small opening presented such an elegant specimen that the Society have now opened the whole and propose to have it restored under the direction of Sir Joshua Reynolds and Mr. Wyatt'.[10] This mention of Reynolds five years after his work for the college had been completed (and in the absence of further payments to him in the accounts) is perhaps more likely to refer to the birth of the idea in 1779 than to prove that the artist was actually involved in the final proposals.

James Wyatt's first recorded appearance at New College was in May 1777, a few months before Reynolds's acceptance of the commission for the west window, so his employment was evidently not at the artist's recommendation, but as a result of his already burgeoning practice within the university.[11] His earliest Oxford commission, the Canterbury quadrangle at Christ Church, begun in 1773, had come only a year after the triumphant opening of the Pantheon in Oxford Street, his first work in architecture, and he later stepped into the shoes of Henry Keene both at Worcester College and at the Radcliffe Observatory, after the latter's death in 1776. As at the Radcliffe and in most of his subsequent work at Oxford, Wyatt collaborated at New College with a local builder named James Pears, who was left to work out many of the details of his designs. The arrangement was one which suited Wyatt's natural indolence well, and which was repeated many times in his career, often making it difficult to decide how much credit should be given to architect or to builder.

The question is particularly relevant to the upper library, where, in 1777, Wyatt's advice was first sought by the college. The pressing need was for more book-space, and Wyatt's immediate response probably contained the seeds of the final solution: the blocking of all except the five central windows on the west side of the room so as to make room for bookcases on all the other walls, and the creation of two deep niches or *exedrae* at either end, also lined with books and screened off by columns—ultimately derived from Robert Adam's library at Kenwood (Plate 59). The idea may have been expressed in a quick sketch, but the surviving set of crude preliminary designs for the room, showing rectangular rather than apsed ends, and particularly comic busts on brackets over the two doors, must be by James Pears.[12] The only direct evidence of authorship is an entry in the order book for 27 May 1777, 'that the Bursars write to Mr. Wyatt to require a positive Answer whether he will undertake the fitting up of the Library or not, if he will not the Bursars proceed . . . to employ some other persons'.[13] Wyatt's reply has not survived, but the likelihood is that he recommended Pears to them, probably making sketches for the latter's guidance, adapting and correcting the more obvious deficiencies of the builder's own scheme. On purely stylistic grounds, it is perhaps not too fanciful to see Wyatt's hand in the form of the bookcases, with slim projecting sections which (though fitted with books) act as pilasters—a much more subtle arrangement than in Pears's design—or in the plaster-work decoration of the apses, with bands of Vitruvian scroll running across the shallow scooped ribs. The Corinthian capitals of the columns and many of the other mouldings which are noticeably weaker and less assured, may, on the other hand, be attributed to Pears, whose name appears alone on the bills, without the endorsement Wyatt was later to make on the accounts for the chapel. It is also noteworthy that, in June 1780, the lower library was ordered 'to be fitted up according to a plan delivered in by Mr. Pears'. In this work, which included laying a new floor, removing the old bookcases projecting from the walls, blocking in the windows at the north-east and south-east corners so as to make room for new shelves against the wall, and altering the form of the sash windows, Wyatt appears to have played no part, and Pears was left entirely to his own devices. It was also at this period that the chamber immediately south of the lower library, above the Chamber of Three, was adapted as the 'Auctarium' (literally the augmentation or annex) and used to house the overflow of books from the other two rooms.

Pears's new form of sash-windows for the two libraries, with larger panes and far thinner glazing bars than Townesend's, was gradually extended to the whole of the Founder's quadrangle and to most of the garden quad over the next two decades. As in the lower library this resulted in the unfortunate cutting away of parts of the medieval arched embrasures, and the filling in of the rest with plaster so as to form plain, splayed reveals. The small windows between the medieval sculptures on the outer face of the gatehouse were also given arched windows in the Gothic taste, which survived until just after the last war. At the same time changes were made to the interior of the warden's lodgings by Dr. John Oglander, including the provision of a Gothic plasterwork frieze in the hall immediately above the gate, and the complete remodelling of the dining room. Originally a fellows' chamber (above that called the Baptist's Head), this had been acquired by the warden earlier in the century in exchange for the ground-floor room on the north side of the gate, now the porter's lodge. Pears, possibly with Wyatt's guidance once again, removed the partitions to make one handsome rectangular room stretching from the warden's staircase to the corner of the quad, and decorated with a typically neo-Classical frieze of alternate tripod perfume-burners and anthemions. The room was slightly reduced in length by Claud Phillimore in 1958–60 to make room for a small pantry at the southern end, but remains otherwise unchanged.

Perhaps the saddest losses the college suffered in the late eighteenth century were Hugh Herland's original timber roofs of the hall and chapel. Yet it would be unfair to blame Pears or Wyatt too heavily for this disaster: by the 1780s the medieval structure of the college had already been in existence over 400 years and it is probable that the timbers had rotted (or been infested with beetle) to such a degree that they were considered past saving. The medieval hall roof had been concealed for centuries by a Tudor ceiling, and it may be that the flat plaster-ceiling inserted by Pears in 1786 below his new roof was therefore thought to be what the Founder had intended. Pears's work was done for £578, and again there is no direct evidence that Wyatt was involved, though he may have given preliminary advice.[14]

The remodelling of the interior of the chapel from 1788 to 1794 was the last, and at the same time one of the most sweeping, of all the changes made to the college in the eighteenth century. By contrast with the hall and warden's lodgings, Wyatt took full control of all the work, as regular payments to him (both for his own drawings, and for London craftsmen contracted by him) make clear.[15] Although part of the medieval reredos immediately above the altar had been uncovered in 1779, it was nearly ten years before the college agreed to a complete restoration scheme, probably because of the large sums of money which had to be raised—a final total of £2,735 for the roof and vault, and £6,959 for the rest of the work, including new choirstalls, organ screen and organ case, all to conform with the Gothic niches of the reredos. A letter written by Thomas Warton in 1789 shows that work was then already far advanced: 'they are new-roofing the Choir of New College Chapel at a considerable expence', he writes, 'woodwork in the Gothic style in a good taste. All the old frontispiece behind the Altar (demolished by Visitor Horne) has been laid open. There are three tiers of niches for statues . . . the canopies and rich tracery all hacked to pieces, with a series of basso-relievo of the life of the Virgin Mary. They talk of restoring as much as they can'. James Pears was again responsible for all the masonry and carpentry work, but much the most important single craftsman was the plasterer, Bernato Bernasconi (father of the more famous Francesco), who was responsible both for the vaulted ceiling and for the ornamental work to the reredos, stalls and screen. Bernasconi's account at New College 'for the Mens traveling expences' between 1790 and 1794 gives valuable evidence of his other activities at this period, notably at Lichfield and Worcester Cathedrals, and at Milton Abbey in Dorset.[16]

James Wyatt's Gothic, from its picturesque beginnings at Sandleford Priory to the monumentality of Bishop Auckland, Fonthill and Ashridge, has not in the past been given the attention it deserves. The criticism made of his cathedral restorations in the early nineteenth century has tended to obscure his important role as a bridge between the frivolous folly-style of the mid-Georgian period and the serious academic approach of the nineteenth-century Gothic Revival. At New College he has been attacked particularly for destroying the remains of the medieval stone reredos[17] and the original roof—yet in both respects there is evidence that Wyatt considered this the best way of returning to the Founder's intentions, and that the fault lay rather in the primitive state of knowledge which prevailed until John Shaw's classification of the different periods of Gothic architecture, and later researches sponsored by the Camden Society. As has already been seen, the low pitch of the chapel roof, in contrast with the timber vault of Winchester chapel, was thought in the 1770s to be incorrect and 'by no means equal to the magnificence of the rest'.[18] It is even possible that Herland's timbers had, like the hall roof, been altered in the early sixteenth century. Wyatt's plaster vault was accordingly intended to restore the chapel to its original proportions. Whether or not it did so, J. C. Stadler's engraving of the chapel in 1814 (Plate 11) shows a clean rib-vault springing from the existing medieval bosses, which is in many ways less disturbing than the hammer-beam introduced by Scott in the following century. As for the niches in the reredos, they were clearly so badly damaged that there was no prospect of patching them up with new stone, and Bernasconi's new version in plaster, which (as far as is known) copied them exactly, was a sensible solution (Plate 12). The carved ornament of the existing Gothic stall-backs was also used by Wyatt as the basis for the new seating arrangements and for the organ screen. The rest of the mid-seventeenth-century stalls were removed to the antechapel, and some of the early eighteenth-century panelling from the sanctuary found its way to another of Wyatt's Oxford commissions, a room adjoining the gallery of his new library at Oriel.

Wyatt's bill 'for Gothic composition in the Chapel' gives a better idea of the richness of Bernasconi's work than any of the early nineteenth-century engravings. The outer face of the screen had '18 Arch'd heads under the organ case very rich with crocketts and pinnacles', and the organ itself '2 very rich cupolas' on the top, either side of the great central arch which gave a view of Reynolds's west window from the main body of the chapel. 'Under the organ loft', perhaps either side of the archway, were '2 figures of Founder and Virgin', in '2 very large and rich niches' and the screen also contained painted glass. The warden's and subwarden's stalls had 'doom [or domed] tops shingled including pinnacles battlements &c', and Bernasconi supplied no less than '832 ornaments to spandrels to open work and front of stalls'. Not all the new work was in plaster, however: there are records of Portland, Windrush and Bibury stone being used, and Mrs. Eleanor Coade's famous artificial stone was used for sixty-nine 'small figures with wings and hands holding a shield', each of which in turn supported a 'Gothic

Pedestal for holding a brass sconce as a light for reading Desk'. The eight extra stalls on each side of the chapel, running eastwards from the original ranges, were also given double 'Gothic Arches with Flower Heads &c as Spandrils' and elbow rests 'with Gothic heads and foliage' in wood, by a carver named Robert Archer. At the same time Wyatt moved the medieval misericords from their original positions to decorate the fronts of the inner choir stalls, a curiously naïve idea, which again reflects the current lack of knowledge about Gothic architecture, rather than pure wilfulness on the part of the architect.[19]

Despite the lapse regarding the misericords, Wyatt's intention to return to the medieval appearance of the chapel is proved by the care with which he supervised the new scenes from the Life of the Virgin above the altar, and the colouring of the reredos. The five medieval 'basso relievo' panels first revealed in 1779 were carefully removed by James Pears in December 1789, and packed up to go to London. At this stage the intention may have been to restore them, but they were obviously too badly damaged and instead the sculptor Richard Westmacott the elder carved five new panels in alabaster, retaining the lines of the medieval composition. Together with the marble altar slab below, these were set up, at a cost of £1,300, in 1793. A year later Westmacott also executed, to Wyatt's design, the memorial to Warden Oglander in the antechapel. In the painting of the reredos, carried out by John Green, Wyatt actually went further towards an archaeological reconstruction than Scott, or even Pearson, were allowed to go a hundred years later: during the uncovering of the niches it was found that their ground colour 'was of a deep ultramarine blue and the exterior edges of the shafts of the niches richly gilt'.[20] A return was accordingly made to this sumptuous colour-scheme, although no attempt was made to restore the sculptures which they originally contained, and which would doubtless have been painted in polychrome. Chalmers records that Wyatt's stalls and organ screen were painted 'white and gold',[21] but if the white was the 'flat dead stone colour' specified in Green's bill (with much 'graining oak colour'), the effect was probably not as startling as it sounds. Unlike Scott's later 'restoration', Wyatt's remodelling of the chapel aroused no hostility, and indeed when the results were first shown, Thomas Warton's friend, Prince, recorded that 'poor Thomas fetched such sighs I could not have thought he could breathe'[22]—a tribute as much to the sensitivity of the architect as to the sensibility of the future Poet Laureate.

The work in the chapel, completed by 1794 (though payments were still being made to Wyatt and Pears in 1797), brings the eighteenth-century alterations to the college to a close, but gradual changes to the garden in these years should also be mentioned. The statue of Minerva was removed from the centre of the Founder's quadrangle in 1789, when the present oval grass lawn was made—shown in John Dixon's charming water-colour for the 1793 *Oxford Almanack* (Plate 6). Probably at the same time, the parterre was finally abandoned, and the formality of the mound itself eroded by replacing the steps with a serpentine walk and scattered planting of variegated trees and shrubs. An engraving made by Joseph Fisher in 1817 shows a small Doric temple at the foot of the mound, which may also have been erected in the 1780s, and which was removed only in 1890.[23] Equally difficult to date precisely is a charming feature of the warden's garden, shown in a drawing made by J. B. Malchair, during the course of 'a lesson in the Art of Perspective to the Lady of Dr. Oglander, the present Warden' in 1786.[24] This is a replica of William Townesend's garden pavilion at the southern end of the garden, apparently painted in *trompe-l'œil* on the high garden wall at the north-west corner, backing onto Hertford College. Whether this was a comparatively recent conceit, or whether its very artificiality suggests that it was made at the same time as the pavilion, in the opening decades of the eighteenth century, it too has long since disappeared.

2. THE MID-NINETEENTH CENTURY: SCOTT'S 'RESTORATIONS' AND THE HOLYWELL BUILDING

Perhaps as a reaction against the radical alterations made to the college by Wyatt and James Pears, the first half of the nineteenth century was one of the quietest periods in its architectural history—what might be called the lull before reform. The port railway in the senior common room, invented by Warden Shuttleworth (1822–40), is symptomatic of its time (Plate 54). It was the custom for fellows gathering here after dinner to sit at small tables placed in a horseshoe round the fireplace; decanters were passed from table to table, but when they reached that nearest the chimneypiece one of the fellows was obliged to rise from his chair and take them across to the table on the other side. Shuttleworth, who 'had seen the principle employed in the collieries of his native Durham',[25] overcame this problem by designing a mahogany ramp to stand in front of the hearth, with a system of balances ensuring that a full decanter placed in the coaster at the upper end would be carried (by virtue of its own weight) safely down a gentle gradient, thereby raising the empty coaster for replenishment.

The warden and fellows certainly took their refreshment seriously at this period; the set of rooms below the warden's dining room was requisitioned as quarters for his butler in 1822; and at the same time the ground-floor room of the muniment tower became a pantry for the fellows' butler.[26] A few minor changes were also made to the chapel in these years: in 1821 W. R. Eginton of Birmingham filled the two empty lights of the window in the north-east corner of chapel with figures of St. Barnabas and St. Paul, and in 1848, a strong wind having blown in Reynolds's 'Nativity' in the centre of the west window, the original stonework tracery was reinstated—to the benefit of its architecture, but to the ruination of Reynolds's composition.[27] Also, about 1830, the figure of St. Michael in the niche in the great pinnacle at the east end of hall was replaced by a replica, the badly-damaged original finding its way to the president's garden at Trinity, where it still remains.[28] The only other important development of the early nineteenth century was the expansion of the junior common room. Originally a small room just inside the arch from the main quadrangle (now the S.C.R. lavatory), it had already in the eighteenth century taken the larger ground-floor room to the east; now, in 1825, it also acquired the room above, made available by the fall in the number of gentlemen commoners—reduced to two or three only by 1851, when there were twenty-three junior or probationary fellows.[29]

The story of the college's rebirth and expansion in the second half of the nineteenth century is told in detail elsewhere in this book: it is enough to say that under the new statutes for Wykeham's two foundations, drawn up in 1857 and effective from 1860, there was an increase of over 100 undergraduates by 1870, and 200 by 1880, when New College was the second largest college in the university. In 1867 it was one of the pioneers in allowing fellows occupied in tutorial work to be married, and in the following year Jowett's choice of New College to share lectures with Balliol was a proof of its new intellectual energy. It is against this background that one must approach the assertive, self-confident restoration work and the programme of new building carried out for the college by Gilbert Scott. Largely due to the activities of the Camden Society medievalists, the Gothic Revival got off to an earlier start at Cambridge than at Oxford, and it is significant that the restoration of the hall roof at New College between 1858 and 1865,[30] had originally been suggested by a party of visiting antiquarians from the other university several years before. Enthusiasm was, as with other new architectural ventures, generated by the younger elements in the college: in 1857 the junior common room pointed out that the original medieval roof of hall must remain (at least in part) above the flat ceiling inserted in the eighteenth century, and offered £1,000 for its restoration if the college were to meet this sum. In the following year it was agreed that this money could be raised over a number of years, and soon afterwards George Gilbert Scott, established since his Martyrs' Memorial of 1841–3 as the leading exponent of the Gothic Revival in Oxford, was invited to submit plans, of which five drawings still remain in the college archives.[31] In the event, very few of Hugh Herland's timbers seem to have been discovered when Pears's plaster ceiling was removed, and it is impossible to tell how accurate Scott's reconstruction of the medieval roof was. The tie-beam construction was, however, far more satisfactory than the hammer-beam later used for the chapel. In scale with the original fourteenth-century corbels on which it rests, and harmonising in colour with the Tudor panelling below, it is perhaps the most satisfactory of all Scott's designs for the college (Plate 36).

The oak used for the hall roof came entirely from the college's own estates at Great Horwood and Akeley in the north of Buckinghamshire, the king oak being felled at Akeley in the presence of the senior fellow on 8 May 1862. But despite this saving, exactly three times the original estimate was spent on the restoration of hall before it reopened in October 1865. Besides work on the roof itself, the builders (Franklins, of Deddington) were paid for restoring the high stone seats below the windows, previously concealed by panelling, encouraged by Scott since 'nearly the same thing exists at Winchester and I find it also in John of Gaunt's Hall at Kenilworth'—an interesting example of his consciously archaeological approach. The panelling itself was stripped of paint and one Buggins was paid £132 for new 'emblazoning', while a carver named John Chapman was commissioned to add the arms of the college's principal benefactors since 1533 to those already set in the panelling behind the dais.[32] Apart from this, the major item of expense was the new heraldic glass provided for the windows by Clayton and Bell—again on Scott's recommendation—the existing lights being moved to the window over the hall staircase. The two windows lighting the dais, filled with royal shields, amounted to £200, while the remaining five, again with arms of benefactors and Bishops of Winchester, cost £60 each.[33] Somewhat harsh in colour, like so much of their work, the effect of these was perhaps the least happy part of the restoration of hall.

Although one fellow was to call Gilbert Scott's new hall roof 'an undoubted failure',[34] it was praised by most contemporaries, and, together with his much admired chapel and library at Exeter College, built between 1854 and 1860, secured for him the commission to build the first new extension planned by the college for a hundred and fifty years. A committee had been formed to consider accommodation for the ever increasing number of undergraduates as early as 1861, and in 1866 the first tentative overtures were made to Merton to acquire some of the houses along the south side of Holywell. Scott was appointed architect in October 1870, and the Holywell Building was finally begun two years later, when his designs were published.[35] Much as one may regret the loss of the charming seventeenth- and eighteenth-century Holywell houses, demolished to make way for Scott's (and later Champneys's) buildings, it must be admitted that the college had little choice over their site. The only possible alternatives—the warden's garden, and a narrow strip of land north-west of the cloisters by New College Lane— were far too cramped and inconvenient to be considered seriously. At the same time it is clear from the preliminary correspondence and estimates that the more glaring faults in Scott's design originated with the college authorities and not with the architect. The least satisfactory feature of his new Holywell Building, consisting initially of the four staircases to the west of the present Holywell gate (Plate 60), was its height, dwarfing and darkening the rest of the street: there is evidence, however, that he originally intended it to be only three storeys in height, containing twenty sets of rooms (at a cost of £13,150), and that the fellows, particularly A. F. Robinson and E. C. Wickham, insisted on the fourth storey, containing an extra eighteen sets (and costing another £3,350).[36] The fact that the college cut down much of the exterior ornament proposed in Scott's initial plans, and also stipulated that water-closets and as many drainpipes as possible should be placed on the Holywell façade, shows that few efforts were made to make this outward-looking elevation any less forbidding—and worse was to come between 1875 and 1877, when two more staircases and a married tutor's house were added immediately to the west in the form of a five-storey tower. Completed in June 1877, only a year before Gilbert Scott's death, this was rather more elaborately decorated—including niches with statues of Edward III, Richard II and Henry VI. It is easy to sympathise, particularly in our own conservation-conscious age, with the indignant reaction of Miss Lloyd, daughter of a Bishop of Oxford, whose charming sketches of old Holywell can be found in an album in the Bodleian. Quoting on one of them a couplet of Christina Rossetti's—'E'en now the devastation is begun, And half the business of destruction done', she adds crisply '6 old Houses demolished by greedy New Coll: to make way for a useless *married* Tutor's House'.[37]

Scott's pliability was not confined to decisions of policy such as the height of the new Holywell Building. In a letter of January 1871 accompanying his first proposals he wrote that 'the plan . . . must be viewed as open to any amount [of] variation in its details. In the slight indication . . . given of the architectural character of the buildings [they are] generally in accordance with the date of the college'.[38] While it would be hard to imagine Burges or Butterfield using such vague phraseology, Scott's Holywell Building (Plate 60) is not as amorphous in style as this might suggest. The design is in the rambling, 'picturesque' vein associated more often with his earlier work such as Kelham Hall, Nottinghamshire (1858), or Broad Sanctuary, Westminster (1852), the row of eight terraced houses next to the west front of the Abbey, than with the more ponderous symmetry of his later projects for town halls and government offices. The influence of Viollet-le-Duc and of French Gothic generally, particularly noticeable in the two projecting staircase turrets of the Holywell Building, castellated and with conical roofs, is, however, also apparent in the famous rejected design for the Foreign Office of 1858, and in St. Pancras, built six years later. In the larger of the two turrets, the windows ascend in a spiral following the line of the stairs, as (most famously) at Blois. Internally, too, these staircases (numbers 4 and 6) are elaborately thought out, partly perhaps because they also act as lobbies to the two large lecture rooms Scott was asked to provide on the ground floor. One has a stair-well in the form of an elongated oval, while the other is pear-shaped, the geometry of the view upwards enlivened by elaborate cast-iron balustrades, using the Founder's rose as a recurring motif, and the panelled wooden ceiling of the conical turret (Plate 61). The lecture rooms themselves have ceilings with chamfered beams and surprisingly playful castellated doorcases and chimneypieces. The other rooms, high ceilinged and designed particularly to afford a 'through draft' in every set, were not provided with sanitation and were virtually impossible to heat—but these considerations were not within the architect's brief and he can hardly be blamed for them. Between ten and fifteen years ago many were converted into more comfortable units for modern living, to the designs of Geoffrey Beard. A certain coarseness of detail on the exterior, and lack of subtlety in the composition as a whole, must, however, be laid at Scott's door. He was at this time both ill and overworked, and a great deal was undoubtedly, therefore, left to the draughtsmen in his office. It is interesting that this was what one disapproving fellow, Charles Mayo, who also attacked Willis's design for the organ, picked on in a broadside written to Warden Sewell (from Fiji) in May 1876: 'the designer of the new buildings in Holywell, whoever he may be, has recorded there his utter incompetence to follow in the steps of the architect of New College. On one side you see genius, on the other the most trumpery office work. I am sure that Mr. Cockerell, or Professor Willis, or Mr. J. H. Parker, or any one who has looked at the style of William of Wykeham closely . . . could bear me out'.[39] Another serious fault, seen in hindsight, was Scott's choice of Milton stone for the Holywell range, against the advice of the builders, Shaw and Jackson, who would have preferred Bath.[40] Compared with the honey-coloured Clipsham stone used by Basil Champneys for the adjoining Robinson's Tower and Pandy, which is still fresh and sharp, Scott's stonework has deteriorated and discoloured to an alarming extent in only a hundred years.

About the same time as the erection of the Holywell Building, various small changes were made to the rest of the college: the present vaulted passage under the dais end of hall was created, and another archway made through the city wall beyond it, so as to give direct access to the new quadrangle from the old,[41] while the upper room of the J.C.R. was extended twelve feet westwards, filling in the original light-well, long rendered useless anyway by Pears's bookcases across the windows at this end of the Founder's library.

The main energies of the college, and its major resources (nearly twice as much as the cost of Scott's Holywell Building), were in the meantime reserved for the chapel. The tide of taste had everywhere turned against James Wyatt's eighteenth-century Gothic and in many of the thirty-nine cathedrals and minsters Gilbert Scott 'restored' all over the country, including Salisbury, Lichfield and Hereford, he had been particularly commissioned to unpick Wyatt's work. But Scott's generation objected more to the materials than to the forms of eighteenth-century church restorations—and this is nowhere more evident than at New College, where Wyatt's reredos and stalls were actually rather closer in style (and in colouring) to the medieval appearance of the chapel than their Victorian successors. What worried the earnest Gothic Revivalists was that these were made of plaster, rather than wood and stone. Under the influence of Pugin's writings, this practice was felt to be inherently dishonest. A committee of fellows first met to consider a restoration of the chapel in 1867, but it was not until 1871 that Scott was asked to draw up preliminary designs and estimates. These were in turn postponed until 1875, when a larger committee was formed and money began to be raised from benefactors. Contract drawings (several of them now in the Victoria and Albert Museum) were drawn up by Scott in 1877, but work had only just begun when, in the following year, he died, leaving his sons John Oldrid and George Gilbert junior to complete the roof, stalls and organ screen over the next two years. The reredos was not completed until 1888, to the designs of J. L. Pearson.

Scott's work on the chapel, and in particular his new hammer-beam roof, has received much criticism. But while he may again be blamed for pliability in the face of opposition, it is clear from his estimates and letters that the idea of the hammer-beam was (like the fourth storey of the Holywell Building) forced on him by the college. His first proposals of 1871 show that he had carefully examined surviving traces of the medieval timbers above Wyatt's plaster-vault, and had come to the conclusion (almost certainly correct) that it had been a tie-beam roof similar to that in the hall—the only difference he suggested was that 'the Ante Chapel might shew its rafters as the Hall roof, while the Chapel proper might have the spaces between its principal timbers richly panelled and perhaps decorated with colour and gilding'.[42] That

Scott's own preference for this type of roof remained unchanged is shown by two letters received by Alfred Robinson, then bursar, in June 1875.[43] In the first, John Oldrid Scott forwarded at his father's request 'the drawing showing the three proposed modes of treating the roof of your Chapel', continuing, 'the drawing itself shows the roof as it appears to have been originally designed [Plate 13] which [sic] on two fly-sheets are drawn the groined ceiling [i.e. a wooden vault below the existing roof] and the hammer-beam roof suggested by some of the fellows'. Exactly a week later, on 14 June, Gilbert Scott followed this up himself with a further explanation of the three alternatives, worth quoting at length for the clarity with which it explains his own order of preferences: 'the first . . . has the recommendation that it is, as nearly as may be . . . the form of the original roof: of the second . . . it may be said that it has the advantage of utilising the existing roof [a considerable saving] and that it has an indirect sanction from the Founder who at Winchester concealed his roof-timbers by oak vaulting. Of the third . . . it must be said that it has neither of these recommendations . . . while destroying [the present roof] it does not reproduce either the pitch or the design of the ancient roof, but wanders away for this type to another building'.

Despite this advice, a majority of the committee, led by Robinson himself, deliberately chose to fly in the face of reason, and the hammer-beam roof was chosen. Scott's own views cannot have been generally aired in the college, for the architect bore the brunt of the opposition from the outset. Three members of the committee itself, Spooner, Mayo and Coker Adams, declared themselves against the scheme. The latter wrote to Robinson in 1879 about 'the new fancy roof, against which the Architect and I voted in vain', and later, in 1881, declared that 'properly speaking the Chapel has not been "restored" at all. Restoration is well defined by Johnson as "the act of replacing in a former state". Now how much of our Chapel has been replaced in a former state?—two corbels'.[44] But forceful though these arguments now seem, W. A. Fearon summed up the general feeling when he pronounced the new hammer-beam 'itself of great beauty, and more ecclesiastical in character' than its predecessors.[45] Ever since Warden Shuttleworth's day, a strong Evangelical strain had run through the college. With a High Church faction in the ascendant it is possible that a more strictly archaeological restoration might have been attempted, but while the fellows professed to admire the Founder's architecture they were not at home with the Catholicism which had inspired it. Significantly it was Warden Sewell who, having had clothes painted over Biagio Rebecca's nude figures of Adam and Eve in one of the north windows of chapel, also had the medieval wall between the warden's study and oratory removed so as to make a larger room for entertainments.[46]

If Scott saw the danger of importing an alien type of roof, based on East Anglian prototypes, and realised also that its steeper pitch would make it visible from a distance above the parapet (particularly at the west end), he may also not have intended the disturbingly red-brown colour of the stained oak used both for it and for the stalls and organ screen. In a letter to Robinson of March 1877, long after the hammer-beam design had been agreed, he wrote that Shaw's tender for the roof 'includes all necessary work but not the coloured or gilded decoration if that should eventually be thought desirable'. Two months earlier he had reported that 'the ancient portions [of the stalls] are highly enriched with gilding upon the original oak and have considerable traces of colour, chiefly red and green—and the carved spandrels are gilded'.[47] Evidently both he and J. O. Scott would have liked to see a return to such painted decoration for all the woodwork, as suggested by Pearson later in the 1880s. Nor can Scott be entirely blamed for another unsatisfactory feature of the restored chapel, the way the canopied stall-backs interrupt the line of the window sills, since, although these were as near as possible replicas of the originals, the college insisted they should be raised on staging so as to allow for two extra rows of choir-stall below them. Coker Adams remarked drily that 'the stallwork must, I think, have been designed by one of the sons . . . for it seems to belong to the 15th century', and although the contract-drawing dated July 1877 is signed by Gilbert Scott himself and the carvers, Farmer and Brindley, it is true that in his last years he came to rely more and more on his assistants—J. O. Scott in particular.[48] None of the New College drawings at the Victoria and Albert bear evidence of his own hand, and a group of designs for the piscina, sedilia, crozier case and reredos niches are products of the short-lived partnership between his sons George Gilbert junior and John Oldrid between 1878 and 1880, terminated by G. G. Scott's breakdown and conversion to Roman Catholicism. The reroofing of the antechapel and the organ case were also carried out by the brothers—the latter less ambitious in scale than

Gilbert Scott's earlier design of 1877, and probably therefore representing an economy on the part of the college.[49] The original estimate made by Scott in 1871 had been for a total of £36,500, though this included replacing all the eighteenth-century painted glass in the chapel: in the end a statement drawn up in 1880, just before the completion of the reredos, accounted for just over £20,000.[50] Three main contractors were involved in the work: George Shaw of Earl Street, Westminster, won the contract for the roof, and also undertook the few structural alterations necessary to the walls; Scott's favourite firm, Farmer & Brindley, who had worked for him at Kelham, Wellington College chapel and elsewhere, were responsible for carving the stalls and organ screen in wood, incorporating where possible the original medieval misericords, stall-backs and canopies, and the two central doors which were the sole survivors of the medieval screen,[51] as well as carving the reredos, sedilia and piscina in stone; while the organ case was made by John Thompson of Peterborough.

One can sense a note of growing frustration in John Oldrid Scott's correspondence concerning the finishing touches to the chapel in 1879 and 1880. If the fellows had rarely taken Gilbert Scott's advice, they were disposed to treat his son in a still more cavalier manner. Against his recommendations they chose gaslight pendants rather than candles; when he pursued his father's idea of painting the roof and organ case, they claimed their funds would not permit it, nor did they even keep two or three old stalls with their original medieval paint 'to be followed . . . at some future time' as he had asked; finally he heard that a red altar frontal 'coming half way down with gold fringe is contemplated', and wrote that he found it 'rather alarming I confess. May I not arrange this? . . . nothing looks worse in a careful restoration than to see such things as curtains, frontals, cushions etc. which have evidently been left to the tender mercies of a tradesman'.[52] Though no details are to be found in the archives, Scott's association with the college came to an end some time in 1880, by which time Wyatt's plasterwork reredos had been replaced by a similar arrangement in stone. The niches, however, remained empty, and the shape of the new hammer-beam roof left an awkward blank space immediately above it. 'That great unlighted gas fire' was how Dr. Christopher Woodforde once referred to the New College reredos, and at no time can it have justified this epithet more fully. Partly on this account, and partly because the fellows were beginning to have second thoughts about the general lack of colour in the chapel, one of the most celebrated of all Victorian church architects, J. L. Pearson, was asked to draw up a report early in 1884, despite a rather lukewarm recommendation from the Dean of Westminster.[53] Pearson's arrangement of sculpture for the reredos, 'suggested by the Te Deum', with a central crucifixion flanked by the apostles, and with rows of prophets and martyrs below, was adopted immediately, although the statues (mostly by Nathaniel Hitch of Kennington) were not completed until 1892.[54] His addition of a Christ in Majesty with flanking angels immediately below the roof-line was an ingenious solution to the problem posed by Scott's hammer-beam (Plate 14). Pearson's other proposals—to decorate the roof 'in light and somewhat delicate tints', taking the Suffolk church of Palgrave as a model, to add figures of college worthies in feigned niches on the blank walls high up between the windows, with a stencilled pattern above them, and to stain the stalls, organ and screen dark brown—were not, however, adopted; nor were Westmacott's carvings immediately above the altar replaced by a triptych or a pair of tapestries as he suggested. At least in part, this was again through lack of money, for the statues alone required an appeal for £3,000 in 1888. Most of them were subscribed by individuals at £30 and £50 each (St. Cecilia was for instance given by Dr. and Mrs. Spooner) and were based on well-known prototypes: St. Stephen and St. George from San Michele in Florence, the Virgin from a picture by Raphael, Archbishop Warham from two portraits at Lambeth, and Bede from a statue at Durham.[55] Hitch, though celebrated in his day, was not especially skilled and the sculptures hardly bear close inspection. But, like Geflowski's slightly earlier figures for the reredos at All Souls, carved under Scott's direction, they give at least some indication of the richness of the original scheme.

3. THE LAST HUNDRED YEARS

With the numbers of undergraduates still expanding rapidly after the completion of Scott's Holywell Building, it was barely ten years before the college considered a new extension on the remainder of the site owned by Merton. Perhaps because of the recent success of his Indian Institute at the end of the Broad, begun in 1883, the new building committee approached Basil Champneys, later architect of Mansfield College—a man of entirely different temperament from Gilbert Scott, wholly eclectic in his sources, but bringing to the Gothic or Renaissance styles equally a hint of Arts-and-Crafts fantasy. Asked to keep the style of his buildings 'definitely different from those of Sir G. G. Scott', Champneys chose a loosely 'Tudor Domestic' idiom with gables, two-storey bay windows, and oriels for the tutor's house, which projected southwards to become virtually a self-contained block.[56] Far smaller in scale than Scott's building (three storeys as opposed to four) it is both more consciously picturesque (Plate 62), and on the north a more tactful addition to the appearance of the street. There is also a capriciousness about the upper string-course with its grotesque bosses (by another Kennington carver, John McCulloch), and the elaborate rain-water heads, which is in total contrast to the high seriousness of the earlier Gothic Revival. Inside the building, an unashamed Arts-and-Crafts style becomes apparent with wrought-iron window catches, linenfold overmantels, and eccentric pierced tracery (including arches lying on their sides) on the staircase.

The intention must always have been to join the two Holywell Buildings at some stage, so it is difficult to see why the college stipulated that they should be in different styles. At any rate, when the time finally came, in 1896, the solution to the problem was reached in a way that would particularly have pleased Scott; his earliest Holywell scheme (of 1871) had included 'a handsome Gateway tower' at the east end of his block,[57] and it may have been this (together with the example of the Founder's muniment tower, forming the junction between the hall and the much lower library range) which gave Champneys the idea of a monumental and again asymmetrical tower as a visual corrective to the long unbalanced wings set back on either side of it. The cost of the gate-tower, and two more staircases fitted in between it and Champneys's earlier block, was £14,225, and both were executed in 1896–7 by the Oxford firm of Benfield and Loxley. The tower, which might otherwise have been ruled an impossible extravagance, was fortunately paid for in part by a fund in memory of Alfred Robinson, which raised a total of £2,620, and after which it was officially known as the Robinson Tower.[58] Exactly when and why Champneys's range to the east of the tower became known as 'Pandy' is uncertain; it would have deeply disturbed E. C. Wickham, who had conceived the idea of tutors' houses in college especially to counteract the pandemonium caused by the undergraduates.

Alternative schemes to the Holywell tower considered by the Robinson Memorial Committee included the building of a new library between the bell-tower and the west end of Scott's Holywell Building, and (since the leases on this site did not fall through until 1899) the conversion of the Founder's and the upper libraries, and the sets of rooms immediately to the south, into one vast galleried room. This last remodelling, which would have involved the destruction of much important medieval and eighteenth-century work, was seriously considered again in 1907 when Champneys drew up plans for both alternatives.[59] Funds were fortunately not forthcoming at this time, and the rest of the architect's work for the college was confined to essential modernisation and restoration work. In 1880 the lower floor of the Long Room was opened up and the 500-year-old cesspit replaced with earth closets, while in 1903 water closets and bathrooms were installed on the floor above; new larders, sculleries and other kitchen offices were also built in 1882 between the kitchen and the city wall, designed by the Oxford architects, Wilkinson and Moore.[60] Electricity was introduced to most parts of the college between 1892 and 1897, while at the same time £3,540 was spent on repairing (and in fact largely replacing) the chapel pinnacles. Champneys's estimate allowed for a different, and tougher, Clipsham stone but specified that there was to be no alteration to the old shapes. It is hard therefore to understand Rashdall and Rait's comment that 'unfortunately, the new pinnacles are thicker and less graceful than the old, though the old seem to have dated only from Wyatt'—nor is such a change evident from engravings and early photographs. Champneys's only other alterations of any significance were the extension of the S.C.R. to the north and J.C.R. to the south, and his creation of a gallery at the east end of hall in 1906–7, by roofing over the space between the Tudor screen and the east wall, and providing access by a circular staircase.[61]

Meanwhile in 1903, the election of Warden Spooner led to a large-scale alteration of the lodgings by W. D. Caroë.[62] Mrs. Spooner, used to life in a bishop's palace, insisted on a minimum of ten resident housemaids and a houseboy. Accordingly extra floors of attic bedrooms were built above the Tudor gallery, on New College Lane, and above the main quadrangle range immediately south of the gate-tower. The latter were ingeniously concealed from view behind the parapet, though at the price of lowering the ceiling above the seventeenth-century stairs. In other ways, however, Caroë increased the grandeur of the staircase by removing the south wall on the ground floor and the south and west walls on the first floor—supporting it by new uprights, continuing the line of Frogley's original newel posts (Plate 40). This re-ordering of the staircase opened up vistas right through the lodgings from the first-floor level, north through the warden's hall to his study, and west down a new gallery to Warden Nicholas's bridge over the lane. Despite Caroë's reputation as an antiquarian-architect, he took surprising liberties with this conversion. The original Tudor gallery was partitioned off, and the new gallery (roughly at right angles to it) although reproducing the pattern of the ribbed ceiling was given an ingle-nook chimneypiece of highly individual design. Much of the old panelling throughout the lodgings was rearranged (and heavily varnished) at this time, and leaded lights were returned to many of the windows which had been given sashes in the eighteenth century. At the same time the triangular courtyard in the centre of the lodgings, gradually reduced in size over the centuries, was finally glazed over to make a servants' hall, and a new entrance made from New College Lane. The Spooners' large family even spilled over the bridge into the eastern end of the barn (previously used by Warden Sewell's servants), the west end becoming a gardener's cottage.[63]

The First World War and the inevitable overcrowding in its aftermath put paid to plans for a new library for the time being, although the sheer weight of the books in the Founder's and upper libraries, and especially in the 'Auctarium' to the south, used as a stack with bookcases on rails, was beginning to endanger the structure of the building. At last in 1937, with the funds raised by the War Memorial Committee standing at £23,500, the Manchester architect Hubert Worthington was, on the strength of his recent Radcliffe Science Library and buildings in St. Aldate's, invited to produce plans for a free-standing block between the bell-tower and Holywell. The new library was begun in 1938 and finished soon after the outbreak of the Second World War, exceeding the original estimates because of the large piles that had to be driven in for the foundations of the southern half, built over what had once been the outer vallum or ditch for the city wall.[64] Influenced by Østberg's Stockholm City Hall and the Paris

Exhibition of 1925, Worthington's building now seems somewhat mannered—particularly in its use of squared Bladon rubble for the walls, and dressed Clipsham stone for the window surrounds, a craze started by Sir Herbert Baker's Rhodes House of 1929 and continued by Giles Gilbert Scott in the New Bodleian of 1937. The discreet use of Baroque motifs, such as the curvature of the front and its double staircase (Plate 8), and the wide central aisle with its emphasis on axial perspectives, at the same time acknowledges a debt to such current literature as Geoffrey Scott's *Architecture of Humanism* and the writings of the Sitwells. The interior is perhaps more successful than the exterior, with much attention paid to materials: an entrance lobby of 'creamy Travertine' and bronze, and different woods used for the corner study rooms—mahogany for the law library, sycamore for the classics, and walnut for the rare books, with waxed English oak in the main reading room. The woodwork was made (and in some instances designed) by Heal's.[65]

The final vacation of the Founder's library, occupied by an Admiralty department, and then reserved as a dormitory for the period immediately after the war, finally came in 1949, and brought with it a heated architectural controversy. The removal of the eighteenth-century bookcases had revealed several of the original blocked medieval windows, and Warden Smith, an unashamed 'Goth', argued for their reinstatement in place of the eighteenth-century sashes looking over the main quadrangle. As a trial the northernmost window was restored to its original form, as it still remains (Plate 7), but it was obvious that unless the Gothic tracery in all the other quadrangle windows was also restored, such a change would make it still less balanced as a composition. The Founder's library, with many of its original features rediscovered or reinstated, was adapted to its present use as a dining room for the senior common room in 1951, and the upper library was also restored at the same time, Pears's long bookcase on the east wall being moved to the west, so as to open up the windows overlooking the garden.[66] The only important alterations made to existing college buildings since then have been the conversion of the Long Room into a gallery for temporary exhibitions or functions with cloakrooms below it (now that sanitation has at last reached every staircase) and, finally, another remodelling of the warden's lodgings by Claud Phillimore between 1958 and 1960, following the election of Warden Hayter. The tide of domestic servants having ebbed since Mrs. Spooner's day, the attic bedrooms designed by Caroë now became undergraduates' rooms, while a small kitchen was formed at the southern end of the dining room. The original medieval kitchen became a self-contained service flat, while above it Phillimore made a new drawing room almost exactly the same shape as the Tudor gallery, sacrificed by Caroë. A small private flat for the warden and his wife was also made in the western end of the barn, overlooking the garden.[67]

Despite the extra rooms acquired by the college over the warden's lodgings and the conversion of many two-room sets in the Holywell buildings into bed-sitting rooms, the end of National Service in 1958 saw another serious shortage of accommodation. The college had, with foresight, acquired the central and northern stretches of Longwall as early as 1921, partly by exchanging houses near Carfax with the city. At that time there was simply a fear that boarding houses were drying up, and there was no thought of actually redeveloping the site. However, to alleviate the acute lack of space, which meant that many under-graduates spent only one year in college, an old member of the college, Harry Sacher, agreed to finance a whole new building in Longwall, built in 1961–63 (Plate 63). True to New College's tradition of archi-tectural innovation the Sacher building, designed by the Cambridge architect David Roberts, was the first in either university to be built by a 'traditional' college solely for graduates; though it may be that its projecting concrete lintels will one day be thought as typical of their time as Hubert Worthington's squared rubble and ashlar. Like the library, the building is kept mostly below the line of the city wall and does not impinge greatly on the rural atmosphere of the garden. The two storeys, above an underground garage, have rooms leading off long corridors in place of the traditional staircase arrangement, and include a middle common room on the ground floor. The paved courtyard between the Sacher building and the city wall is a wholly successful feature. What is less successful is the Longwall front, disturbingly horizontal in emphasis, and monumental in scale, compared with the irregular eighteenth- and early nineteenth-century houses on either side. The building nevertheless received a Civic Trust commendation in 1963 'for the contribution it makes to the local scene'.[68] Six years later, in 1969, the college also built Bodicote House further down Longwall to the south, to provide rooms for twenty-one undergraduates. The design here, by Geoffrey Beard of the Oxford Architects Partnership, shows a far greater sensitivity to its surroundings, retaining both the scale and the articulation of its Georgian neighbours, while remaining wholly contemporary in style.

Our own century has seen the acquisition of more important individual works of art by the college than any similar period of time since the Founder's death. In the antechapel, W. R. Lethaby's tablet to Alfred Robinson and Eric Gill's war memorial of 1921 perhaps come into this category. But foremost among them is the 'Lazarus' by Jacob Epstein, set up inside the west door of chapel in January 1952 (Plate 67). One of the two works exhibited by Epstein at the Festival of Britain, and one of his acknowledged masterpieces, it was bought at the instigation of Warden Smith with money raised by old members and by the Pillars of Wisdom Trustees, beneficiaries of T. E. Lawrence's will. The 'Lazarus' has been called 'the most haunting statue in Oxford' and indeed when Kruschev visited Oxford he said that the memory of it kept him awake at night.[69] Epstein was also responsible for a bronze bust of Warden Smith, now at the north end of the dais in hall. On the opposite side of the antechapel to Lazarus, flanking the central archway through the organ screen, is a pair of panel paintings of the Annunciation (Plates 64 and 65), the work of Bartolommeo Montagna of Vicenza (c. 1450–1523), while in a case near the altar is a 'St. James' by El Greco, given to the college by A. E. Allnatt in 1963 (Plate 66).[70] A fine portrait by Romney of Bishop Bathurst was bought by the college in 1943— most commendably from the proceeds of a sale of surplus port. An abstract sculpture by Barbara Hepworth, which stands in the courtyard between the Sacher building and the city wall (Plate 63), was given partly by Mrs. Sacher and partly by subscription from old members in the same year. The latest of the college's additions, the new organ case in the chapel, designed by G. G. Pace, can also be regarded as abstract sculpture, though described by Pevsner as 'rather spiky for its setting'.[71]

No account of the architectural history of New College would be complete without some reference to the cleaning and refacing of its buildings in our own times. If 'restoration' obsessed the fellows in the nineteenth century, preservation has been their main concern in the twentieth. In some areas progress was made early on: Champneys's work on the chapel pinnacles in 1902 was followed in 1904 by a report on all the medieval sculpture by Caroë, who inaugurated a general programme of stabilising, cleaning and removing crude later repairs.[72] Between the wars the very serious flaking of the Headington stone used for the garden quad had begun to give cause for anxiety and in 1928–31 the north range was entirely refaced. But it was not until 1957 that concerted action was taken, due to a great extent to the pioneering work of one of the college's lecturers and research fellows, W. J. Arkell, whose *Oxford Stone*, published in 1947, laid down the guidelines for the work of the Oxford Historic Buildings Fund—itself largely the brainchild of Warden Smith. Between 1957 and 1969, the fund raised £180,000 for the college, and during this time practically all its buildings received some attention (under the direction of the college architect, Geoffrey Beard) from the refacing of the main quadrangle to the eradication of death-watch beetle and dry rot in various roofs, the removal of cast-iron bars from the tracery windows of the cloisters, the repair of the wrought-iron garden gatescreen, and the conversion of the beer cellar. The college was particularly lucky in having a gifted sculptor among its lay clerks, Michael Groser, who was responsible for much of the new carved work required: bosses, gargoyles, coats-of-arms or full-scale statues, such as the St. Michael in the great niche at the east end of the hall roof. Stone from the Clipsham quarries was used throughout this restoration, except for the plinth in the front quadrangle, which is of Purbeck burr.[73] It is heartening that the college buildings should be approaching, in some cases, their seventh century of existence in better repair than at any time since the Founder's death.

REFERENCES

1. Woodforde, 16–20; N.C. MS. 958 (Building Chest Book 1732–66).
2. Ed. Mrs. Paget Toynbee, 'Horace Walpole's Journals of Visits to Country Seats', Walpole Society, vol. XVI, (1927–8), 25.
3. Woodforde, 20–38; Wale was paid 5s. for his drawing, which has since disappeared (N.C. MS. 958).
4. College Order Book, 30 March 1775, N.C. MS. 960; Woodforde, 38.
5. For Jervais's and Reynolds's work, see Woodforde, 39–55.
6. Ed. W. Cotton, *Sir Joshua Reynolds' Notes and Observations on Pictures* (1859), 58–9.
7. Ed. Mrs. Paget Toynbee, *The Letters of Horace Walpole* (Oxford 1904–5), xii, 447; xiii, 336.

8. Ed. C. B. Andrews, *The Torrington Diaries 1781–94* (1936), i, 54; Thomas Warton, *Verses on Sir Joshua Reynolds' Painted Window at New College Oxford*, printed for J. Dodsley in Pall Mall, 1782.

9. Woodforde, 59–60; see p. 245 below.

10. Rashdall and Rait, 72; Daniel Prince quoted in J. Nichols, *Literary Anecdotes and Illustrations of Literary History 1817–58*, iv, 740.

11. Wyatt may also (as previously suggested) have recommended Biagio Rebecca to the college as early as 1772.

12. N.C. MS. 1144 ('Estimate for work in the Library at New Coll:', 1777–8); the drawings (which have affinities with Henry Keene's lower library at Christ Church) are in N.C. MS. 1167; two sheets of designs for neo-Classical torchères (1199), probably intended for the room, are more assured, and may possibly be by Wyatt himself. For Pears's independent work at Oxford, see Colvin, 629.

13. *V.C.H.*, 149.

14. *V.C.H..*, 148; Smith, 120–1.

15. N.C. MS. 1203 ('Mr Wyatt's accounts', 1788–94).

16. The elder Bernasconi has previously been known only for his work on the long demolished ballroom and drawing room at Claydon, Bucks.; see Geoffrey Beard, *Decorative Plasterwork in Great Britain* (1975), 205.

17. Smith, 114.

18. See Chapter V, *n.* 36.

19. An abstract, and the individual bills, are to be found in N.C. MS. 1203.

20. A. Chalmers, *A History of the Colleges . . . of Oxford* (1810), i, 135.

21. Ibid.

22. Nichols's *Literary Anecdotes*, op. cit., 740.

23. A copy of Fisher's engraving is in the Bodleian, G. A. Oxon. a. 56, fo. 29; Joseph Skelton in his *Oxonia Antiqua Restaurata* (1823) claimed that the pillars of the temple came from Cannons, demolished about 1750 after the death of the Duke of Chandos, but it was evidently not in the garden at the time of Mrs. Lybbe Powys's visit to the college in 1759; it is possible that the Duke of Chandos's gift of money towards Robinson's screen (Chapter VI, p. 224) gave rise to two successive legends: first that the screen, and later that the temple, came from Cannons.

24. The drawing, in the Ashmolean Museum, was reproduced for the 1929 *Oxford Almanack*; H. M. Petter, *The Oxford Almanacks* (1974), 113.

25. Rashdall and Rait, 85.

26. *V.C.H.*, 150.

27. Woodforde, 59–61.

28. A. Vallance, *The Old Colleges of Oxford* (1925), 39.

29. Smith, 126–8.

30. N.C. MSS. 2450, 3149; Sherwood and Pevsner, *Oxfordshire* (1974), 170, incorrectly date the hall restoration to 1877–81; for this and all subsequent nineteenth-century building, see H. E. Bell, 'Victorian Builders at New College' (typescript), N.C. MS. 3593, and George, 53–67.

31. N.C. MS. 5601; there is also a perspective drawing in the Victoria and Albert Museum (D. 496–1908) showing the roof as executed, except for a different form of pierced spandrel.

32. Scott's correspondence, and the scheme for the arrangement of the arms, is in N.C. MS. 3149.

33. N.C. MS. 5656 (scheme and drawing), 3149 (estimate).

34. Charles Mayo; N.C. MS. 3146.

35. *The Builder*, 19 October 1872.

36. N.C. MS. 2455; Bell, op. cit., 8–9.

37. The album, entitled 'Oxford Sketches', and containing water-colours made from about 1865 to 1896, is in MS. Top. Oxon. c. 406.

38. N.C. MS. 2455.

39. N.C. MS. 3146; but cf. the reactions of the antiquary, Edward Freeman, who, in a letter to G. G. Scott of 27 July 1879, called his father's New College work 'of special importance, as the return to plain English and commonsense in Oxford buildings, after so many years of Ruskinian tomfoolery' (ex. inf. Gavin Stamp).

40. W. J. Arkell, *Oxford Stone* (1947), 26.

41. H. E. Bell, op. cit., 7; the new quadrangle was grassed at the same time with turf from Stanton St. John.

42. N.C. MS. 2455.

43. Both in N.C. MS. 3230.

44. N.C. MS. 3146.

45. Letter of 17 January 1876 (N.C. MS. 3232); Fearon also gave £2,000 towards the hammer-beam roof.

46. Smith, 43.

47. N.C. MS. 3231; see also J. O. Scott's letters to Alfred Robinson of 24 April and 30 May 1879.

48. N.C. MS. 3146; the contract drawing is in the Victoria and Albert Museum (D. 489–1908).

49. Ibid., D. 488–96 inclusive.

50. N.C. MSS. 2455, 3231.

51. N.C. MS. 3142, Farmer and Brindley's specification.

52. N.C. MS. 3231.

53. N.C. MS. 3140.

54. Pearson's report is in N.C. MS. 3152, and the estimate for the work in 3142; Hitch also worked for Pearson at Peterborough Cathedral, Westminster Abbey and St. Augustine's, Kilburn.

55. H. E. Bell, op. cit., 20–1; N.C. MS. 3140.

56. N.C. MS. 3147; drawings in 9585.

57. N.C. MS. 2455.

58. Champneys's work was illustrated in *The Builder*, 8 April 1899; N.C. MS. 829 (minutes of the Robinson Memorial Committee).

59. N.C. MS. 1155.

60. Plans and correspondence in N.C. MSS. 11676–7.

61. N.C. MSS. 3224, 3227, 3208, 3237; Rashdall and Rait, 88.
62. N.C. MSS. 9383 (Caroë's plans) and 3522 (notes by Wardens Spooner and Hayter on alterations to the lodgings).
63. Plans for further alterations and additions to the barn by Sir Robert Lorimer (N.C. MS. 9391) seem to have come to nothing.
64. N.C. MSS. 3226 (appeal), 3130; articles in *The Builder*, 30 April 1943, and *Architectural Review*, June 1942.
65. Drawings in N.C. MS. 9382.
66. A detailed account of these changes can be found in Smith, Appendix III.
67. N.C. MS. 2791 (notes by Warden Hayter); Mark Girouard, 'The Warden's Lodgings, New College', *Country Life*, 5 April 1962.
68. *New College Record*, 1975–6, 7–8; N.C. MS. 2811.
69. N.C. MSS. 2807, 14,097; James Morris, *Oxford* (1965), 223.
70. *New College Record*, 1945–6, 1960–1; the Montagna panels, given by G. R. Y. Radcliffe, were formerly at Badger Hall, Salop, and are recorded as being bought at Padua in the 1840s (other panels from the same altarpiece are in Westminster Cathedral); the El Greco was until 1959 in the Del Monte Collection.
71. *New College Record*, 1963–4; Sherwood and Pevsner, op. cit., 171.
72. N.C. MS. 8710.
73. A full account of the refacing can be found in *Oxford Stone Restored* (ed. W. Oakeshott), (1975), 83–8.

PART THREE

Traditions and Possessions

VIII

Music and Musicians

PAUL R. HALE

The Founder established from the start that New College was to have a musical future. He counted 'the advancing of divine ritual' among his objects, and thus provided in his statutes for ten chaplains (one of whom was to act as precentor and another as sacrist) and for three clerks and sixteen choristers. Seven canonical 'hours' and seven masses were to be sung daily (fellows had to attend only one), with named persons prayed for, both in a litany for the living and in commendation for the dead. From 1394 some instruction in singing—and in grammar—was evidently given to the choristers, since payments were made to an *informator choristarum*. As Frank Harrison has written:[1]

The statutes of New College, Oxford, did not expressly require the singing or teaching of polyphonic music, nor did the chapel books given by the Founder include books of polyphony (they included eleven noted Antiphonals, nineteen Graduals and thirteen Processionals). In preparation for Henry VI's visit to the college in 1442–3 certain Masses, probably for the King's good estate, were added to the Graduals in the choir, and in the same year the informator (John Francis) received for the first time an additional payment for teaching the antiphon of the Virgin, which was followed by prayers for the King. In 4–5 Edward IV (1464–5) the 'King's Mass' was again 'noted', and the Bursars' Roll for 1494–5 also has a payment *pro missa Domini Regis*. The first definite mention of polyphonic music is in 1470–71, when three books of *cantus fractus* were repaired, and later entries in the Rolls show the building up of a considerable repertory.

One of these entries refers to one John Tucke (F. 1499–1507), who wrote and 'noted' a mass in 1505–6.

The role of the *informator choristarum* became more clearly defined during the fifteenth century, when it is apparent that he was responsible for the choristers' education as well as their singing; he also acted as organist. His importance in college may be estimated from the fact that he received twice the salary of a chaplain. Entries for copyists occur regularly in the bursars' rolls from the fourteenth to the nineteenth centuries, and through them we get a fairly clear idea of what music was being sung in the chapel. The deed listing the books given to the choir in 1458 by William Porte (F. 1418–23) records that he and his wife Joan gave *Orgona* [sic] *magna pro choro*. This is not in fact the first mention of an organ: the earliest reference seems to be in 1449 when 10s. was allowed to Thomas Wootton *pro pipa antiquorum organorum* in part payment *pro factura magne pipe organorum*. This organ probably stood on the screen which then as now divided the antechapel from the chapel, while Porte's organ was most likely 'in a loft supported by wooden pillars, joining to the vestry door on the north side of the upper end or high altar'.[2] Repairs were carried out in 1484–5 on both the organ *in choro* and the organ on the pulpitum, and in 1488–9 on the 'smaller organ' by William Wotton (presumably a relative and successor of Thomas). In 1536–7 the sum of £25 6s. 10½d. was paid for organs made over a two-year period, and by 1540 the college possessed no less than four organs, one of which was in a Jesus-chapel. One or more of the instruments seems to have been removed in 1548, re-erected in the time of Mary I, and again removed in 1571.[3]

A new organ costing £60 was built in 1597–8 by John Chappington, and to coincide with this an organist, William Wigthorpe, B.Mus. (Oxon), was appointed. Wigthorpe lasted until 1610, and must therefore have known Thomas Weelkes, the famous composer, who took his B.Mus. from New College in 1602. Weelkes, who was an outstanding writer of madrigals as well as of a quantity of fine church music, was Organist of Winchester College in 1600 and after supplication for his degree at New College moved to Chichester as organist of the cathedral. He was certainly one of the finest musicians ever to have been associated with New College even though he may never have been truly in residence.

Bishop Horne's commissaries had visited the college in 1566–7 and had decreed, among other things, how music should be used in chapel. Psalms were to be sung before and after sermons, and there was to be 'no turning to the East in papistical fashion when the *Gloria Patri* was sung'. They had also advised that 'choristers should spend most of the day in learning to sing as well plane song as composite'. However, over the next forty years or so such instructions must have been relaxed, and, if the quality of the chapel music in the early years of the seventeenth century reflected the money spent on it, it must have been very fine. Indeed we have testimony to that effect, for in the words of the historian Antony Wood: 'A.D. 1605. They [King James I and his entourage] went to New College where they were entertained with a royal feast, and incomparable music.'[4] In 1611 Wigthorpe was followed by William Meredith, who appears to be the first organist to have been buried in the cloisters (January 1637). On his tombstone he is described as *Vir pius et facultate sua peritissimus*; another epitaph upon him is found in Wood: 'here lyes one blowne out of breath, Who liv'd a merry life and dyed a *merry death*'.[5] Meredith was succeeded by one Pink (Christian name unknown), who lasted but three years, when Simon Coleman took the position.

After the fall of the city to the parliamentarian forces at the end of the Civil War, a Puritan visitation was held in 1647. This has been noted by Wood, who had been earlier 'translated to New College School'.[6] The choristers' school had originally been situated in the undercroft, then divided into 'dark, gloomy chambers'.[7] but some time làter (possibly after the visitation of 1549) had been moved to the cloisters, where its presence is noted in the Computus Roll for 1587. In 1626 some attics had been opened up in the roof between the hall and the kitchen, which seem to have been designated for the choristers, no doubt as sleeping quarters. Before the Civil War the school was situated between the west end of the chapel and the cloisters; but in 1642, while scholars trained for the King's service in the quadrangle—to the delight of the choristers, some of whom 'could never be brought to their books again'[8]—the cloisters were converted into an arsenal and the school removed to a room at the east end of hall which had probably been a part of the servants' quarters. Wood describes his new schoolroom as 'a dark, nasty room and very unfit for the purpose, which made the scholars complaine, but in vaine'.[9] Grown too many for this room, the choristers were later housed in the two vestries adjoining the chapel. Wood also tells us how, in May 1647, after the defeat of the royalists, when the parliamentary forces were guarding the arsenal, the clerks and choristers 'had the audacity to celebrate the Prince's birthday by a bonifier on the Mound in College Walks'.[10]

The organ *in choro* was taken down at the parliamentary visitation, and the organist, Simon Coleman, was expelled from the college on 22 June 1649, together with many of the chaplains and fellows: one Miles was appointed in Coleman's place in 1650. In 1657 Crouch took over, and in 1660, when choral services were resumed, William (?) Flexney. He too lasted a short time, as did his successor Robert Pickhaver, who was appointed in 1662 and on moving to Winchester College was succeeded in 1664 by William King. Before Pickhaver, the organist's salary had been for many years £6 13s. 4d. per annum. In Pickhaver's time this was raised to £20, and on appointing King (who was obviously highly recommended to the college) the warden and fellows passed a motion fixing his salary at £50 per annum, payable quarterly, and agreed that he should play the organ upon Surplice Days and Litany Days only, unless he should be by some of the House desired at any other time. King (son of George King, Organist of Winchester Cathedral), under whom chapel music picked up its standard again, is remembered today by a tablet in the cloisters, and he must have appreciated the new organ which was built in 1662–3 by Robert Dallam.

The construction of this organ, some of whose pipework survived in the organ until 1967 and is now in store, is well documented. Dallam had been recommended to the college by Edward Lowe, the University Professor of Music and Organist of Christ Church, and by Philip Timber, 'Chaunter' of Westminster Abbey. He received for his work the sum of £443 12s. 7d., of which sum 'ten pounds was borrowed'. The case, made by Mr. Harris the joiner, cost no less than £162 12s., and Mr. Taylour and Mr. Hawkins charged £100 'for Gilding & painting' it. The new instrument was placed on the screen, between chapel and antechapel, where its successors have stood to this day. From the contemporary papers of Warden Woodward we learn that Lowe suggested that the pitch of the organ should be a semitone lower than the Christ Church organ, whereas Dallam considered that a quarter of a tone would be sufficient. This is a clear indication that there was no standardisation of pitch at that time. When Woodward and the fellows discussed with Dallam his designs for an organ case they 'conceived that to be fittest which was open in the midst, and might let in more light from the Western Window in our Chapel'. This would seem to indicate an arch-shaped case, which is exactly what the much later Ackermann print of the chapel shows (Plate 11), although the organ, and indeed the chapel, had been much rebuilt by then. Robert Dallam's advanced ideas are shown in his original scheme for the New College organ, which if it had been built, would certainly have been one of the finest in the land and probably the largest, but the college settled on a smaller scheme. Dallam had oversight of the organ until his death, which occurred at Oxford on 31 May 1665. He was buried in the cloisters, opposite to the west door of the chapel, where his tombstone can still be seen, as well as a memorial tablet on the wall. A large donation (£100) for the 1663 organ came from Dame Frances Freake, of Hannington, Wiltshire, and 'as a return of thankfulness unto the aforesaid lady for her great liberality, Mr. Warden thought fit to send unto her a free and voluntary promise of freely admitting into our College six children of any poor men, such as in charity she would please to choose to be Choristers of the College'.[11] This generous promise can hardly have pleased the new organist, William King, or aided him in his endeavours to keep musical standards high.

The new organ seems not to have lasted long before considerable repairs were necessary, for in 1672 William King wrote 'An Account of w^t is wanting in ye organ, & w^t is to be mended, taken by ye Organist ye 10th day of June, 1672'. The many faults listed in this document include poor tuning, general dirtiness, 'dumb' pipes, pipes needing renewal, the poor condition of the trumpet stop, uneven keys, ciphers, soft case-pipes and inadequate bellows. King concludes that a 'Mr. Harris' should do the work and declares that he 'hath ye Report of all ye fellowes of Winchest^{er} to bee a very honest man'. The last two lines refer to Renatus Harris who, though fiercely rivalling another builder, Bernard Smith, shared with him the distinction of becoming the finest organ builder in England at the close of the seventeenth and start of the eighteenth centuries. He received only £10 at this time, so it would seem that not all the organist's requirements were complied with. The final mention of the Dallam name occurs in 1714, when yet another member of the family was paid £4 'by order of Mr. Harris, Organ Maker'.

An ancient musical custom of New College was recorded by Aubrey, writing about the year 1690:

the fellows of New College, have time out of mind, every Holy Thursday, betwixt the hours of eight and nine, gonne to the hospitall called Bart'lemews near Oxford, when they retire into the chapell, and certaine prayers are read, and an antheme sung; from thence they goe to the upper end of the grove adjoyning the chapell (the way being beforehand strewed with flowers by the poor people of the hospitall), they place themselves round the well there, when they warble forth melodiously a song of three, four or five parts; which being performed, they refresh themselves with a morning's draught there, and retire to Oxford before sermon.

Wood has a similar version of the same custom, but adds that 'they sung a song of 5 parts, lately one of Mr. Wilbye's *principium* "Hard by a christall fountaine" '.[12] In two footnotes he adds 'New College men made a choice of Holy Thursday every year because Magdelene men and the rabble of the town came on May Day to their disturbance' and, pointedly, 'by the prevalence of the Presbytery these customes vanish'.[13] There is no trace of a revival of the custom after the Restoration, and Hearne, writing in 1729, speaks of it as having been long in desuetude.

William King died on 17 November 1680 and was buried in the cloisters, where his tombstone may still be seen. His successor in the same year was Richard Goodson (senior), B. Mus., who was appointed University Professor of Music in 1682. In 1691 or 1692 Goodson was appointed Organist of Christ Church and left New College in about March 1692. He does not seem to have been replaced immediately for no organist's salary was paid during 1693. Instead, a member of the choir, one Perry, was paid £5 a quarter for teaching the choristers music. Some mysterious circumstances surround Goodson's eventual successor in 1694, one Read (described by Wood as 'a young hot-head'[14]), for we learn that 'Read committed suicide, ript up his own belly on Low Sunday, 15 April, and died Wednesday 18 April 1694 the College paid the expenses of his funeral'.[15] In Read's place was appointed a distinguished musician—John Weldon, who was after-wards (1708) Gentleman Extraordinary of the Chapel Royal (a musical establishment of great importance at that time) and organist and second composer to the king (1715). Weldon was a pupil of Purcell and wrote a quantity of church music which in style was typical of the time, and some of which was highly esteemed.

In 1702 Weldon was succeeded by Simon Child who held the post for thirty years. During this time Renatus Harris was paid £35 (in 1714) for lowering the pitch of the organ 'from Gamut in De Sol-re to Gamut proper' (i.e. one note lower), and in 1716 £160 for 'a new stop and altering the organ'. The cost shows this to have been a major overhaul. In 1726 a new bellows was provided for £10. At this period the organ was under the successive care of Renatus Harris (d. 1724), his son John (d. 1743 or 1744), John's partner and successor John Byfield, senior (d. 1757), and the last-named builder's son John Byfield, junior. Byfield senior was paid £50 for a new manual department for the organ—an 'Eccho and Swelling Organ' in 1735. Richard Church was appointed organist in 1732, and although he held the post for a remarkable forty-four years, he 'was esteemed a good musician, but not a very brilliant player'.[16] Despite the latter criticism he was also Organist of Christ Church from 1741, and from 1732 to 1736 was a lay clerk at Magdalen as well. He resigned both posts early in 1776, and, dying in July of that year, was buried near the path leading towards the High Street in the churchyard of St. Peter-in-the-East (now the library of St. Edmund Hall).

Richard Church's successor was one of the greatest characters ever to work in New College chapel—'greatest' in more ways than one, for he was considered to be the 'largest man in England'. This was Dr. Philip Hayes, and his influence, musical and otherwise, made itself felt at New College from 1776 to 1797. One of his successes in college was to oust the chaplains from their common room (now the Song Room), which they had taken over on the school's translation to the old Congregation House at St. Mary's in 1694 (owing to the large numbers in the school at that time), and have the college fit it up 'for the use of the Organist, in order that he may therein instruct the Choristers in the Art of Singing'. He must also have had a hand in getting the organ overhauled in 1776 at a cost of £330 15s. by Byfield's successor, Samuel Green. Philip Hayes's father, William, had been Professor of Music at Oxford and Organist of Magdalen College, and his son was to succeed him in both these posts in 1777, to which he added a similar position at St. John's College in 1790, holding all these appointments until 1797, when he died in London. Hayes was buried in St. Paul's Cathedral after a memorial service sung by the combined choirs of St. Paul's, Westminster Abbey and the Chapel Royal.

Hayes was such a well-known figure in his day that one may be forgiven for dwelling at some length on his personality, which made up perhaps for the musical barrenness of the times in which he was living. 'I remember', wrote George Valentine Cox (Master of New College School from 1806 to 1857), 'being taken to his house in my very early days to have my voice tried; he had been, for many years, remarkable for his state of obesity, and I have not forgotten the awe I felt at the huge projection over the keys of his harpsichord, contrasted with his delicate, small hands, and accompanied with a soft velvety voice.' The professor also held the appointment of Gentleman of the Chapel Royal, which necessitated occasional trips to London.

According to John Bumpus:[17]

Occasionally Dr. Philip made his journey to London in a chaise. At that time it was common to see upon the chimney-piece of the public room of an inn an announcement of the want of a 'companion in such a conveyance. The Doctor (whose unwieldy person rendered his travelling in one of the 'six insides' of the time a matter of considerable inconvenience) on one occasion accepted the first companionship that offered at the 'Star'; and to avoid the toil of a walk from his house in Holywell it was arranged that he should be taken up there. On the morning appointed, the inquirer for a companion jumped into the chaise—luggage all right—and, dashing up to the Doctor's door, he saw a figure little less than the great Daniel Lambert, supported by a servant on either side, slowly advancing from the wall. In amazement, he hastily lowered the front glass, roaring out, 'Post-boy—hoy! is that the gentleman we are to take up?' 'Ees, sir, that be Doctor Phil Hayes.' 'Fill chaise, by—,' replied the traveller; 'he shan't come in here; drive on, drive on,' thus leaving the poor Doctor to get on his journey as well as he could. Hence the sobriquet with which he is invariably associated, 'Phil Chaise'.

Hayes's nephew wrote of his uncle:

Dr. Philip Hayes was organist of New College (his favourite College), also of S. John's College, and S.M. Magdalen College; was elected organist of Christ Church, and ousted by a man named Norris. Often went to London and purchased pictures, and presented them to the College. Very fond of works of *vertu*: a lazy dog, fond of good living, in fact, a gourmand: fine temper, good looking, handsome man. Could have married well in his younger days, when his person was slender: during the latter part of his life very stout, weighing 20 stone. When at low water, took William his 'Caleb Quotem,' with him (one of the finest cooks of the day) and drove in his carriage to Town. Composed music, of which he disposed; and returned home full of money.

That musical standards under Hayes might not always have been of the highest is borne out by an extract from the *Torrington Diaries* of the Hon.

John Byng, who was evidently visiting Oxford in 1781: 'July 8th, 1781. The chapel services at the colleges being so early, that we hurry'd away from our dinner in hopes of hearing an anthem sung by a famous singing boy of New College . . . we were baulk'd of our intention, as the anthem was very ill sung, and the service most idly perform'd, by such persons as I should suppose had never learnt to sing or read tho the warden himself attended . . . good breeding is scarcer here than elsewhere.' Just before this comment was written, in about 1780, the choristers' school had been removed from St. Mary's back to the undercroft, where it seems to have remained until the 1860s. A piece of paper stuffed in a statue in the chapel by a chorister the year before Hayes's death reads: 'When this you find, recall me to your mind, James Philip Hewlett, Subwarden's chorister, 26th April, 1796. [Apparently written during Evensong] Yeates just gone out of chapel, making as if he was ill, to go to Botleigh with Miss Watson. Mr. Prickett reads prayers. Mr. Lardner is now reading the second lesson. Mr. Jenks reads the first. Slatter shams a bad Eye because he did not know the English of the theme and could not do it. A whole holiday yesterday being St. Mark. Only the Subwarden of the Seniors at Prayers.'

'Improvements' to New College chapel had been completed by James Wyatt in 1794.[18] They included a rebuilt organ, to all intents and purposes new, which was installed by Samuel Green, who, it will be remembered, had followed Byfield in 1776. Green in fact had been a partner with the younger Byfield, setting up by himself in 1772, which could explain why he carried out the work in 1776. Indeed, Green was the first builder to work on the New College organ not actually to be related to Robert Dallam. The work on the organ took place over six years in order to fit in with Wyatt's restoration work. Green's bill for £844 8s. 0d. shows that he renewed virtually all the mechanical parts of the organ and provided some new pipework which included some sham front pipes 'all Semicircular of Wood' (Plate 11). There were 173 show pipes (many of these being on the antechapel side), all of which were gilded. The case in which the organ stood can be seen, from Ackermann's print, to be arch-shaped with the third manual (the Choir Organ) just visible, being built into the gallery front. This would make it very similar to the case we imagine Dallam to have constructed, except for the enormous amount of 'Gothic Composition' which was called for, with canopies, pinnacles and crockets in abundance. The organ case and screen were apparently 'coloured both sides', and this decoration, together with the gilded organ case pipes, must have given a sumptuous appearance: in fact we know that Dallam's original case-pipes were painted, as some of them survived inside the organ in full use until 1967. Green died on 14 September 1796, but his firm continued to look after the organ until 1803.

One of Dr. Hayes's pupils was the Reverend Gilbert Heathcote, an able clerical musician and an ardent Wykehamist. He was born in 1765, and after his time at Winchester College and New College, latterly under Hayes's tutorship, was successively fellow of New College (1788), fellow of Winchester College and afterwards the holder of several livings and cathedral posts, dying in 1829. His compositions, most of which remain in manuscript, are numerous and his Evening Service in G was popular at New College for a long time. He is worthy of particular mention as being the editor of the most recent edition of *Harmonia Wykehamica. The Original Music in Score, of the Graces used at Winchester and New College in Oxford. Also the hymn 'Jam lucis', the Song of 'Dulce Domum' and the Song of 'Omnibus Wykehamicis' as performed at the Anniversary Meeting in London of Gentlemen educated at either of the above Colleges.* These meetings of Wykehamists commenced in 1758 and were held until 1800 at the 'Crown and Anchor' in the Strand, and subsequently at Willis's Rooms and elsewhere. The hymn 'Iam lucis' has an interesting background. It also appears as No. 1 in the New College hymnbook (of which more later) and was originally composed by John Bishop (Organist of Winchester College from 1695). Bishop's setting of the *Te Deum, Benedictus, Cantate Domino* and *Deus Misereatur* was always used on the Founder's commemoration days at New College and at Winchester. Bishop's tune, called *Ilsley* but later sometimes called *Bishop* or *Winchester College* was written for the 100th Psalm and adapted by its composer for *Iam lucis orto sidere*, to which words it is meant to be sung during the season of Easter, changing to *Te de profundis, summe Rex* for the rest of the year. It forms part of the college grace, other parts of which are furnished by John Reading, who preceded Jeremiah Clark (of 'Trumpet Voluntary' fame) as Organist of Winchester College (1681–92). The other item mentioned on the title page—*Omnibus Wykehamicis*—was a glee written by Hayes's equally distinguished father, William.

Heathcote did us valiant service by penning a little booklet, still in existence in the college library, entitled *Catalogue of the Music books in New College Chapel, November 1794*. From the first few pages of this we can tell what was the staple fare of the time. It was indeed a very comprehensive library, including most of the published church music of the day, all bound in such collections as Boyce's. On the next few pages he lists the items to be found in these collections, and categorises them as having been performed, or not having been performed, since the reopening of the chapel after Wyatt's alterations. A remarkably large current repertoire is thus displayed, and one commendably broad in scope, though concentrating in general on the eighteenth century. Composers represented include Aldrich, Battishill, Bishop, Blow, Byrd, Clarke, Croft, Gibbons, Green, Handel, P. Hayes, W. Hayes, Hine, Humphrey, Kelway, Kent, King, Nares, Purcell, Rogers, Tallis, Travers, Tye, Weldon and Wise.

On Hayes's death in 1797 Isaac Pring was appointed in his place. Pring was described in the notebook of Henry Leffler (*c.* 1800), as a young man 'of very promising Musical talents who was educated under Mr. Hudson, the Master of the Choristers at St. Paul's Cathedral'. He 'came to Oxford as assistant to Hayes in June 1794 in which capacity he very much recommended himself to the Warden and Society by the general propriety of his conduct and by the steady attention which he paid to the duties of his situation'. Pring was, however, only to enjoy his position as Hayes's successor for two years since he died of a pulmonary consumption in September 1799. His burial in the cloisters is recorded in the chapel register, but there is no trace of his tomb. His successor, William Woodcock, B.Mus., lasted from 1799 until his death in 1825. Woodcock had been assistant organist at Christ Church and was then a lay clerk there and at Magdalen, St. John's and New College, resigning all these on his appointment as Organist of New College.

From about 1803 comes an account by G. V. Cox in his *Recollections of Oxford* of the ancient custom whereby for many years the members of college were summoned to dinner by 'the agency of two little choristers who at a stated moment, started from the College gateway, shouting in unison and in lengthened syllables *Tempus est vocandi à manger, O Seigneurs*. It was their business to make this sentence (itself a remnant of older times) last out till they reached with their final note the College kitchen. For the last 30 years or more since the choristers' duty *ministrandi in aula* was discontinued, a bell from the Tower has called to dinner'. How interesting that the choristers were still required to act as servants as late as 1770!

In 1825 Alfred Bennett, B.Mus., was appointed Organist of New College. He was born in Chichester in 1805, his father being the cathedral organist there from 1803 to 1848. Bennett graduated B.Mus. from Oxford in 1825 and in the same year was appointed to both New College and the University Church. In 1829 he was the co-editor of a collection of Anglican chants which for a long while was considered to be definitive. Following the success of this he was, in 1830, preparing for the press a selection of sacred works arranged from the great masters, when he was killed in a coaching accident. He had been travelling to the Worcester Music Meeting (now the Three Choirs Festival) on the stage-coach *Aurora*, which, being overloaded, turned over near Severn Stoke and killed several of its occupants, including the unfortunate Mr. Bennett. His body was brought back to Oxford and buried in New College cloisters, quite a large subscription being raised for his young widow and infant son.

His successor, Dr. Stephen Elvey, was to have as distinguished a career as any of his predecessors, striving after high standards both musically and academically throughout his thirty years in the position. Whilst he was undoubtedly a fine musician, his control of the choristers was perhaps not what it should have been, for we read in the Reverend W. Tuckwell's *Reminiscences of Oxford* (1907), with regard to the 1830s: 'As for the [Magdalen] chorister boys, they ran wild. . . . The New College brats were not under better discipline.' Elvey came to Oxford from Canterbury, where he was born, and as a boy (in the cathedral choir) lost a leg in a shooting accident. With a wooden substitute he was able to manage the pedals: 'notwithstanding this disadvantage, few performers could give greater effect to Handel's choruses in Wykeham's beautiful Chapel'.[19] He held in plurality the post of Organist of the University Church (from 1845) and of St. John's College (from 1860) in addition to that of New College. While at New College he published his *Psalter pointed*, which remained in daily use in the chapel despite various alterations until it was finally supplanted in 1928.

Glee clubs flourished in great numbers in the second half of the nineteenth century. New College had a very active society, founded in 1839 with as its object 'the performance of Glees, catches, rounds, canons, and Madrigals, or any similar kind of English Music'.[20] The club, under the initial secretaryship of the Reverend W. B. Heathcote (presumably a relative of Gilbert Heathcote), had a formidable set of seventeen rules, which included a terminal subscription of 5s., fines of 1s. for being late for meetings, and of 6d. for talking during the singing of a piece! Rule 17 was added in 1846, obviously at the prompting of Dr. Elvey, keen to keep the musical standard up: 'that the Conductor have the power of putting a veto on a proposed Glee or Madrigal when it appears to him that the voices of the Choristers are unequal to take the treble part efficiently'. The first meeting was held on Thursday 14 March 1839 and the pieces performed were all glees of the period, though the evening concluded with Byrd's *Non nobis Domine*. Succeeding meetings had much the same fare, with a few items by Morley, Tallis, Gibbons, Weelkes and Wilbye to give some variety. Most of the music seems to have been donated by various members and several of the volumes are still in the college library. At the first meeting Mr. J. M. Holland, who was secretary and treasurer in 1841 and 1842, gave a copy of Morley's collection of canzonets and madrigals, while Heathcote gave copies of four more glees, and the Reverend J. E. Sewell (later to be warden) gave one sovereign.

The lists of members show us who were the musical New College men at the time. In addition to those already mentioned, the Reverend Henry Havergal (Chaplain of New College and Christ Church) was an interested amateur, and was responsible for an edition of *The Preces and Litany set by Thomas Tallis for Four Voices* (1847), in the introduction to which he shows considerable insight into the background of this music. There is a copy in New College library given by Havergal which shows in a printed list that several senior members of New College subscribed to its publication. Havergal was also responsible (in the same year) for a beautifully illuminated catalogue of the Christ Church collection of the church music of Robert Whyte (d. 1574). Frequent secular concerts in hall continued for the next fifty years or so. Handel's *Samson* was given in June 1847, and many 'open' glee concerts were given, usually finishing with *Dulce Domum* and *God save the Queen*. Copies of music continued to be donated and the catalogue drawn up in 1867 shows that a large collection had by then accrued. Other concerts took place in hall, as is shown by the programme of an 'Entertainment' given by the boys of New College School on Tuesday 20 December 1870. It consisted of madrigals, glees, part-songs, a piano duet, recitations and two scenes from Shakespeare—a very well-balanced and accomplished pro-gramme of some length. This indicates the flourishing condition of the school, which during the 1860s occupied premises at 26 and 28 Holywell. At some time No. 6 New College Lane became the school-house, and No. 19 Holywell the boarding quarters: there were about sixty pupils.

Towards the end of Elvey's time certain changes were made in the statutes of the choir. These were passed by the Visitor on 10 November 1858: they concerned the replacing of several of the vacant chaplaincies with choral scholarships, the first departure from the Founder's intentions as regarding the choir. The additional statutes stated that there should be between eight and ten choral scholars, who must be members of the university and of the Church of England. They were to be elected by examination and their tenure of office was five years, the warden and college being empowered to extend or curtail that period. There was also a resolution that 'one of the Chaplains shall be elected annually by the Warden and Fellows to hold the joint office of Chanter and Sacristan, and shall receive the additional stipend of £50 per annum'. Dr. Elvey must have worked hard to acquire a more youthful element in the choir, but with his death the next year (1860) the impetus seems to have gone and choral scholarships were abandoned in 1864. On 1 June 1864 a new choir statute was passed omitting choral scholars altogether. It was now laid down that the choir was to consist of three chaplains, eight lay clerks and sixteen choristers. The sum of £1,400 was set apart for the stipends of chaplains and lay clerks, the former to receive not less than £120 a year each, while the latter, significantly, were to receive 'such as the Warden and Officers shall think fit'. A precentor was to be appointed annually from amongst the fellows or chaplains, whose job it was 'to ensure the due performance of the choral service, and the maintenance of discipline amongst the members of the choir'. The lay clerks' pension fund was established at the same time.

Dr. George Benjamin Arnold followed Elvey, and set to work to improve the condition of the music books in chapel. Many accounts for new books and music, re-bound volumes and music copied by hand, are found for the years 1861 to 1863. The music bought was very much in the same idiom as the music already in the repertoire, Gounod's *Last Judgement* and some works by E. J. Hopkins (Organist of the Temple Church) being the most up-to-date purchases.

On Dr. Arnold's translation to Winchester, where he succeeded S. S. Wesley as organist in 1865, Dr. James Taylor was appointed. He stayed until 1901—a period of much change in the college and chapel. In 1867, a committee was set up 'to consider whether it is desirable to shorten or alter the Morning Service, and to make recommendations to the College accordingly'. In fact it resolved to shorten the office of Mattins, sung every morning as a full choral service, chiefly by the omission of the Canticles, the new form being 'modelled upon the forms now in use at Corpus and at Merton: the form, in the case of Merton, having been adopted under the express sanction of the Archbishop of Canterbury, after an appeal to him as Visitor of the College'.[21] Ten years later, in 1877, the Reverend Coker Adams, an old member of college, then of Saham Rectory, Thetford, wrote to Warden Sewell outlining several proposals for altering the chapel services. Adams mentioned the music several times, usually critically, and considered that some of his changes might perhaps lessen to some extent the number of strangers who

> *To church repair,*
> *Not for the doctrine but for the music there.*

He claimed that his proposed time for the weekly sermon (5 p.m. before Evening Prayer)

might render desirable the adoption of less prolonged services for the Canticles, the excision of the quasi-recessional Hymn, and the postponement for a quarter of an hour of the College dinner. But what is there to regret in any of these results?

At this point he called for 'the restoration of the Voluntary on the organ, which for so many years used to be played on every Sunday, Saturday, Holy-day, and Eve . . . [using] those pleasing and sacred melodies by which the reading of the Holy Scripture used to be preluded'. He complained of the increasing floridness of Evensong compared with the barrenness of Mattins, went on to plead for the introduction of Choral Communion, and lamented the small part that the chaplains played at Morning and Evening Prayer, for at that time the preces and responses were sung by a member of the choir, and the lessons read by members of college. After some paragraphs on the correct clerical dress for chapel, Adams launched an attack on the choice of music, criticising the use of oratorio and cantata extracts as anthems and declaring that the use of what is at least technically called florid harmony, such as that of Purcell or Croft, must be retained, unless the character of our Services is to be entirely altered. And I, for one, could never propose that we should confine ourselves to Gregorian Tones or to harmonies of Tallis and Marbeck. [On the other hand] there is something essentially theatrical about the tone and manner of most Oratorios which at once, on its appearance, turns a church into a concert-room. A few of Handel's sacred airs, such as *But thou didst not leave* might have been written for a Cathedral. But in most of them, even when the words are taken from Scripture, the effect, powerful though it may be, is not devotional, but sensational only.

Sewell's reply to Adams's long letter was short: '. . . I have come to the conclusion that it is not desirable, at all events at the present time, to make any of the changes suggested.' However, Adams's proposals were put to a general meeting on 10 October 1877, and a committee reported on 27 March 1878 that several of Adams's proposals should be adopted: that the sermon should be at 5 p.m. on a Sunday, the voluntary before the first lesson restored, a hymn sung before the Litany instead of in the middle of it, more short anthems sung at Mattins rather than hymns, and so on. But most of Adams's more controversial resolutions were turned down. However, although much controversy may have raged over the chapel services, at least one sensitive and gifted listener has recorded his appreciation of the music. In May 1876, the Reverend Francis Kilvert, on a visit to Oxford, wrote in his diary of Evensong at New College: 'the Chapel was filled with people. There were "High Prayers", a magnificent tempest of an Anthem, and a superb voluntary after the service. . .'.[22]

Relatively little work had been done to the Green organ over the previous hundred years: Bishop had been paid £96 10s. in 1830 for 'new pedal pipes, etc.', and he tuned the organ for some years longer, though a local builder named Rowse also did minor repairs to this and the organ in the Song Room at the same time. The organ in the Song Room still exists: it was built *c.* 1670 by Bernard ('Father') Smith (mentioned above as being the rival of Renatus Harris) and might have been donated by Dr. Hayes, for in the college meeting of 27 March 1783, it was 'ordered that the Bursars pay Dr. Hayes twenty guineas for the organ now in the Music School for the purpose of teaching the Quiristers'. Over the years this little organ must have deteriorated badly, for on 16 June 1841 the Warden and Thirteen resolved 'That the old organ in the Song Room be sold, and a good one purchased for a sum not exceeding £80'. A new organ was accordingly ordered for such a sum, and the warden (Dr. Williams) begged that he might be allowed to make a gift of it to the college. The old Smith organ was not apparently sold, for in June 1845 it was found by Sir John Sutton in the college brewhouse, as he says on a note pasted inside, 'full of hops'. Sutton purchased it from the warden and fellows for £10 and took the instrument to Jesus College, Cambridge, his own college (in which chapel there were already two organs). The organ was sold at Sotheby's some years after Sutton's death and was acquired by Captain J. Lane of Snaresbrook, Essex, who sold it to the London organ builder Noel Mander, who restored it and in whose music room it still remains. Mr. Mander kindly lent the instrument to the college in 1967 while the chapel organ was being rebuilt. Its successor in the Song Room had but one more stop and has itself now disappeared without a trace.

The old chapel organ had evidently begun to deteriorate ten years or so before it was finally replaced, for in May 1863 Bishop cleaned it for £15 and did some work to the mechanism of one of the departments for a further £3.10s. In 1867 he submitted an estimate for a new Swell Organ, some other additions, new bellows and a refurbished console for £454. The organist, Dr. Taylor, obviously wanted a far more radical reconstruction and so we find the warden (Dr. Sewell) writing to Henry Willis in February 1872 asking him to look at the organ, to advise and to estimate. Willis inspected the old organ on Friday 8 March together with Dr. Taylor and Dr. Hopkins (of the Temple Church). Their report suggested scrapping the existing instrument and building a new one, using certain old stops where appropriate. A specification was drawn up, with several of the most distinguished features later crossed out— finance then as now proving a considerable obstacle. Willis's scheme entailed using the old case, with the central arch filled in with pipes, thus hiding the west window 'but really that will be no loss'.[23] The estimate was for £1,500 (£1,320 if a 32 foot stop were omitted). The scheme met with the approval of Professor Ouseley (who advised that the old stops by Dallam and Green be retained, their stop knobs being marked to show the derivation of the pipework) but a note of dissension came from Scott, who considered it inadvisable to fill in the central portion of the case. So a compromise was reached in which Willis would only fill the lower part of the arch and compress his mechanism and wind-supply as best he might. He achieved this with much ingenuity.

All seemed set for Willis to go ahead with the work when a fellow of New College—Charles Mayo—stepped in, writing to the warden and suggesting that Willis's plans and intentions were far from ideal. Dr. Mayo was taken seriously enough for there to be considerable delay in awarding the contract and for some acrimonious correspondence to follow between Willis and the warden. The organ was not finally installed until the end of September 1874.

Dr. Charles Mayo was a notable amateur musician of New College. He was a doctor of medicine and seems to have been a remarkable man, travelling all over the world not only as a doctor but also as a journalist. There survive in the college archives many pages of his organ designs for New College chapel, and for theoretical instruments of great economy of material. There are descriptions of several ingenious devices and some beautiful coloured drawings and water-colours of his plans for New College chapel (which included removing the window above the vestry door and building a large organ chamber there, outside the building, which was to contain a five manual organ together with 40 foot pipes on the opposite wall!).

The Willis organ did not remain undisturbed for very long, for in 1877 plans were being drawn up for Scott's refurbishing of the chapel and the organ had to come out. The idea was to preserve the old case in which the organ had been built, but this was found to be impossible as it had been nailed together and could not have been taken down and reassembled. Scott therefore provided a new case of much the same shape as the old, at the very considerable cost of £1,084 2s., the new screen costing even more—£1,755 16s. 2d. Willis took the organ down in 1878 and re-erected it in June and July 1879 with one slight mechanical improvement. Scott then decided that the large case-pipes ought to be of pure tin (an expensive proposal at £280, but a very fine one) and so Willis produced a tin speaking front east and west of the case and made some other alterations to the case-pipes so that more of them would be speaking pipes. These alterations were completed in October 1879 and Willis's account of £405 settled.

The Order of Service for the 500th Commemoration of the Founder, on 14 October 1879, still survives. At Morning Prayer the psalms were 145, 146 and 147 and the Canticles were sung to Parry (1848–1918) in D. The anthem was *Now my God, let, I beseech Thee* by William Sterndale Bennett (1816–75). At Evening Prayer the psalms were 112, 122, 132 and 133, the Canticles being sung to Garrett (1834–79) in D, and the anthem was *Sing, O Heavens* by Arthur Sullivan (1842–1900). All this service music was remarkably modern at the time and shows considerable progress from the music lists of only a few years before.

The organ continued to be blown by hand, and since this proved unsatisfactory after a number of years, plans were drawn up for a hydraulic machine to blow the instrument. This was installed in a new blowing chamber designed by Champneys and built at the foot of the organ loft stairs in 1901. This was Dr. Taylor's last act as organist, for he died in the same year: a memorial tablet to him may be seen in the cloisters. As well as striving for high standards in the chapel, he must also have encouraged the college's own music-making, for in the last twenty-five years of the century many notable concerts were put on in hall, which often included major choral or semi-operatic works. The commemoration concert on 12 June 1883 featured *Alexander's Feast* by Handel, and the 'Entertainment' given on 16 December 1897 included, as well as musical items, several scenes from Shakespeare's *The Merchant of Venice*. To Taylor must also go much of the credit for the college hymnbook, which was published by Novello's in 1900. Five hundred copies were printed and many copies of the second (1910) printing still exist, as do the plates. The book includes hymns by many notable composers and authors and several musicians connected with New College, the second edition containing one by Hugh Allen, Taylor's successor as organist. One of Taylor's undergraduate pupils destined to achieve great things was Sidney (later Sir Sidney) H. Nicholson, who, born in 1875 and educated at Rugby and New College, went on to be Organist of Westminster Abbey and to found the English School of Church Music (later the Royal School of Church Music).

Sir Hugh Allen (he was knighted in 1920) was one of the most dynamic and capable musicians ever associated with New College. Born in Reading in 1869, he was taught by Dr. F. J. Read, who in 1887 took him to Chichester Cathedral where he became his assistant. After taking his Oxford B.Mus. in 1892 he went as organ scholar to Christ's College, Cambridge, where he had a remarkably varied five years. In 1897 he was appointed Organist of St. Asaph Cathedral where he only remained a year before moving to a similar position at Ely. Allen was appointed Organist and Master of the Choristers at New College in 1901, gaining a fellowship in 1908 (in those days a rare distinction for an organist) and he soon brought the choir up to that level of excellence from which it has never since slipped, while increasing and broadening the repertoire enormously. Allen ran the Oxford Bach Choir (and later *the* Bach Choir), formed an orchestral society to accompany it (now the Oxford Orchestral Society) and started the annual Bach Festivals. Indeed by 1920 Allen was acknowledged to be perhaps the greatest conductor in the country of Bach's choral music.

In 1918 he was appointed Professor of Music at Oxford, and on his appointment to the Royal College of Music as Director in 1919, ceased to be organist at New College in order to run these posts efficiently, though retaining his rooms and his fellowship. Allen returned his fellowship money to the college, hoping, as he wrote in a letter of 18 March 1919, that £100 of it would be put towards a music exhibition to provide an assistant organist. This system worked, often with members of other colleges gaining valuable experience in this way, until 1962 when the first organ scholar on the Margaret Bridges Foundation was elected and the post of assistant organist became unnecessary. Allen retired from the Royal College of Music in 1937 and remained tremendously active until his death in 1946. In his 'retirement' he retained his rooms at New College and lived at Bosham with his wife. Much of his time (he was still professor at Oxford) was spent in reorganising the University Music School in its new premises in Holywell and in getting the department recognised as a faculty (which he succeeded in doing in 1944).

After a tragic accident in which he was knocked over by a motor bicycle near the Martyrs' Memorial, Allen lay in hospital, unconscious, for a few days before dying on 20 February 1946. A memorial service was held for him in New College chapel on 1 March, in which his successors as Organist of New College, Dr. (later Sir) William Harris, Dr. (later Sir) John Dykes Bower, Dr. Sidney Watson, and Dr. H. K. Andrews, took part. The choir was augmented by singers from Magdalen and Christ Church and sang Parry's *Never Weather-beaten Sail* and Psalm 16 (one of Allen's favourites—the psalm sung in his first service at New College). A further memorial service was held in Westminster Abbey on 11 March and his ashes, at his own desire, were scattered at sea.

Hugh Allen deserves a chapter to himself, for his influence on the amateur and professional, choral and instrumental music-making of the country as a whole, and of Oxford in particular, was well-nigh unique. Allen's sense of humour is illustrated in several stories, from choristers under him at New College and in the Bach Choir. Here is one from his retirement, told by Cyril Bailey: 'Once when walking with a friend down St. Giles' in Oxford, Allen saw an organ-grinder—"I must play that organ" he declared. Giving the man a coin and telling him to go and get a drink he pulled his hat over his eyes and seized the handle. As he tootled away a benevolent gentleman approached and gave him 6d. "Thank you, sir", said Allen, "I was once Director of the Royal College of Music, but now I have come to this." "Oh my man," said the benefactor, "stick to the truth: it will serve you better." ' One of Allen's musical achievements was to 'discover' and arrange the aria *Jesu, Joy of man's desiring* from Bach's Cantata No. 147 which the choir sang at the wedding of one of Warden Spooner's daughters on 3 September 1912. This was the first performance in modern times of a work which is now immensely popular—partly through the playing of it by Dame Myra Hess, who herself learned of it from Allen.

It is fortunate that two choristers from Allen's time have written accounts of their days at New College School. The school moved to new buildings in Savile Road in 1903, the premises it still occupies. One of the choristers at the time was Philip Hilton, who had been admitted in 1900 at the age of nine. Mr. Hilton describes the conditions in 19 Holywell—the old boarding house:

There was one bathroom for all, family and boys alike, and only one W.C. in the house, but two down the yard for the daytime use of boys. We had one bath per week . . . the water heated by an antiquated gas boiler. This latter was really dangerous . . . the thing would explode . . . and a boy would be dragged naked and dripping wet out of bath and room.

Mr. Hilton mentions that in the practice room (the Song Room) there was a small organ, hand-blown [the 1841 instrument]; 'many of the stops were out of commission and many of those that functioned produced the weirdest sounds, helped by my seniors who used to take out the pipes and strike the desks with them [!], thus furthering their destruction'. Allen had a grand piano put in on his arrival, and the organ was no longer used: it evidently disappeared in the next few years. Of Hugh Allen, Mr. Hilton's first remarks are: 'as organist and choir-master he taught us much that was beyond our vocal requirements, and every single boy loved him with a love that was little short of personal devotion'.

The other account is by J. H. Alden, who joined New College School in 1910 after his voice trial with Allen, in which 'I can remember singing a hymn tune in one key while he played it in another. At the last chord he played my note and said that I was wrong; I told him he was wrong and that seemed to settle things'. Dr. Alden says that every morning 'we went to Chapel by 8.00 a.m. to sing a hymn (Litany on Wednesdays and Fridays) at which one or two boys consistently "passed out" [they never had breakfast before the service]', which indicates that the morning service was getting less and less elaborate. Dr. Alden also mentions that the choir used sometimes to sing the Bach motets (*Jesu, Priceless Treasure* was somewhat abridged) on consecutive Fridays. These would have been heard by the poet Robert Bridges who often walked in to Evensong on a Friday night (always an unaccompanied service). Bridges and Allen collaborated in revising the pointing of the psalter, in order to encourage a style based on speech rhythm. The carol services, Alden tells us, were 'sung from the Ante-chapel; a handful of strings accompanied where suitable. Someone played the organ at various spots and the general programme was taken largely from the Cowley Carol Book. No one was allowed to sit in the Ante-chapel; the main Chapel was crammed. The strings sounded well; the Pastoral Symphony from the *Christmas Oratorio* and *the* tune from *Sleepers, wake* were perennial'. The service list for the 1910 carol service suggests that Allen was very forward-looking and catholic in his taste; works by Bach, Brahms and Buxtehude were performed in addition to the more traditional carols.

Dr. Alden remembers Parry's *Songs of Farewell* being given their first performance in the chapel, with the composer in the organ loft; he also remembers Allen playing the *1812 Overture* from several different versions which he (Alden) had to rotate as necessary. Allen, with New College Choir and the Oxford Bach Choir, gave first performances of many works which are now famous, including Vaughan Williams's *Sea Symphony* and Parry's *Jerusalem*. The concert programmes from Allen's time show many of the great musicians of the time playing or conducting at New College, often performing their own works—Vaughan Williams, Parry, Stanford, Tovey, Harwood, Parratt and Myra Hess being among them.

Allen's successor was Dr. William Harris. Born in 1883, Harris was an organ scholar at the Royal College of Music in 1899. He came to New College in 1919, moving on to Christ Church in 1929, where he stayed until 1933. In that year he moved to St. George's Chapel, Windsor, and remained there until his retirement in 1961. He died in 1975. Harris was a professor of harmony and organ at the Royal College of Music from 1921 to 1953 and conducted the Oxford Bach Choir from 1926 to 1933. Sir William numbered his New College days as among his most happy and fulfilling, and expressed his belief that the trebles at New College were the best he ever had in a long and varied career. Harris's great anthem *Faire is the Heaven* was written for New College Choir and given its first performance in the antechapel in 1926.

Among Harris's pupils were Dr. J. H. Alden, who had returned to New College as an undergraduate, and R. E. Ellison, who was an undergraduate between 1922 and 1925. Mr. Ellison writes of Harris: 'He was a fabulously talented musician, a composer of outstanding gifts, particularly in the field of church music, a first-rate organist and the sort of musician who could play at sight an eight-part anthem with all the parts, but for the bass, in the C clef, and with only a figured bass to guide the accompaniment. He was always a most charming friend and it was a privilege to have known him.'[24] Sir William Hayter (warden 1958 to 1976, and in Harris's days an undergraduate) remembers the notable pianissimo singing of the choir, which he describes as 'almost a whisper, especially in the responses'.[25]

Harris maintained the organ recital series, giving three himself on Sunday evenings in his first term. The organ, however, began to show distinct signs of wear and so in May 1925 the college issued an appeal for money to rebuild the instrument. This met with a splendid response, and with the sum collected (£2,653 10s. 10d.) Dr. Harris was able to do more to the organ than mere repairs. In 1926 this work was carried out by Messrs. Rushworth & Dreaper of Liverpool, who transposed some stops, revoiced others and supplied a new electric blowing plant as well as carrying out major reconstruction of the action and wind supply. This Rushworth rebuild lasted until a new instrument was constructed in 1968 by Messrs. Grant, Degens & Bradbeer.

During the Easter term of 1927, Harris and the choir made a recording with H.M.V. of some items including *Lord, for Thy tender mercy's sake* (Farrant), *My soul, there is a country* (Parry) and *Justorum*

Animae (Stanford) which for some reason was never released. Harris used to tell the story of Sibelius's visit to New College, whither he was brought by Vaughan Williams. Apparently Sibelius asked Harris to play the organ to him, which he did, performing the Bach Prelude and Fugue in A minor. At the conclusion of this, the great composer came upstairs and putting his arm round Harris's shoulders exclaimed 'Artiste!' (for he spoke no English). Harris later found his cigar butt stubbed out on the chapel floor.

Harris was succeeded as organist by Dr. John Dykes Bower who came to New College from Truro Cathedral. It was Dykes Bower who, together with Boris Ord, Organist of King's College, Cambridge, organised the first New College versus King's College choristers' cricket match, in 1930. This was held at Cambridge, and the home team won. Both sides then sang Evensong in Kings' Chapel. Although Dykes Bower still had no organ scholar to help bear the burden, there were many fine musicians at New College at this time, few of whom were reading music however, as Hugh Allen did not get the Faculty of Music established as such until 1944. Many of these were involved in a particularly memorable concert given on Saturday 20 June 1931. This included Mozart's Sonata in D for two pianos, played by John Dykes Bower and Norman Tucker (then an undergraduate at the college, later Director of Sadlers' Wells Opera), and Stanford's *Songs of the Fleet* which were given by Keith (later Sir Keith) Faulkner (until 1974 Director of the Royal College of Music) and the choir. Termly Sunday evening sacred concerts in the antechapel were the custom for many years, and that given on 8 November 1931 contained an excellent balance of fine choral music—Palestrina, Parry, Brahms, Tallis and Byrd all being represented. Bach motets were also perennial favourites at these concerts.

In 1932 a Bach organ recital was given by Dr. Albert Schweitzer. This was one of many he gave in Oxford in order to raise funds for his mission hospital. He is remembered by Norman Tucker as 'a good, if not distinguished player, and an austere, unassuming man'.[26] Another distinguished musical visitor was Leopold Stokowski who knew Hugh Allen well. Stokowski visited Oxford on more than one occasion, and Sydney Watson, Sir John Dykes Bower's successor in 1933, remembers that on one visit he 'came every morning to the boys' practice. He said he enjoyed that more than anything else during his stay in England because it opened his ears to a different sense of music from all else that came his way. I think he was quite sincere about this'.[27] Sir John left New College in 1933 for Durham Cathedral, becoming Organist of St. Paul's Cathedral from 1936 to 1968.

Coincidentally with the arrival of Dr. Watson a music exhibition was founded by H. W. B. Joseph, in memory of his wife Margaret, daughter of the poet Robert Bridges, who, it will be remembered, had close connections with New College Choir and with Allen. Although originally intended to facilitate musical research, the Margaret Bridges Foundation has since supplied a long line of organ scholars as well as other college musicians. The first Margaret Bridges Scholar was Norman Tucker, who was awarded it for the distinction of his piano playing. The first organist on the Margaret Bridges Foundation was Ian Parrott (1934–7) who is now Professor of Music at University College of Wales, Aberystwyth. A contemporary of his was Humphrey Searle, the composer, for whom Allen arranged a travelling scholarship to study with Webern in Vienna. Sydney Watson remembers 'that he came home slightly dashed after his first term there because Webern spent a great deal of time in showing him fifteen ways of resolving the Diminished Seventh. I told him that he might have learned that by staying with me!'[28] Dr. Watson also remembers 'one hilarious Gaude when Sir Hugh Allen, Sir William Harris and Sir John Dykes Bower, who were all there, insisted on coming upstairs to sing with the choir in the madrigals. They were all rather merry and they did not sing very accurately but I don't think that the audience knew that'.[29] When Dr. Watson moved to Winchester College (whence he proceeded to Eton and, ultimately, Christ Church) there was a brief interregnum, filled by Thomas Tunnard, the organ scholar, whose commitments to the college VIII meant that Allen—for the first time in years—had to play for Evensong for a week, probably the last time he ever did so—in Eights Week 1938.

With Sydney Watson's departure this chapter closes, recounting as it has the story of New College music from the founding of the college to the Second World War, and the writer's successor will have the task of describing Dr. Watson's successors—to date, Dr. H. K. Andrews (organist 1938 to 1956), Meredith Davies (1956 to 1958), Dr. David Lumsden (1958 to 1976) and Edward Higginbottom (1976–).

REFERENCES

1. Frank Harrison, *Music in Medieval Britain* (1958), 157–8. I am indebted to Messrs. Routledge & Kegan Paul for permission to quote from this work, and to the Oxford University Press for permission to quote from Cyril Bailey, *Hugh Percy Allen* (Oxford, 1948). My thanks are also due to Dr. Francis Steer for making the New College archives so readily accessible to me, and to Mrs. Mary Young for allowing me to study the Leffler notebook. The author hopes to provide further details on the history of New College organs in a work that is now in preparation.
2. Wood, *Colleges*, 198.
3. Bursarial Accounts, New College, *passim*.
4. Wood, *Annals*, II, 286.
5. Wood, *Colleges*, 217.
6. Notebook of Warden Sewell, in New College library office, 210. Wood, *Life*, I, 49.
7. Rashdall and Rait, 57–8.
8. Wood, *Life*, I, 53.
9. Ibid., I, 69.
10. Rashdall and Rait, 170.
11. Sewell Notebook, 169.
12. Wood, *Life*, I, 289.
13. Rashdall and Rait, 248.
14. Wood, *Life*, II, 450.
15. Ibid. See also pencilled notes in New College library copy of *The Organ*, IX, no. 35 (Jan. 1930).
16. John S. Bumpus, *A History of English Cathedral Music* (1908), 215.
17. Ibid., 291–2.
18. Above, Chapter VII, 240–4, for Wyatt's 'improvements' to the chapel.
19. Bumpus, op. cit., 429.
20. Rules of New College Glee Club, 1839.
21. Report of the Chapel Services Committee, 1867.
22. *Kilvert's Diary*, ed. W. Plomer (1971 edn.), III, 318.
23. Letter to Warden Sewell from Henry Willis, 18 March 1872.
24. Letter to the author from Mr. R. E. Ellison.
25. Letter to the author from Sir William Hayter.
26. Letter to the author from Mr. Norman Tucker.
27. Letter to the author from Dr. Sydney Watson.
28. Ibid.
29. Ibid.

IX

The College Plate

CHARLES OMAN

The college's collection of plate is of unusual distinction because of the survival of a number of early pieces, including relics of the Founder and gifts made in the fifteenth and sixteenth centuries.* In his statutes the Founder ordained that the chapel plate should be kept on the top floor of the muniment tower and the secular plate on the floor below. He can hardly have expected that the priests would enjoy climbing to the top of the tower to collect the necessary plate before mass each morning, so we may suppose that only the pieces for occasional use were kept there. Since there are no signs of aumbries in the chapel it is likely that the chalices were kept in the lower muniment room immediately above the room now used as the treasury, which had been assigned in the Founder's statutes for the keeping of vessels of brass and pewter not in daily use.

The Founder made no bequest of plate for the chapel, probably because he had provided sufficient in his lifetime. There would certainly have been a chalice and paten for each of the five altars, those for the high altar being more elaborate than those for the altars in the ante-chapel. There would have been a silver cross provided both with a foot for use on the altar and a staff for carrying in processions; a pair of cruets, a censer and incense-boat and perhaps a pax. The lesser furniture for the minor altars may have been of copper-gilt or pewter, since we cannot assume that New College was inaugurated with any-

*One of the principal difficulties in disentangling the history of the college plate is that the first complete inventory was compiled by Messrs. Walford & Spokes in 1913. Previous lists were made on the occasion of the transfer of responsibility for part of the plate by the bursars to a new warden or a new butler. Most remarkable is the lack of information regarding the chapel plate in medieval times.

thing like the lavishness with which Archbishop Chichele was to fit out All Souls. The Founder must have assumed that later generations would supplement his gifts, as they certainly did.

By his will the Founder bequeathed to the college his pastoral staff: no doubt he assumed that it would be consigned to the top floor in the muniment tower except on special occasions such as a visitation by the Bishop of Winchester.[1] It was never entirely forgotten, for there is mention of its being brought down to the bursary in 1617, but it has been only since 1753, when it was rediscovered, that it has been kept in chapel. Since then its artistic importance has never been in question, but its exact significance has been a subject for dispute. Its general design (Plate 68) conforms with that of the other surviving pastoral staffs of the fourteenth century and of continental origin. There has been a tendency, for this reason, to ascribe a foreign origin for it, in Montpellier, Paris, or Italy. But the piece does not display any stylistic or technical features which would rule out London goldsmiths. It is, however, rather more open to doubt whether it was commissioned by Wykeham. When compared with the continental examples a date around 1370 seems rather late; it carries no device connected with the Founder (unlike Bishop Foxe's crozier at Corpus,) and it is tempting to suppose that he may have obtained it from the executors of his predecessor, Bishop Edington, who had been consecrated in 1346.[2] However, it is clear that the Founder had a special devotion to the Virgin Mary, to whom he dedicated his two colleges, and the representation on the crozier of the Annunciation may be compared with the sculptural groups over the entrance and above the stairway to hall. In all three the Founder is shown kneeling to the Virgin's left, in the position of a donor.

The Founder also bequeathed to the wardens of both his colleges a silver-gilt covered cup and ewer for their own use and that of their successors. We can obtain from the archives only hints regarding the other pieces of secular plate which he had provided. A very full inventory made in 1508,[3] which appears to include all the college's secular plate, lists as his gifts a great *pece*[4] with a cover, a standing *pece* with a cover, both gilt, a spice-plate, and thirteen *peces* called 'bollys' with two covers and a spoon, all of silver.* It is not possible to identify

*The 'xiii peces called bollys' given by the Founder were evidently entirely of silver, and not mazers.

any of these with certainty in later lists, and perhaps they were rather overshadowed by later acquisitions. The Founder also bequeathed to the college his mitre, dalmaticals and sandals, of which the mitre, twice reconstructed in the present century, alone survives. Associated with the Founder, but not named among his bequests, are five lengths of hinged band decorated with crystals, pearls and enamels (now believed to have been a lady's girdle), and an exquisite jewel in the form of a crowned Lombardic M. This contains within the arches of the letter minute figures of the Archangel Gabriel and the Blessed Virgin Mary in gold, with the pot of lilies on the central vertical stroke. The pot is carved out of a ruby, the lilies have a stalk of gold, leaves of translucent green enamel, and flowers of mother of pearl. Two rings are also traditionally associated with the Founder: the smaller is a plain gold ring set with a single ruby (and Bishop Edington left a ruby ring to the Founder), but the larger ring, set with an irregularly shaped crystal over green foil, is of silver-gilt.

The list of plate in the 1508 inventory is most impressive and the more important pieces were mostly given by persons who are depicted in the delightful drawing in the Chaundler manuscript (Plate 1). The college had benefited more from the second rank of clergy than from the bishops who appear in the illustration, since Chichele and Waynflete had the well-being of their own foundations to consider. Two outstanding donors were Hugh Sugar, Treasurer of Wells, and Richard Andrewes, Dean of York. The former had contributed three covered cups, two ewers and basins[5] and also two ewers for wine (weight 14 ounces). The latter had given a standing *pece*, two great salts (one with a cover) all gilt, and a dozen silver spoons. By 1508 there had been time for Wykehamists who had missed portrayal in the Chaundler manuscript to rise to eminence and give or bequeath plate to the college. At least three of the listed pieces can be recognised. One is described as a 'gilt standing *pece* with a cover gilt and partly enamelled on the knop' the gift of the Bishop of Hereford. This can be recognised as the Warden's Grace Cup (Plate 69) which has scratched underneath 'Ric' de Mayhew', who was a fellow 1457–71 and Bishop of Hereford 1504–16. Also scratched underneath is a device of a hand grasping a cross rooted in a heart, which may be intended to identify *arbor crucis* with *arbor vitae*, in the tradition of St. Bonaventure. The bowl is attached to the foot by a bayonet joint and the knop on the cover closely resembles that on the Giant Salt at All Souls, which shows traces of green cold enamel. In the cup probably only the berry finial was coloured, perhaps with cold enamel.

Warden Hill's salt (Plate 70) is grouped with the *peces*[6] although there is a separate section for salts. It is the most exuberant of all the surviving examples of late medieval plate and is unique in its perfect preservation. It is surprising that a warden should have come by such an expensive piece, but the inscription round the foot does not suggest that it was a gift. It is a punning version of the Vulgate Psalm 104, verse 6, and reads **Super WA montes TER stabunt HIL aque M.** English goldsmiths appear to have been experimenting in ways of adding colour to their work, but the idea of setting the sides of the lid with six panels of red glass overlaid by an imbricated pattern in gold foil is unique.

Seven coconut cups appear in the 1508 inventory, two of which were without covers, so that it may be presumed that the two medieval examples (now without covers) were listed. They are both outstanding. The earlier shows the nut held by six branches of an oak tree, the stem of which is encircled by a collar of Lombardic letters D linked back to back (Plate 71). The roots are confined in a paled enclosure within which are holes, probably for rabbits (now missing). If we assume that the initial D is that of the donor we may attribute it to Robert Dalton who was admitted to the college in 1472, left in 1485 and after collecting various benefices became a prebendary of Chichester.[7] The second coconut cup (Plate 72) has the nut held by three straps with feathered borders linking the lip-band which is engraved **ave maria gracia plena dominus tecum benedicta.** At the junction of the bowl and the stem are three demi-figures of angels carrying scrolls inscribed, respectively, **cristus, ihesus** and **maria.** The stem is decorated with overlapping feathers whilst the richly decorated foot is supported on three little angels carrying scrolls inscribed **ave maria.** The decoration provides no clue to the identity of the donor but both of these very important pieces must date around 1500.

It is difficult to analyse the plate listed in the 1508 inventory since some of the categories which it includes are no longer represented. There were more than a score of drinking vessels of major importance besides some fifteen lesser ones. Besides these were the nuts which have already been mentioned, three great salts and eleven lesser ones (mostly made to fit one on the top of another in twos or threes). Besides Canon

Sugar's ewers and basins there were five and a half dozen spoons and also one reputedly given by the Founder.

Acquisitions had come not only by bequest—the Grace Cup does not appear in Bishop Mayhew's will—and a few years after the 1508 inventory Archbishop Warham made over to Warden Porter four pieces, the descriptions of which have given rise to much discussion.[8] The credit for discovering when the Monkey Salt (Plate 73) was acquired goes to Mr. H. E. Bell[9] who saw that it must be 'the gilt salt, sumptuously made, with a monkey seated on a cushion with a cover, weight 51 ounces'. So far so good, but a lot of problems remain. The ruby eyes of the monkey and the finely finished base resting on three wodewoses or wild men, richly deserve the description 'sumptuously made' but the piece is manifestly not in its original condition. The cover was probably lost at an early date since the salt is not recognisable in the later sixteenth-century inventories, nor is it mentioned amongst the plate lost or saved at the time of the Civil War. It had perhaps been put away in the muniment tower and forgotten. It was probably rediscovered towards the end of the eighteenth century, when the plain guilloche band was added to replace something which had been lost between the cushion and the base. H. C. Moffat,[10] who did not know of the connection with Warham, dated the piece early sixteenth century and this dating was accepted by Bell. It might date a little earlier, since it may have been given to the archbishop, who is not credited with exotic tastes.

A large standing cup weighing 34 ounces and a smaller one weighing 20 ounces, both of silver-gilt, have certainly disappeared, but the last item on the list has been much discussed. This is the Celadon bowl mounted in silver-gilt and having 'W Warh Cantua' scratched in what may be seventeenth-century script under the foot. The description of this piece is tricky but it may be rendered 'a cup without a foot, made like a mazer with a stone of variegated colour with a base and with straps on the handle (?) and on the sides with a cover of silver completely gilt of the weight of 41 oz.'[11] The difficulty arises partly from the fact that the writer of the list was unfamiliar with the practices regarding the description of plate. Ordinarily only the weight of the silver was recorded but the scribe both in this case and in that of the Monkey Salt, gave the all-in weights including the non-metal parts. It is obvious that the 41 ounces would have to have included the weight of quite a substantial coloured marble bowl and that the present porcelain one must have been substituted at some later date. It is not a very good fit. The romantic tale connecting it with the visit to England in 1506 of the Archduke Philip must be discarded together with the belief that the bowl provides early evidence of the importation of Chinese porcelain into England. Likewise it cannot be taken for granted that the mounts of the bowl belong to the object mentioned in the 1516 document, since Warham survived until 1532 and may have presented it at a later date.[12]

In 1553 the chapel plate of Winchester College was seized at the same time that the Privy Council ordered a levy on the plate of the cathedrals and churches. The seizure was illegal, since Winchester ranked as part of the University of Oxford (just as Eton was of Cambridge) and was specifically exempted. The plate of the university chapels remained intact at the accession of Elizabeth I, but its survival was, of course, offensive to the Protestant hierarchy. Since the Crown showed no dispostion to get involved, it was left to the Visitors to bring pressure to obtain its destruction. Although there were Catholic sympathisers amongst the fellows there is no record of any concerted effort to preserve the chapel plate as there was at All Souls. Since Visitors had no power to seize it, they could only press the wardens and fellows of the colleges to convert it to secular use, thus preserving the capital which it represented. New College must have accepted this thesis since, when a visitation was held by Bishop Horne in 1566, the emphasis was upon the religious shortcomings of the fellows and nothing was said about the plate. It is likely, however, that one or perhaps two medieval chalices remained in use until late in the century, since the two communion cups bear respectively the hall-marks for 1590 and 1599. The two surviving pieces of the medieval chapel plate probably owe their preservation to having been mislaid in the top room of the muniment tower. The pax (Plate 74) with its representation of the Crucifixion within a frame delicately engraved with birds and foliage is akin to one of the woodcuts used by Richard Pynson in a Sarum Missal of about 1500.

After 1508 succeeding lists of the plate seem to have been made for special purposes. The list made in 1565 for Warden White,[13] records Warden Hill's salt and two coconut cups, and also 'a broad bowle gylt w^t m^r porters name in the bottom'. William Porter had been warden 1494–1520, and the sad fate of his cup will be told later. An inventory made on 23 December 1589[14] lists two more coconut cups and 'ii greate colledge potts weighing xx oz.' This is an early reference to a type of drinking vessel much favoured at one time in academic circles and of which the college still possesses one made in 1675 (Plate 76). Up to this time the warden had been responsible for everything, but when Warden Ryves took office on 24 May 1599 he was charged only with a dozen miscellaneous items.[15] Amongst them were Canon Sugar's ewer and basin, a set of six goblets with a cover with Warham's arms, one large and one medium (bell) salt, three silver bowls with the Founder's arms (perhaps refashioned out of Wykeham's benefactions), and a dozen spoons. The collection probably represents what was considered appropriate for the warden's personal needs.

It may have been about the same time that a category of buttery plate was inaugurated, though we only get a first glimpse of it in a list dated 15 November 1611. It consists of six 'bowls' and goblets, eighteen 'pots',[16] three smallish salts and fifty-six spoons. Another list dated 4 May 1625[17] records seven 'bowls' or goblets, twenty-three 'pots', seven small salts and forty-six spoons. Seven years later four 'pots' and one spoon had been lost but the number of 'bowls' and goblets had risen to twelve. These were described as 'lately in the custody of Joseph Frape, Butler'.[18]

By the time of the election of Warden Ryves the chapel plate consisted only of one communion cup of 1590 and another of 1599. The Prayer Book service, which prescribed the administration of the cup to all communicants, led to a greater consumption of wine. To obviate the lengthening of the service by repeated consecrations, it was preferable to have a vessel in which consecrated wine could be kept ready to replenish the chalice. Some colleges (All Souls and Magdalen), allocated an old possession for this purpose but Warden Ryves in 1602 presented two handsome flagons. Whereas Warden Ryves's benefaction may be deemed over-generous, that of Warden Pinke who gave in 1641 an almsdish (diameter 10 inches) seems to have been carefully calculated to meet the actual needs of the small congregation of a college chapel.

The history of the plate during the Civil War and the Commonwealth is very involved. At an early stage of the war King Charles issued a circular letter to the colleges asking them to lend their plate and promised repayment at a rate of 5s. per ounce for silver and 5s. 6d. for gilt. A list of the plate sent by the colleges is preserved at the Bodleian[19] but New College is not mentioned. There is no doubt that New College responded to the appeal but the self-despoilment was not complete. There is a list of plate delivered by Warden Pinke to the bursars in 1636[20] at the bottom of which has been added 'All the Plate above written, at the time of ye Siedge of Oxon, was given to Charles ye firste except (1) the Plate for ye communion and (2) the 3 Indian Nutts.[21] The cover of ye Indian Nutt was given also for at this time, 1662, ye Coll. hath it not'. The puzzling thing is that the plate listed does not seem to correspond with what we know of either the warden's or the buttery plate. This rather suggests that it may have been from a reserve stored in the muniment tower. Since the plate is said to have been *given* to the King at the time of the siege it may refer to a date about 1644 and not be connected with the appeal for a *loan* in 1642.

Warden Pinke died on 2 November 1647, and the fellows, disregarding the prohibition of the Parliament, elected Dr. Stringer in his place. He was *de facto* warden until January 1649, when George Marshall was imposed by the Parliament. The latter's take-over was complicated by his inability to find out much about the affairs of the college, since most of the senior fellows had been ejected. He appears to have assumed that no secular plate survived and there remains a bill from a local goldsmith, Thomas Berry, for £26 9s. 6d. for supplying a great salt, two trencher salts, a tankard, a porringer and a dozen spoons.[22] It was not until nearly two years later that he discovered a chest put away by Warden Stringer, containing a ewer and basin, two flagons, three tankards, sixteen cups of various types, a sugar-box with spoon and sixteen spoons. Most of the pieces were probably of recent date.[23] There is no reason to suppose that Warden Marshall ever learnt about the medieval plate which must have been concealed in the muniment tower, and the whole collection was probably forgotten until late in the eighteenth century when the injudicious repair was done to the Monkey Salt. Another piece fared much worse. Amongst the senior common room plate is a salver bearing the 1783 hall-mark and inscribed underneath 'Gul. Porter Custos, 1494, dono dedit'. This was probably refashioned from the 'broade bowle gylt w^t Mr Porter's name in the bottom' listed in the 1565 inventory.

It will be seen that at the Restoration the college, thanks to Warden Stringer's treasure chest and Warden Marshall's purchases, was probably better supplied with everyday plate than any other in the university. None of the latter pieces, however, have survived in their original state, although a few extant pieces bear inscriptions showing that they were made from their silver. This may be taken as evidence of the growth of antiquarianism, which ensured that the names of past benefactors came to be engraved on the refashioned pieces, since there is little evidence that the bursars were so scrupulous during the 263 years prior to the Civil War.

During the reign of Charles II administrative changes were made which affected the plate in several ways. Wykeham's statutes had forbidden the college to those not on the foundation, but gentlemen commoners had come to be tolerated, although they might not be lodged within the college. In 1677 this disability was removed so that the field from which gifts and bequests of plate might be expected was somewhat extended. But since Winchester commoners were not often members of wealthy families the benefit was only marginal. It might have been otherwise had the palace begun by Charles II at Winchester been completed and Winchester College become a school for the sons of the aristocracy. However, the college is indebted to the early commoners for some handsome tankards, some of which have been damaged by the addition of spouts at a later date.

More important was the appearance of a new category of common-room plate. Up to this time much help has been obtained from the archives but from now on the pieces are left to tell their own tales since no catalogue was compiled before 1913. It is not possible to trace the development of the various categories with any confidence. Vessels for wine and beer might be allocated to the warden, buttery or the senior common room (or to the junior common room when that made its appearance). Vessels for tea and coffee went to the common rooms, which were more prone to accept silver bric-à-brac.

The post-Restoration plate has not the same artistic importance as that which survives from before the Civil War. The Spanish Ambassador's Cup (Plate 75) is, however, outstanding. For long it was believed to have been made to replace one given by Don Francisco Chacon y Valenzuela, who had lodged in the college when the Court had removed to Oxford at the time of the Plague. But this cup was stolen when thieves broke into the buttery on 6 November 1675 and stole 'near 200^{li}. of plate'.[24] The credit for correcting the story of the cup is due to David Ogg, who was able to show that it was the gift of a later Spanish Ambassador, Don Pedro Ronquillo, who was entertained in the college at the time of the Oxford Parliament of 1681 and who referred to his intended benefaction in a letter to Warden Beeston. It bears the hall-mark for 1680–1 and the mark of Jacob Bodendick, who was born at Limburg-am-Lahn and who became one of the most prosperous London goldsmiths after having come to terms with the Goldsmiths' Company.

Apart from the Spanish Ambassador's Cup the college is rather weak in Charles II plate. The only college pot or tun bears the 1675 hall-mark and a curious inscription referring to a story now forgotten (Plate 76).[25] Also amongst the buttery plate is a pair of tankards with lion thumb-pieces, one with the 1677 hall-mark and the other that for 1679 (Plate 77). They are uninscribed and the arms engraved upon them may not be original. Among the senior common room plate is a tankard of about the same date but stamped with a goldsmith's mark *R.T. above a rosette* repeated four times. It is probably provincial.

The only piece of any importance representing the late Stuart period is a tankard presented by Edward Chute of the Vyne. It was made by John Jackson and bears the 1697 hall-mark but has a spout added in the nineteenth century.

During the reign of George II the bursars had a campaign to bring the plate up to date by refashioning pieces which were either worn out or out of fashion. These included several late Stuart pieces. Their preference was for good reliable work and they patronised two London goldsmiths much favoured by the bursars of other Oxford colleges. It is not clear whether they dealt direct or passed their orders through a local goldsmith. Edward Pocock supplied mugs and tankards between 1728 and 1732, but John Swift supplied five tankards and two mugs in 1749, one tankard and six mugs in 1750, and another tankard in 1753. A pair of sauce-boats was provided in 1763. The best example of the work of Pocock is a fine large tankard with the hall-mark for 1732 (Plate 78) made out of a piece given by Charles Wither, commoner, in 1680. A pair of tankards with the hall-mark for 1749 shows the best of Swift's work. One was made from a piece given by Charles Newsham of Chadshunt in 1693 (Plate 79) and the other from one given by William Pynsent, commoner, 1697.

The only important additions made in the second half of the eighteenth century are a pair of soup tureens. The earlier one belongs to

68. The Founder's Pastoral Staff.

69. The Warden's Grace Cup, *c.* 1480.

70. Warden Hill's Salt, *c.* 1490.

71. Coconut-cup mounted in silver-gilt, *c.* 1490.

72. Coconut-cup mounted in silver-gilt, *c.* 1500.

73. Archbishop Warham's Salt (The Monkey-Salt), *c.* 1500.

74. Silver Pax, *c.* 1500.

75. The Spanish Ambassador's Cup, 1680.

76. College pot or tun, 1675.

77. Tankard, 1677.

78. Tankard, refashioned 1732 from one given in 1680.

79. Tankard, refashioned 1749 from one given in 1695.

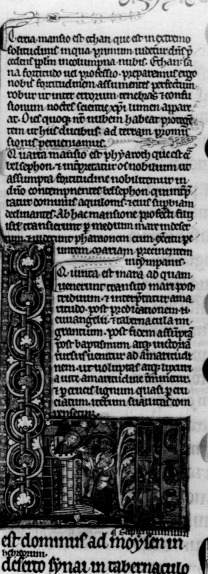

80. A book given by William of Wykeham.

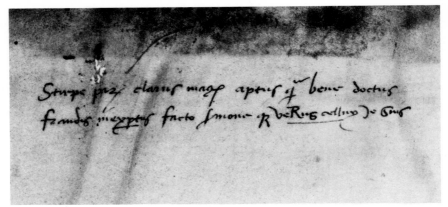

81. Inscription of ownership of John Russell.

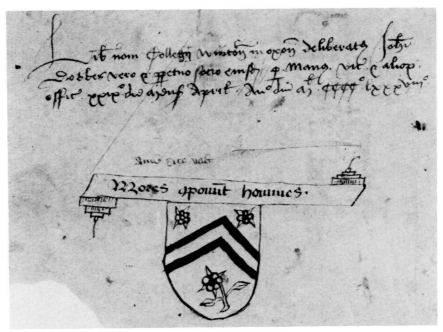

82. A book from the circulating collection.

hic iacet Iohēs london in artib3 magz ac sacre
theologie scolaris necnon huȝ alme vniuersitatis
scriba qui obiit xiiȝ die Augusti Anno dm̄ m̄
ccccc viij cuius aīe propicietur deus amen

83. Memorial brass to John London, Fellow 1494–1508.

84. Bust of Michael Woodward, Warden 1658–75.

the buttery and bears the 1766 hall-mark and that of George Baskerville and William Sampel. It was the gift of Peregrine Bertie. The second has the mark of Edward Conen and the hall-mark for 1775. It was the gift of Gilbert Clarke, commoner, and is allocated to the senior common room. A set of candlesticks was given to the senior common room in 1768 by Rowland Ffrye. A pair of 16½ ounce oval salvers bearing the mark of Richard Rugg and hall-marks for 1783 have inscriptions which tell that they were made from plate given by Warden Porter, 1494, and Warden Coxed, 1729. Whilst the loss of the former of these pieces is to be deplored, that of the latter is to be regretted because of the scarcity of early eighteenth-century plate in the collection.

The chapel plate did not suffer during the Civil War and the only important addition made between the Restoration and the age of Victoria was a large gilt alms dish presented in 1666 by John Nicholas, who became warden nine years later.[26] The rim is embossed with cherubs, floral scrolls and cartouches enclosing arms and donative inscriptions. It is curious that the centre is left plain instead of being engraved with the sacred monogram. This peculiarity is shared by the alms dish which he presented to Winchester in 1681, two years after he had become warden there.

The plate acquired during the nineteenth century is mostly unimportant, consisting largely of articles recently devised for the greater comfort of the fellows (covered dishes, toast-racks, etc.) and partly of copies of the Georgian pieces in daily use. When Georgian pieces were presented they were often spoilt by embossed decoration as was the tankard presented in 1845 by William Trapier of Charleston together with the recipe for mint julip. If it is possible to excuse redecoration, an exception might be made in favour of a tankard presented in 1836 to the junior common room, which is embossed with a very spirited rendering of the story of Tam-o'-Shanter. It is not clear whether the candlesticks shown upon the altar in chapel in early nineteenth-century engravings were of brass or of silver. In 1886, however, was acquired a handsome pair made in the late fourteenth-century style, gilt and with enamelled decoration.[27]

The acquisitions made in the present century show greater variety. Of historical interest is a small waiter, given by the late Lord Donoughmore, made by William Egan of Cork during the period in 1922 when that city was occupied by the Republican forces and communication with the Dublin assay office severed.

In the eighteenth and nineteenth centuries the majority of pieces were of standard design but recently there has been a swing towards ones specially designed. One of the first of these is a standing bowl in the senior common room, given in 1916 in memory of Leslie Whitaker Hunter but bearing the Birmingham hall-mark for 1911 and the mark of George Payne of Oxford.

More recently Leslie Durbin has made a number of pieces for the different sections of the college plate. The buttery has a bread basket made in 1960 in memory of Warden Smith. The senior common room has a seven-branched candelabrum made in 1961 and given by seven members of the Llewellyn-Smith family. For the chapel he has made a chalice and paten, a ciborium, and a wafer-box, in addition to the cross and candlesticks which illuminate the altar.

REFERENCES

1. R. Lowth, *The Life of William of Wykeham, Bishop of Winchester* (1759), appendix, xxxix.
2. This was suggested in 1906 by W. St. John Hope (*Archaeologia*, LX, 472) who made the unnecessary suggestion that the staff might have been Edington's but the crook Wykeham's.
3. *Liber Albus*, 9.
4. A *pece* generally referred to some sort of cup but the word might describe a piece of plate of any sort.
5. In 1599 a ewer and basin 'with a garnishing of sugar loaves' was transferred to Warden Ryves for his use (N.C. MS. 1750).
6. *Itm una pecia deaurat' stans cu' copclo ex done m^{ri} Walti' hylle nup Custodis.*
7. Dalton was a person of some importance. This makes him a more likely donor than the Mr. Dogett who also gave a coconut cup.
8. *Liber Albus*, f. 16v, dated 16 April 1516.
9. *The Treasures of New College, Oxford*, n.d.
10. H. C. Moffat, *Old Oxford Plate* (1906), 66.
11. 'Unum ciphum non stantem factum ad modum murre cum lapide varii coloris cum pede et ligament' super ansem et in lateribus cum coopertorio argenteo et integre deaurato ponderis xli unc.' (*Liber Albus* f.16v.). An alternative translation might read: 'a cup (not a standing one), fashioned like a mazer, with a stone of variegated colour, with a foot and with binding bands on the handle and on the sides, with a silver cover gilt inside and out, of the weight of 41 ounces.'
12. He certainly made later benefactions of plate since in the short list of plate issued in 1599 to Warden Ryves were 'Six gilt goblettes wth Archbishoppe Warhams arms on the toppe of the cover' (N.C. MS. 1750).

13. N.C. MS. 1748.
14. N.C. MS. 1750.
15. N.C. MS. 1136.
16. Were these mugs or 'college pots'?
17. N.C. MS. 1178.
18. N.C. MS. 880.
19. Bodley MS., Tanner 338; Moffatt, op. cit., x.
20. N.C. MS. 989.
21. The third 'Indian Nutt' still survives. It bears the 1584 hall-mark and was given by Katherine Bayley of Sarisbury, Hants.
22. N.C. MS. 1143.
23. There are no earlier mentions of flagons or of a sugar-box. The only donor mentioned is Dr. Barker, Dean of the Arches, who had given 'one faire Gilt Bole' which was probably like the standing cup which he had given to Winchester in 1632. The inventory of this collection was deposited in the Herts. Record Office by Sir Walter Halsey, Bart. A transcript is in the College Archives (2817).
24. Three thieves were involved, Smith, Ingram and another who is not named. The death of the butler, two days earlier, probably made their task easier. The loot was taken to London and sold for melting. Ingram denounced Smith who was hanged. *Life and Times of Anthony Wood* (Oxford Hist. Soc.), XXI, 325, 327, 371, 390.
25. 'Tenebrionibus Surreptum Johannes Gunter L L B Firmarius de Birchanger denuo in lucem edit.' Birchanger was a college living and perhaps Gunter had discovered the piece amongst the goods of a former incumbent?
26. Paten-covers were supplied for the Elizabethan communion cups in 1741. They bear the mark of Richard Bayley.
27. I have not been able to discover the designer and the maker's mark: F S does not seem to be recorded at Goldsmiths' Hall.

X

Thoughts on the Archives[1]

FRANCIS W. STEER

In his original scheme for the buildings of New College in 1379, William of Wykeham provided a tower—almost a fortress—in which to store the evidences relating to his own extensive endowments and those of subsequent benefactors. This *turris chartularia*, a handsome building in the north-east angle of the front quadrangle, also serves as an entrance to the college hall. The tower is about 26 feet by 23 feet externally and some 55 to 60 feet high; niches sheltering a figure of Our Lady (retaining slight traces of original colouring) flanked by those of the Archangel Gabriel and the Founder in attitudes of adoration are distinctive and lovely features of the west front. A sun-dial was formerly high up on the south wall of the tower.

In the north-east corner of the tower is a spiral stone staircase leading to two lofty muniment rooms, each about 22 feet by 19 feet, situated one above the other; a third muniment room (used for modern records) is at the top of the staircase leading to the hall and is incorporated in the eastern range of the front quadrangle. These three rooms, each with massive iron-clad doors fitted with intricate locking devices, still serve the purpose for which they were designed. As muniment rooms, they violate every rule laid down in modern manuals of archive administration; the walls and ceilings—the latter with simple lierne vaults—are of plastered stone, and the floors are of attractive, fourteenth-century, patterned tiles; the small windows do not open and are protected by iron grilles and heavy oak shutters; ventilation depends on draughts up or down the staircase; electric light and heat (both used sparingly) and smoke detectors are the only concessions to twentieth-century usage.

Yet in 600 years, the documents stored in these rooms have not suffered any deterioration except in one small area where rain once penetrated the lead roof. One therefore echoes what an old member of the college once wrote, 'Who is wiser than our Founder?' Sir Ernest Barker, in an eloquent passage in *Age and Youth*, also refers to the 'sense of the majesty and magnificence of the Founder . . . in the matter of architectural planning'. Wykeham's 'new college', rather like the 'new forest', seems to be the essence of stability and of history.

The furnishing of the muniment rooms is interesting. The Founder provided five or more great oak chests each measuring 8 feet 6 inches by 2 feet 3 inches by 2 feet 3 inches and each secured by three locks, plus an elaborate system of draw-bars kept in position by padlocks. The chests, of timber 1⅜ inches thick, must have been built *in situ* because they are far too large to go up the spiral staircase and much too heavy to move. Three of these chests survive, two having been cut up to form the ends of eighteenth-century presses. Lacking divisions or trays, the chests must have been extremely inconvenient for storage purposes, as the records, either in small charter boxes, as rolls, or as books, would have been piled on top of each other, and a lot of time could have been spent searching for a particular item. By the sixteenth century, when the chests were probably full, an enormous press of fifty-four heavy oak drawers, with cupboards below, was constructed in the first-floor muniment room; in the seventeenth century various smaller nests of drawers were made of pine; in the eighteenth century two very substantial presses comprising drawers, shelves and cupboards were erected in the top muniment room. Other storage equipment has been introduced as required, so New College has a collection of 'archival furniture' representative of periods from the fourteenth to the twentieth centuries.

The confusion which faced the present writer in the muniment rooms in 1956 was daunting. The floors were partially hidden by tin and wooden boxes filled with documents; cupboards were stuffed with hundreds of account and manorial court rolls; drawers were full of papers; shelves accommodated bulging parcels (many of them split open) of title-deeds and leases. On the top of one press was a collection of shallow boxes of the type used in old-fashioned drapers' shops to store reels of cotton, plus sundry packages and a wickerwork travelling hamper; in those containers were ancient documents of all classes, which Warden Sewell had taken from the muniment rooms and must have retained in the lodgings until his death when, mercifully, someone had the sense to restore these miscellaneous and immensely valuable records to safe custody. In addition to the chaos, there was a pall of dust and the webs of generations of spiders over almost everything. The cleaning, sorting, listing, numbering and arranging of about 14,000 groups of documents and books was strenuous and dirty work; however, the result was satisfying and this great series of archives is now accessible and any item can be produced if its catalogue reference is quoted. To the credit of the college and other benefactors, the catalogue was published at the end of 1974; one hopes that it is a boon to scholars.

We must now consider some of the classes of records which have survived. There are copies of the statutes in various forms leading up to the final sealed version; there are title-deeds and manorial court rolls which came with the acquisition of property and often antedate the foundation of the college; numerous royal letters patent and papal bulls testify that William of Wykeham took no chances whatever with his temporal or spiritual superiors—he was well aware of the definition of a muniment. For example, there is an impressive group of notarial and other instruments concerning the dispute with the incumbent of St. Peter-in-the-East regarding privileges which the Founder obtained for his college to the detriment of the vicar's income; these documents alone show with what determination such causes were fought.[2]

A summary may be useful at this stage before a description and discussion of particular classes of archives is given. The foundation of the college is represented by deeds of title to the site, the foundation charter, the statutes, grants of privilege and protection (incidentally, William of Wykeham did not waste money on richly illuminated documents), and by the title-deeds of his endowments and those of his contemporaries, or near contemporaries, who were such generous benefactors. Every aspect of the college finances is shown in hundreds of account rolls and associated documents dating from the foundation to the present time, but with some gaps. The internal management of the college and its buildings is covered rather less completely, although records are fairly copious from the Restoration. The manorial and estate archives are virtually complete from the time of the acquisition of a property; the administrative papers for estates are patchy and tend to be of a decidedly miscellaneous character.

Surviving correspondence is mostly from the eighteenth and nineteenth centuries and is disappointing. The records of the activities of members of the college and its officers are sparse, although the registers of protocols (long declarations in Latin by newly appointed scholars/fellows to observe the statutes of the college), with their very interesting notarial attestations, dating from 1450, are invaluable genealogical material. The long series of 'Suggestion Books', besides telling us of the grievances of members of the junior common room, shows a dramatic decline in the use of the English language, and, more seriously, of good manners as we reach the 1970s.[3]

The collection of estate maps, although large, contains very few examples of cartographic art; such documents must be regarded as administrative records, rather than beautiful pictorial records to be put away and forgotten. The seals on early deeds are a specialised interest, but of prime importance to students of heraldry. The great cartularies and registers of leases[4] are not only convenient to use, but save wear and tear on original, and precious, documents.

With the exceptions of the early hall books and some bursars' rolls which are invaluable for giving the names of persons, and building and other charges, respectively, the college is relatively badly off for administrative records until about the third quarter of the seventeenth century when there are many which reflect almost every facet of college life. Of course, there are unfortunate gaps in nearly all classes of records, as they have been at the mercy of generations of administrators and custodians who pleased themselves as to what they kept or destroyed. Frequently, too, books, in particular, were bought for a specific purpose, but within a few years developed into confused memoranda bearing no relationship to the original subject.[5] Account rolls, although in great quantity, are difficult to use, and the true state of the college finances at any given date can only be established by the painstaking researcher.

Some idea of the diversity of the archives may be gained when it is mentioned that there are ninety-five classes relating primarily to college affairs; such records include accounts of all types, and others concerning the college administration, its benefactors, buildings, chapel, the Founder and Founder's Kin, immunities and privileges, libraries, progresses (i.e. inspections of estates), the Visitor and warden, and, most important, the members. For the latter, the great volumes each labelled *Registrum Protocollorum* are unique[6] and provide the material on which to base an assessment of the social status of members of the college and the areas whence they came. Among special classes of records may be noted those of James Woodforde (1740–1803) which are mainly of family interest rather than of the diarist himself,[7] and a large and important collection of the Rev. Sydney Smith's (1771–1845)[8] letters which are to be included in the edition of his voluminous correspondence by Mr. Alan Bell.[9] The college received the letters, some books, and various other records of Alfred, Viscount Milner (1854–1925) in 1934; the bulk of those archives has been deposited in the Bodleian Library, but the college has retained an impressive quantity of illuminated addresses and certain personal records.[10] The very miscellaneous papers of Warden Alic Halford Smith (1883–1958) reflect his many activities,[11] especially his concern for Oxford and the controversial road schemes for the city (which aroused such passionate feelings in the hearts of many people and which still remain an unsolved problem).

When one considers the sheer bulk of parchment and paper which has accumulated over the centuries and which, under various headings, offers opportunities for studying the administrative, economic and architectural history of the college, there is a sense of disappointment at the comparative paucity of records relating to its social history. For example, the absence of the correspondence and diaries (in any appreciable quantity) of wardens and fellows is to be deplored; but it must be accepted that a man's official letters, sometimes mixed up with his private papers, present difficulties to widows or executors and are too often the objects of wholesale destruction at times of bereavement or when day-to-day demands are heavy and the significance of letters and papers is not realised.

New College has had many benefactors who, besides giving lands and money, donated books, jewels, plate, vestments, pictures and other valuables. Among the major benefactors may be mentioned, in addition to the generous Founder, Thomas Beckington, William Warham, Robert Sherburne, William Fleshmonger, Christopher Rawlins, Michael Woodward, Charles Parrott, Alfred Ernest Allnatt, and Harry Sacher.[12] Lists of benefactions assist in the understanding of art and of gracious living, and in learning about what books were available before and in the early days of printing; we can also understand the sense of gratitude and devotion which men of all ages have felt towards the college to which they owe so much. As to life in college, buttery and kitchen books going back to the seventeenth century provide first-hand, accurate information about what was eaten and drunk, and what it cost. For example, a Mr. Bowles had a dinner on 21 November 1772[13] comprising fish (10s.), roast beef (5s. 2d.), salad and potatoes (1s. 4d.), New College pudding (a speciality!) (1s. 6d.), brawn (2s.), and mince pies (2s.)—a total cost of £1 8s. 6d., a sum which, if converted into modern money, suggests a pretty expensive dinner-party, and we are not told what wine was consumed in addition. Films showing tables loaded with roast peacocks, swans and herons, dishes of sturgeon and other rare fish, are all very romantic, but do not present the true, everyday gastronomic habits of past generations any more than, in our own time, fellows of Oxbridge colleges spend every evening drinking large quantities of excellent port!

The religious life in a place like New College raises questions which can only be answered from its archives. What services were held? What chaplains, organists and choirs were employed and at what cost? What was spent on the adornment of the chapel, and was it common for one idea—say the introduction of a new style in stained glass[14]—to be copied by one college from another in much the same way that the installation of new and expensive organs was fashionable in the 1960s and 1970s. Colleges were patrons of the arts if we include sculpture and achitectural ornament; alterations to existing buildings and the erection of others (not always an enhancement to Oxford's beauty) to provide extra accommodation,[15] is also a matter for the written and the pictorial record. New College is fairly rich in this way, especially for the nineteenth century, but, alas, scarcely a plan has survived, although there is plenty of correspondence.

As some of its fellows were (and still are) trustees or members of governing bodies, New College has amassed extensive collections of documents relating to Thame School, Bedford School, the Lambourne Almshouses and so forth. In the case of Thame School, the records[16] are preserved in five sixteenth-century chests made for the purpose; the contents of one chest comprises title-deeds and other documents still preserved in their original leather-covered charter boxes or coarse linen bags with contemporary labels pasted or stitched on them. One copy of the statutes of the school (founded by John, Lord Williams of Thame by will in 1559) is bolted into the usher's desk to signify that 'he taught on the statutes'.

Turning to estate records, these occupy the greatest amount of space in the muniment rooms. The estates have always been the life-blood of a college and their archives are not only evidences of title but they shed light on many aspects of human activity. We have records such as manor-court rolls, title-deeds, leases, surveys and maps, correspondence, agreements, accounts of every sort, tithe records, details of advowsons, charities and schools, taxation, timber transactions, law suits, and so on in considerable bulk. Estates were acquired, in the earlier years, either by bequest or by purchase with accumulated funds; in some counties there was a sound policy of consolidating land holdings by buying small acreages as they came on the market to add to the principal estate. Conversely, fairly small properties in parts of the country a long way from Oxford were often sold because they were not economic units, but the early records of such estates were usually retained. A college owning rich agricultural land, or property in London, Oxford or some other prosperous town, was receiving a substantial income which enabled it to improve or increase its buildings, enrich the emoluments of its fellows and, by careful husbanding of surplus revenue, enabled it to acquire yet more lands and, incidentally, increased responsibilities which, in turn, created more and more administrative records. With the purchase of property came title-deeds; in the case of early gifts or investment, such documents, as already stated, antedate the foundation of the college and often carry heraldic and other seals which are important aids to a highly specialised branch of learning.[17]

The college has had (and in many instances retains) property in London and twenty-eight English and Welsh counties; the major holdings were in Berkshire, Buckinghamshire, Essex, Gloucestershire, Hampshire, Norfolk, Oxfordshire and Wiltshire. Such a wide variety of estate-records enables scholars to compare, for example, the revenue of one college with another, the differences in the administration of estates owned by absentee landlords and those owned by wealthy resident landlords, and to assess what influence a college imposed on a particular locality. The historian will seek to answer such questions as: Did the richer foundations always attract a certain class of student?

Were the inhabitants of a parish more favourably treated by private than corporate landlords? What were the social and academic backgrounds of great benefactors and what prompted them to make these substantial gifts? Only the close study of contemporary archives—national or otherwise—can give clues to the answers to such fascinating problems.

It is in the great cartularies, the lease registers, the bailiffs' and bursars' rolls, the registers of members of the college, estate correspondence, the reports made by the warden when on progress, and the minute books of the governing body that so much information lies on college life and on the lives of others who were dependent on the foundation in one way or another. But the search can be tedious and sometimes unrewarding because of inexplicable gaps in records. The importance of estate archives so far as local history is concerned is obvious, although the correct interpretation of such documents is not so simple as some local (and usually untrained) historians imagine.

The accounts for any one manor or land holding are usually straightforward; difficulties arise, however, when an attempt is made to compile a 'statement of account' or balance sheet for a college and its possessions in any one year because of variations in accounting systems and in the time of year when a particular account was submitted.[18] On a rather lower level, accounts and vouchers (there are thousands of the latter dating from the mid-seventeenth century at New College) are a valuable source of information on the prices of commodities, labour and building maintenance.

By reason of our sister foundation at Winchester, we have archives relating to that college and evidences (not in great quantity) submitted by applicants for admission to New College on the grounds that they were Founder's Kin.[19] T. F. Kirby's book, *Winchester Scholars* (1888), Warden Sewell's manuscript register (a monument of industry) of New College men, and the forthcoming catalogue of the Winchester College archives are basic sources, but it would be an immense contribution to the history of New College if someone would accept the task of collecting impressions (whether printed or in manuscript is immaterial) of members during their time at Oxford.[20]

Items which are not strictly archives in the generally accepted sense of the term have also found their way into the muniment rooms; there are minor literary manuscripts of which none is likely to add significantly to scholarship, large quantities of photographs, engravings and newspaper cuttings, an outstanding collection of keys dating from the late fourteenth century to the early nineteenth, examples of seal and charter boxes and other containers, labels, spikes on which vouchers were impaled,[21] and even a pen-knife which an unfortunate clerk lost in the documents relating to Donhead St. Mary, Wiltshire. Such objects, like the presses and fittings mentioned earlier, are worth preserving as evidence of how archives were kept; in time, such trifles become museum pieces.

To attempt a description of all the classes of documents held by New College is impossible within the space at my disposal;[22] it is also unnecessary because the printed catalogue[23] lists, in some detail, the type, quantity and dates of all the records, and there are general and sectional prefaces plus numerous references in footnotes. Efforts are made to preserve modern records as, for example, memoranda on the reconstruction of the warden's lodgings, 1958–60, and correspondence, drawings and specifications relating to the organ installed in 1969, but administrators of colleges, rather like persons in charge of business houses, are not always aware that the papers they accumulate, and frequently destroy when storage space becomes a problem, are materials for future historians. The attitude is understandable, but the losses are great and the absence of records leaves many questions unanswered and unanswerable.

The trained historian knows, or ought to know, that any restrictions imposed by an archivist are usually in the general interest of scholars as a whole. This observation is from a lecture given by the late Sir Hilary Jenkinson[24] in 1947 in which he outlined the respective roles of the archivist and the historian. As one who had a foot in both camps, Jenkinson was aware that while the custodian was not necessarily the best interpreter of the records in his care, he must sometimes be allowed the pleasure and privilege of following up his own discoveries. Sir Hilary took as his text, 'Thou shalt not muzzle the ox when he treadeth out the corn';[25] a metaphor perhaps not entirely apt where historical records are concerned. We must, however, allow the 'ex-archivist' a few mouthfuls of corn, although reminding him that his primary duty is to tread; it is hoped, however, that he will not tread on many, if any, toes belonging to historians.

An institution of the antiquity, size and importance of New College attracts scholars from all over the world who wish to study various aspects of social, economic and agrarian history. Records, whether they date from the fourteenth or any other century, provide basic material for research; modern records should be preserved with the same care as those of earlier periods because, at some point in time, such evidence will be required. The college buildings are glorious examples of architecture, and men who spend a brief three years (in some cases, many more) in such surroundings cannot fail to be impressed by the munificence of the Founder. But many members of New College who have ascended the worn steps to hall probably have no idea of the documentary treasures in that lovely tower of which the steps form but a part. The author of this short and inadequate essay asks that those who read it and possess any documentary evidence relating to the college will arrange for its eventual deposit in the Founder's *turris chartularia* for the benefit of our successors.

REFERENCES

1. This essay is based, to a considerable extent, on the introduction to Francis W. Steer, *The Archives of New College, Oxford: a Catalogue* (1974), and on a short essay, 'In that tower . . .', in *New College Record, 1972—3*.
2. *The Archives of New College, Oxford* (hereafter abbreviated to *Archives*), esp. 83–6.
3. The earliest record of the junior common room to survive is an account book begun in 1793.
4. *Archives*, 47–9, in particular.
5. Ibid., 47–9, for examples; the *Liber Albus* and the Great Register Book (MSS. 9654, 9655) demonstrate that this type of confusion existed from 1400 to 1855.
6. Ibid., xiv, 100; these records cover the period 1450 to 1841.
7. Ibid. 112–21.
8. Ibid., 111, 112.
9. To be published by the Clarendon Press.
10. *Archives*, 106–9.
11. Ibid., 145–53.
12. See also H. Rashdall and R. S. Rait, *New College* (1901), 238–42, and *Oxford University Calendar*.
13. N.C. MS. 8727.
14. On this subject, see C. Woodforde, *The Stained Glass of New College, Oxford* (1951).
15. See A. H. Smith, *New College, Oxford, and its Buildings* (1952), but more recently, the Sacher building and Bodicote House have been built in Longwall.

16. *Archives*, 426–33, and references there quoted; see also Francis W. Steer, *Thame School and its Founder* (1975). For Bedford School, see *Archives*, 155–61, and J. Godber, *The Harpur Trust, 1552–1973* (1973).

17. The early deeds listed in *Archives*, 513–26, are a rich quarry for students of sigillography and palaeography.

18. An important discussion on accounting is provided by G. R. Batho in his introduction to *The Household Papers of Henry Percy, Ninth Earl of Northumberland (1564–1632)* (1962).

19. See G. D. Squibb, *Founder's Kin: privilege and pedigree* (1972).

20. There have been appeals for such recollections, but the response has been poor. It must be admitted, however, that Sir William Hayter's request for anecdotes about W. A. Spooner brought many recollections— some truthful and others probably apocryphal—of that distinguished warden (see N.C. MSS. 14394, 14395).

21. Spikes or other pieces of wire have rusted during the centuries with resulting damage to some of the documents filed on them.

22. There are over 14,000 groups of documents; of this number, there are, of course, single items, but it is not unusual to have a bundle comprising a hundred or more papers, so perhaps the muniment rooms contain upwards of 150,000 'pieces' all of which have had to be sorted and classified. For what one may expect to find in a college muniment room, see also W. A. Pantin's 'PreliminaryNote' in *Oxoniensia*, vol. 1, 140–3.

23. See *n.* 1.

24. 1882–1961; Deputy Keeper of the Public Records. His lecture, *The English archivist: a new profession*, was published in 1948. See also N.C. MS. 9292 and *Archives*, 427, *n.* 3, and Sir Frank Stenton and Francis W. Steer in *Archives: the Journal of the British Records Association*, vol. 2 (1953–6), 382–6, 402–4.

25. Deuteronomy, xxv. 4.

XI

The Medieval Library

R. W. HUNT

More manuscripts survive from the medieval library of New College than from that of any other Oxford or Cambridge college. For the most part they are still in its possession, but a few have strayed to other collections. Our knowledge of the contents of the library is further enlarged by the lists of books preserved among the muniments. In the present chapter I have tried to combine all these different sources. New College was the first Oxford or Cambridge college in which a library room was part of the original plan. Like the rest of the college it was on an ample scale, and a collection of books was provided by the Founder. The library was on the first floor of the east range of the quadrangle, over the bursary, the gate and the chamber south of the gate. It was entered by a staircase at the north end. The room was 70 feet long by 21 feet wide, and was lit by nine windows on each side. The original mullions and transoms of the northern window on the east side, which was covered about 1480, can now be seen inside the room. This arrangement of a room running north and south with windows looking east and west was preferred in the Middle Ages, since it gave the best light to the early-rising reader. Two-sided lectern-desks ran out from the walls between the windows. These desks have vanished, but in the course of repairs in 1949, when the eighteenth-century plaster was removed, the profile of the end of a case was visible on the wall. The apex of the lectern-desk was 5 feet 6 inches from the floor,[1] the same height as those later installed in Duke Humfrey's library.[2] Between the desks ran benches. When the room was fully furnished it would have contained sixteen desks, eight on each side, and four half-desks, two

317

against the wall at each end. To judge from the two manuscripts still in their medieval bindings (MSS. 61, 129, both gifts of William Warham), the books lay on the desk with their back covers uppermost. At the bottom of the front cover is a loop of iron to which a chain would have been attached, the other end of which was linked to a bar running the length of the desk. A label protected by a piece of horn, giving the contents of the book, was nailed to the upper part of the back cover. The chain was long enough for the book to be removed from the sloping desk and to be placed on a shelf below, thus making room to house more volumes than could be accommodated on the desk.[3] The maximum capacity for such a room was about 500 volumes. The only surviving evidence for the arrangement of the books is a note in the first volume of a large Bible given by Thomas Beckington (MS. 3),[4] which runs: 'For difficult words both in the prologues and in the text go to the books of Roger of St. Edmund[5] on the next desk on the right, and for difficult words in the text go to the book (not named) on the Astronomy desk.'

The earliest evidence of the occupation of the library comes from 1388–9, when there is a payment in the accounts for the binding and repair of diverse books for the library. In 1390–1 21d. was paid for rushes to be strewn on the floor. Three years later there is a payment of 2d. for the chaining of two books. In 1402 the windows were glazed, and in 1445 a ceiling was put in.

William of Wykeham laid down careful regulations concerning books in his statutes (rub. 61). There was to be an annual review of the books of the college in the possession of fellows before the warden and all the fellows, and a review each term before the warden or subwarden, the deans and bursars, to see that none was missing. No book was to be alienated or to go out of the college except for binding or repair. Loans of books to fellows were to be on the basis of an annual selection (*electio*) with special provision for the twenty students of civil and canon law, who might borrow a set of the text books for their whole period of study, 'provided that they do not possess such books of their own'. The remainder of the books left over after the fellows had made their choice were to be chained in the common library with iron chains. This clause is qualified by one in which it is enjoined that the wishes of donors in the disposition of their books should be respected. Finally, rules are made about keys to the library. In these regulations the stress is laid upon making books available for loan to fellows for their individual use. It appears that the distinction between a reference collection of chained books and a circulating collection, which became the regular pattern for college libraries, was not yet fully accepted.

Wykeham also made handsome provisions of books (Plate 80). There is a list of his gifts in the college register, the *Liber albus*, drawn up *c.* 1400.[6] It comprises 136 volumes of theology, thirty of philosophy, forty-three of canon law, and thirty-seven of civil law, a total of 246 volumes. These gifts were made over a considerable period of time. A list of four philosophical texts, which had apparently been purchased, is on the dorse of the first surviving bursars' roll (1376–7). Two of them are identifiable[7] in the list of books given by the Founder, and one, the Commentary of Albertus Magnus on Aristotle's Meteorologica, is still in the collection (MS. 229). Ten years later (Michaelmas Term, 1387) there is an entry in the hall books to the effect that 'five menservants of his lordship [i.e. Wykeham], came here on Wednesday to supper bringing books'.[8] Warden Sewell stated that the Founder gave £100 for books on 16 June 3 Henry IV, i.e. 1401,[9] but the source for this statement has not been found. Further there is an entry in the list of civil law books: 'A copy of the Code bought from moneys of the lord [i.e. Wykeham], by the hands of William Reede', who was fellow 1391–8.[10] Against a large number of the books a price is given: of the five copies of Peter Lombard's Book of Sentences, for example, two are unpriced, three priced. Probably the priced books were borrowable, the unpriced books were chained in the library.[11] In the accounts for 1388–9 there is a payment of 12d. to the stationer (i.e. the university stationer), for pricing books. To judge by the regulations of the university in 1439 such a price was to be 'notably higher than the book's market value (*verus valor*) to encourage borrowers to take care'.[12] The total of the books priced comes to £126 8s. 11d., but since the unpriced books are among the more valuable the total cost was probably at least double the £100 given by the Founder.

Where did the books come from? Among the twenty-six surviving volumes there is no trace of any book being copied specially for the college. Oxford was a place where secondhand books could be bought. Two of the books had previously belonged to Lewis de Charlton, Bishop of Hereford 1361–9 (MSS. 101, 117). It was also becoming common practice for monastic institutions to dispose of unwanted books. Some of the glossed books of the Bible probably came from such a source, but the earlier inscriptions of ownership have been too thoroughly erased to be legible even under the ultra-violet lamp.

Another part of the foundation collection came from the bequest of William Rede, Bishop of Chichester 1369–85. Rede had been a fellow of Merton College, of the generation of distinguished logicians, mathematicians and astronomers. He 'had got together perhaps the largest, to us at least certainly one of the most interesting, private libraries that an Englishman had ever yet formed'.[13] In his will, dated August 1382, there are two clauses relating to New College:[14]

Item to the College of St. Mary Winton 50 books and twenty pounds of gold. Item I bequeath to the same College 50 precious books of theology and canon law which I formerly put down (intitulavi) to the Cathedral church of Chichester, and a cup, praying and beseeching in the bowels of Jesus Christ my venerable father and lord the Lord Bishop of Winchester that he protect and defend at law (in iusticia) my will and my executors.

Thirteen volumes of his bequest survive. The inscriptions of gift entered in them fall into two classes, a simpler form stating that the book came from the gift of Rede (MS. 55), and a more elaborate form, which runs: 'The book of St. Mary Wynton in Oxford to be chained in the common library and for the common use of the scholars of the same and especially of those to be taken in future from the diocese of Chichester by the kindness of the Bishop of Winchester' (MS. 120). The books with this form of inscription clearly belong to those originally intended for Chichester. There must have been negotiations: Wykeham was anxious to build up the library, William Rede was concerned to make sure that his testamentary dispositions should be carried into effect. He had already, eight years before, made over a hundred volumes to his old college, Merton, twenty-five to Exeter College, and ten to Queen's. The only way he could increase the number available to New College was by diverting those intended for his cathedral library, but adding a condition that scholars should be taken from the diocese of Chichester.[15]

The number of Rede's books in the lists[16] falls far short of the hundred volumes bequeathed. It comprises fifty-seven of theology, three of philosophy, and four of canon law. A further volume of theology (MS. 96) is found in another part of the lists without a donor's name,[17] a second volume is in the list of philosophy books given by the Founder (MS. 264),[18] and a third is among the medical books (MS. 171) for which no donors' names are given. What happened to the others we cannot tell.

Rede was one of the few medieval book owners who was careful to record the source from which he obtained his books. His chief benefactor as a young man was Mr. Nicholas of Sandwich, 'clerk, scholar, and country gentleman', lord of the manors of Bilsington and Folkestone in Kent. In MS. 134, a copy of Thomas Bradwardine's De causa dei contra Pelagium, Rede noted that he had it written from funds provided by 'his reverend lord, Mr. Nicholas of Sandwich' while he was fellow of Merton.[19] The note continues: 'Pray therefore for the same (i.e. William Rede) and for his benefactors and for the souls of the faithful to be delivered from purgatory.' An interesting volume of sermons (MS. 92) was put together by Rede, partly from a collection of Oxford University sermons of the academic year 1292–3, which Nicholas of Sandwich caused to be reported and afterwards gave to him, partly from a volume of sermons of John de Shepey, Bishop of Rochester 1352–60, which he bought from the bishop's executors, and partly from a collection made by Thomas Trillek, Bishop of Rochester 1364–72, also bought from the bishop's executors. Five other volumes of the bequest (MSS. 55, 70, 96, 97, 120) came from the same source. Another (MS. 306) he had bought from the executors of Simon Islip, Archbishop of Canterbury 1349–66.

The books of the Founder and of Rede formed a basic collection of theological works. There was a good provision of Bibles, and a set of glossed books, complete except for Kings, with multiple copies of the Psalter and Pauline Epistles, both with the gloss of Peter Lombard. There was a considerable number of medieval commentators, but the names of the authors are rarely given in the lists and cannot be identified unless the volume happens to survive. Thus 'Postillae super Ysaiam' can be identified as the work of the thirteenth-century Dominican, Guerric of St. Quentin (MS. 40), not a common text. 'Postillae super Matheum' is the work of the Carmelite doctor, William de Lidlyngton (fl. 1300) (MS. 47), and is the only known copy. Among the few authors named is Richard Fishacre, the early Oxford Dominican, with a Commentary on the Psalter, not known to survive. There was a complete set of the Commentaries of Nicholas de Lyra, then the standard commentator, and a copy of William of Nottingham's (d. 1334) huge commentary on the Gospel Harmony of Clement of

Llantony. The texts of the works of the fathers, *originalia* as opposed to extracts included in later compilations, were less well represented, except for Gregory the Great, though there was a fair selection of Augustine. There was only one volume of Ambrose, and none of Jerome. There were three copies of the 'Opus imperfectum in Matheum' that went under the name of John Chrysostom, but is in fact the work of an Arian of the fifth or sixth century. The standard texts, the 'Historia Scholastica' of Peter Comestor and the 'Sentences' of Peter Lombard, were present in multiple copies. Other eleventh- and twelfth-century writers included Anselm, Hugh of St. Victor, and Bernard (but only Sermons). For the late twelfth and early thirteenth centuries there were works of Stephen Langton, Innocent III, Alexander Nequam and William de Montibus. There was the 'Summa' of William of Auxerre and Richard Fishacre on book I of the Sentences. A feature I cannot account for is the presence of three copies of the Life of St. Thomas Becket. Of the great scholastics Thomas Aquinas is well represented, but stands almost alone. There is one volume of Bonaventura, but the work is not specified. Of the Oxford masters of the fourteenth century there is only Duns Scotus on book I of the Sentences and Bradwardine's De causa dei contra Pelagium.

The philosophy list chiefly consists of texts of Aristotle, with commentaries of Averroes, Albertus Magnus and Thomas Aquinas. One of Walter Burley's commentaries is included, that on the Physics. The civil law list is made up of multiple copies of the texts of Roman law, no doubt with the standard apparatus, though this is not indicated in the list.[20] The named commentators are few, and not up to date: Azo, Roffredus of Benevento, and Cynus of Pistoia (1270–1336/7). The canon law list is likewise made up of multiple copies of the texts, but the representation of the commentators, down to Johannes Andreae (c. 1270–1348), is fuller. There were also medical books from the beginning, but the list was not drawn up till the mid-fifteenth century, and does not give the names of donors. The same is true of astronomy.[21]

The lists in the *Liber albus* give us the names of other early donors. The significant point about them is that they were men who had connections with Wykeham. To give an example, Sir William Walworth, the wealthy London merchant and Lord Mayor, and early benefactor of the London Charterhouse, who is best remembered as the killer of Wat Tyler, made Wykeham his executor, and bequeathed to the college in

1385 a Bible, Durandus, Rationale divinorum, Legends of the Saints and the Pauline Epistles 'well glossed'.[22] Occasionally we get a glimpse of the negotiations that must have accompanied the gifts. In the bursars' rolls for 1409/10 there is a payment of 3s. 11d. for the expenses of Mr. John Sarger, then the subwarden, and William Overley riding to the Dean of Lincoln to have communication with him about books to be bequeathed to the college. The Dean of Lincoln was John de Shepey, who had been 'official' of the see of Winchester, and the upshot was that he bequeathed a set of civil law books. A manuscript which can be assigned to this group by the dates of the donor, though his connection with the Founder is not known, is the copy of the Decretals, glossed (MS. 184), bequeathed by William de Deighton, canon of St. Paul's, London, and prebendary of Tottenhall (c. 1371–91) 'pro exercicio doctrine scolarium eiusdem collegii'. It contains a memorandum which shows that the gift included the other canon law texts, which have not survived. The surviving volume is one of the most splendid books in the whole collection, a great folio, measuring 18¼ x 11½ inches, the fine white parchment looking as fresh as when it left the Bolognese workshop to which art historians give the name of Pseudo-Niccolo. Its margins are unsullied by later annotations, but the neat running titles in various hands show that it was used by the fellows.

The growth of the library depended on gifts. A few lists of such gifts were entered in the *Liber albus*, but usually only when there was some condition to be fulfilled. Thus in 1459, when William Porte, fellow 1419–23, gave twenty-four books, of which three survive (MSS. 26, 86, 154) together with chalices, service-books, vestments and great organs in the choir, the college undertook to commemorate William and his wife, Alice, among the chief benefactors.[23] For the most part we are dependent on the inscriptions in the books themselves, but many of these have disappeared in the course of rebinding. There are fifty manuscripts which appear to have belonged to the college before the Reformation but are without indication of provenance. Nevertheless we have a record of the names of over fifty donors, beginning with men admitted full fellows in 1386. Arranged by decades the figures are as follows, the numbers in parentheses denoting the number of volumes:

| 1386–9 | 8 (28) | 1442–9 | 8 (117) |
| 1390–9 | 5 (40) | 1451–9 | 6 (8) |

1400–9	6 (15)	1466–9	4 (6)
1410–9	3 (42)	1474–5	2 (62)
1421–7	3 (18)	1481–6	4 (23)
1430–8	9 (27)	1496	3 (1)

The years in this table are those in which a man became a fellow, and do not give a fair indication of the growth of the library. From this point of view it is important to bear in mind that there might be a long interval between the time when a man was fellow and the time when his books reached the college. Thus the books of Andrew Holes, fellow 1414–20, did not arrive till 1470. The table is inadequate in another way: our knowledge of the number of books a man gave is very incomplete. Thus the entry for the year 1496 represents one surviving manuscript (MS. 187), the gift of Thomas Jackson, fellow 1496–1510, and an unknown number received from Thomas Bentley, fellow 1496–1508, and from John Fremantle, fellow 1496–1520. The following table shows by decades the number of books known to have been received, leaving out of account the gifts of the Founder and of William Rede. The numbers in parentheses denote the number of donors:

By 1400	6 (4)	1461–70	44 (10)
1401–10	31 (4)	1471–80	20 (4)
1411–20	51 (7)	1481–90	112 (6)
1421–30	27 (4)	1491–1500	5 (5)
1431–40	5 (4)	1501–10	78 (5)
1441–50	10 (4)	1511–20	5 (3)
1451–60	34 (3)	1521–30	10 (3)

The majority had only one or two volumes to give, common texts at that, to add to the stock of circulating copies, but they were sometimes copies out of the ordinary run. Richard Willis, fellow 1474–89, and warden of the college at Higham Ferrers 1504–23, gave a Decretum with the gloss and much added apparatus (MS. 210), in which the three surviving initials are good examples of the 'Channel' style of the early thirteenth century. He added the condition that the man to whom it was assigned should be bound to hand it over to anyone leaving the college on account of any contagious illness and studying in the country. It is a sharp reminder of the 'almost continuous plague' which afflicted

Oxford.[24] A few of the books are more out of the way. The Distinctiones on the Psalter of Michael of Meaux (MS. 36), written in the early thirteenth century, was a gift of William Ware, fellow 1386–96, through William Malton, fellow 1409–19. John Chinnor, fellow 1442–52, gave Rhabanus Maurus on the Pentateuch (MS. 29), also written in the early thirteenth century. It had been given to him by Thomas Lustcyll, fellow 1425–40. They are instances of the way Carolingian and twelfth-century writers were rediscovered in the fifteenth century. William Person, fellow from 1430 until his death in 1435, gave a copy of the Letters of Peter of Blois (MS. 127) for the use of a bachelor who has determined, i.e. one who has reached the final stage before inception as M.A. It contains a colophon stating that it was written by W. Sengleton in the New College of Winton, the only book we know to have been written in the college. It is a little book, written in an ugly hand, but is textually a valuable copy, because it preserves the names of some of the addressees not otherwise known.

It would take too much space to go through all the donors, and I shall concentrate on the principal gifts. These came mainly from men who had served most successfully in Church and State. Thomas Chaundler, fellow 1437–50, Warden of Winchester College 1450–4, Warden of New College 1454–75, at the beginning of his Collocutiones (MS. 288),[25] a work in praise of William of Wykeham and dedicated to Thomas Beckington, fellow 1408–20, King's Secretary and Bishop of Bath and Wells, a key figure in the advancement of Wykehamists, included a picture in which the most distinguished old members were portrayed (Plate 1). The earliest is Thomas Cranley,[26] warden 1389–96, from whose gift nine volumes of theological works survive. Like Rede he had the habit of entering in them a note of acquisition. He had bought the Historia Scholastica of Peter Comestor (MS. 104) from John Brown, stationer, presumably in Oxford, from whom he also bought a volume of sermons (MS. 88). Five of the volumes he bought at Chester or Liverpool, no doubt on his way to or from Ireland. Gregory's Moralia in Job was bought from a priest at Chester, a volume of devotional works, including one which Fr. Aubrey Gwynn restored to Cranley's predecessor, Patrick, Bishop of Dublin 1074–84[27] (MS. 91), and Fishacre's Commentary on the Sentences (MS. 112) from Frater Ricardus Tarbok at Chester, and part of the Summa theologica of Thomas Aquinas (MS. 122) from a priest at Liverpool. One wishes that

Cranley had recorded more detail. We should be interested to know more of the priest in Liverpool who owned part of the Summa. Yet another copy of Ps. John Chrysostom, Opus imperfectum in Matheum (MS. 52), was bought in 1403 from Mr. Nicholas Whyt, who has not been identified. Only MS. 109, a twelfth-century copy of Peter Lombard's Sentences, books I and III, has no note of provenance.

Cranley had owed his earlier training to Merton College. Thomas Beckington,[28] whom we have already mentioned, owed his to the two foundations of William of Wykeham. He gave a 'large and precious Bible' in four volumes, which was written in France by a scribe named Philip of Troyes and finished in 1290 (MSS. 3–6). The bursars' roll for 1464–5 records payments of 10s. for four deerskins, of 4s. for twelve skins of red leather, of 22d. for white skins for binding it, as well as of 2s. 8d. for four pairs of clasps and of 2d. for bosses. The next year the college received 33s. 8d. from Beckington's executors for the binding of the Bible and of other books to be placed in the chapel. Like nearly all the manuscripts it was rebound in the seventeenth century in plain reversed calf. His only other surviving gift is a very handsome copy (MSS. 189–90) of the Distinctiones on the Decretals by Henry de Bohic, a Breton who taught at Paris (d. c. 1350).[29] The pictures have been cut out, but the borders are good Parisian work of c. 1380. Both it and the Bible were probably spoils of the French wars.[30]

Andrew Holes, a younger contemporary of Beckington, fellow 1414–20, was King's proctor at the papal curia in Rome and Florence, and held the chancellorship of Salisbury and the archdeaconries of York and Wells. He died in 1470, and directed his executors to distribute his canon law books to the libraries of the colleges in Oxford not having such books.[31] The executors, of whom one was John Baker, fellow 1438–54, appear to have interpreted his directions widely. New College certainly received three canon law books (MSS. 201, 209, 219) and perhaps two more (MSS. 218, 224), but it also received other notable volumes: the complete works of Cyprian (MSS. 131–2), the letters of Jerome (in private ownership), works of Lactantius (MS. 133), speeches of Cicero (MS. 249), Boethius De consolatione philosophiae (MS. 265), the Commentary of Thomas Aquinas on the Pauline Epistles (MS. 63), the Dialogue of Giovanni Conversini of Ravenna (MS. 155), and Petrarch's Letters (MS. 268). In a well-known passage in his memoirs, Vespasiano da Bisticci, the Florentine bookseller, speaks of the number of volumes Holes had had copied, so many that they needed to be transported to England all the way by ship. The surviving volumes make the statement credible.[32] The books were either written for or acquired by Holes in Florence. The Cicero was partly copied by the Florentine scribe, Antonio di Mario; the Giovanni Conversini is the dedication copy, and had belonged to Coluccio Salutati.

The gift of Richard Andrew, fellow 1421–33,[33] stands in sharp contrast. Fourteen volumes of his gift to New College survive, and five of his gift to All Souls.[34] They are miscellaneous in origin, and almost all books copied in the thirteenth and fourteenth centuries, though one is earlier, Jerome on the Epistles to Philemon, Galatians and Ephesians (MS. 62), a French book of the twelfth century, probably Cistercian. Canon law predominates. Andrew also had an interest in letter writing. The gift includes the letters of Petrus de Vineis (MS. 158), who worked for the Emperor Frederic II, and of the early French humanist, Nicholas de Clamanges (MS. 128), as well as an anonymous treatise on the art of letter-writing (MS. Bodley 310, fol. 148).

William Say, fellow 1430–43,[35] was a theologian, not a lawyer. The bursars' roll for 1469/70 records payments for nine dozen chains and the making of new lectern-desks, part of which was for books bequeathed by Say. Mr. Richard Mayhew, fellow 1459–71, was paid 19s. 10d. for riding to London to receive them, for making an indenture, and for a barrel (*pipa*) to convey them to Oxford. Only eight volumes survive, five of which contain Latin classical texts. MS. 252, written in the first half of the twelfth century, contains Cicero's Philippics, Seneca, De beneficiis and De clementia, with other contents. It is one of the few manuscripts which contain all fourteen speeches, and it preserves some words which have fallen out of the other manuscripts.[36] MS. 250 contains the later rhetorical works of Cicero which had been discovered at Lodi in 1421. It was copied in Italy by an English scribe, Thomas Candor, who had learned to write humanistic script. MSS. 277–9 contain Livy, Decades I, III, IV, copied in Florence c. 1430–40. It is the first copy of the three decades, then believed to be all that had survived of Livy, which is known to have reached England. The fourth decade is of textual importance.[37] The other three volumes are patristic: Hegesippus (MS. 150), Gregory's Moralia, part II (MS. 39), a copy probably made for Say, and letters and treatises of Cyprian with other works (MS. 130). The last is a finely written book, executed in England *c.* 1200, probably from a Cistercian house, but it has lost all trace of earlier ownership. The first leaf and the right-hand half of the second are replacements of the fifteenth century. It is one of a small group of English manuscripts of letters of Cyprian which appear to depend on a fourth-century manuscript, of which a fragment was discovered at Arundel Castle early this century and was acquired in 1920 by the British Library (MS. 40165 A).[38] It is one of the rare instances where a manuscript written in later antiquity and presumably brought to England in Anglo-Saxon times, can be shown to be the ancestor of a distinct tradition.

These early donors were included by Chaundler in his picture. The next two considerable gifts, those of John Russell, fellow 1449–60,[39] and of William Warham take us into the age when printed books had begun to make their appearance, and contain both manuscripts and printed books. In a letter of thanks, dated 18 November 1482, copied into one of the college registers, the writer speaks of Russell's great love for the college, which, well known before, was made plain when he gave 105 beautiful books, 'hidden treasures of learned men and so eagerly awaited for the increase and adornment of the study of the best sciences'.[40] Unfortunately no list was entered, and only ten manuscripts and five printed books can be identified. They usually contain an inscription with a punning allusion to his name and the date 1482 (Plate 81):

> Stirpe parum clarus magis aptus quam bene doctus
> Fraudis inexpertus facto sermoneque Ve *Rus. celluy* je suis.

The manuscripts include Pliny's Natural History (MS. 274), a selection of Plutarch's Lives (MS. 286), the later letters and the Bucolicum carmen of Petrarch (MSS. 267, 269), and Boccaccio's De casibus virorum illustrium (MS. 263). The latter was bought from William Brygon, canon of Salisbury, from whom Russell also bought a volume relating to the Council of Basel (MS. 138) and a Vergil (MS. 271). The Vergil is an early fifteenth-century copy, probably Florentine, to which the 'Thirteeenth book' of the Aeneid by Mafeo Vegio was added in the hand of the English humanistic scribe, Thomas Candor, already mentioned. Candor is also the scribe of another volume containing grammatical works of Guarino of Verona (MS. 256). Russell gave also a printed Vergil (Strasbourg, 1469). Among the other printed books are Plutarch's Lives in Latin translation (Venice, 1478), in which are some annotations by Russell, and the Margarita poetica of Albertus de Eyb (Strasbourg, s.a.). I mention this because three years earlier the college had received from Robert Mason, fellow 1438–54, a manuscript of this work (MS. 307), which was copied from the edition printed at Rome in 1475. The scribe, perhaps Mason himself, since the hand does not look professional, even copied the colophon in which it is stated that the book was not written by pen but printed by a new kind of art by Udalricus Gallus *alias* Han, a German from Ingoldstadt. Now Robert Mason was a considerable pluralist. At the time of the gift he was Archdeacon of Northumberland, which he visited by deputy; Rector of Richmond, co. Yorks; Canon and Prebendary of Norton and Rector of Gateshead, both co. Durham; and Canon of Lincoln. It was surely not that he could not afford to buy a printed copy, but that there was no shop in his neighbourhood where he could buy one. Russell went on diplomatic missions, one of which took him to Bruges where he bought the Mainz Cicero, the earliest printed edition of a Latin classical text, in 1467, the year after it was published.[41]

The gifts and bequest of William Warham, fellow 1475–88,[42] outshone any since the time of the Founder, as befitted the most distinguished alumnus of the century. He made a gift of twenty-five manuscripts in 1508. They are nearly all theological works which from their contents might have been gifts of the Founder. Further gifts followed in 1516 and 1523, which we know of only from the letters of acknowledgement entered in the college registers.[43] The fullest letter is that of 1523, in which the writer speaks of works of the choicest authors in many disciplines. Warham had offered, he writes, to procure for the college the works of any other author they wanted, sparing no expense, even if they had to be brought from the furthest isles. Finally, in his will, Warham bequeathed his canon and civil law books and the pricksong books from his chapel to New College, and his theological books to All Souls. There survive seventeen manuscripts and forty-one printed books. Six volumes of the manuscripts and all the printed books are legal, except for a set of Erasmus's edition of Jerome, a presentation copy from the editor and two volumes of a set of Origen (Paris, 1512), and the works of Petrarch (Basel, 1496). Among the legal manuscripts is another set of the Distinctiones of Henry de Bohic (MSS. 185–6), a finely written copy, which was executed in one of the Parisian workshops that produced books for Jean, duc de Berry. It still retains its pictures. The other manuscripts include two twelfth-century English copies of letters of Augustine and Jerome (MSS. 126, 129), and the commentaries of Bede on Acts and on the Song of Songs (MSS. 57, 42), and of Alexander Nequam (d. 1217) on the Song of Songs (MS. 43). These last are written in imitation English twelfth-century script. Their bindings are Canterbury work. Presumably they were commissioned by Warham and executed at Canterbury. There are handsome copies of Nicholas de Gorran's Commentaries on Luke and the Pauline Epistles (MSS. 53, 61), and Duns Scotus on the Sentences, books I–III (MS. 113). Leonardo Bruni's translation of Aristotle's Politica and Ethics (MS. 228), written in 1452 by the English humanistic scribe, John R(ussell), stand rather apart, but may be connected with two volumes of humanistic interest[44] which were given to him by his friend, Robert Sherborne, fellow 1474–86.[45] Sherborne himself appears to have been a considerable benefactor to the library, but there is no record of the books he gave.[46]

I have deliberately refrained from giving any estimate of the total number of books, because the evidence is so fragmentary. The best indication is provided by the purchases of 295 chains for books in the library entered in the bursars' rolls for the fifteenth century. Since only forty-four expenditure rolls survive for this century, we cannot estimate the total number of chains bought, but the number recorded fits in with other evidence that the library room was becoming inadequate by the third quarter of the fifteenth century. Another room, now the senior common room, was built in 1479–80 over the mid-fifteenth-century extension to the Chequer. At first it was called the new library, later it came to be called the law library,[47] and it may well have been intended for law books from the beginning. The only books known to have been placed in it are three volumes of civil and canon law (MSS. 172, 178, 204), the gift of William Speckington, fellow 1469–87, as executor of Hugh Sugar, fellow 1435–52 (d. 1489). Sugar was Beckington's chancellor, Treasurer of Wells, and a friend of Chaundler, who included him in his pictures of college notables. He provided funds for the building, and his arms were formerly in the painted glass.[48] The college admitted him to its confraternity in 1473. Of the internal arrangements we know that it contained desks with chained books, and that provision was made for other books. Behind the present panelling are fifteenth-century recesses for shelves.

It is time now to ask what was the connection between the manuscripts and the studies pursued by the members of the college. The evidence varies a good deal from faculty to faculty. The books for the arts course provide little evidence except for two volumes. One is the copy of Albertus Magnus on the Meteorologica of Aristotle, which reached the college in 1376–7.[49] It has no annotation until the second half of the fifteenth century, when it was annotated by Robert Sherborne and another fellow. The other is a chance survivor from the circulating collection (MS. 289). It contains short tracts on logic and natural philosophy written chiefly by Oxford masters of the late fourteenth and fifteenth centuries. These were not on the syllabus, but were studied by sophists, i.e. undergraduates, alongside the Aristotelian texts. The general title of the book is 'Liber communis sophistarum'. It is a rather tattered paper book, and its interest lies not in its annotations, for which the margins are too narrow, but for the names of the fellows, seven in all, through whose hands it passed, beginning with Thomas Chaundler in the 1430s and ending with John Dobbs, fellow 1488–98, to whom it was delivered by the subwarden and other officials on 29 April 1488 (Plate 82). Below this last inscription are the arms of the college with the motto in its Latin form 'Mores componunt homines'. It is amusing to find Robert Sherborne as an undergraduate scribbling in it a tag then in circulation:[50]

Est mea mens mota pro te, speciosa Magota.

It should be added that his name was afterwards erased, but it comes up as clear as day under the ultra-violet lamp.

In civil and canon law the texts with their apparatus were the stuff of the course, and many of the surviving copies show much sign of use, but it would require expert knowledge of the two laws to make sense of the annotations. I give one slight example from a copy of the Apparatus of Innocent IV on the Decretals (MS. 187), which must be one of the last legal manuscripts—as opposed to printed books—to have been received. It bears the name of Thomas Jackson, fellow 1496–1510, and had once belonged to Adam de Orleton, Canon (later Bishop) of Hereford, who had a supplementary tract added at the end while he was attending the Council of Vienne in 1311. It has good quality English thirteenth-century miniatures, and contains much annotation in a succession of hands throughout the fourteenth and fifteenth centuries. There are five brief notes in the hand of Jackson, of which one (fol. 295^v) draws attention to the position of the clerk who engages in hunting (De clerico venatore).

In theology the copies of the Sentences which circulated among the fellows have disappeared. The surviving copies are those which were chained in the library, and they do not contain fifteenth-century annotation. There are other theological books which do contain such annotation, for example the Michael of Meaux, which had belonged to William Ware, one of the early fellows, but I have not succeeded in identifying the hands.

Rather surprisingly it is the medical books which are the most informative. As we have seen, the list of these books in the *Liber Albus* is an addition made in the middle of the fifteenth century. It is divided into two parts, thirty-seven volumes presumably available for lending, and fourteen headed 'Books of medicine chained in the library'. The descriptions of contents are very summary: fifteen volumes are simply called 'Liber medicine'. No donors' names are given. Five volumes survive from the first part, three from the second.

The Founder had made provision for two fellows to study medicine, and from an early date advantage was taken of this provision. The earliest recorded names are those of John Wittenham, fellow 1388–1412, who is known not because he was a doctor but because he headed the delegacy for condemning Wyclif's books in 1411, and Robert Thurbarn, fellow 1388–1413, and Warden of Winchester from 1413 until his death in 1450. An entry in the bursars' roll for 1401/2 of a payment of 16d. for the binding of a 'text of medicine' and for a new cover for it shows that the provision of medical books also goes back to the Founder's time. From the will of John Mottisfont, fellow 1390–1411, who died in 1420, we learn that he bequeathed two medical books, which can be identified in the list by the opening words of the second leaf.[51] The next recorded donor is John Bowring, a fellow of Exeter College, who bequeathed MS. 169 in 1427. Two more books (MSS. 166, 167) had belonged to Henry Beaumont, another fellow of Exeter College, who died in 1415, but we do not know when they reached New College. John Swanage, fellow 1413–23, deposited Averroes's Colliget

(MS. 163) as a pledge in the Turvyle chest in 1419, together with two other medical books identifiable in the list of borrowable volumes.[52] MS. 163 bears no inscription of gift, but must have been an early acquisition. The same is true of three other extant books which are identifiable in the lists (MSS. 164, 165, 170) but which contain no inscriptions of gift. MS. 170 contains the pledging note of Thomas Buckett, fellow 1446–60, who graduated B.M. in 1455 and D.M. in 1459.[53] He was the donor of the Pharmacopaea of Mesue the Younger (MS. 168). From his will we learn that John Green, fellow 1401–16, bequeathed in 1434 John de Gaddesden's Rosa medicine.[54]

It is a feature of the medical books that we can identify some of the fellows who used them. In a copy of Isaac on Fevers (MS. 167, fol. 124) there is a marginal note which reads like a jotting of a lecture or disputation: 'Edmond. How dost thou argue that crises are good or bad, and this according to times, in acute illnesses?'[55] Edmond is Thomas Edmonds, fellow 1435–51, who supplicated for his D.M. on 6 February 1450 on condition that he might count lecturing on the Aphorisms of Hippocrates, studying and practising for eight years, together with an academic exercise, for the complete course. This dispensation, or 'grace', as it was called, was granted on condition that he contributed 40s. to the fabric of the new Schools.[56] Such asking for 'graces' was in flat contradiction of the Founder's injunctions. Edmonds was given a Book of Medicine for his use by Robert Thurbarn, already mentioned, with the condition that it should pass to the college on his death, and that any fellow studying medicine should have the use of it inside and outside the college when he was summoned to visit the sick, a welcome hint that these were practising doctors.[57] Another fellow who entered his name in three of the manuscripts (MSS. 163, 167, 170) was Robert Sherborne, whom we have already met as an annotator. He was one of the fellows who proceeded to the study of medicine. In the copy of Averroes's Colliget he wrote against a passage on the principal signs of illness: 'Jhesus mercy. Lady help' (MS. 163, fol. 37). Richard Burgess, fellow 1486–1503, is not known to have had a degree in medicine, but he wrote his name in a thirteenth-century copy of the Ars medicine, the standard collection of texts used all over Europe (MS. 166, fol. 129^v), and there are many notes in his distinctive humanistic hand elsewhere in this manuscript, and in MSS. 163, 167, 170.[58] He studied carefully the verses of Gilles de Corbeil on urine with the commentary ascribed to

Gilbert the Englishman (MS. 170, fol. 258–61). Records of degrees at Oxford for the late fifteenth century are lacking, but apart from the evidence of these notes a printed book owned by him is also medical. On leaving New College he became Warden of St. John's Hospital, South Weald, co. Essex, and died three years later. The man who made the most mark as a doctor was Thomas Bentley, fellow 1496–1508. The copy of Averroes's Colliget (MS. 163) was lent to him, presumably after he had vacated his fellowship on marriage. He witnessed the will of Thomas Linacre,[59] the effective founder of the Royal College of Physicians (1518), probably as his physician. He was an early member of the Royal College, and held office in it, becoming president in 1526, 1529, 1530. He made a bequest of books to New College, as we know from the bursars' rolls for 1539/40, in which there is a payment of 18d. for the carriage of books given by Dr. Bentley and a payment of 21d. for their repair and chaining in the library, but none has been identified.

Following the list of medical books is one of books of astronomy, consisting of only two items: 'A book of astronomy', and 'Another book of astronomy', the second being in English. The Founder had put astronomy on the same footing as medicine, allowing two fellows to study it after graduating M.A., a puzzling provision, since in the university statutes astronomy is only recognised as part of the requirements for the B.A. and M.A. course. Three astronomical (or astrological) manuscripts have survived. One is a copy of Ptolemy's Almagest (MS. 281), a set text for the M.A. course.[60] It was given by John Farley, fellow 1451 until his death in his early thirties, c. 1464, and Registrar of the University from 1458. The manuscript was written in the late thirteenth century, but left unrubricated. The decoration is of Farley's time, and the bill for the work is entered in the manuscript. The margins contain chiefly thirteenth-century apparatus, but also a few in Farley's beautiful humanistic hand. He also wrote his name in Greek letters, as he did in the University Letter-Book, in a collection of astrological tracts given to the college in 1431 by Henry Jolypace, Chamberlain of St. Paul's, London (Bodl. MS. Auct. F. 5.29, S.C. 2635). The third manuscript contains Ptolemy's astrological work, the Tetrabiblos, known in Latin as the Quadripartitum, given by Thomas Driffield, fellow 1467–76. By his time it had come to be a regularly accepted set text in substitution for the Almagest.[61]

We have so far been concerned with books related to the curriculum.

Any survey would be incomplete which did not mention the humanistic interests among the fellows. As far as the library goes, it was not until the books were received of Say (1469), Holes (1470) and Russell (1482) that such interests were reflected in its holdings. To the same period belongs the entry in the bursars' roll for 1479/80 of a payment of 2d. to the Winchester carrier for 'bringing us the book (*codex*) of Laurentius Valla' most likely the *Elegantiae*, the guide for those wishing to write in the revived classical style. Apart from this the only evidence we have is the emergence of Italian humanistic script, which can be traced back a generation earlier. Thomas Chaundler did not succeed in mastering it fully himself, but he chose it for the copying of his writings, and one of the copyists he employed was the young fellow of the college, John Farley,[62] already mentioned. He was the first Oxford man of the fifteenth century known to have attempted to learn Greek, and we should surely have heard more of him if he had not died in his early thirties. As we have already seen, Sherborne in his annotations showed an easy mastery of the new script, which he also used as Registrar (1480–6) in the University Letter-Book (Registrum F).[63] His predecessor as Registrar was William Grocyn, fellow 1467–81, who like Farley wrote his name in the Letter-Book in Greek letters, and used the new script. Grocyn's later career is well known, but the early development of his interests in the new learning is hidden from us. Again we have Russell's humanistic script in the inscription in his books and in the annotations in his Plutarch, but we cannot follow the stages by which he became, in Sir Thomas More's judgement, 'one of the beste learned menne that England hadde in hys time'.[64]

The gifts of the later fifteenth century comprised, as we have said, both manuscripts and printed books. As more and more printed books became available, the growth of the library increased considerably. The college was, after Magdalen, the first Oxford college to buy printed books to modernise its library. £27 was spent in 1544–5.[65] Printed books superseded manuscripts for working purposes, and it was inevitable that many manuscripts should be discarded and sold for waste. The Oxford bookbinders from the 1530s had a large supply which they used as end-papers for their bindings. There was also some deliberate destruction for ideological reasons, and this is documented for New College. In an often-quoted letter of 1535, Dr. Richard Layton, the Royal Visitor of the University, reported to Thomas Cromwell his progress in carrying out the King's injunctions to establish public lecturers in Latin and Greek. He gloats over the banishment of Duns, that is Duns Scotus, who is made to stand for outmoded studies, and continues: 'And the second tyme we came to Newe College, affter we hade declarede your Injunctions we found all the gret Quadrant Court full of the leiffs of Dunce, the wynde blowing them into evere corner; and there we found one Mr Grenefelde a gentleman of Bukynghamshire gathering up part of the said bowke leiffs (as he saide) there to make him sewells or blawnsherrs[66] to kepe the dere within the wode thereby to have the better cry with his howndes'.[67] Mr. Grenefelde can be identified as Edward Grenville of Wotton Underwood. The books destroyed in this way were probably volumes from the circulating collection, books like those 'found in the studies of the scholars of Winton' in 1479, of which a list happens to survive.[68] There are three works of Duns Scotus in it. But destruction was not confined to Duns. Two lists of about this time are known, one made by John Leland, the other by a scholar unknown. They contain chiefly books out of the common run, of classical, medieval, and Italian humanist writers, and the majority of them, whether works of Seneca, Roger Bacon, Boccaccio, or Leonardo Bruni have disappeared without trace. One is reminded of the dictum that it is impossible to weed a library without making mistakes.

The largest gift received in the middle of the sixteenth century, though its extent cannot be fully distinguished, was that of books and manuscripts of Cardinal Reginald Pole (d. 1558),which came through the good offices of his friend, companion, and executor, the Venetian patrician, Alvise Priuli. The manuscripts were Greek, of which there were then virtually none in Oxford, except at Corpus Christi College. Only seven have Pole's initials in them, but there are fifty Greek manuscripts which came into the possession of the college before the end of the century, and the probability is that the majority were Pole's. The works contained in them are of the Greek fathers, especially John Chrysostom, and of commentators on Aristotle, with some grammar and rhetoric. The only volume which by any stretch could be called literary is that containing the Speeches of Aristides (MS. 259). Two volumes, or rather one volume now bound in two (MSS. 240–1), are of special interest. They contain commentaries on the Nicomachean Ethics and were copied in 1497 at Reading for Thomas Linacre by

Johannes Serbopoulos, a Greek refugee scribe. It is the collection of commentaries on the Ethics which was translated into Latin by Robert Grosseteste, and it is very likely that the exemplar used by Serbopoulos was Grosseteste's own copy, and that it came from the Franciscans at Oxford, who inherited Grosseteste's books. The volumes are marked for the printer, and were used for the Aldine edition of 1536.

A gift of four manuscripts in 1583–4 shows another new direction of interest. They are objects of an historical character, collectors' pieces. The donor was Thomas Martin, fellow 1540–54, a civilian who took his doctorate at Bourges. He became a Master in Chancery, and was concerned in affairs of state in the reigns both of Mary and of Elizabeth. He was a man of wide interests, including horticulture, a devoted Wykehamist, and the author of the first printed Life of William of Wykeham. The printed books he bequeathed are unusual, and include Livy in French, Italian, and Spanish, Thucydides in French, Hakluyt's Principal Navigations, two geographical works of Abraham Ortelius, and Polydore Vergil on Inventors in Spanish. His manuscripts are a Wycliffite New Testament (MS. 67), Gower's Confessio Amantis (MS. 266), with illumination of good quality, a thirteenth-century illustrated Apocalypse (MS. 65), which had been executed for Johanna de Bohun (d. 1283), wife of Sir Humphrey de Bohun, and Geoffrey of Monmouth's History of the Kings of Britain, which bears the *ex libris* of the Cistercian Abbey of Belleperche (diocese of Montauban) (MS. 276).

Printed books multiply much faster than manuscripts, and it became necessary to make another extension of the library in 1585–6. Attics, with windows looking east onto the garden, were constructed in the roof above the northern end of the library, the dormers of which can be seen in Loggan's engraving.[69] The furnishing of this room is not known for certain, but it may be that the books were chained on flat shelves rather than on desks.[70] It was coming to be seen that in this way a great many more books could be housed in a given space, a mode of furnishing familiar to us from its adoption by Sir Thomas Bodley for the university library. In 1602–3 a beginning was made with its introduction into the main library at New College, but it took some years to complete the work, and it is not easy to follow its progress from the bursars' rolls. There are still considerable payments in the rolls for 1613/14 and 1614/15 for ironwork for the stalls and for locks. In 1619 there first appears in the rolls the payment of £1 a quarter to one of the fellows for the care of the books (*pro cura librorum*). The first librarian was Thomas Man, fellow from 1615 to 1632, when he became Vicar of Hornchurch, a college living in Essex. He was probably responsible for the workmanlike catalogue of the manuscripts, dated 1624, in which they are arranged by subject (theology, medicine, civil law, canon law, arts) and given the numbers which they have borne ever since.[71] At this time or later in the century the manuscripts were collected together in the upper library, and probably put in locked cupboards, because from their bindings we can see that they were no longer chained. Antony Wood in his account of the college in his *History and Antiquities*, speaking of the conversion of the law library to a senior common room in 1675 says: 'At which time, or soon after, the books therein were translated to the Manuscript Library which was then enlarged by windows built next to the quadrangle.'[72] The details of this enlargement are not known. The whole upper library was remodelled in its present handsome form in 1778.

Man's list was not the first. In 1598 Thomas James, fellow 1593–1602, and Bodley's first librarian, had drawn one up which was published in 1600 with lists of manuscripts in other Oxford and Cambridge colleges under the title *Ecloga Oxonio-Cantabrigiensis*, the first published catalogue of manuscripts in this country. His list for New College is numbered from 1 to 285, but since he sometimes put more than one volume under the same number, the actual number of volumes is nearer 340. When we compare this list of James with that of the 1624 catalogue, it is disconcerting to find that ninety-three volumes listed by James are no longer there, and that fifty-eight volumes not listed by James are described, all of which, as far as we can judge, were in the possession of the college before 1598. Some of the losses are as surprising as they are regrettable. It is hard to see why a Suetonius (a gift of Warham) and a Tacuinus De conservatione sanitatis, both described as elegantly written, and the latter illustrated, should have been discarded. Among the theological books it is particularly regrettable that the Commentary on the Psalms by Richard Fishacre, already mentioned,[73] should have disappeared. What happened we cannot tell. Thomas James gave to the Bodleian in 1601 three of the volumes he listed as well as a fourth which is not in his list.[74] The loss of a Greek manuscript from Pole's gift happened while the list was in the press, and is recorded in an indignant note. James says that it was stolen at the

Encaenia of 1599 in the throng of visitors to the colleges and their libraries. A few years later it reappeared in the possession of Thomas Allen of Gloucester Hall, who gave it to the Bodleian. Sir Thomas Bodley wrote to James in 1608: 'I pray yow add in the margin [of the Benefactors' Register] the gift of his Greek MS. For though it was purloined from your College we had not had it, but by his gift.'[75] These few books are the exceptions. The remainder were seemingly discarded, and used as waste. There are two volumes of fragments (MSS. 362–3), for the most part used as wrappers of the annual accounts of the college manors.[76] About half of them are from service books, no doubt thrown out of the chapel, but among the others are two leaves of the Speculum historiale of Vincent of Beauvais, which served as wrappers for rolls of 43 Eliz. I (1600–1). A copy of this work was listed by James (no. 229). Two leaves of Anselm's Monologion may well have come from James no. 233. Parchment was useful stuff. In 1965, in the course of repairs to the chambers on the south side of the quadrangle it was found that the beams had been lined with leaves of medieval manuscripts. They are not in very good condition, but they appear to come from three or four volumes, among which I can distinguish a Commentary on the Pauline Epistles, a thirteenth-century legal manuscript, and a polyphonic music book.[77] Losses since the seventeenth century are negligible. One Greek manuscript from Pole's gift strayed to the royal collection, now in the British Library.[78]

A few more medieval manuscripts were received in the seventeenth century, including the first oriental manuscripts. William Ferrars, a Turkey merchant of London, who is described in the Library Benefactors Book as an *alumnus* of the college,[79] gave an Arabic work on law (MS. 296) and three Greek manuscripts. He had probably acquired them in accordance with the directive issued in 1634 by King Charles I, inspired by Archbishop Laud, to the Turkey Company, requiring that 'every ship at every voyage shall bring home an Arabic or Persian manuscript book'.[80] The most famous English illuminated manuscript in the collection, the Psalter illuminated by William de Brailes (MS. 322) was given by Henry Howell in 1693. He is described in the Library Benefactors Book as of London, the son of Thomas Howell, Bishop of Bristol.[81] At the same time he gave a fine sixteenth-century Flemish Book of Hours (MS. 323). In 1705 Thomas Mompesson, fellow 1684–1713, gave another copy of Gower's Confessio Amantis (MS.

326), interesting for the connections of the family with the college. It was made for John Mompesson (1432–1500), M.P. for Wilton 1453–4, and perhaps 1470–1, and holder of other county offices. One of his executors was Henry Mompesson (1464–1509), doctor of laws, perhaps his son, who was fellow 1479–81, when he was beneficed. Another member of the family, John Mompesson, was fellow 1618–13. Lastly Anne, widow of Robert Wetherell, fellow 1784–1814, and Rector of Newton Longville, gave a thirteenth-century St. Albans Psalter (MS. 358).

New College has very extensive muniments, but they concern almost exclusively the financial and legal affairs of the college. The manuscripts we have been reviewing allow us to get a little nearer to the studies and interests of the men trained in the college in the fifteenth century who made their mark in Church and State. It is one of the less well-recognised functions of a great and ancient foundation to act as guardian of such a storehouse of treasures. The administration of a collection of medieval manuscripts is no light task, and E. W. B. Nicholson, when Bodley's librarian, conceived the plan of suggesting to colleges that they should deposit their manuscripts in the Bodleian Library, where there was staff adequate to deal with them. New College deposited its collection in 1907. They have been freely available to scholars, and selected manuscripts have been exhibited from time to time. In recent years the college has withdrawn a selection every summer to form part of an exhibition in the chapel, where they are seen by many visitors as part of the history of the college.

Acknowledgments. The writing of this chapter would not have been possible if Dr. A. B. Emden had not worked out the careers of the fellows in his *Biographical Register of the University of Oxford to 1500* (Oxford, 1957) and *1501–40* (Oxford, 1974). I have not given references to it. Spelling of surnames has generally been modernised; when this has been done the form given by Emden is shown in italics in the index, after the form used in this chapter. Mr. N. R. Ker generously allowed me to use his extracts from the bursars' rolls. Mrs. E. Temple, who is making a handlist of illuminated manuscripts in Oxford college libraries, has allowed me to draw on her work. I wish also to thank the librarian and the archivist of New College, and their assistants, who have patiently helped with my many enquiries.

REFERENCES

1. Smith, 54 and Plate 58.
2. J. N. L. Myres, 'Recent discoveries in the Bodleian Library', *Archaeologia*, vol. 101 (1967), 163. Fig. 4 facing p. 163 gives a good idea of what the library of New College would have looked like.
3. For methods of chaining see N. R. Ker, *Records of All Souls College library 1437–1600* (Oxford Bibliographical Society, n.s. XVI, 1971), appendix III, 173–4. MS. New College 49 (Bodley), to which Mr. Ker refers, has been shown by Dr. David Howlett to have come from from Gloucester (now Worcester) College, Oxford, and did not reach New College till the sixteenth century.
4. All references to manuscripts in the text in this form are to the manuscripts of the college deposited in the Bodleian Library (see p. 340), and catalogued by H. O. Coxe, Oxford, 1852, reprinted with addenda, 1972 (*Catalogue of the manuscripts in the Oxford Colleges*, vol. I). Manuscripts which have strayed into other collections are given their full press-marks.
5. This text is to be found in one of the Founder's gifts, now MS. Bodley 238 (S.C. 2050).
6. *Archives*, 47, no. 9654. Printed by A. F. Leach in *Collectanea* III of the Oxford Historical Society 32 (1896), 223–41.
7. The books can be identified because the opening words of the second leaf are given, a common method of identification from the fourteenth century onwards, for which see Ker, *All Souls*, appendix IV, 175.
8. Historical Manuscripts Commission, *2nd Report* (1871), appendix, 133[b].
9. He entered it in his interleaved copy of the section on the college from A. Wood, *History and Antiquities*, ed. J. Gutch (Oxford, 1786), 130, which is kept in the library office.
10. Leach, 241: 'Codicem emptum [Leach wrongly read 'Codices empti'] de pecuniis Domini per manus Willelmi Reede.'
11. This was suggested by Leach, 218. The same holds true of the list of Rede's gift.
12. *Statuta antiqua universitatis Oxoniensis*, ed. S. Gibson (Oxford, 1931), 260.
13. R. A. B. Mynors, *Catalogue of manuscripts in Balliol College, Oxford* (Oxford, 1954), xiv.
14. Printed by F. M. Powicke, *Medieval books of Merton College Oxford* (Oxford, 1932), 88.
15. Sussex is included in the list of counties from which scholars were specially to be drawn in the statutes (rub. 2).
16. Printed by Leach, 223–5.
17. It is the last item on p. 230: 'Tractatus de penitentiis, cum aliis' of which the opening word of the second leaf, accidentally omitted by Leach, is 'ingratitudo'.

18. It is the third item on p. 234: 'Boycius de consolatione philosophiae.'
19. Powicke, op. cit., 28.
20. The surviving copy of the Code (MS. 173) from the Founder's gift has the apparatus.
21. See below, pp. 332–4.
22. S. Bentley, *Excerpta historica* (London, 1831), 141. I owe the reference to Mr. R. H. Bartle.
23. See ch. I, p. 33.
24. H. E. Salter, *Registrum cancellarii Oxon. 1434–1469* (Oxford Hist. Soc., 93–4, 1930–1), ii, 358, and see ch. I, p. 17.
25. N.C. MS. (Bodley) 288 is the dedication copy, which Beckington left to Wells. It reached New College probably between 1598 and 1624. About the same time its sister manuscript, the Allocutiones, came to Trinity College, Cambridge, from Thomas Neville (d. 1615); for both volumes see M. R. James, *The Chaundler Manuscripts* (Roxburghe Club, 1916).
26. See ch. I, p. 22.
27. *The writings of bishop Patrick* (Scriptores latini Hiberniae I, 1955).
28. See ch. I, pp. 24, 26.
29. P. Fournier, *Histoire littéraire de France*, 37(1938), 158, who does not notice the New College manuscripts, remarks that many of the copies of this work are 'plutôt des manuscrits de luxe que des exemplaires faits pour l'usage quotidien de praticiens; ils trouvaient leur place dans les librairies des riches amateurs'.
30. I owe this suggestion to Dr. Jonathan Alexander.
31. In the will, printed in *Somerset Medieval Wills 1383–1500*, ed. F. W. Weaver (Somerset Record Society 16, 1901), 213, the other books are not mentioned, nor are the monies, which according to the bursars' roll for 1469/70, were received from the executors for the fellows and scholars.
32. I am much indebted to Miss A. C. de la Mare for allowing me to draw on her unpublished work on the books of Holes.
33. See ch. I, p. 25.
34. His gift to All Souls was mainly of law books. A list of thirty-three, of which two survive, is printed by Ker, *All Souls*, 19–20. He also gave some theological books, of which three survive; see Ker, op. cit., 5.
35. See ch. I, p. 22.
36. It is *o* in the edition of A. C. Clark (Oxford, 1916).
37. It is the leading manuscript of the ψ class, first distinguished by A. H. McDonald in his edition (Oxford, 1968), xv–xvii. For its history see A. C. de la Mare in *Livy*, ed. T. A. Dorey (London, 1971), 178.
38. See *New Palaeographical Society*, II, 101, and M. Bévenot, *The tradition of manuscripts; a study in the transmission of St. Cyprian's Treatises.* (Oxford, 1961), 52–3.
39. See ch. I, p. 24.
40. Registrum dimissionum ad firmam 1480–1528, fol. 2ᵛ (*Archives*, 47, no. 9757).

41. It is in Cambridge University Library; see J. C. T. Oates, *Cat. of the 15th Cent. printed books in the University Library of Cambridge* (Cambridge, 1934), no. 28.
42. See ch. I, pp. 28–9.
43. 1508: Leach, 233–4, and more fully N.C. MS. 2887 (*Archives*, 91); 1516; Reg. dimissionum ad firmam 1480–1528, fol. 50; 1523; ibid., fol. 79ᵛ.
44. London, British Library, MS. Harley 2741, and Manchester, John Rylands Library, MS. Lat. 211.
45. See ch. I, p. 24.
46. In the Reg. dimissionum ad firmam 1528–44 (*Archives*, 47, no. 9758), pp. 141–2, is a long letter of thanks to Sherborne from the Warden and all the scholars of Wykeham's college for the gift of furnishings for the chapel. It is dated v kal. Mart., i.e. 25 Feb. The year is not given, but is probably 1535. In it reference is made to Sherborne's earlier gifts to the college of property and of 'libri optimi' for the library.
47 It is called 'Nova libraria' in the bursars' rolls for 1479/80 and 1515/16. In the rolls for 1593/4 and 1608/9 it is called the 'Law library'.
48. C. Woodforde, *The stained glass of New College, Oxford* (Oxford, 1951), 65. The Registrum referred to by Woodforde at *n.* 4 is Sewell's Register, and Sewell does not give his source.
49. See p. 319, above.
50. Magota is a form of Margareta. The verse is recorded by H. Walther, *Proverbia sententiaeque latinitatis medii aevi* (Göttingen, 1963–9), no. 7607 from one fifteenth-century English manuscript. It is also found as a fifteenth-century addition in another English manuscript, Bodleian Library, MS. Laud Misc. 500, fol. 131v.
51. They are the first and sixth items in Leach, 243.
52. The pledging notes are printed in the reprint of Coxe's *Catalogue of Manuscripts*, vol. I (above, *n.* 4), after p. 124. The two other books are identifiable by the opening words of the second leaf as the second and last item in the list of borrowable books, Leach, 242–3.
53. 'Cautio Magistri Thome Boket exposita pro uno libro qui intitulatur Gilbertinus super . . . et habet unum supplementum 2° fo. *caloris.*' (fol. i), erased, but legible under the ultra-violet lamp.
54. *Registrum Henrici Chichele*, ed. E. F. Jacob (Canterbury and York Society, 1938–47), ii, 514. It is probably one of the two copies at the end of the list of chained books, Leach, 244.
55. 'Edmond. Quomodo argues crises esse bonas vel malas, et hoc secundum tempora, in acutis egritudinibus?'
56. *Register of Convocation 1448–63*, eds. W. A. Pantin and W. T. Mitchell (Oxford Hist. Soc., n.s. 22, 1972), 52.
57. *Liber Albus*, fol. 14ᵛ, not printed by Leach.
58. He was Registrar of the University 1492–1502, and the letters he entered in Registrum F are in the same hand.
59. For Linacre's will see J. M. Fletcher in *Essays on the life and work of*

Thomas Linacre, eds. F. Maddison and others (Oxford, 1977), 171. Bentley's membership of the Royal College of Physicians escaped Dr. Emden in his *Biographical Register*, but is noted in the copy with his manuscript additions in the Bodleian Library, with reference to W. Monk, *Roll of the Royal College of Physicians, London* (London, 1878), i, 24.

60. *Register of Convocation 1448–63*, xxxi, xxxiii. Dr. Fletcher does not mention the provision in the New College statutes.

61. See the entries ibid., 109, 129. On 23 October 1453 William Child, fellow 1443–6, was granted a grace that lecturing on the Quadripartitum would fulfil the requirements of the course; ibid., 153. He bequeathed a book (*textum*) unspecified, according to the bursars' roll for 1487/8.

62. *Duke Humfrey and English humanism in the fifteenth century*: Bodleian Library exhibition catalogue (1970), nos. 34–6.

63. *Register of Convocation 1448–63*, 416.

64. *History of King Richard III*, ed. R. S. Sylvester (1963), 24.

65. N. R. Ker, 'Oxford College libraries in the 16th century', *Bodleian Library Record*, 6 (1957–61), 482.

66. See O.E.D. s.vv. shewel and blancher, things set up to turn the deer from a particular direction.

67. H. Ellis, *Original letters*, 2nd series, vol. II (London, 1827), 61.

68. It is entered on the last leaf of Bodleian Library, MS. Digby 31, and is printed in Macray's Catalogue (Quarto Catalogue IX); but Macray misread the last two lines, which should read: 'Quodlibetum Duns, in quaterno pergamenali, Duns super primum Sententiarum.'

69. Smith, 74.

70. Ker, 'Oxford College libraries', 508 *n.* 4. Mr. Ker took the reference in the bursars' roll for this year to an 'upper librarie' to mean the law library, but Warden Smith's account seems to me the right one.

71. The main series ends at 289; MSS. 290–5 are an appendix of miscellaneous books listed in the same hand, which no doubt turned up after the numbering was done.

72. Ed. Gutch, iv, 198.

73. See above, p. 321.

74. MSS. Bodley 238 (S.C. 2050), a gift of William of Wykeham, Bodley 798 (S.C. 2656), donor unknown, Bodley 709 (S.C. 2668), a gift of Richard Andrew, and Bodley 310 (S.C. 2121), a gift of Richard Andrew.

75. *Letters of Sir T. Bodley to T. James*, ed. G. W. Wheeler (Oxford, 1926), 177. It is MS. Auct. E. 4.9 (S.C. 3080).

76. Listed by N. R. Ker, *Pastedowns in Oxford bindings* (Oxford Bibliographical Society, n.s. V, 1954), 185–7.

77. Now kept in a box in the library.

78. It is MS. Royal 16 C. XIX, formerly MS. 248. It was identified by E. Lobel, 'Cardinal Pole's manuscripts', *Proceedings of the British Academy* 17 (1931), 98.

79. *Archives*, 51, no. 3582: 'Gulielmus Ferrers generosus Mercator

Londinensis ad Turcas [*sic*] quondam huius Collegii alumnus.' Inside MS. 298 Sewell copied the entry and after *alumnus* added 'perhaps Gen(tleman) comm(oner)'.

80. *Cal. State Papers Domestic, Charles I*, 1633–4, 477; *Bodleian Library Quarto Catalogue*, II, Laudian (1973), xix.

81. 'Henricus Howell Thomae Episc. Bristol. Filius Civis Londinensis Colleg. Novo Honoris ergo DDCG.'

XII

Memorials at New College

FRANCIS W. STEER

Except for recumbent effigies, canopied or other altar tombs, and wooden plaques, the memorials in New College chapel and the cloisters to the west of it illustrate the fashions in commemorating the dead from 1403 to the present time. The chapel was consecrated late in 1382 or early in 1383 and the cloisters in 1400;[1] the right of burial within the college precincts was the subject of a bitter and protracted quarrel with the vicar of St. Peter-in-the-East at the end of the fourteenth and during the early years of the fifteenth centuries.[2] The powers of the Founder and the college's advisers were greater than could be mustered by the vicar of St. Peter's church; although the dispute was not settled until 1415, the fact that Warden Richard Malford was buried in the chapel in 1403 demonstrates that the college exercised its autonomy regardless of, what the final judgement might be.

At the present time there are 187 identifiable memorials in the chapel and cloisters; there are twenty-nine brasses and nineteen mural monuments in the chapel and 139 identifiable on the walls or in the pavement of the cloisters. To describe all of them in detail would exceed the space allotted for this essay, so only the more important will be mentioned, either by reason of the persons commemorated or because the memorials have special artistic merit. In his edition, 1786, of Anthony Wood's *History and Antiquities of the Colleges and Halls in the University of Oxford*,[3] John Gutch records eight mural monuments, twenty-seven brasses, eight slabs and three unknown types of memorial in the chapel or antechapel, twenty-six brasses, fifty-eight slabs in the pavement, nineteen mural monuments and four epitaphs not specifically described as to type in the cloisters: a total of 153, dated between 1403 and 1781. Of the chapel memorials mentioned by Wood, only three (brasses to William Holmegh (1434), Philip Carmarthen (1446), and Henry Wriothesley (1486)) have disappeared, but of the cloisters memorials only fifty-two out of 107 survive; the losses are twenty-five brasses, five pavement slabs, one tablet and four unspecified.

Reforms in religious practices in the sixteenth century and the ravages of the Civil War in the seventeenth accounted for the destruction of buildings, memorials and other treasures in many parts of the country; but as Wood's *History* of the colleges and halls was originally carried up to 1668 and continued to almost 1695 when the author died,[4] blame for losses at New College should perhaps be attributed to the post-Civil War period. Brasses on walls tend to corrode more quickly than those in pavements (although it is obvious that the continual passage of feet over stone or brass will be detrimental to survival); but such a loss of memorials from the cloisters points to deliberate removal (perhaps for the value of the metal) rather than fair wear and tear. The gradual obliteration of lettering on gravestones is understandable, but several now in the cloisters have been identified from a variety of sources.

So far as the chapel is concerned, there have been major 'restorations' involving the removal of memorials (especially brasses in slabs) from the east end and, presumably, the central aisle, to the north-west area of the antechapel where a few are partially obscured by seating.[5] No reliable pictorial representations are extant showing the chapel before Scott's 'improvements' in the last quarter of the nineteenth century, but as Wood refers to the transfer of monuments from the 'inner' chapel to the 'outer' chapel, we may perhaps assume that in New College chapel, as in many parish churches, the more exalted the person, the nearer to the altar was his place of burial.

Of the memorials in the antechapel (there are none in the chapel itself) we must first deal with some of the twenty-nine brasses, ranging from that of Richard Malford, 1403, to that of Thomas Hopper, 1623. These brasses are important not only by reason of the persons they commemorate but because they show the changes in ecclesiastical, academic and civilian costume over 220 years. Malford (1403), Cranley (1417), Hill (1494), Rede (1521) and Young (1526)[6] were all wardens of the college and are shown wearing ecclesiastical vestments.[7] The effigy of Nicholas Ossulbury (1453/4), another warden, has been lost, but the inscription survives. Other ecclesiastics include John Desford (1419), who has a half-effigy partially obscured by seating: Rector of Colerne, Wilts., he does not appear to have been a fellow of New College. A half-effigy of John Fry (1507) shows him holding a chalice and wafer. Examples of academic costume are depicted on the brasses of John Louth (1427), Professor of Civil Law, William Hawtryve (1441), 'Decretorum doctor', Geoffrey Hargreve (1447), Walter Wake (1451), Thomas Hill (1468), Richard Wyard (1478, but mutilated), John Palmer (1479) and John London (1508),[8] scribe of the university (Plate 83). Only the shield remains of the brass to Thomas Gascoigne, D.D. (1457), who was not a member of the college.[9] Thomas Fleming's brass (1472) shows an emaciated figure in a shroud; it is the only example of this type of memorial in the college and is partially obscured. A brass to a notary, c. 1510, with an inkhorn and penner has lost its inscription.

Of other brasses in the antechapel, mention must be made of that to Walter Baily (1592), physician to Queen Elizabeth I; his career was the subject of various papers by L. G. H. Horton-Smith,[10] and his escape from what could have been an alarming situation regarding the death of Amy Robsart is described by Sir Walter Scott in his introduction to *Kenilworth*. The brass of Hugh Lloyd, D.C.L. (1601),[11] Chancellor to the Bishop of Rochester and Master of Winchester College is on the west wall of the antechapel. There is also the brass to Anthony Aylworth (1619), son-in-law of Walter Baily, and his successor, first as Regius Professor of Physics, and later as Physician-in-Ordinary to Queen Elizabeth I.[12]

The brass to Thomas Hopper (1623) is on the east wall of the antechapel. He was the son of John Hopper of Loxley in Warwickshire. Thomas gave 500 books to the college library, practised medicine in Oxford for twenty years and died aged fifty-five; his wife Agnes is commemorated on the same brass, which was designed by Richard Haydocke[13] and includes figures of Aesculapius and Fortune, with circles, triangles, etc.

The granite slab, with an inlaid cross and marginal inscription, in the antechapel covering the grave of Dr. David Williams (warden, born 1786, died 1860) was paid for by the college; it was executed by F. A. Skidmore of Coventry at a cost of £104 17s. 6d. and although ordered in 1860 was not delivered until 1862.[14]

Of the mural monuments in the antechapel, if we exclude the brasses already mentioned to Lloyd (1601) and Hopper (1623) and the war memorials to be noticed below, we have twenty, ranging in date from 1613 to 1930. Nine are to wardens or former wardens, i.e. Robert Pinke (1647),[15] Michael Woodward (1675), Richard Traffles (1703),[16] John Oglander (1794),[17] Samuel Gauntlett (1822), Philip Nicholas Shuttleworth (1842), David Williams (1860), James Edwards Sewell (1903) and William Archibald Spooner (1930). The first three monuments are large and of exceptional quality; they have busts of the deceased and cartouches of arms among other embellishments. One wonders if any are the work of William Byrd, the sculptor and mason, who was employed at New College in the last quarter of the seventeenth century.[18] Gauntlett's Latin epitaph was composed by his successor, P. N. Shuttleworth (afterwards Bishop of Chichester); Williams, in his turn, composed Shuttleworth's epitaph, which is on a marble tablet on the north wall. Sewell's brass plate ranks as *art nouveau* and Spooner has a stone tablet of no great artistic merit.

John Harmar (or Harmer),[19] Professor of Greek and a translator of the New Testament, has an alabaster and black marble memorial incorporating cherubs, emblems of mortality and his coat-of-arms. The elaborate monument to Hugh Barker, LL.D. (d. 1632) is by Nicholas Stone, who charged £50 for it;[20] the lawyer's bust is in a recess and there is an achievement of his arms. He was Master of the Prebendal School at Chichester where the celebrated John Selden was a pupil. A portrait of Barker's father, also Hugh, painted in 1596 at the age of sixty is in the old bursary and a monument to another Hugh Barker (1683/4–1690) is on the west wall of the cloisters. The monuments to Harmar and Barker were formerly on the south wall of the chapel, but had been moved to their present positions by 1786.[21] Small stones marking the graves of these two men in the 'chancel' have disappeared as has that for Henry Beeston, warden, 1701.[22] Five other graveslabs, including those of Wardens Pinke, Traffles and Purnell, ranging in date from ?1632 to 1764, noted by Gutch, have been removed.

Of lesser, but nevertheless interesting, memorials, there is on the west wall that to William Gother, LL.B., who died in 1766, aged thirty-one; it incorporates musical instruments and his family arms.[23] Alfred Robinson (died 1895, aged fifty-three) who was bursar for twenty years has, as his principal memorial, the Holywell gate tower which bears his name; the memorial in the antechapel is an uninspired effort in red marble. Near by is a brass to commemorate the repaving of the antechapel by Philip Bury Duncan,[24] who gave £150 for the purpose and was thanked by the Warden and Thirteen for his generosity on 13 November 1839, although the date on the brass is 1841. Martin Wall (1747–1824), an eminent physician, has an unimpressive monument which includes the arms of him and his wife Maria, who died in 1841, aged ninety.[25]

On the north wall of the antechapel is the important memorial, by Humphrey Hopper, to Charles Burlton (1799–1836), fellow of the college, 1820–36, appointed chaplain at St. Petersburg, 1836,[26] who died in Rome on 12 January of that year and was buried in the Protestant cemetery. This large monument shows a female weeping over a tomb; the Latin epitaph was composed by the Rev. W. Lisle Bowles,[27] a relation of Burlton's. To keep, as it were, within the family, Henry Bowles, M.D. (d. 1765, aged sixty-five) has an elaborate memorial further along the same wall; the monument bears the words 'J. Townesend Fecit' in a very prominent position. Henry Bowles was a fellow of the college for forty-seven years, and John Townesend, the fourth of that name, appears to have been a member of a London and Oxford family of sculptors who flourished from c. 1660 to 1784.[28] The tablet to Philip Nicholas Shuttleworth (already mentioned on p. 349) is the last on this wall; he died in 1842 aged sixty.

On the northern limb of the east wall is the marble tablet, designed and executed by Grimsley of Oxford, to David Williams (see p. 348) and the large memorial, with arms, to Henry Blackstone, M.B. (d. 1778, aged fifty-six). There have been many Blackstones at New College and this Henry, who practised as a physician in Reading, afterwards became Rector of Paulerspury, Northants, and then Vicar of Adderbury in Oxfordshire.[29] The epitaph on the tablet to Henry Darell Stephens (d. 1840, aged thirty-six) was composed by the Rev. J. S. Ogle; Warden Sewell noted that 'the College was engaged in an important law suit respecting the tithes of Hornchurch [in Essex], in which Mr. Stephens undertook to maintain the interests of the Society, when they were deprived of his valuable services by his sudden death'.

Michael Woodward's splendid monument is on the southern limb of the east wall (Plate 84); near it is the tablet by Eric Gill and H. J. Laurie Cribb, erected in 1930[30] to three German members of the college—

Prinz Wolrad-Friedrich zu Waldeck-Pyrmont, Freiherr Wilhelm von Sell, and Erwin Beit von Speyer—who fought and died for their own country in the 1914–18 War. There are brasses to Edward Charles Wickham (d. 1910)[31] and to Thomas Hopper (see above, p. 348). Warden Traffles's fine monument has also been noticed already (p. 349).

The south wall is occupied by the 1914–18 war memorial executed by Eric Gill in Hopton Wood stone in 1921 at a total cost of £1,123 5s. 6d.;[32] it records 228 names which, together with the inscription at the top, comprise some 5,085 letters and figures for which Gill was paid £271.

THE CLOISTER MEMORIALS

When Thomas Jefferson said that all men are created equal, he must have forgotten Pope's line, 'some are, and must be, greater than the rest'. The truth of both quotations is demonstrated by the memorials in New College cloisters, which record wardens, statesmen, profound scholars, undergraduates and college servants. Some of the memorials are fine examples of the sculptor's art, some are humble and worn slabs in the pavement, some show to what low levels letter-form, use of materials and design can reach; but whatever praise or criticism may be allotted to an individual memorial, it must be accepted that all of them were erected as acts of piety and all contribute to the history of the college and its members. As a list of the monuments, with notes of the armorial bearings on them, existing in 1974 will be deposited in the college archives,[33] only a selection of the more important and interesting of them is included in this essay.

Entering the cloisters by the doorway near the chapel and turning left we have, on the east wall, tablets to (1) Sir Hugh Percy Allen (1869–1946), college organist and Heather Professor of Music;[34] (2) Percy Ewing Matheson (1859–1946), fellow for sixty-five years;[35] (3) Hastings Rashdall (1858–1924), Dean of Carlisle;[36] (4) Thomas Holden Ormerod (d. 1818, aged twenty-one);[37] (5) John Baron Moyle (d. 1930), bursar for twenty-eight years; (6) David Samuel Margoliouth (1858–1940), Laudian Professor of Arabic;[38] (7) Gilbert Charles Bourne (1861–1933), Professor of Zoology;[39] (8) John Scott Haldane

(1860–1936), physiologist and philosopher;[40] (9) Alfred, Viscount Milner, K.G. (1845–1925).[41]

In the south wall of the cloister, note the tablets to (10) Sir John Linton Myres (1869–1954), Wykeham Professor of Ancient History and college librarian[42] and (11) Sir John Sealy Edward Townsend (1868–1957), Wykeham Professor of Physics.[43] Near by is the elaborate wall memorial, erected by himself six years before his death, to (12) Henry Brome (d. 1667, aged eighty-six), and a tablet to (13) Herbert Hall Turner (1861–1930), Savilian Professor of Astronomy.[44] Further west are tablets to (14) Hugh Todd Naylor Gaitskell (1906–63), Chancellor of the Exchequer and leader of the Labour Party,[45] (15) John Galsworthy (1867–1933), playwright and novelist,[46] and three commemorating members of the college who died in the 1939–45 War. A large bronze plaque with figures is to the memory of the seven New College men killed in the South African War, 1899–1902. In the pavement are slabs to (16) Alfred Bennett, organist (d. 11 October 1830, aged twenty-five), who was killed in an accident to a coach while on his way to a musical festival at Worcester, and to (17) William Meredith (d. 1637/8), another college organist.[47] An elaborate memorial with cherubs' heads and coat-of-arms is to (18) Scroggs Goad (d. 1723) of the Inner Temple; he was Founder's Kin, a chorister, and eventually a fellow of the college, 1688–1723; and in the pavement is a small slab marking his grave. Another organist (19) William King (1624–80)[48] lies under a ledger stone; one of his successors (20), Dr. James Taylor (1865–1900), has a tablet on the wall and so has (21) Richard Stephen Creed, D.M. (1898–1964), fellow, 1925–64.[49] The brass plate to (22) Richard Dyke, chaplain (d. 1604), was put up in 1623–4; the bursars' roll for that year records payments to one Yorke, of 6s. 4d. for the brass and £1 10s. 0d. for engraving it. At the end of this south cloister is the elaborate cartouche with cherubs, emblems of mortality, and arms in memory of (23) Laurence Saintloe, who died of smallpox on 6 July 1675 aged twenty-six.

In the west of the cloisters is a ledger stone to (24) Paul Acton (d. 1686/7, aged twenty-nine), chaplain, and a tablet with drapery, cherubs' heads and a shield of arms to (25) Josias Calmady (d. 1701, aged seventeen).[50] The inscription on (26) George Harvey's tablet is now illegible,[51] and that on the slab to (27) Giles Raymond (d. 1675, aged twenty-two) is also badly worn. A tablet commemorates (28)

Francis Evers Beddard (1858–1925), F.R.S., Linnæan Medallist and 'Professor of the Zoological Society'; another is to (29) Francis Basil Riley (1893–1927), 'victim of an unknown fate at Chengehow, Honan Province, China'. The monument to Hugh Barker (1632) in the antechapel has been mentioned (p. 349), and here is that to his namesake (30) Hugh (1683/4–90), son of Hugh Barker of Great Horwood, Bucks.; the tablet, surmounted by a shield of arms, was erected by his brother, Richard, *nuper hujus Coll. Superioris Ordinis Commensalis*.[52] A black-and-white marble tablet is in memory of (31) Alice Bourdillon George (d. 1893, aged forty-nine) and Hereford Brooke George (d. 1910, aged seventy-three).[53] Mention should also be made of the memorial to Harold Thomas Beresford Hope (d. 1917), after whom a scholarship in the college is named.

Among the memorials in the north walk of the cloisters is a ledger stone to (32) Matthew Finch (d. 1665, aged twenty-seven), and near it was another covering the grave of his uncle (33) Bartholomew (d. 1668, aged fifty-nine), 'late Master of the Society of the Cooks of the University of Oxon., and Cook of this College'.[54] A small slab marks the grave of (34) Thomas Hayward (d. 1768), warden from 1764 to 1768; another is to (35) William Gother (1766), whose monument in the antechapel is mentioned on p. 349; another, very worn, is to (36) William Finch (d. 1695), who gave a pair of silver candlesticks to the chapel but they were stolen by burglars in January 1849. A ledger stone marks the grave of (37) John Taylor (d. 1686, aged twenty-eight), the college gardener; another (illegible except for the date 1675) is for (38) Thomas Symons, the college manciple; a third is for (39) John Louch (d. 1825, aged 74), the college butler.[55] A decayed tablet (40) to Peter Woodgate (d. 1590) is of interest by reason of his Latin epitaph having been composed by John Hoskyns, sen., 'a most celebrated wit of this College'.[56] East of the bell-tower is the tablet to (41) Alic Halford Smith (1883–1958), warden from 1944 to 1958;[57] near it is one to (42) Dr. Martin Wall (d. 1824) and his wife (d. 1841) who have a memorial in the antechapel (see p. 350). At the extreme east end of this cloister walk is the rather decayed tablet to (43) Thomas Lydiat (1572–1646), Rector of Alkerton, Oxfordshire, divine and chronologer.[58]

The remaining part of the cloisters is the northern limb of the east range. A slab marks the grave of (44) James Edwards Sewell (1810–1903), warden from 1860 to 1903;[59] next is a ledger stone to (45)

Paul Barcroft (d. 1715/16, aged twenty-three), the son of William Barcroft, Treasurer and Canon of Chichester Cathedral. The fine memorial to (46) Herbert Albert Laurens Fisher (1865–1940), warden from 1925 to 1940,[60] is on the wall. Near the gateway to the west door of the chapel is the recut tablet to (47) Robert Dallam (1602–65),[61] 'who built an organ in this chapel'; a ledger stone with a long Latin inscription marks Dallam's grave. He is described as *Instrumenti Pneumatici (quod vulgo Organum nuncupant) peritissimus Artifex* and apparently belonged to an armigerous family. A more recent tablet (48) commemorates R. H. S. Crossman (1907–74), whose published *Diaries* have caused agitation in political and other circles.

A tablet to (49) Horace William Brindley Joseph (1867–1943), philosopher[62] and his wife, Margaret Bridges, is to the south of the chapel gateway; next are memorials to (50) Edward Bowles (d. 1714, aged twenty, from smallpox);[63] to (51) Giles Feild (d. 1629, aged twenty-one), son of Dr. Richard Feild, Dean of Gloucester;[64] to (52) members of the Erle family (monument erected in 1860); to (53) Sir Henry Erle Richards (1861–1922) and his brother, Owen William Richards (1873–1949); to (54) Francis Fearon (d. 1822, aged twenty-five) and (55) William Andrewes Fearon (1841–1924), Headmaster of Winchester College.[65] A small slab in the pavement marks the grave of (56), John Field, college butler who died in 1753.

Enough has been written to provide an outline of the various styles of memorials at New College and of the variety of persons to whom they relate. There are ample illustrations of the brasses, but very few of the monuments have been photographed: a pictorial record of them would be desirable as would the restoration and repainting of such as are in poor repair. Errors of grammar and even of wording occur in some of the printed transcripts of epitaphs, but this is understandable when a memorial is worn or decayed. Our debt to Anthony Wood and, of course, to Warden Sewell for their industry in recording is manifest. Wood's diaries and papers are an invaluable source of information; he, like Sewell, noted memorials which have been lost.[66]

By an Order in Council, 21 July 1855, the discontinuance of burials beneath the chapel and antechapel of New College (among others) was effected.[67]

Note on Surnames. The spelling of surnames has generally been modernised; when this has been done the form given by Emden, *BRUO*, is shown in italics in the index, after the form used in this chapter.

REFERENCES

1. Francis W. Steer, *The archives of New College, Oxford: a catalogue* (1974) (hereafter abbreviated to *Archives*), 83 and *V.C.H. Oxfordshire*, vol. 3 (1954), 144.
2. *Archives*, 85, 86.
3. Hereafter abbreviated to Wood, *Colleges*; see also H. C. P. Dobrée, 'A catalogue of the brasses in New College, both past and present' in *The Journal of the Oxford University Brass-Rubbing Society*, I (June 1897), 41–67. In Warden Sewell's annotated copy of Wood in New College library are many important notes about memorials. It should also be noted that in Rudolph Ackermann's *History of the University of Oxford* (1814), the view of the interior of New College chapel shows a tiled floor without memorial slabs (Plate 11). See also the index to *Archives* under the heading, New College: cemetery, chapel, cloisters, and monuments.
4. See preface to Wood, *Colleges*. See also A. Clark (ed.), *The Life and Times of Anthony Wood, antiquary, of Oxford, 1632—1695, described by himself* (Oxford Hist. Soc., 5 vols., 1891–1900), hereafter referred to as Wood, *Life*.
5. The chapel was repaved with black, white and grey marble in 1637, but the brasses of Thomas Cranley and John Young were not moved at that time; *V.C.H. Oxfordshire*, vol. 3 (1954), 146.
6. For Young, see also J. Watney, *Some account of the Hospital of St. Thomas of Acon, in the Cheap, London, and of the plate of the Mercers' Company* (1892), 63–108.
7. For references to illustrations of the New College brasses, see M. Stephenson, *A list of monumental brasses in the British Isles* (1926), 414–16.
8. Not to be confused with his namesake, the infamous warden who held office from 1526 to 1542.
9. At a college meeting held at 8.15 a.m. on 1 December 1936 the only item of business was to consider an offer by the Rev. W. B. Gascoigne to replace this brass at his own expense; an inscription was drafted by Professor (afterwards Sir) J. L. Myres, but the gift of a replacement was declined (N.C. MS., 11708).
10. See his book, *The Baily family of Thatcham and later of Speen and of Newbury all in the county of Berkshire* (1951).
11. See *Dictionary of National Biography* (hereafter abbreviated to *D.N.B.*).
12. See L. G. H. Horton-Smith, 'New College Brasses: Oxford', in *The Genealogists' Magazine*, vol. 11, 93, 94.
13. Haydocke (see *D.N.B.*) was also a physician; he composed the epitaphs on the brasses (now lost) to John Halswell (1618) and Esdras Booth (1627) formerly on the west and east walls of the cloisters respectively (see Wood, *Colleges*, 205, 215, 221). Haydocke was the donor of the

painting in the possession of the college commemorating the Gunpowder Plot (see *Archaeologia*, vol. 84, 27–39). Haydocke was also responsible for the brasses to Henry Robinson, Bishop of Carlisle (d. 1616) and Provost Henry Airay (d. 1616) in The Queen's College chapel (see J. R. Magrath, *The Queen's College*, vol. 1, 1921, 206–9) and to Erasmus Williams (d. 1608), rector, in Tingewick church, Buckinghamshire. Hopper's gift of books to the college reminds us that many others, before and after his time, were benefactors in various ways. Some of those men have memorials in the college, but others are commemorated elsewhere. See also R. Hutchinson, 'Dr. Richard Haydocke, brass engraver and "Sleeping Preacher" ', in *Transactions of the Monumental Brass Society*, vol. xi, part vi, 396–401, R. Strong, *The cult of Elizabeth* (1977), 16, and K. J. Höltgen, 'Richard Haydocke: translator, engraver, physician', in *The Library*, fifth series, vol. 33 (1978), 15–32.

14. Note by Warden Sewell. Skidmore also submitted a design for a wrought-iron gate for the entrance to the chapel (N.C. MS. 5631).

15. This monument was provided by Ralph Brideoake (1613–78; see *D.N.B.*), Bishop of Chichester, in 1677, thirty years after Pinke's death. The warden died following a fall downstairs.

16. Traffles desired that his epitaph should begin, *Hic situs est Ricardus Trafles, Humilis Peccator*, but the present wording, composed by William Bradshaw (1671–1732; see *D.N.B.*), Dean of Christ Church and afterwards Bishop of Bristol, disregarded the wish. See C. E. Doble and others (eds.), *Remarks and collections of Thomas Hearne*, vol. 1 (1885), 10; Hearne describes Bradshaw as 'a vile Whigg, but a man of Parts' (vol. 3, 120), says he is commonly called 'the old Man' (vol. 5, 361) and was 'a very great drinker' (vol. 11, 138); he was a fellow of New College, 1695–1718.

17. Oglander's marble tablet, with drapery, was designed by James Wyatt and carved by Richard Westmacott.

18. See R. Gunnis, *Dictionary of British Sculptors, 1660–1851* (n.d.), 55 and K. A. Esdaile, *English Church Monuments, 1510–1840* (1946), 17 and Plate 97. See ch. VI, pp. 209ff.

19. 1555?–1613; see *D.N.B.*

20. For Barker, see *D.N.B.* Stone executed the monument to Sir Thomas Bodley in Merton College chapel. See also H. Walpole (ed. by J. Dallaway), *Anecdotes of Painting in England*, vol. 2 (1816), 62. For this Hugh Barker, see also J. Buxton, '*Peplus*: New College Elegies for Sir Philip Sidney', in *The Warden's Meeting: a tribute to John Sparrow* (1977), 25.

21. Wood, *Colleges*, 200.

22. Warden Sewell records the discovery of Warden Beeston's grave in the chapel on 5 May 1879. 'In removing the earth on the North side of the Chancel of the Chapel this day, preparatory to the erection of the new wood work a grave was discovered close to the wall at the door of the old vestry. It was bricked over—but the top fell in. From fragments of the lid of the coffin which I saw put together, it was ascertained to be the grave

of Henry Beeston—the following letters & figures being discovered in nails on the lid —

H.B.
Aged 72
1701

Dr. Beeston died in May 1701 & as he is described in the admissions to Winchester College as having been 13 years of age at Michaelmas 1643, there can be no doubt of the identity of this grave with his place of sepulture. The bricks, which enclosed it, looked as fresh as if newly placed there.'

23. The monument was formerly on the south wall (Wood, *Colleges*, 211). Gother's grave is covered by a slab in the north cloister.

24. 1772–1863; see *D.N.B.* He was Keeper of the Ashmolean Museum, 1826–55 in succession to his brother.

25. See *D.N.B.*, and tablet and gravestone in the north cloister.

26. According to T. F. Kirby, *Winchester Scholars* (1888), 297.

27. 1762–1850; see *D.N.B.* Edward Bowles who died, aged twenty, of smallpox in 1714 has a memorial, erected by Thomas Bowles in 1724, in the east walk of the cloisters, and the Rev. Christopher Erle (d. 1817, aged fifty-seven) and his wife, Margaret Bowles, have a memorial near by.

28. R. Gunnis, *Dictionary of British Sculptors, 1660–1851* (n.d.), 398, 399.

29. T. F. Kirby, *Winchester Scholars* (1888), 238.

30. N.C. MS. 3195. The erection of this tablet demonstrates, very forcibly, that sense of brotherhood which membership of New College inspires in all right-thinking people.

31. 1834–1910; see *D.N.B.* Headmaster of Wellington College; Dean of Lincoln. See also L. Ragg, *A memoir of Edward Charles Wickham* (1911).

32. N.C. MS. 3190; *Archives*, 68, 69; E. R. Gill, *The inscriptional work of Eric Gill* (1964), 58. Gill was assisted in this great work by H. J. Laurie Cribb, Denis Tegetmeier and David Jones. See also W. Shewring (ed.), *Letters of Eric Gill* (1947), 147, 148 and R. Speaight, *The Life of Eric Gill* (1966), 187. Gill also executed the memorial tablets to Sir H. E. Richards (1922) and G. C. Bourne (1933), both in the east cloister, and John Galsworthy (1933) in the south cloister.

33. The material on which this paper is based, and other extensive notes, will be given to the college after, or before, the decease of the present writer.

34. *D.N.B.*; portrait by J. S. Sargent in the senior common room; see also C. Bailey, *Hugh Percy Allen* (1948).

35. Portrait in the Chequer.

36. *D.N.B.*; author, with R. S. Rait, of *New College* (1901).

37. He had obtained both the Latin and English verse prizes at the preceding Commemoration 'and his death was generally lamented' (Sewell's notes). J. Shergold Boone (1799–1859; see *D.N.B.*) of Christ Church, who had

obtained both prizes in a similar way the year before, wrote lines on Ormerod. The tablet is by J. Bacon of London.

38. *D.N.B.*; Obituary by G. Murray, in *Proceedings of the British Academy*, vol. 26.
39. *D.N.B.*; *Archives*, 369.
40. *D.N.B.*
41. *D.N.B.*; for the Milner Papers at New College, see *Archives*, 106–9; portrait in hall.
42. *D.N.B.;* Obituary by T. J. Dunbabin, in *Proceedings of the British Academy*, vol. 41.
43. *D.N.B.*
44. *D.N.B.*
45. See *Who was Who, 1961–1970.*
46. *D.N.B.*; *Archives*, 99.
47. Wood, *Colleges*, 217, quotes an epitaph made on Meredith:
    > Here lyes one blowne out of breath,
    > Who liv'd a merry life, and died a merry death.
48. *D.N.B.*; Wood, *Colleges*, 218, *n.* 111.
49. See *Who was Who, 1961–1970.*
50. A large, but decayed, ledger stone covers his grave.
51. He died in 1753, another victim of smallpox (Wood, *Colleges*, 223); a small diamond-shaped stone marks his grave.
52. Richard was a scholar of New College, fellow 1685–1703, and fellow of Winchester College; see T. F. Kirby, *Winchester Scholars* (1888), 14, 202.
53. *D.N.B.* H. B. George was a fellow of the college for fifty-four years and the author, *inter alia*, of *New College, 1856–1906* (1906).
54. Wood, *Colleges*, 228; Bartholomew's gravestone cannot now be recognised. His epitaph was composed by the Rev. Philip Smyth, afterwards Rector of Worthen, Salop.
55. He was butler for forty-five years. Sewell noted slabs for Tobias George (d. 1808, aged seventy-four) and Thomas Dewson (d. 1833, aged forty-nine), both college butlers, but the stones are no longer recognisable, and neither is the tablet near the bell-tower door to William Bragge, M.A. (1761–1840), who was steward of the college for thirty-five years. Another example of the disappearance of monuments is afforded by that of Giles Vie (d. 1628). Wood, *Colleges*, records it (p. 231) but Sewell notes that: 'This tomb stone now covers the drain from the East side of the first Quadrangle, just in front of the Arch Way under the Library. I saw it there, on the drain being opened, Aug. 23. 1851.'
56. See Wood, *Colleges*, 231, and J. Buxton, op. cit. (*n.* 20 above), 24–6, for references to John Hoskyns.
57. See foreword by Sir Christopher Cox to A. H. Smith, *Selected Essays and Addresses* (1963). Bust by Epstein in the hall.
58. *D.N.B.* He greatly assisted John Selden in the preparation of *Marmora Arundelliana* (1624).

59. *D.N.B.*
60. *D.N.B.* See also, H. A. L. Fisher, *An unfinished autobiography* (1940) and D. Ogg, *Herbert Fisher, 1865–1940: a short biography* (1947). Portrait in hall.
61. *D.N.B.*; *Archives*, 12, 67; Wood, *Colleges*, 213; see ch. VIII, p. 270.
62. *D.N.B.*
63. See also *n.* 27.
64. 1561–1616; see *D.N.B.* under Field.
65. The families of Bowles, Erle, Richards and Fearon were all related.
66. For example, to Thomas James (1573?–1629) first librarian of the Bodleian who was 'buried toward the upper end' of the chapel, and Isaac Pring, organist (d. 1799, aged twenty-two) who was buried in the south cloister. Camden, in his *Remains concerning Britain* (1674 edn.), 521, 522, quotes the epitaph, written with a coal in the north cloister to Peter Woodgate (d. 1590); the story is repeated by Wood, *Colleges*, 231, *n.* 112.
67. *Archives*, 69.

EPILOGUE

Epilogue

PENRY WILLIAMS

When Wykeham founded New College, the collegiate movement in European universities had already gathered considerable momentum. Even so, his establishment was in many ways revolutionary. Before 1379 the Oxford colleges were small institutions, averaging only about ten fellows apiece and accommodating men who had already graduated: the notion of a college for the teaching of undergraduates was as yet unknown in Oxford. True, King's Hall, Cambridge, had been admitting undergraduates from the early part of the fourteenth century, and Wykeham may perhaps have been imitating that remarkable royal foundation. If so, he carried the innovations of King's Hall a good deal further and placed his college upon a more permanent base. To begin with, New College was far larger than any of the other secular Oxford colleges, which scarcely held more than seventy fellows between them in 1379. Then the establishment of Winchester College three years later was designed to provide Wykeham's Oxford college with boys already proficient in Latin; and this double foundation was copied later by Henry VI at Eton and King's, Cambridge. Above all, the Founder and his advisers created buildings which were carefully designed for the close-knit community that he envisaged. The influence of the architecture of New College upon later medieval Oxford was enormous and is still obvious today. In many different ways the college became the prototype for later foundations in both Oxford and Cambridge.

For nearly two centuries it was remarkably successful. Its endowments were adequate without being excessive; it acquired enough benefices to provide livings for its members; it produced distinguished servants of Church and State; it possessed both the finest library in either university and a magnificent collection of ecclesiastical and secular plate. The Founder was held in deep and proper reverence, while his statutes were rigidly observed. Towards the end of the fifteenth century the college produced the most distinguished of the early English humanists, William Grocyn, while Archbishop Warham became one of the most generous and perceptive patrons of scholarship. The strong tradition of humanist learning generated by these men was still alive in the middle of the sixteenth century, when New College became the principal centre of the new Catholic learning.

With the Elizabethan settlement the intellectual vigour of the college began a slow decline. The Catholic scholars went into exile; fervent Protestants were attracted to other colleges. The devotion shown by New College to its Founder's statutes prevented it from admitting commoners in any number or from accepting boys who had not been to Winchester. The college was thus isolated from some of the most invigorating influences of Reformation Oxford. At the same time its fellows began increasingly to value their physical comforts, and the college became more secular in its outlook. One should not exaggerate the falling-off: New College continued to produce able and interesting men, but it was no longer the college which showed the way to others. Indeed, by the end of the sixteenth century it was something of an anachronism.

The attractions of material pleasures and the reassuring wealth of the college further dampened the intellectual ardour of its fellows after the Restoration. Yet, although the college then entered a scholarly wilderness, its building activity was abundantly fruitful. While the additional storey in the front quadrangle was aesthetically unfortunate, the garden quadrangle was a triumph of architectural ingenuity and taste. Even if this passion for building was aroused primarily by a desire for greater privacy and for the fees paid by gentlemen commoners, the fellows were not wholly secular in their interests. The fine new Dallam organ was installed in 1662–3 and a new reredos erected a few years later. The history of New College in the late seventeenth and early eighteenth centuries shows that institutions are not all of a piece. Intellectually the college may have been moribund; but its musical and architectural achievements were splendid.

Admittedly, during the middle years of the eighteenth century, the fellows were almost exclusively preoccupied with political intrigue and the competition for livings. Little building was done and the musical standard seems to have been low. But in the last quarter of the century, interest in building—especially in ecclesiastical building—revived. The Reynolds window—at the very least a remarkable object—was installed; and the whole interior of the chapel was dramatically remodelled by James Wyatt, one of the outstanding architects of his day.

Although the first half of the nineteenth century saw little building at New College, there was a slow beginning of educational reform. In the university at large the introduction of honours examinations in 1801 had set off a fierce debate about the system of teaching. New College men, allowed to proceed to degrees without entering for university examinations, remained aloof from this argument. Many of them, as Founder's Kin, were anxious to maintain every vestige of privilege. Yet there was a minority of reformers under the leadership of Warden Shuttleworth; and the surrender of the college's exemption from university examinations began the process by which it moved back into the mainstream of university life. Shuttleworth's departure to Chichester checked, although it did not halt, this movement. But only external agencies could supply the pressure needed to shift the majority. The change, when it came, was dramatically swift. Within twenty years between 1850 and 1870 New College had abolished the priority given to Founder's Kin, admitted scholars from schools other than Winchester, accepted commoners, and allowed its fellows to marry. By the last quarter of the century it had achieved an academic and athletic eminence rivalled only by Balliol, Christ Church and Magdalen. At the same time the appearance of the college was drastically altered. Domestic buildings were razed in Holywell to make room for the vast Gothic range required for the new intake of commoners. Under the dominant evangelical mood of the fellows, immense sums of money, far larger than the cost of Scott's new building, were spent on his transformation of the interior of the chapel, with results for which Scott himself cannot be entirely blamed.

These changes prepared the way for a golden epoch between the two world wars. This was not a period of dramatic reform, in spite of the dynamic personality of Warden Fisher. But to describe it as a time of consolidation suggests a quality of coagulation quite false to the confident and successful history of those years, when the college produced a lavish harvest of talent.

It is too early to attempt a history of the college since the end of the Second World War, and personal reminiscence would be either anodyne or embarrassing. But a few paragraphs are needed to round off this volume. When Warden Fisher died in 1940 the college did not at once choose his successor; but in 1944 Alic Smith, fellow and tutor in philosophy and subwarden for most of the war years, was elected warden. He presided over the college until his death in the summer of 1958. By then, the college had already pre-elected their next warden, Sir William Hayter, at that time Deputy Under-Secretary of State at the Foreign Office. On his retirement in 1976 Dr. Arthur Cooke, Tutorial Fellow in Physics since 1946, became the forty-second warden of New College.

In many ways the college has changed more under these three wardens than it did under Fisher, although the changes have been neither as dramatic nor as fundamental as those presided over by Sewell. The years after 1945 were followed by a large and rapid increase in numbers, as the college took in men whose university careers had been interrupted or postponed by the war. I doubt whether those of us who were then up quite realised the magnitude of the effort put out by the college on our behalf—though we were, I think, aware of our good fortune. In 1938 there had been 233 undergraduates in residence; by Michaelmas term 1948 there were 435, taught by a fellowship body no larger than it had been before the war. The number of junior members declined during the 1950s to 364 in 1957, and then rose again with the ending of national service, to more than 400 in 1960; and it has remained above 420 during the 1970s. However, this figure conceals important changes in the composition of the college. In 1950, 308 men were reading for honours schools, forty-seven for higher degrees; in 1974 there were 343 undergraduates and eighty-three graduate students in residence. Research students, few in number before the war, now make up about a fifth of those reading for degrees. The balance between arts and sciences has also shifted: in 1950, 223 men were reading for undergraduate degrees in arts, eighty-five in sciences; by 1977 the comparable figures were 235 and 130.

The fellowship body has expanded slowly but considerably to meet this growth in numbers. In 1938 there had been twenty-seven fellows, about seventeen of whom taught undergraduates. The number remained below thirty until 1957, when there were thirty-two, twenty-one of whom were tutorial fellows. By 1970 the total had reached forty-one, and in 1976, when Warden Hayter retired, it was forty-three, of whom thirty had some responsibility for teaching undergraduates. The range of subjects grew with the numbers. In 1938 the college had tutorial fellows in classics, philosophy, ancient and modern history, English, economics, law, mathematics, physiology, physics and chemistry. By 1976 there was a tutorial fellow in almost every honours school.

The physical appearance of the college has also been transformed, within and without, over the last thirty years. The first major work after the war involved the restoration of the Founder's library and the Wyatt library, both infested with death-watch beetle. A few years later, in 1957, began the enormous enterprise of cleaning, repairing and restoring the buildings of the whole university. The erosion of centuries was checked by the Oxford Historic Buildings Appeal, whose birth owed much to Warden Smith. In New College the familiar subfusc patina was removed from the front quad, the garden quad and the cloisters, to reveal an unexpected and golden splendour.

In 1958–9 the college began to modernise the New Buildings in order to make them more comfortable and to provide more accommodation. With the gradual disappearance of the old-style Oxford landlady it has become more common and more necessary for all colleges to provide housing for their members. A generous gift by Mr. Harry Sacher, an old member of the college, then provided money for the Sacher building, designed by David Roberts and intended for the accommodation of graduates. With its completion in 1963 the college had 270 rooms for its junior members, compared with 165 before the war. It was now possible for all undergraduates to live in college for at least two years. The building of Bodicote House, by Geoffrey Beard, the purchase of houses in north Oxford for graduate flats, and various minor additions have raised the total to 347 in 1978. Building and conversion have not all been utilitarian. The upper storey of the Long Room, no longer needed for baths, has been transformed by Geoffrey Beard into a charming gallery for meetings, parties, dances and exhibitions. In the chapel, the

old Willis organ was replaced after long service in 1969 by an entirely
new instrument designed by Messrs Grant, Degens & Bradbeer, with a
screen by G. G. Pace.

One final change, perhaps the most important, certainly the most
controversial, will take effect in the college's sixth-centenary year. In
1963 New College was the first of the men's colleges in Oxford to
consider the admission of women: the proposal was defeated. The issue
was raised again in the early 1970s, but although the governing body
changed its statutes to enable the college to admit women, it decided, in
characteristic compromise, not actually to accept them as junior
members; it did, however, allow itself to elect a woman fellow.
Eventually, in 1977, the college agreed to admit women as undergraduate and graduate members: the first cohort will arrive in October
1979.

New College has seen two great periods in its history: the first two
centuries and the last hundred years. Yet it has produced very few men
of the highest national renown. Unlike Balliol and Christ Church, it has
housed few political celebrities. Nor have New College men made a
mark in the creative arts: there are no great New College poets,
painters, or, with the exception of Thomas Weelkes, composers. The
ranks of its successful graduates—and they are many—are paraded
towards the back of the stage, somewhat out of the public eye: their
worlds lie in administration, learning, the law and the Church. Perhaps
the intentions of the Founder have been fulfilled in this modest yet
confident distinction.

A Note on Further Reading

John Buxton, *New College, Oxford: a Note on the Garden* (Oxford, 1976).

Hereford George, *New College, 1856–1906* (Oxford, 1906).

William Hayter, *New College* (1962).

William Hayter, *William of Wykeham, Patron of the Arts* (1970).

William Hayter, *Spooner: a biography* (1977).

A. H. M. Jones, 'New College', in *Victoria County History, Oxfordshire*, III (1954), 144–62.

C. E. Mallett, *A History of the University of Oxford* (3 vols. 1924–7).

H. Rashdall and R. S. Rait, *New College* (1901).

A. H. Smith, *New College and its Buildings* (Oxford, 1952).

Francis W. Steer, *Misericords at New College, Oxford* (1973).

Francis W. Steer, *The Archives of New College* (1974).

Selby Whittingham, *Medieval Portrait Busts at New College, Oxford* (1973).

C. Woodforde, *The Stained Glass of New College, Oxford* (Oxford, 1951).

A full list of printed works relating to New College will be found in E. H. Cordeaux and D. H. Merry, *A Bibliography of Printed Works relating to the University of Oxford* (3 vols. Oxford, 1968), III, 671–80.

APPENDIX

Wardens of New College

Nicholas Wykeham, 1379–89
Thomas Cranley, 1389–96
Richard Malford, 1396–1403
John Bowke, 1403–29
William Estcourt, 1429–35
Nicholas Ossulbury, 1435–54
Thomas Chaundler, 1454–75
Walter Hill, 1475–94
William Porter, 1494–1520
John Rede, 1520–1
John Young, 1521–6
John London, 1526–42
Henry Cole, 1542–51
Ralph Skinner, 1551–3
Thomas Whyte, 1553–73
Martin Culpepper, 1573–99
George Ryves, 1599–1613
Arthur Lake, 1613–17
Robert Pinke, 1617–47
Henry Stringer, 1647–8
[George Marshall, intruded by the
    Parliamentary Commissioners, 1649–58]

Michael Woodward, 1658–75
John Nicholas, 1675–9
Henry Beeston, 1679–1701
Richard Traffles, 1701–3
Thomas Braithwaite, 1703–12
John Cobb, 1712–20
John Dobson, 1720–4
Henry Bigg, 1725–30
John Coxed, 1730–40
John Purnell, 1740–64
Thomas Hayward, 1764–8
John Oglander, 1768–94
Samuel Gauntlett, 1794–1822
Philip Nicholas Shuttleworth, 1822–40
David Williams, 1840–60
James Edwards Sewell, 1860–1903
William Archibald Spooner, 1903–25
Herbert Albert Laurens Fisher, 1925–40
Alic Halford Smith, 1944–1958
William Goodenough Hayter, 1958–1976
Arthur Hafford Cooke, 1976–

Index

N.B. Italicised spellings are those used in Emden's *Biographical Register*. (W) means Warden.

Adam 173
Adam the Joiner 164
Adams, Coker 251–2, 281
Adderbury 8, 31, 104
Agas, Ralph 202
Ainsworth, *Aynesworth*, Henry 25
Albertus Magnus (MSS.) 319, 331
Alden, J. H. 288
Allen, Sir Hugh 108, 112, 285–8, 291, 351
Allnatt, Alfred E. 260, 310
Allnutt, H. 126
All Souls College 24, 45, 47, 56, 120, 161, 188; glass, 188, 235; plate, 298; MSS., 327, 329
Allsop, H. C. B. G. 134
Alton Barnes 30, 104
Amicabilis Concordia 20
Andrew, Richard 20, 25, 31, 327
Andrewes, A. 135
   Richard 295
Andrews, H. K. 291
Antechapel 17, 169–70; memorials, 347–51
Aquinas (MSS.) 322, 325
Aranyi, Jelly d' 140
archives (see also Muniment Tower) 306–16
Arkell, W. J. 261
Arnold, George B. 280
Ashcroft, Peggy 139
Ashley, Lord 59
Ashton, Hugh 134
astronomy 20, 83, 318, 322, 334
Auctarium 240, 257
Averroes (MSS.) 322, 332–4

Ayliffe, John 60–1, 214
Aylworth, Anthony 348

Bailey, Cyril 141
Baily, Walter 348
Balliol College 72–3, 89, 96, 138, 153
barber 56
Barcroft, Paul and William 354
Barell, John 33
Barker, Sir Ernest (quoted) 307
Barker, Hugh 349, 353
Bartlemas Hospital 272
Bassett, Reg 118
Beard, Geoffrey 249, 260–1, 367
Beckington, *Bekynton*, Thomas 14, 20, 24, 25, 26, 29, 32, 194, 310, 325
Beckington 25
Bede, statue of 254; MS. of, 330
Bedford School 64, 311
Beeston, Henry (W) 349, 356 n. 22; grave, 356
Bell, H. E. 297, 262 n. 30
Bell, Henry 213
Bell-tower 45, 55, 152, 154–5, 176–7
Belloc, Hilaire 128
bells 163, 177, 277
Benbury, William 33
Benfield and Loxley 255
Bennett, Alfred 278, 352
Bennett, Mary (née Fisher) 125, 127–31, 143
Bentley, Thomas 324, 334
Berlin, Sir Isaiah 108, 130, 141
Bernard, John 154
Bernasconi, Bernato 241–2

Betton, Sir John 159
Bigg, Henry (W) 61–2
Bilson, Thomas 51
Bishop, John 276
Blackstone, Henry 350
Bobart, Jacob 225
Bodendick, Jacob 302
Bodicote House 259, 367
Bodley, Sir Thomas 339
Body, John 49
Bolney, Bartholomew 35
Bones, John 28
Booth, Richard 228
Boscherville Abbey 8
Bourchier, Thomas (Archbishop) 199
Bourne, G. C. 98–9
Bowles, Edward 353
    Henry 350
Bowra, Sir Maurice 109
Bowring, John 332
Bradshaw, William (Bishop of Bristol)
    356 n. 16
Bradwardine (MS.) 321
Brailes, William de (MS.) 339
Braithwaite, Thomas (W) 60
brasses 346–8
Brent, Thomas 25
Bridges, Margaret 291, 353
    Robert 288
Brocas, Sir Bernard 33 (also Edward and
    John)
Brown, John 36
Brown, William 162, 176, 188
Buckett, *Boket*, Thomas 333
Buckingham, Duchess of 10
Burgess, Richard 333
Burghers, Michael 212, 219, 223, 225
Burlton, Charles 350
Burrard, Harriet (Lady Rooke) 236
bursars receipts, rolls, 11, 40 n. 16, 51; key
    of, 182; parsimony of, 128; pilfering by, 51;
    plate, 302; praise of, 113; rudeness of, 90;
    vigour of, 86
Bursary, Old 180–1
Butler, Francis 210
butlers (commemorated) 358 n. 55
Buxton, John 138–43
Byng, John (quoted) 275
Byrd, William 209–17, 349

Candor, Thomas 327
Carmarthen, *Carmardyne*, Philip 347
Caroë, W. D. 200, 256–7, 259, 261
Carracci, School of 238
Cecil, Lord David 109, 143

celibacy 6; dispensed with, 91
Chacon y Valenzuela 301
Chalner, Robert 38
Champneys, Basil 249, 255–6, 260–85
Chandos, James Brydges, Duke of 224,
    262 n. 23
chapel building of, 4, 154, 169–75, 193,
    206–8, 219–20, 228–9; Reformation and,
    47; Mary I and, 48–9; under Elizabeth
    I, 49–50; eighteenth century, 238;
    nineteenth century, 88, 250–4; twentieth
    century, 260; music in, 119, 267–91
chaplains 4, 12, 76; reduction of, 82;
    rooms of, 216, 228
Chapman, John 246
Chappington, John 268
Charlton, Lewis de (Bishop of Hereford) 319
Charterhouse 160, 322
charters, foundation 7, 153, 154, 308
Chaundler, Thomas (W) 14, 22, 25, 26,
    165, 178, 325
Cheesman, G. L. 100
Chequer 193–5, 210
chess 11
chests 14, 15, 180, 307
Chevington, Richard 161
Chichele, Henry (Archbishop) 24, 25, 32,
    188
Chichester Prebends at, 28; MSS. from, 320
Child, the 87
Child, Simon 272, 344
Chinnor, *Gynnor*, John 325
choir and choir-school 55, 80, 95, 107, 201,
    203, 267–91
choristers 4
Christ Church 58, 103
Church, Richard 273
Chute, Edward 302
Cicero (MS.) 326–7; Mainz edn, 329
Civil War 55–6, 205–6, 269, 299–300
Clark, Colin 118
    Jeremiah 276
Cliffe, Michael 29
Clipsham stone 209, 249, 256, 258, 261
cloisters 17, 55, 152, 154–6, 162, 175–7,
    205, 218, 269; memorials in, 351–4
clubs, societies, etc. 135, 139, 278–9
Coade stone 242
Cobb, John (W) 60
Cobham, Lord (and college) 160
coconut cups 296
Cohen, Lord 109
Coker, Henry, John and Thomas 235
Cole, Henry (W) 47–8, 198
Coleman, Simon 269

Collins, William   65
Commissions of Inquiry, etc. (see also
    Visitations)   1850: 68, 78; 1854: 81–3;
    1873: 86, 89–90; 1877: 89, 97
committees, college   92
common rooms   senior, 63, 210, 244; junior,
    213, 245–6, 249; suggestion-books, 306
commoners (see also gentlemen commoners)
    excluded, 44, 76–7; admitted, 81
commons   12, 15
Compton, Sir Edmund   109
Conduit Chamber   184, 201
cook   submission of, 56; memorial to, 353
Cook, E. T.   101
Cooke, Arthur (W)   366
Cooke, Henry   219–20, 228, 238
Coole, Richard   28
Cooper, Duff (Vicount Norwich)   110
corbels   173, 178, 251
Cotswold stone   155, 169
Courtenay, William (Archbishop)   173
Courtney, W. L.   100
Cowley Marsh   99
Cox, Sir Christopher   108, 124, 139, 140,
    142; as Dean, 127
Cox, G. V.   274, 277
Cox, Cokkys, Laurence   32
Coxed, John (W)   228, 303
Cranley, Thomas (Archbishop of Dublin)
    (W)   9, 22, 325, 347
cricket   99, 140; choir, 290
Cromwell, Thomas   45
Crossman, Richard   108, 109, 123, 130, 139,
    141–2, 354
Crouch (organist)   270
Cruston, William   32
Culpepper, Martin (W)   201
Curtis, Lionel   101

Dallam, Robert   206, 270–1, 275; memorial,
    353
Dalton, Robert   296
Decretals (MSS.)   323, 326, 331
degrees, exemption from University   66–7
Deighton, William de   323
Dew, John and Job   209
Dixon, John   244
Dobbs, John   331
dogs   11, 50
Donoughmore, Lord   303
Doone, Francis   205
Duncan, Philip B.   350, 357 n. 24
Dunkeld, Bishop of   156
Dunns Scotus (MSS.)   27, 322; ripped up, 46,
    366

Durbin, Evan   118, 122
Dykes Bower, Sir John   290–1

Eccles, Lord   109, 118
Edmonds, Thomas   333
Edward III   149, 151, 173
Edward IV   15, 33
Edwards, George   213
Edyall, James   37
Eginton, W. R.   245
El Greco   260
Elizabeth I   34, 47, 49; Wykehamist
    ancestry, 42 n. 59
Ellison, R. E.   289
Elvey, Stephen   278–80
English, study of   108
Epstein, Jacob   141, 260
Erasmus   28, 329
estates of the college   administration 11, 57,
    164; 1660: 92–5, 96–7, 104–6; 1871
    (records of), 312–13
Estcourt, William (W)   13
Eton College   20, 21, 91, 189, 363
Exeter College   6, 28, 138, 186, 332
Eyre, John   234

Farley, John   26, 34, 334–5
Faulkner, Sir Keith   290
Fearon, W. A.   251, 354
fellows under the Founder's statutes   age of,
    17; careers of, 29–31; comforts of, 45, 53,
    58, 244; dress of, 11; drunkenness of, 59,
    63; execution of, 49; expulsions of, 56, 67;
    factions among, 16, 38 (1526), 45–6
    (1530), 48 (1551), 57 (1660s), 58–9, 60–3
    (eighteenth century), 74 (nineteenth
    century); food of, 12, 15–16, 63, 178, 311;
    incompetence of, 79; marriages of, 35, 37;
    mortality of, 17, 26; non-residence of, 52;
    numbers of, 7, 16, 44–5; obscurity of, 31,
    52, 64–5, 72, 76, 204; ordinations of, 30,
    32–3, 65; provenance of, 31, 33–4, 37;
    rooms of, 18, 58, 183–5, 201–4, 215; song
    of, 272; stipends of, 9 (1398), 15 (fifteenth
    century), 65 (eighteenth century), 80
    (ninetheenth century); studies of,
    20–30, 318, 331–4; Fellows, tutorial
    1857–1914: 74–5, 82, 91; 1918–39: 107–8,
    139, 142; marriages of, 245, 248, 255–6;
    philistinism of, 247–9, 251–3, 259;
    numbers 1938–76: 367
Ferrars, William   339
ferrets   11
Field, John   354
Fiennes family   52; Celia, 58, 218

Finch, Matthew and Bartholomew   353
Fischer, Bram   134
Fishacre, Richard (MSS.)   321, 322, 325, 338
Fisher, H. A. L. (W)   92, 101, 108; quoted, 72; Buxton on, 142–3; Mary Bennett on, 128–9; Rees on, 125–6; Robbins on, 112–14; Woodcock on, 134; memorial, 353
Fisher, Mary (see also Bennett, Mary)   125
Fisher, Mrs.   129–30, 132
Fitch, Sir Lambert   227
Fleshmonger, William   310
Flexney, William (organist)   270
football   11; Sparrow at, 123
Founder's Kin   31, 33, 52, 58, 65, 66, 77–8, 309; privileges abolished, 82
Fowler, John   49
Franklin, Jeremiah   226, 228
Freake, Frances   271
Fremantle, John   324
Frogley, Richard   210–11
Fry, John   348

Gaitskell, Hugh   109, 118, 122, 352
Galsworthy, John   110, 352
Garbrand, John   51
garden   202, 217–19, 225–6, 244; magic of, 119, 120
garden quadrangle   212–17, 220–4; gate screen, 224–5
Gaudes   159
Gauntlett, Samuel (W)   65, 349
Gee, E. A.   149
general strike   109
gentlemen commoners   45, 212, 301
George, Hereford   74–100, 353
Germans (commemorated)   351
Gielgud, Sir John   139
Gilbert, Thomas   31
Gill, Eric   260, 350
Glazier, Thomas   175, 177, 187
Goad, Scroggs   352
Godber, George   110
Golding, Christopher   62
Gome, John   19
Goodson, Richard   272
Gother, William   349, 353
graduate students   127, 367
Greek, study of   26, 46, 108, 335, 336
Green, Grene, John   29, 333
   Samuel   275
Greenhurst, Ralph   32
Grocyn, William   27, 36, 335
Groser, Michael   261

Grosseteste, Robert   337
Gutch, John   346

Hackett, Sir John   110
Haldane, J. S.   101, 108, 112
   J.B.S.   101, 108
Halévy, Elie   130
hall   84, 177–8, 195–7, 227–8; gallery of, 256
Hankey, Robin   118
Hankford, Richard and William   34
Hansford, Robert   21
Harding, Clement   29
   Thomas   45, 47
Hardy, G. H.   108, 112, 114; Rees on, 124–5; Robbins on, 116–18
Hare, Augustus   66
Harlech, Lord   109
Harmar, John   349
Harpsfield, John and Nicholas   45, 46–7
Harris family   270–3
Harris, Sir William   286, 289–90
   William   204
Harrow School   91
Hartington, Marquess of   223
Harvey, John   149
Hassall, Christopher   139
Havergal, Henry   279
Hawkes, Christopher   140
Hawtryve, William   348
Haydocke, Richard   54, 348
Hayes, Philip   273–6, 282
   William   276
Hayter, Sir William (W)   107, 258, 289, 366
Hayward, Richard   32
   Thomas (W)   353
Headington   16, 115
Headington stone   155, 169, 209
Heal's   258
Hearne, Thomas   61, 228, 272
Heath, A. G.   100
Heathcote, George   67
   Gilbert   276
Hegel, G. W. F   100
Henderson, H. L.   139
Henry   II and III, 173; Henry IV, 22, 24, 156; Henry VI, 14, 15, 20, 22, 24, 189; Henry VII, 22, 24, 25; Henry VIII, 36, 38, 45, 195
heraldry, arms etc.   10, 197, 203, 212, 217, 246–7, 299, 330, 349
Herbert, Lord   135
Herbert, Sir Alan (A. P.)   135
Herebright of Cologne   175
Herland, Hugh   152, 156–64, 176, 179, 240

Heveningham, Thomas 36
Hewlett, James Philip 275
Hichens, W. L. 101
Higginbottom, E. 291
Hill, *Hylle*, Thomas 347
 Walter (W) 21, 26, 27, 296
Hilton, Philip 287–8
Hitch, Nathanael 254, 268 n. 54
Hoadley, Benjamin (Bishop of Winchester) 62
Hoare, Samuel 110
Hobbes, Thomas 208
Holden, William 27
Holes, Andrew 26, 324, 326
Holland, J. M. 279
Holmegh, William 21, 347
Holywell Buildings 247–50
Hooke, John 64
Hopper, Humphrey 350
 Sir Thomas 54, 347
Horman, William 21, 271
Hornchurch 10, 95, 104, 350
Horne (Bishop of Winchester) 50, 194
Hoskyns, John 54, 353
Housewife, *Huswyfe*, Roger 35
Howell, Henry 339
Howley, William (Archbishop) 65
Hoyer-Millar, Derick (Lord
 Inchyra) 109
Hulyn, John 157
Hunt, Robert 38
Hurst, Robert 25
Hussey, Sampson 19
Huxley, Sir Julian 108, 112
hymn-book, New College 276, 285

Ickenham, William 152, 164
income, college fourteenth century, 8;
 fifteenth century, 10–16; sixteenth–
 seventeenth centuries, 53, 55, 58;
 1775–1850: 65, 70; 1850–1915: 86,
 95, 96–7, 98, 103–4, 105
Inge, Hugh (Archbishop of Dublin) 22

Jackson, *Jacqueson*, Thomas 324, 331
Jacobitism 62
James, I 269
James, Thomas 35, 338, 359 n. 56
Jane, Thomas 24, 25
Jay, Douglas 109, 123
Jeans, Sir James 135
Jenkinson, Sir Hilary (quoted) 314
Jervais, Thomas 235–7
Jewel, Bishop 47, 51
Johnson, Frances and Elizabeth 236
Jolypace, Henry 334

Jones, A. H. M. 148
Joseph, H. W. B. 100–1, 108; fear of,
 124; Robbins on, 114–15; Woodcock
 on, 133–6; as Socrates, 139;
 memorial, 353
Jowitt, Lord 110

Ken, Bishop 58
Kerr, Philip (Marquess of Lothian) 101
Keys, Roger 189
Kidwelly, Geoffrey 34
Kilvert, Francis (quoted) 282
King, William 271
King's College, Cambridge 20, 189
King's Hall, Cambridge 183, 363
Kingscot, *Kyngescote*, John (Bishop of
 Carlisle) 19, 34
Kingsmill, *Kyngesmyll*, John 36, 51
Kirby, T. F. 313
kitchen 178–80; chimneys, 195, 228;
 extensions, 256; books, 311;
 warden's, 185–6
Knight, *Knyght*, William 28
Knole 199
Kruschev, Nikita 260
Kynow, Thomas 30

Lambourne Almshouses 311
Lane, New College 155, 209
Laud, William (Archbishop) 52, 53, 204,
 339
Lavender, Richard 29
law, civil and cannon, study of, 20,
 22–5, 37–8, 41 n. 48, 81, 108, 323;
 law library, 194–5, 330
Lawrence, C. W. 92
 T. E. 260
Layton, Richard 46, 335
lectures university, 5, 75, 136–7,
 141; college, 73, 344 n. 61
Lee, Lancelot J. 86, 90
 Thomas 61
Leicester, Earl of 198
Lely, Sir Peter 207
Lethaby, W. R. 260
Lewis, Owen 47
Liber Albus 319, 322, 332
librarian 338
library Founder's, 29, 47, 182–3, 194–5,
 227, 258, 317–45; upper, 337–8;
 Wyatt, 239–40; law 194–5, 330;
 new, 257–8
Lichfield, *Lichefeld*, John 32
Lidlyngton, William de (MS.) 321
Lincoln College 90, 186

Linge, Abraham van   204
livings,college   30–1, 53, 59,64, 79
Livy (MS.)   327
Llewellyn-Smith family   304
Lloyd, Hugh   348
   Miss   248
loans   1420: 13; 1461: 14
Loggan, David   165, 199, 209
Lombard, Peter (MSS.)   319, 322, 326
London, John (W)   38, 45–7, 197, 198
   Edward   46
   John (scribe)   348
Long Room   50, 184–5, 213, 223, 256, 367
Longford, Lord   109
Louth, John   348
Lowe, Edward   270
Lowth, Robert   64–5
Lucas, John   34
Lucy, William, & Co.   225
Lumsden, David   291
Lustcyll, Thomas   325
Lybbe Powys, Mrs.   218, 220, 262 n. 23
Lydiat, Thomas   353
Lynd, Maire   125–6, 129

McCulloch, John   255
McGregor, D. H.   136
Magdalen College   22, 72, 95, 153, 161, 186,
   188, 277; School, 21; tower, 176; beds, 183
Maidstone, Thomas   152, 163
Malford, Richard   347
Mallowan, Sir Max   110
Malton, William   325
Man, Thomas   338
   John   45
Manchester Grammar School   91
Mander, Noel   283
Margoliouth, D. S.   101, 108
Marlborough College   86
Marshal, John   47
Marshall, George (pseudo-warden)   56–7,
   300
Martin, Thomas   45, 337
Martyn, John   152
Mary, the Blessed Virgin   4, 8; Mrs.
   Spooner as, 87; representations of,
   157, 163, 172, 173, 241, 242, 294,
   306
Mary I   48
Mason, Robert   29, 329
Mason, William   236
Massachusetts   54
Matheson, P. E.   351
Matthiessen, F.O.   110
May, Hugh   207

Mayhew, *Mayew*, Richard   22, 128, 327
   Nicholas   25
Mayo, Charles   249, 251, 284
medicine, study of   54, 332–4
Membury, Simon   158–9
memorials, monuments, etc.   260, 346–59
Meredith, William   269, 352, 358 n. 47
Merton College   5, 7, 45, 84, 138, 169, 182,
   185, 210, 221, 247, 281, 320, 326
Michael of Meaux (MS.)   325
Miles (pseudo-organist)   270
Milner, Lord   101, 108; papers, 310
   Lady   130
mint julep   303
misericords   171–2
modern history, study of   74, 108
modern languages, study of   108
Molina, Count   58
Molson, Hugh (Lord Molson)   109
Mompesson family   339–40
monkey salt   297, 300
Montagna, Bartolommeo   260
More, Henry   36
   Sir Thomas   335
Mottisfont, John   332
mound   202, 205, 217–18, 226, 244
Mundyn, John   49, 50
Muniment Tower   148, 180–1, 219, 293,
   300, 306–8
Murray, Gilbert   101, 141
   Lady Mary   130
Myres, Sir John   101, 141
   Nowell   110, 140

New College, Toronto   192 n. 64
Newport, Andrew   19
   John   36
Newton Longville   14, 27, 48, 104, 340
Nicholas, John (W)   62, 210–11, 214–15, 303
Nicholson, Sir Sidney   285
Non-licet gate   216, 218
Normanton, Lord   237
North, William   29
Norton, John   25
   Richard   163

Oaksey, Lord   109
oaths, fellows'   8, 16, 81
officers, college   21, 64
Ogg, David   69, 101, 301
Oglander, John (W)   240, 243, 244, 349
Oman, Sir Charles   85, 98, 101
Orchard, William   161, 176
organs   268–91, 367–8
Oriel College   8, 63, 67, 163, 242

Orleton, Adam de (Bishop of Hereford)   331
Ossulbury, Nicholas (W)   348
outrider   57
Oxford town   5, 121, 153
Oxford, Thomas of   159

Pace, G. G.   260, 368
Packett, *Pakett*, William   21, 42 n. 55
Palmer, Hugh   21
'Pandy'   255–6
Parker, Sir Henry   220
Parrott, Charles   310
   Ian   291
pax   298
Payne, Humfrey   140
Pears, James   238–9
Pearson, J. L.   254
Peckitt, William   234–7
Pembroke, Earl of   55
Pendlebury, John   140
Person, *Perysson*, William   325
Peter of Blois (MS.)   325
Peterhouse, Cambridge   182
Phelps Brown, Henry   118, 133
Phillimore, Hon. Claud   240, 258
Philpot, John   45
Pickhaver, Robert   270
Piddington, Richard   221
Pinke, Robert (W)   53, 55, 299, 349
Pink (organist)   269
plate   29, 58; Oman on, 293–304
Plot, Dr.   on roofs, 171; on Long Room, 184
Pole, Reginald (Cardinal)   336–7
popery   17, 47–9, 88, 269
port railway   244–5
Porte, William   15, 33, 268, 323
Porter, William (W)   298, 300, 303
portraits   198, 357 nn. 34, 35
P.P.E.   108, 118, 136
Price, William   233–4
Prichard, H. A.   100, 136–7
Prince, Daniel   238, 243
   Thomas   61
Pring, Isaac   277, 359 n. 66
professors   imposed, 83, 91; cost of, 105
progress, warden's   57, 309
pudding, New College   311
Puritans   51, 364
Purnell, John (W)   62, 349

quadrangle, front   as built, 6, 7, 165–9;
   altered, 208–9; statue in, 220, 244; new,
   248–9
Queen's College   6, 7, 54, 138, 160, 170
Quinbey, John   45

rabbits   10, 12
Radcliffe, G. R. Y.   112, 128, 264 n. 70
Radcliffe, Lord   109
Radclive   21
Radnor, Earl of   62, 238
Rait, R. S.   148, 256
Rashdall, Hastings   95, 100, 148, 256
Rastell, John   47, 49
Rawlings, *Rawlyns*, Henry   19
Rawlins, Christopher   310
Read (suicide)   272
Rebecca, Biagio   234, 252
Rede, William (Bishop of Chichester)   320
Rede, John (W)   21, 27, 347
Redyng, John   197
Reede, William   319
Rees, Goronwy   120–6
reform   pre-1850, 66–8; post-1850, 73–102
Reformation   36, 38, 44–51, 200
Reilly, Sir Patrick   109
Requests, Court of   25
Reredos   172–3, 219, 238, 254
resignations   17–19, 84–5
Reynolds, Sir Joshua   235–8
Rhodes House   258
Richard II   9, 22, 152, 154, 173
Richards family   354
Robbins, Lord   112–19
Roberts, David   259, 367
Robinson, Alfred   74, 85, 92, 96, 247, 251,
   255, 349
   Croke   88
   Thomas   224–5, 228
Romford   95
Ronquillo, Pedro   302
roofs   162, 171–2, 208–9, 240–2; hall, 177,
   246; kitchen, 179; chapel, 250–2
Routh, Martin   98
rowing   98–9, 107
Ruskin College   132–3, 139
Ruskinian tomfoolery   263 n. 39
Russell, John   10, 15, 24, 27; MSS., 328
Ryves, George (W)   299

Sacher, Harry   310, 367
Sacher building   259, 367
St. John's College   84, 277
St. Pancras Station   248
St. Peter-in-the-East   308
St. Thomas Becket (MSS. vitae)   322
Salvesen, Harold   112
Sampson, John   163
Saunders, Nicholas   47, 49
Say, William   22, 25, 327
Saye and Sele, Lord   55

scholars   before 1857, see fellows under
        the Founder's statutes; after 1857, 82, 133
Schweitzer, Albert   290
science   98, 108
Scott, Sir Gilbert   73, 246–53, 284
    George Gilbert   250
    John Oldrid   250–3
    Giles   258
seals   180, 309
Searle, Humphrey   291
Selby, Thomas   161
Sengleton, W.   325
Serbopoulos, Johannes   337
Sewell, James (W)   74, 85, 252, 279, 281;
        MSS., 313; memorials, 349, 353
Shepey, John de (Bishop of Rochester) 321, 323
Sherborne, Robert   24–5, 28, 197, 310, 330,
        331, 333, 343 n. 46
Sheridan, Mrs.   236
Sherriff, R. C.   132–3
Shirt, the   85
Shuttleworth, Philip (W)   66–7, 244–5,
        251, 349
Sibelius   290
Sidney, Sir Philip   54
Simeon, Geoffrey   22, 125
Simonds, Lord   109
Skinner, Ralph (W)   48
Slype   221
Smith, Alic (W)   108, 128, 133, 148, 180,
        182–3, 186, 304; Robbins on, 115; quoted,
        176; bust of, 260; Historic Buildings
        Fund, 261, 367; papers, 310
    Bernard   282
    George   221
    Sydney   310
Snareston, William   21, 29, 42 n. 55
socialism, Wykehamical   122
Society, the New College   110
Spanish Ambassador's cup   302
Sparke, William and Charles   228
Sparrow, John   123
Speckington, *Spekynton*, William   330
Spence, Joseph   64
Sponle, John   161
Spooner, W. A. (W)   86–7, 92, 101, 107,
        251, 254; diet of, 186; household of, 256;
        anecdotes of, 316; memorial, 349
Stadler, J. C.   242
staircases   183, 215, 227
Stanbridge, John   21, 27
Stanton St. John   104, 105, 263 n. 41
Stapleton, Thomas   47, 49
statutes, Founder's   7, 9, 11, 26–7, 30, 39 n. 2,
        45, 78, 82, 85, 155, 180, 267, 280, 293, 318;

of 1882, 90–1; ordinances of 1857, 83,
        85, 88
Steeple Morden   8
Steer, Francis   39 n. 2, 40 n. 25, 148; on
        Archives, 306–16; memorials, 346–56
Stephens, Henry Darell   350
Stockholm City Hall   257
Stonesfield   176
Stringer, Henry (W)   55, 300
Sturgeon, Richard   32
subwarden   26, 275, 323
Sugar, Hugh   25, 194, 295, 299, 330
Sumner, Bishop   80–2
Sutton, Sir John   283
Swanage, *Swanych*, John   332
Swift, John   302

taxation, exemption from   10
Taylor, A. E.   100
    James   281–5
Taynton, Richard of   169
Tenison, Thomas (Archbishop)   60
Thame School   311
theology, study of   20, 21; books, 320–2,
        325, 332
Thorpe, J. H.   234–5
Thurbarn, Robert   29, 333
Timber, Philip   270
Tingewick   8
Townesend, John   350
    William   225, 227–8, 244
Traffles, Richard (W)   217, 349, 356 n. 16
Trapier, William   303
Tresham, Sir Thomas   202
Trill, *Tryll*, John   19
Trillek, Thomas (MS.)   321
Trimnel, Charles   60, 61
Tucke, John   267
Tucker, Lord   109
    Norman   140, 290–1
Tutors' Association   78–9

undergraduates   6, 18, 77; numbers
        1873–1977, 91, 103, 366; arrogance of,
        107; illiteracy of, 309; rowdiness of, 99;
        strike by, 79; Rees on, 121–2; Woodcock
        on, 133; post-war, 109
University of Oxford   5, 65, 67, 98
Upper Heyford   21, 29
Upton, Nicholas   34
Uvedale, Nicholas   149

van Thulden, Theodore   207–8
Versailles   214
Vineis, Petrus de (MS.)   327

Visitations (Commissions of Inquiry,
    Investigation, etc.) 71 n. 47; 1385,
    1393: 8; 1535:46; 1549: 47; 1560s: 50,
    268, 298; 1576: 51, 194; 1647–58: 55, 56;
    1850: 68; 1852: 78, 81–2
Vivian, Dr. 56
von Uffenbach 217, 218

Wadham College 210
Walker, Gilbert 118
Wallop family 35
wall, city 5, 153, 168, 221, 249
Wall, Martin and Maria 350, 353
Walpole, Horace 233, 234, 237
Walworth, Sir William 322
Wardens of New College list of, 370;
    elections of, 8, 38, 60–2; intrusion of,
    56; deposition of, 48, 56; lodgings of,
    16, 127–9, 185–8, 198–201, 240, 256–7;
    staircase of, 211; barn of, 156, 158, 187–8,
    257, 259; bridge of, 209; garden of, 244;
    servants of, 198, 245, 256; studies of, 21–2,
    85, 113–14, 148; stipends of, 13, 66, 96,
    105
'Warden and Thirteen' 27, 51, 63, 83
Wardens of Winchester (see Winchester)
Ware, William 325, 332
Warham, William (Archbishop) 10, 24,
    25, 28, 32, 138, 197, 310; plate, 297–8;
    books, 328–30
Warton, Joseph and Thomas 65, 235, 237,
    241, 243
Watson, Sydney (quoted) 290
Watts, Henry 37
Waynflete, William (Bishop of
    Winchester) 20, 21
Weelkes, Thomas 268
Weldon, John 272
Wellington, Duke of 67
Wellington School 87
Wells, Welles, Thomas, D. D. 28
    Wellys, Thomas 36
    H. G. 130
Wesley, S. S. 281
West, Benjamin 235
    Rebecca 130
Westbury, William 21
Westmacott, Richard 243
Weston Longville 63, 64
Wetherell, Robert and Anne 340
Whaddon 84
Wheeler, J. W. 128
Whigs 60–1, 66, 356 n. 16
White, Thomas (W) 48–9, 298
    John 54

Whitney, J. H. 110
Wickham, E. C. 74, 85, 87–8, 247, 255, 351
Wigthorpe, William 268
Wilberforce, Lord 109
Wild, John 208
Willebury, William 155
Williams, David (W) 52, 78, 85, 282–3, 348
    John (Lord) 312
Willis, Henry 283
    Richard, Welleys 324
Wilson, Angus (quoted) 110
Winchester Bishop and See, 1, 8, 21, 33, 49,
    60, 61, 62, 67, 81; Edington, 151, 294;
    Morley, 216
    College, 6, 7, 16, 29, 52, 65, 72, 77, 81, 84;
    Warden of, 62
    Palace, 149, 214
windows chapel, 47, 155, 170–1, 173–4,
    233–40; unglazed, 183–4; hall, 177, 247;
    oriel, 187; library, 182, 204, 258
    (Smith's); garden quad, 215; sashed,
    222, 226–7
Windsor Castle 149, 151
Witney lime 155
Witt, Sir John 118
Wittenham, Wyttenham, John 332
Women exclusion of, 50, 89, 129, 368; Rees
    on, 125–6; Buxton on, 138–9; admission
    of, 368
Wood, Anthony (quoted) 58, 59, 178, 201,
    205, 217, 269, 271, 338
Woodcock, George 110, 132–7
    William 277
Woodforde, Christopher 149, 253
    James 63, 310 (papers)
Woodgate, Peter 353
Woodington, Thomas 28
Woods, Margaret L. 130
Woodward, Sir Llewellyn 115
    Michael (W) 57–8, 205, 208, 310; on
    organ, 270; memorial, 310
Woolf, Virginia 130
Woolley, Sir Leonard 101
Wootton, Thomas 268
Worthington, Hubert 257–8
Wotton, Sir Henry 54
Wren, Sir Christopher 160, 210, 214
Wriothesley, Wrattisley, Henry 347
Writtle 95, 105
Wyatt, James 234, 238–44
Wyclif, John 332, 337
Wykeham, Nicholas (W) 8, 21, 156
    Thomas 13, 33
    William of foundations of, 2–10, 149–56,
    164–89; influence of, 188–9; wisdom of,

307; crozier of, 294; rings of, 295;
treasure of, 13–15, 293; vestments of,
295; arms of, 10, 40 n. 24
Wylot, John   152
Wynford, William   151, 156–64
Wyse, William   152, 164, 176

Yevele, Henry   156–64, 176
York Minster   234

Yorke, Eric   108, 139
Young, *Yonge*, John (W) (Bishop of Gallipoli)
22, 347
Yonge, John   28
Younger, Kenneth   109

Zimmern, Sir Alfred   101
Zouche, Richard   53
Zulueta, Sir Philip de   102